ATLAS OF AMERICAN HISTORY

ATLAS OF
AMERICAN HISTORY

ATLAS OF AMERICAN HISTORY

SECOND REVISED EDITION

Charles Scribner's Sons • New York

Copyright © 1984 Charles Scribner's Sons

Library of Congress Cataloging in Publication Data

Main entry under title:

Atlas of American history.
    "Prepared by the Scribner Reference Books
Division"—Introd.
    Rev. ed. of: Atlas of American history /
Kenneth T. Jackson, editor.   Rev. ed. © 1978.
    Includes index.
    1. United States—Historical geography—Maps.
I. Jackson, Kenneth T.   Atlas of American history.
II. Scribner Reference Books Division.
G1201.S1A8 1984   911'.73   84–675413
ISBN 0–684–18411–7

5 7 9 11 13 15 17 19   V/C   20 18 16 14 12 10 8 6 4

The paper in this book meets the guidelines for permanence and durability of
the Committee on Production Guidelines for Book Longevity of the Council
on Library Resources.

CONTENTS

CONTENTS

IV COLONIAL WARS OF THE INDIANS, FRENCH AND BRITISH / 57

V THE AMERICAN REVOLUTION / 75

VI THE NEW NATION / 93

CONTENTS

VII   THE CIVIL WAR AND RECONSTRUCTION   / 147

VIII   THE END OF THE FRONTIER   / 167

CONTENTS

IX   THE UNITED STATES AS A WORLD POWER, 1898–1984   / *183*

X   SOCIAL AND ECONOMIC DEVELOPMENTS / *205*

CONTENTS

XI CURRENT ISSUES, 1978–1984 / *243*

INDEX / *255*

INTRODUCTION

Aᴏ ꜰᴛᴇʀ ᴛʜᴇ ᴘᴜʙʟɪᴄᴀᴛɪᴏɴ of the *Dictionary of American History* the need became apparent for a concise, easy to use, authoritative atlas of American history. Historian James Truslow Adams was appointed editor in chief. Assisted by an advisory council of sixty-four historians and researchers, he followed the premise that a historical map must be easily understood without the clutter of distracting information. It was also decided that each map would connect in area and in time with those maps immediately preceding and following so that the reader would be able to follow American history chronologically. Accuracy was of the greatest importance to Adams and his co-workers; and it is for this reason that the reader will not find places that did not exist during the period considered. The emphasis of that edition was on discovery, exploration, settlement, and territorial organization—all of which describe history through places, because to a large extent location explains occurrence. Both the American Revolution and the Civil War are treated with especially great detail so the reader can follow invasions and battles as the wars unfold in the movements of troops.

The 1978 Revised Edition, under the supervision of Kenneth T. Jackson, proceeded chronologically as well, making insertions where there were gaps in the original version of the *Atlas of American History*. Indian Tribal Groups, Indian Wars Before 1690, and Indian Reservations were significant additions as were the maps showing areas of settlement in 1700, 1800, 1850, and 1890. This edition also continued the earlier coverage of transportation by adding Commercially Navigable Waterways, Railroad Passenger Lines, and the Interstate Highway System. Most of the new maps showed twentieth-century developments in human rights, the economy, population, immigration, and the nation's rise to being a major force in foreign affairs. The reader finds locations of important events in the Spanish-American War, both world wars, Korea, Vietnam, and interventions in the Caribbean and Middle America. Major military bases on the continent and abroad shed light on America's military strength.

The *Atlas of American History* Second Revised Edition, prepared by the Scribner Reference Books Division, follows the same attention to clarity and detail. In a few instances we found it necessary to alter maps of the prior editions. For example, we added the Norse voyages (*ca.* 1000) and Jacques Cartier's voyage of 1535 that now appear on the map of the Discovery of America. National forest areas were added to the map on National Parks. As part of the map on Railroad Passenger Lines the reader will find a comparative table of passenger miles travelled by rail and by air. Some maps from the earlier editions have been updated with statistics from the 1980 census.

The new chapter, Current Issues, 1978–1984, continues treatment of the economy and supplements material shown in earlier chapters with attention to recent developments in nuclear energy and national security and changes to the environment. The maps showing personal income per capita for all states and the total number of unemployed as a percentage of the civilian labor force, also shown for all states, will aid the reader in seeing the effects of the economy from 1978 to 1982. The range of years was decided upon to avoid combining conflicting sources that had different approaches to the calculation of statistics.

The map of nuclear power plants includes only plants licensed as of May 1984. The Nuclear Regulatory Commission evaluates reactors constantly, often changing the status of their operation. For this reason we have omitted those plants that were subject to license review, although these plants were most likely in operation. Nonetheless, the reader gets a clear picture of the number of plants in use and their locations.

Throughout the work on the Second Revised Edition it was the intention of the editors to maintain the high standards set by the earlier editions of the *Atlas*. The editorial staff recognizes the controversial nature of two of the maps—Intercontinental Ballistic Missile Complexes and Hazardous Waste. We include them as representations of contemporary history, taking note of the national concern directed toward the environment and defense. It is the publisher's hope that the *Atlas* again proves to be a genuinely useful aid to the better understanding and interpretation of American history.

ATLAS OF
AMERICAN HISTORY

I   AMERICA AT THE TIME OF DISCOVERY

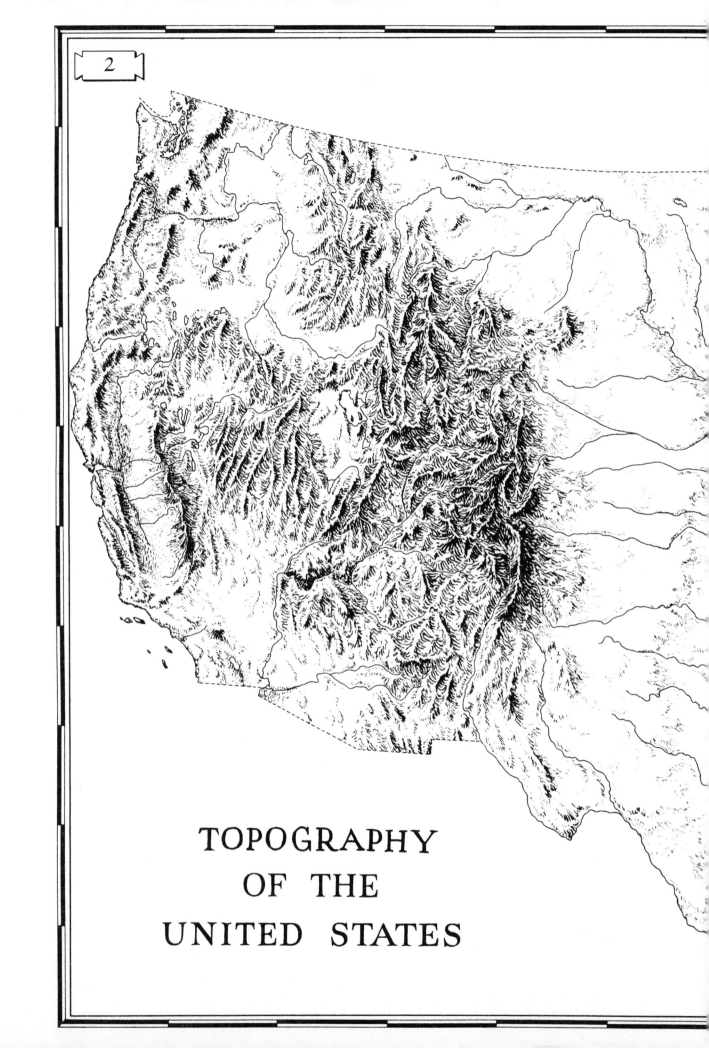

TOPOGRAPHY
OF THE
UNITED STATES

Drawn under the supervision of Lloyd A. Brown

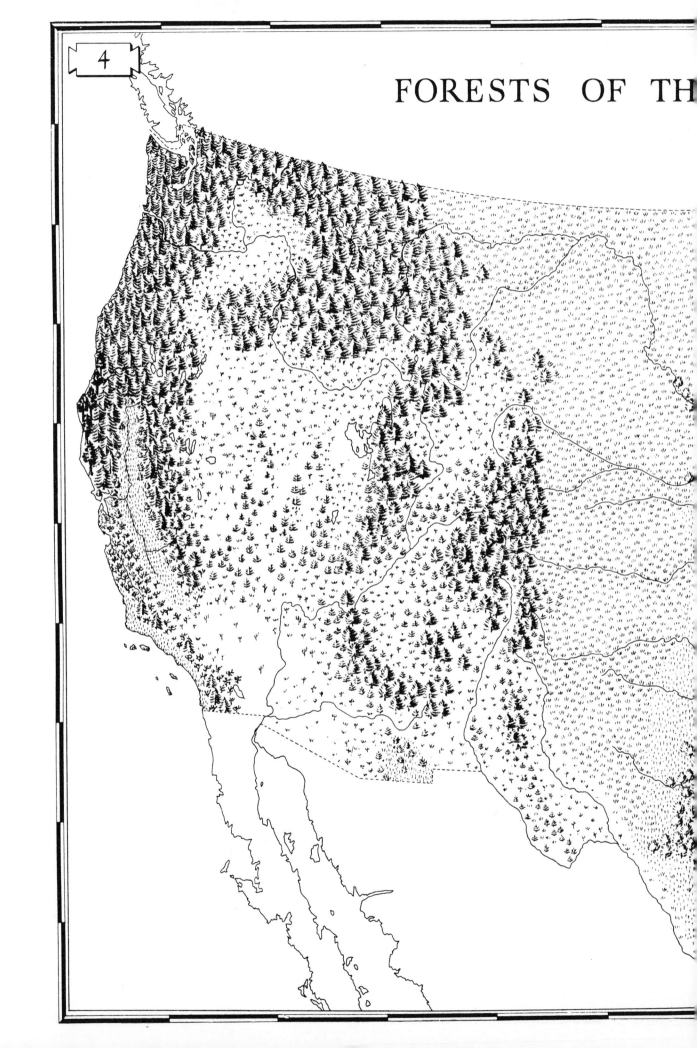

4

FORESTS OF TH

NITED STATES

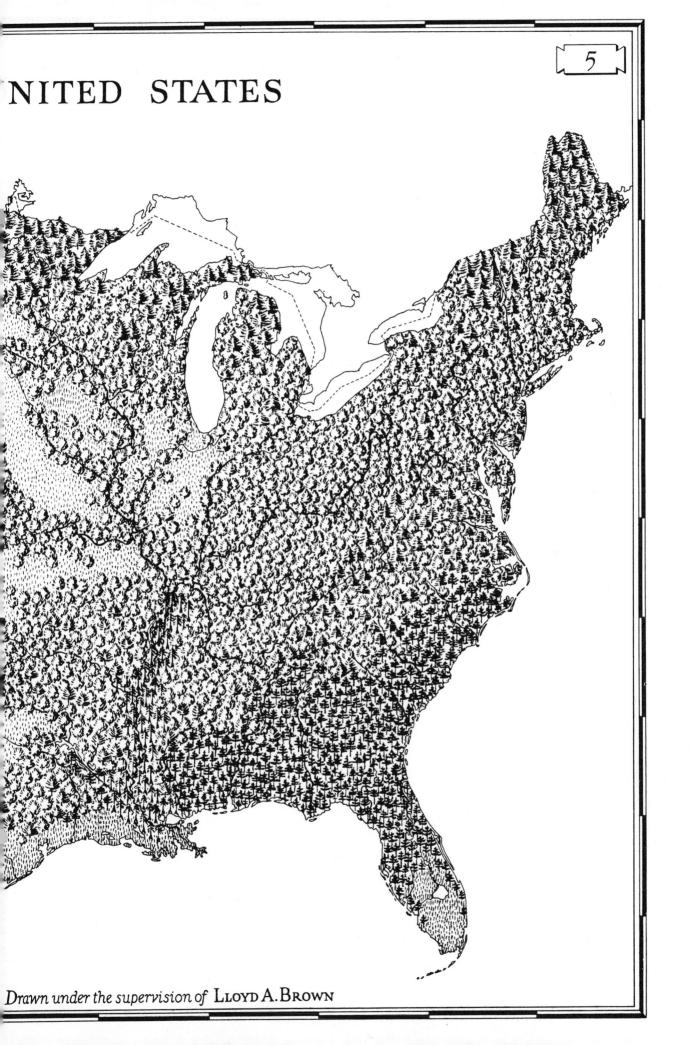

Drawn under the supervision of LLOYD A. BROWN

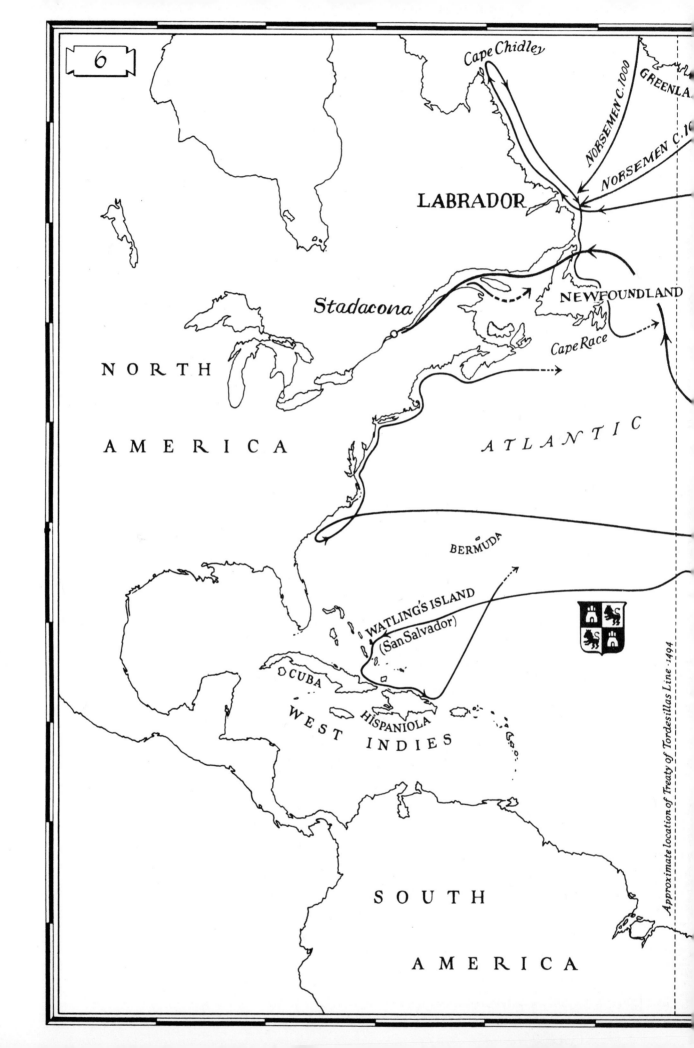

6

Cape Chidley

NORSEMEN C.1000

GREENLA

NORSEMEN C.1(

LABRADOR

Stadacona

NEWFOUNDLAND

Cape Race

NORTH

AMERICA

ATLANTIC

BERMUDA

WATLING'S ISLAND
(San Salvador)

CUBA

WEST   INDIES

HISPANIOLA

Approximate location of Treaty of Tordesillas Line 1494

SOUTH

AMERICA

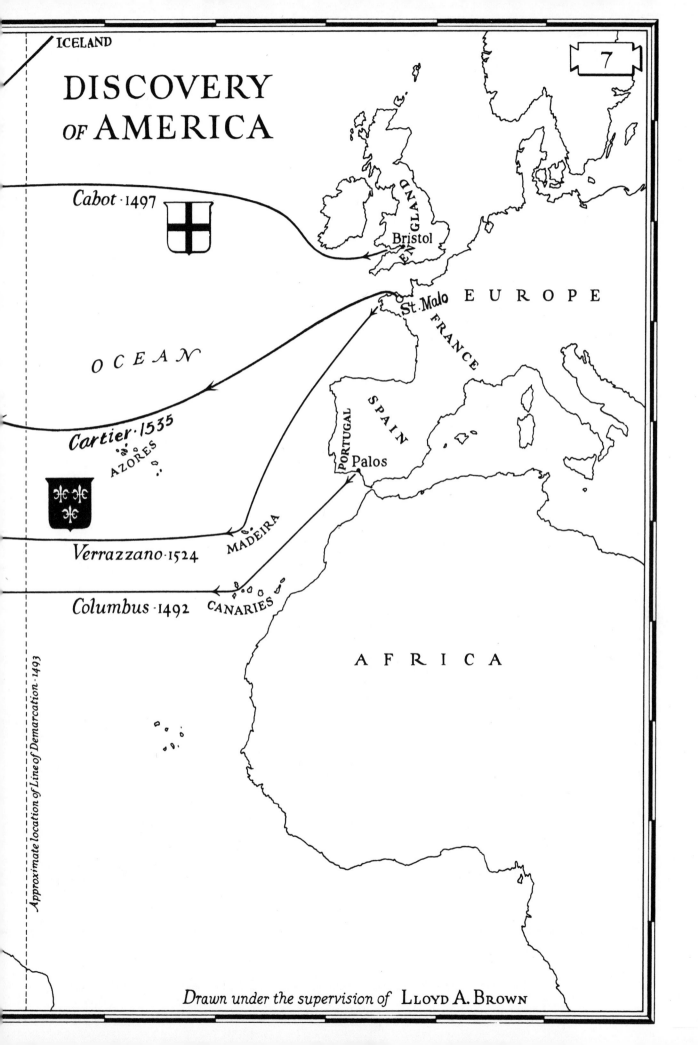

ICELAND

DISCOVERY
OF AMERICA

Cabot · 1497

Bristol

ENGLAND

St. Malo   E U R O P E

FRANCE

O C E A N

SPAIN

PORTUGAL

Palos

Cartier · 1535

AZORES

Verrazzano · 1524

MADEIRA

Columbus · 1492

CANARIES

A F R I C A

Approximate location of Line of Demarcation · 1493

Drawn under the supervision of LLOYD A. BROWN

8

MAKAH
QUINAULT
TWANA
SANPOIL
ASSINIBOINE
HIDA
YAKIMA
COEUR d'ALENE
BLACKFEET
DAKOTA
MANI
CHINOOK
FLATHEAD
SIOU
TILLAMOOK
NEZ PERCÉ
CROW
CAYUSE
SNAKE
BANNOCK
ARIKARA
YANK
KLAMATH
YUROK
WIYOT
PAIUTE
SHOSHONI
MAIDU
PAVIOSTO
CHEYENNE
OM
POMO
MIWOK
SHOSHONI
PAWNEE
UTE
ARAPAHOE
COSTANOAN
PAIUTE
SALINAN
NAVAHO
KIOWA
MOHAVE
ZUNI
WICHITA
CHUMASH
HAVASUPAI
HOPI
CAHUILLA
YAVAPAI
COMANCHE
PACIFIC OCEAN
PAPAGO
APACHE
KICH
APACHE
MESCALERO
LIPAN APACHE

Each tribal group is shown in the area it
occupied at the time of its first encounter
with white settlers. Because tribal groups often
ranged widely, many of the locations shown here were
only temporary.

MILES

0   100   200   300   400

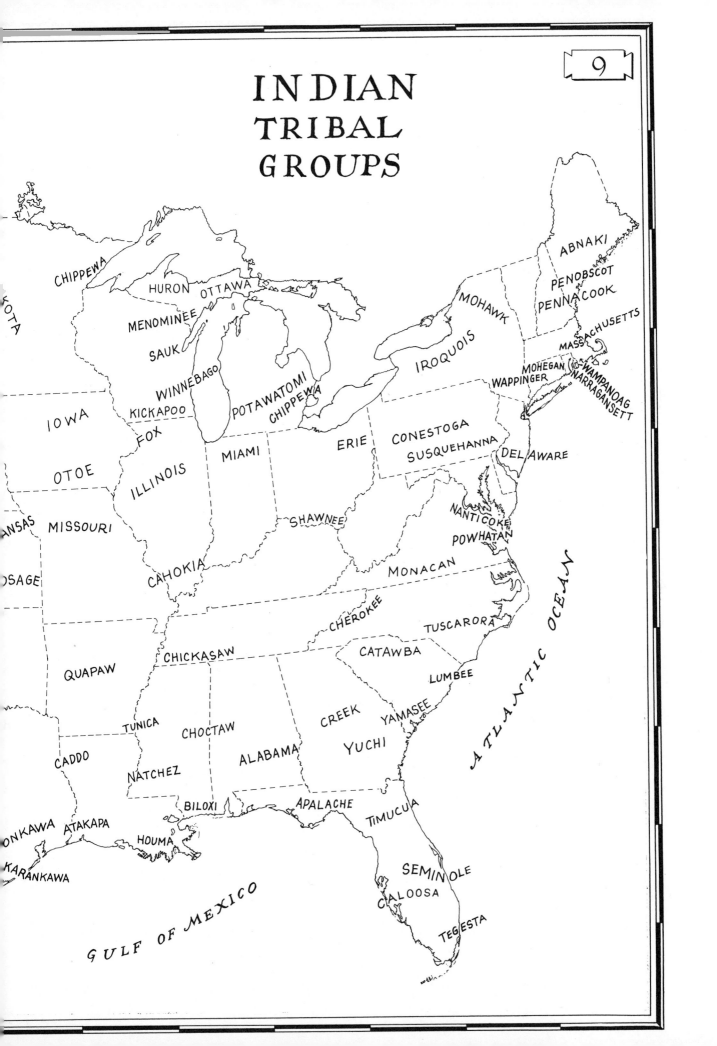

INDIAN TRIBAL GROUPS

II FRENCH AND SPANISH EXPLORATION AND SETTLEMENT

SIXTEENTH CENTURY

(Arkansas River)

QUIV

Grand
Cañon

(Little Colorado River)

Tusayan
(Hopi)

Jemez

Taos

Cardenas

Tovar

Cibola
(Zuni)

Tiguex

Cicuye
(Pecos)

(Canidian)

River)

Acoma
(Acuco)

(Colorado River)

QUERECHOS

(Gila

River)

Army Returns

Chichilticalli

(Pecos

(Colorado

(Brazos)

Melchior Diaz

Suya

Arizpe

River)

Sonora

Ures

(Rio Grande)

River)

Batuco

Yaquimi

Fuerte

Santa Barbara

PACIFIC

Sinaloa

(Rio Grande)

OCEAN

Culiacan

San Blas

Tampico

Compostela

- - - - - *Juan Ponce de Leon · 1513*
—•—•— *Panfilo de Narvaez · 1528*
—o—o— *Alvar Nunez Cabeza de Vaca · 1528-1536*
—o—·—o— *Hernando de Soto · 1539-1542*
—··—··— *Luis de Moscoso · 1542-1543*
Francisco Vazquez de Coronado · 1540-1542
—x—x— *Principal Route*
—x—x—x— *Subsidiary Explorations*
—x—x— *Hernando de Alarcon · 1540*
·········· *Beltran-Espejo Expedition · 1582-1583*

•Mexico City

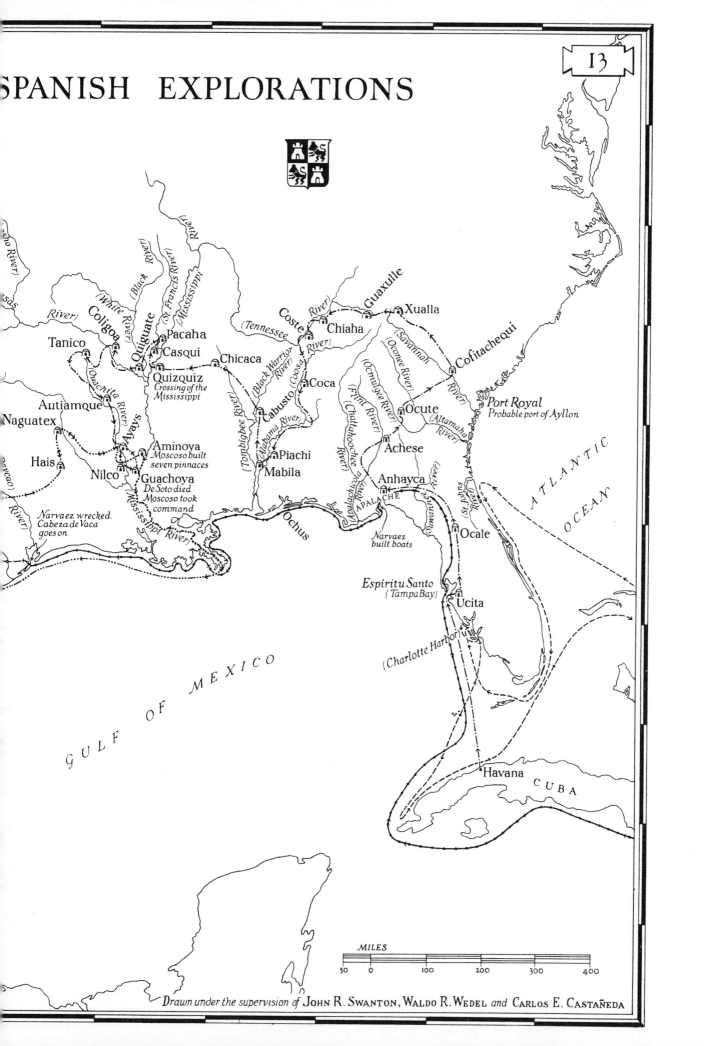

SPANISH EXPLORATIONS

13

Tanico
Coligoa
(White River)
(Black River)
(St. Francis River)
(Mississippi River)
Pacaha
Casqui
Quiguate
Chicaca
Autiamque
(Ouachita River)
Ayays
Naguatex
Quizquiz
Crossing of the Mississippi
Hais
(Bayou)
Nilco
Aminoya
Moscoso built seven pinnaces
Guachoya
De Soto died. Moscoso took command
(Tombigbee River)
(Alabama River)
Cabusto
Piachi
Mabila
(Black Warrior River)
(Coosa River)
Coste
Chiaha
Coca
(Tennessee River)
Guaxulle
Xualla
Cofitachequi
(Savannah River)
(Oconee River)
(Ocmulgee River)
(Flint River)
(Chattahoochee River)
Ocute
Port Royal
Probable port of Ayllon
(Altamaha River)
Achese
Anhayca
APALACHE
(Apalachicola River)
(Suwannee River)
Ochus
Narvaez built boats
(St. Johns River)
Ocale
Narvaez wrecked. Cabeza de Vaca goes on
(Mississippi River)
Espiritu Santo
(Tampa Bay)
Ucita
(Charlotte Harbor)

ATLANTIC OCEAN

GULF OF MEXICO

Havana

CUBA

MILES

50   0   100   200   300   400

Drawn under the supervision of JOHN R. SWANTON, WALDO R. WEDEL *and* CARLOS E. CASTAÑEDA

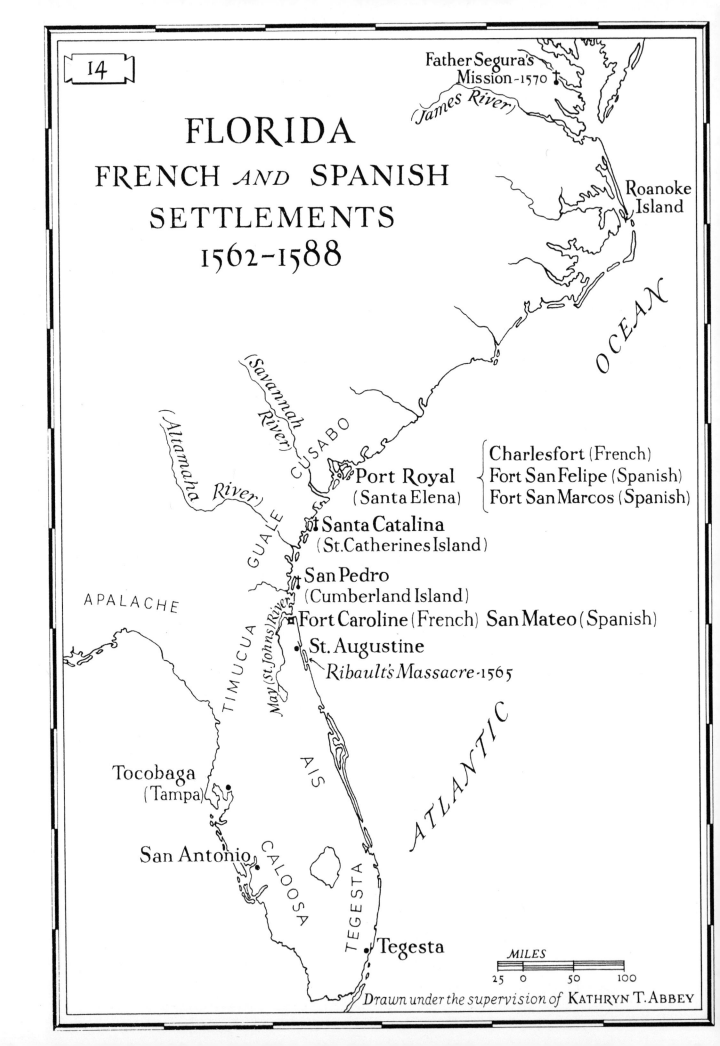

14

FLORIDA
FRENCH *AND* SPANISH
SETTLEMENTS
1562–1588

Father Segura's
Mission·1570

(James River)

OCEAN

Roanoke
Island

(Savannah River)

(Altamaha River)

CUSABO

Charlesfort (French)
Fort San Felipe (Spanish)
Fort San Marcos (Spanish)

Port Royal
(Santa Elena)

Santa Catalina
(St. Catherines Island)

GUALE

APALACHE

San Pedro
(Cumberland Island)

Fort Caroline (French) San Mateo (Spanish)

TIMUCUA

May (St. Johns River)

St. Augustine

Ribault's Massacre·1565

Tocobaga
(Tampa)

AIS

ATLANTIC

San Antonio

CALOOSA

TEGESTA

Tegesta

MILES

25 0   50   100

Drawn under the supervision of KATHRYN T. ABBEY

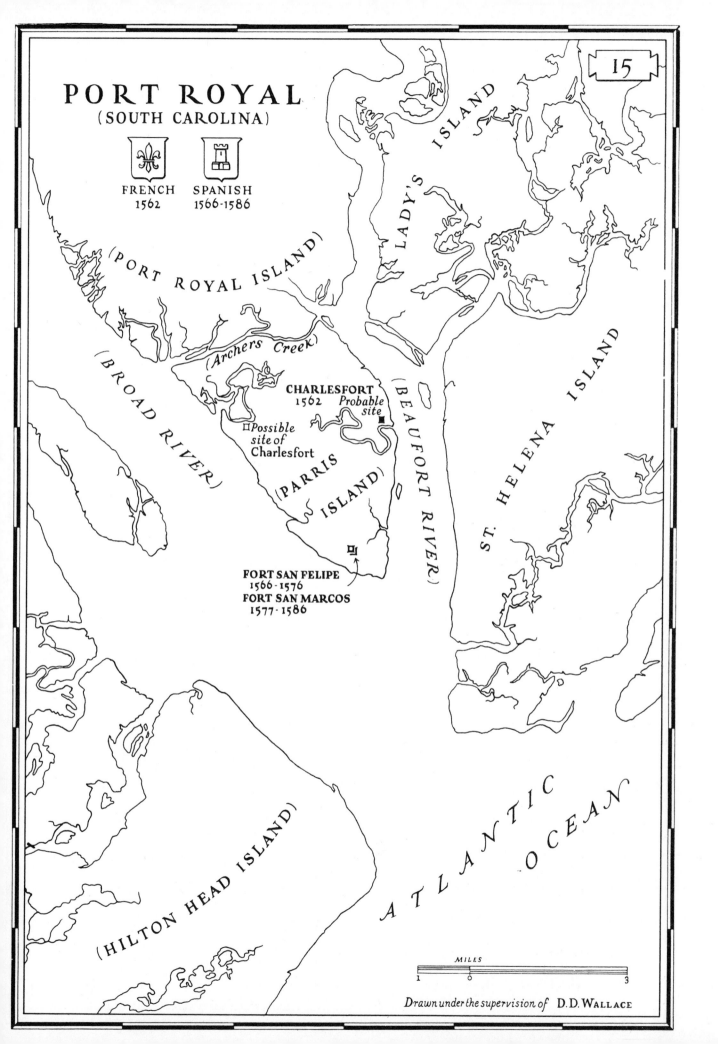

15

PORT ROYAL
(SOUTH CAROLINA)

FRENCH
1562

SPANISH
1566-1586

(PORT ROYAL ISLAND)

LADY'S ISLAND

(BROAD RIVER)

Archers Creek

CHARLESFORT
1562
Probable site

□ *Possible site of Charlesfort*

(PARRIS ISLAND)

(BEAUFORT RIVER)

ST. HELENA ISLAND

FORT SAN FELIPE
1566-1576
FORT SAN MARCOS
1577-1586

(HILTON HEAD ISLAND)

ATLANTIC OCEAN

MILES
1   0   3

Drawn under the supervision of D.D. WALLACE

16

Lac Superieur

Sault Ste. Marie

St. Ignace

Michilimackinac

St. Mary's River

Lac Huron

Mission du St. Esprit

MENOMINEE

Baye des Puans

WINNEBAGO

Marquette died (1675)

FOX
SAUK

Mississippi River

River

Fox River

St. François Xavier

MASCOUTEN
MIAMI
KICKAPOO

Portage

Wisconsin

Lac des Ilinois (Michigan)

Des Plaines River

St. Joseph River

Portage

Kaskaskia Village

Illinois River

Kankakee River

Lac Erie

Illinois Village

PIASA

(Missouri River)

(Ohio River)

DISCOVERY
OF THE
MISSISSIPPI
JOLLIET and MARQUETTE
1673

(Arkansas River)

Mississippi River

Arkansas Village

MILES
50   0   100

Drawn under the supervision of JEAN DELANGLEZ

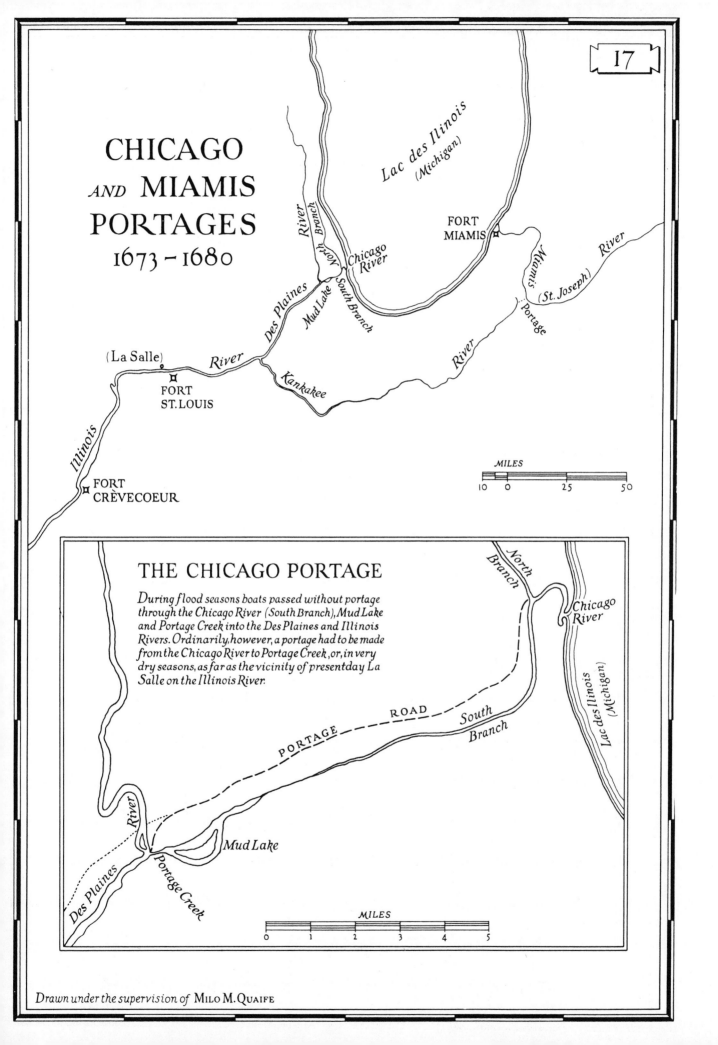

CHICAGO AND MIAMIS PORTAGES
1673 – 1680

Lac des Ilinois
(Michigan)

River

North Branch

Des Plaines

Chicago River

Mud Lake

South Branch

FORT MIAMIS

Miamis

(St. Joseph)

River

Portage

(La Salle)

River

FORT ST. LOUIS

Kankakee

River

Illinois

FORT CRÈVECOEUR

MILES

10   0   25   50

THE CHICAGO PORTAGE

During flood seasons boats passed without portage through the Chicago River (South Branch), Mud Lake and Portage Creek into the Des Plaines and Illinois Rivers. Ordinarily, however, a portage had to be made from the Chicago River to Portage Creek, or, in very dry seasons, as far as the vicinity of presentday La Salle on the Illinois River.

North Branch

Chicago River

Lac des Ilinois (Michigan)

PORTAGE ROAD

South Branch

Des Plaines River

Portage Creek

Mud Lake

MILES

0   1   2   3   4   5

Drawn under the supervision of MILO M. QUAIFE

NEW FRANCE
TO 1673

LAC SUPERIEUR

CHIPPEWA

Sault Ste. Marie

OTTAWA
(Refugee)

St. Ignace

HURON

OTTAWA

Mission
du St. Esprit

Michilimackinac

Manitoulin Island

SIOUX

MENOMINEE

Baye des Puans

LAC HURON

HURON
(Refugee)

POTAWATOMI

HURON

St. Marc

SAUK

Nicolet, 1634

Otinawatawa

WINNEBAGO

St. François
Xavier

LA

OUTAGAMI
(FOX)

Niagara

MIAMI-
MASCOUTEN

NEUTRALS

LAC DES ILINOIS
(Michigan)

MIAMI

River

LAC ERIE

ERIE (CAT)
NATION

ILINOIS

Mississippi

La Belle Rivière (Ohio)

APPALACHIAN

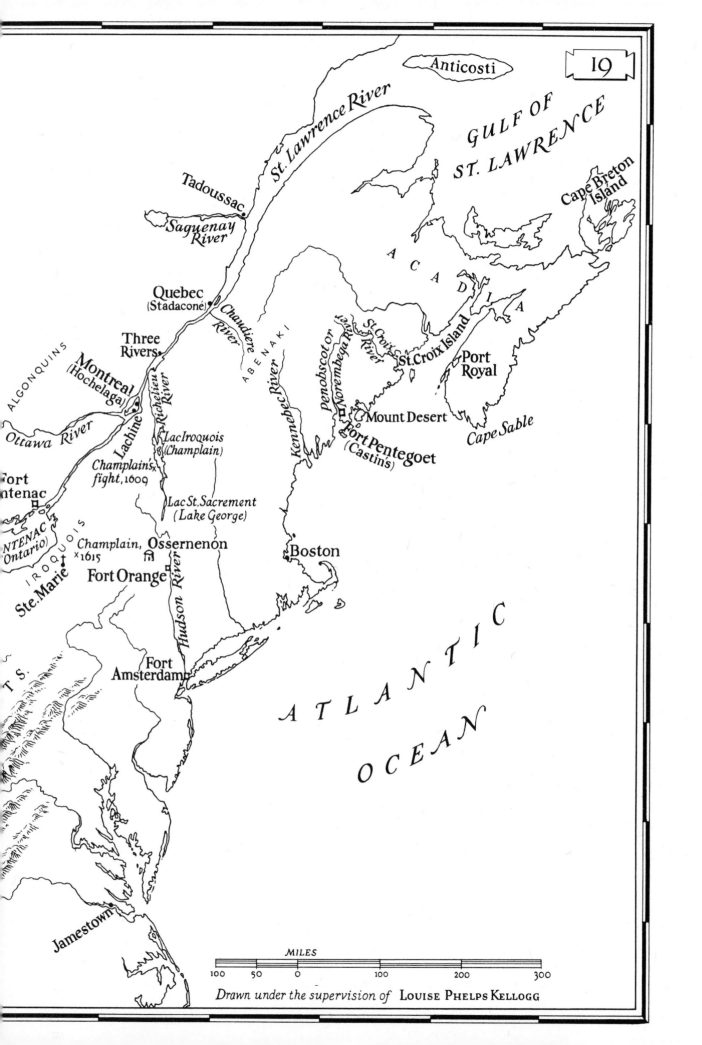

Anticosti

St. Lawrence River

GULF OF
ST. LAWRENCE

Tadoussac

Cape Breton
Island

Saguenay
River

A C A D I A

Quebec
(Stadaconé)

Chaudiere
River

St. Croix Island

Port
Royal

Three
Rivers

Penobscot or
Norembega River

St. Croix
River

ALGONQUINS

Montreal
(Hochelaga)

Richelieu River

ABENAKI

Kennebec River

Mount Desert

Cape Sable

Ottawa   River

Lachine

Lac Iroquois
(Champlain)

Fort Pentegoet
(Castin's)

Fort
ntenac

Champlain's
fight, 1609

Lac St. Sacrement
(Lake George)

NTENAC
Ontario)

IROQUOIS

Champlain,
×1615

Ossernenon

Boston

Ste. Marie

Fort Orange

Hudson River

T S.

Fort
Amsterdam

A T L A N T I C

O C E A N

Jamestown

MILES

100   50   0   100   200   300

Drawn under the supervision of LOUISE PHELPS KELLOGG

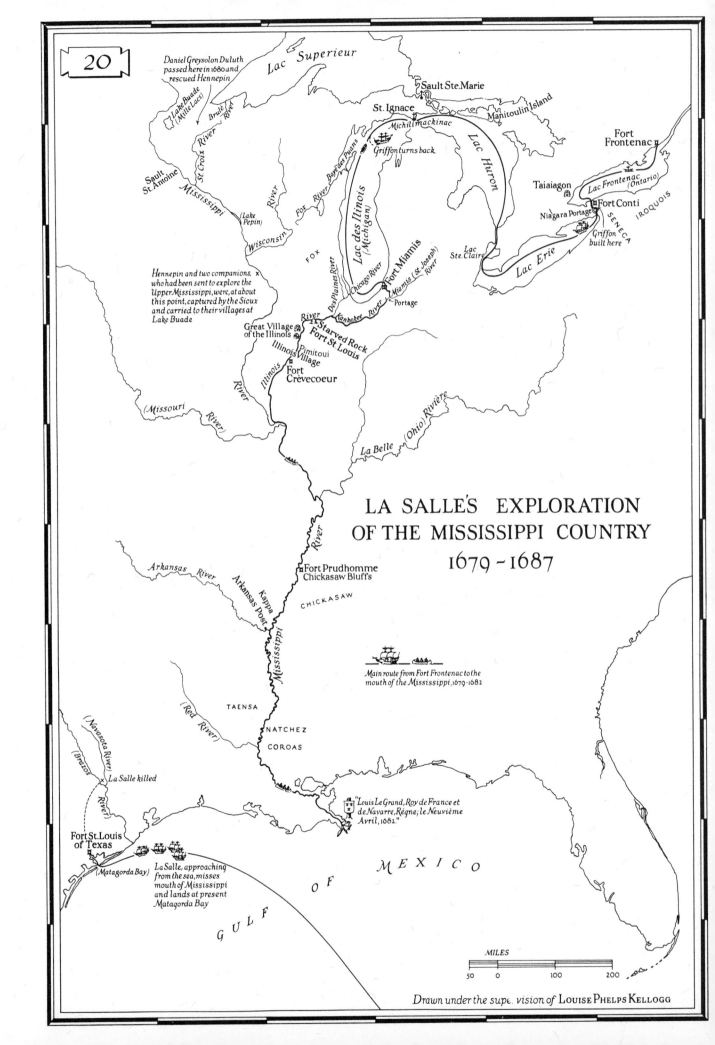

20

Daniel Greysolon Duluth
passed here in 1680 and
rescued Hennepin

Lac Superieur

Sault Ste. Marie

St. Ignace

Manitoulin Island

Michilimackinac

Griffon turns back

Fort Frontenac

Lake Buade (Mille Lacs)

St. Croix River

Brulé River

Fox River

Bay des Puans

Lac Huron

Taiaiagon

Lac Frontenac (Ontario)

Sault St. Antoine

Mississippi

Wisconsin River

(Lake Pepin)

FOX

Lac des Ilinois (Michigan)

Fort Conti

Niagara Portage

SENECA

IROQUOIS

Griffon built here

Lac Ste. Claire

Lac Erie

Hennepin and two companions,
who had been sent to explore the
Upper Mississippi, were, at about
this point, captured by the Sioux
and carried to their villages at
Lake Buade.

Fox

Des Plaines River

Chicago River

Fort Miamis

Miamis (St. Joseph) River

Portage

Kankakee River

Great Village
of the Illinois

River

Starved Rock
Fort St. Louis

Pimitoui
Illinois Village

Fort
Crèvecoeur

Illinois

(Missouri River)

River

River

La Belle (Ohio) Rivière

LA SALLE'S EXPLORATION
OF THE MISSISSIPPI COUNTRY
1679 ~ 1687

Arkansas River

Arkansas Post

Kappa

Fort Prudhomme
Chickasaw Bluffs

CHICKASAW

Mississippi

River

Main route from Fort Frontenac to the
mouth of the Mississippi, 1679-1682

(Red River)

TAENSA

NATCHEZ

COROAS

(Navasota River)

(Brazos River)

La Salle killed

"Louis Le Grand, Roy de France et
de Navarre, Règne; le Neuvième
Avril, 1682."

Fort St. Louis
of Texas

(Matagorda Bay)

La Salle, approaching
from the sea, misses
mouth of Mississippi
and lands at present
Matagorda Bay

GULF   OF   M E X I C O

G U L F

MILES

50   0   100   200

Drawn under the supervision of LOUISE PHELPS KELLOGG

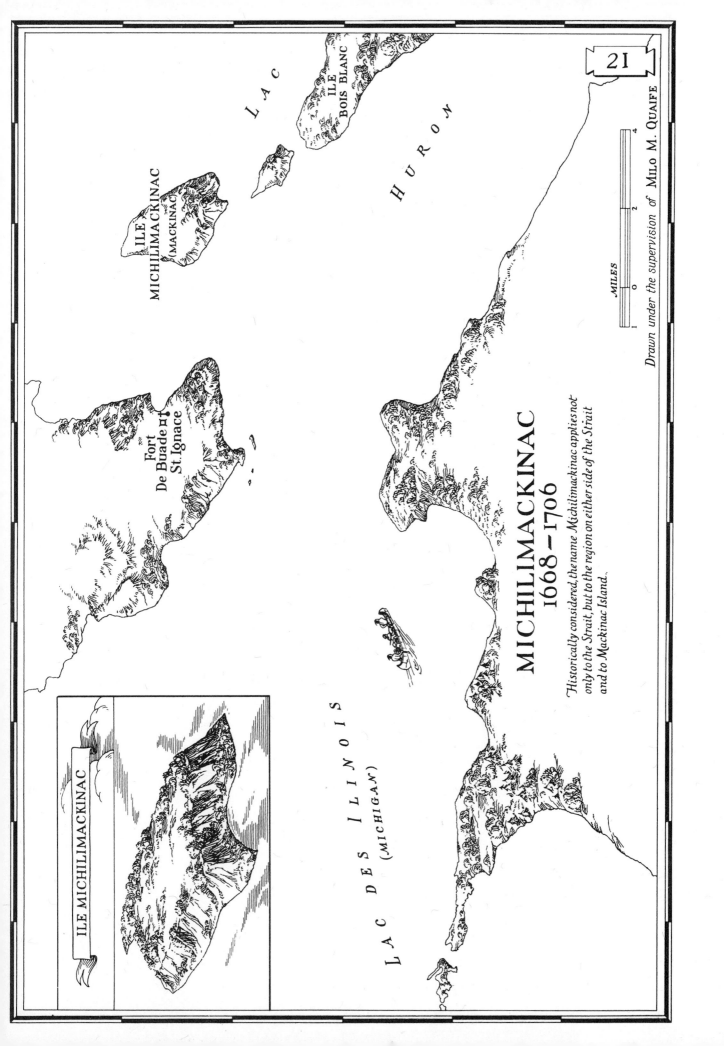

21

L A C

ILE
BOIS BLANC

L A C

H U R O N

ILE
MICHILIMACKINAC
(MACKINAC)

Fort
De Buade et
St. Ignace

L A C   D E S   I L I N O I S
(MICHIGAN)

MICHILIMACKINAC
1668–1706

*Historically considered, the name Michilimackinac applies not
only to the Strait, but to the region on either side of the Strait
and to Mackinac Island.*

MILES
1   0   2   4

Drawn under the supervision of MILO M. QUAIFE

ILE MICHILIMACKINAC

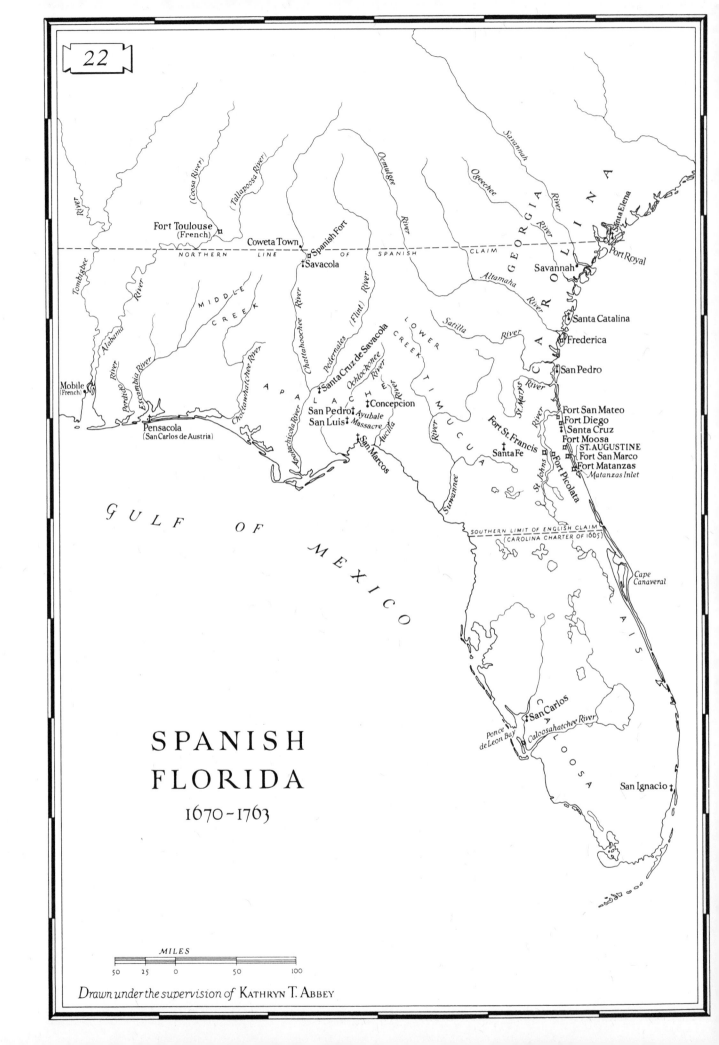

22

Fort Toulouse
(French) □
Coosa River
Tallapoosa River
Coweta Town ● □ Spanish Fort
† Savacola
NORTHERN LINE OF SPANISH CLAIM

Tombigbee River
Alabama River
M I D D L E C R E E K
Ocmulgee River
Chattahoochee River

G E O R G I A
Savannah
Ogeechee
River
● Santa Elena
● Port Royal
Savannah

C A R O L I N A

Altamaha River
Satilla River

† Santa Catalina
⊡ Frederica
† San Pedro

Perdido River
Escambia River
Choctawhatchee River
Apalachicola River

† Santa Cruz de Savacola
Pedernales (Flint) River
Ochlochonee River

L O W E R   C R E E K

Mobile
(French) □

Pensacola
(San Carlos de Austria)

A P A L A C H E E
San Pedro † ● Concepcion
San Luis † Ayubale † Massacre

† San Marcos

Aucilla River

T I M U C U A

Suwannee River

St. Marys River

Fort St. Francis †
† Santa Fe

St. Johns River

Fort San Mateo ⊡
Fort Diego †
Santa Cruz †
Fort Moosa ⊡
ST. AUGUSTINE ⊡
Fort San Marco ⊡
Fort Matanzas ⊡
Matanzas Inlet

Fort Picolata ⊡

G U L F   O F   M E X I C O

SOUTHERN LIMIT OF ENGLISH CLAIM
(CAROLINA CHARTER OF 1665)

A I S

Cape
Canaveral

Ponce
de Leon Bay
● San Carlos
Caloosahatchee River

C
A
L
O
O
S
A

San Ignacio †

SPANISH
FLORIDA
1670–1763

MILES
50 25 0   50   100

Drawn under the supervision of KATHRYN T. ABBEY

23

TRANS-MISSISSIPPI - FRENCH & SPANISH
1600 — 1750

Assiniboine

River

Lake Winnipeg

Fort La Reine

VERENDRYE

Grand Portage

Lake Superior

Missouri River

Mantanne Village

Red River

Fort St. Antoine

Yellowstone River

SONS

VERENDRYE

Minnesota River

Chippewa River

Wisconsin River

Lake Michigan

Fort d'Huillier

Fort Beauharnois

Missouri River

COMANCHE (PADOUCAS)

North Platte River

Platte River

South Platte

VILLASUR

PAWNEE

DU TISNE

BOURGMONT

Illinois River

Fort Orleans

Cahokia

MALLET BROTHERS

Kansas River

OSAGE

Orage River

Fort de Chartrês

Kaskaskia

Colorado River

UTE

NAVAHO

San Gabriel

Jemez

Zuni

HOPI

Santa Fe

Taós

San Juan del los Caballeras

Canadian

River

Arkansas

River

River

Ste. Genevieve

Mississippi

Ohio

Acoma

Pecos

ONATE 1601

LA HARPE

Arkansas Post

YUMA

ONATE 1604-05

Albuquerque

Colorado or Red

River

TEJAS

Gila River

San Xavier del Bac

APACHE

Pecos River

Brazos

Trinity

Nacogdoches

Natchitoches

Tubac

El Paso

San Gabriel del Guevavi

Fronteras

Casa Grande

Rio Del Norte

ONATE 1598

(Rio

San Juan Bautista

ST. DENIS

San Antonio Missions

San Francisco de los Tejas

Sabine River

Los Adaes

Fort Rosalie

Baton Rouge

New Orleans

GULF OF CALIFORNIA

River

Chihuahua

Grande)

GULF OF MEXICO

MILES

50   0   100   200   300

	Oñate	1598-1605
	St. Denis	1714-1716
	Bourgmont	1714-1724
	Du Tisne	1719
	La Harpe	1719
	Villasur	1720
	Mallet Brothers	1739-1740
	Verendrye	1738-1739
	Verendrye Sons	1742-1743

Drawn under the supervision of WALTER PRICHARD & CARLOS E. CASTAÑEDA
The Verendrye routes drawn under the supervision of O. G. LIBBY

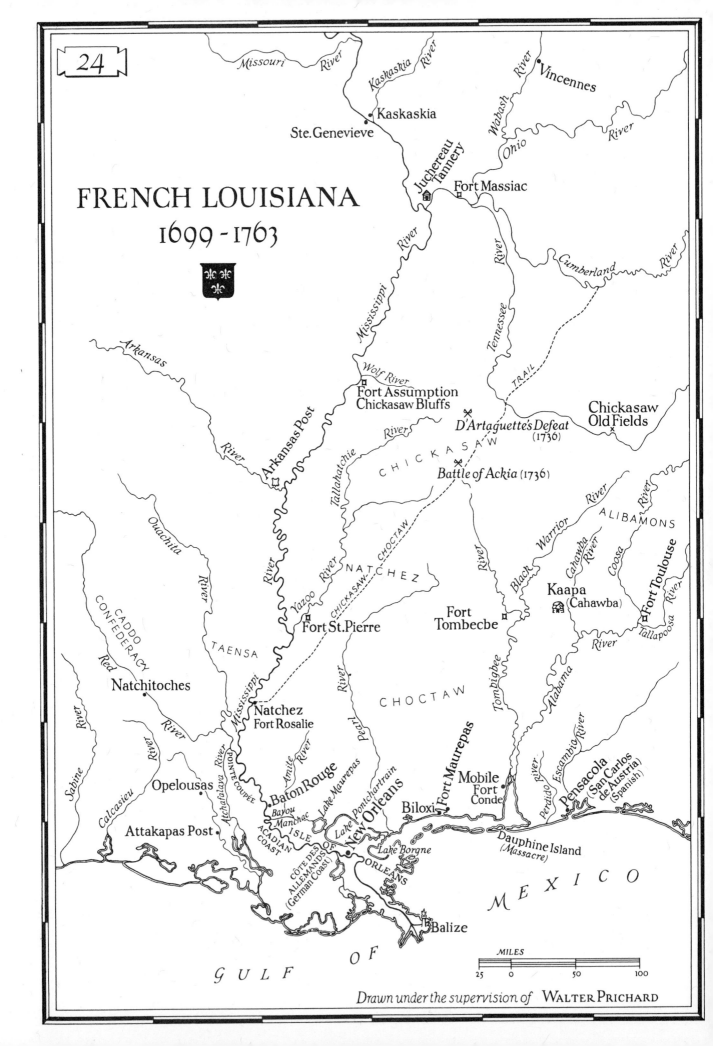

24

FRENCH LOUISIANA
1699-1763

Missouri River

Kaskaskia River

Vincennes

Kaskaskia

Ste. Genevieve

Juchereau Tannery

Fort Massiac

Wabash River

Ohio

Mississippi River

Tennessee River

Cumberland River

Arkansas

Wolf River

Fort Assumption
Chickasaw Bluffs

TRAIL

D'Artaguette's Defeat
(1736)

Chickasaw
Old Fields

River

C H I C K A S A W

Battle of Ackia (1736)

Tallahatchie River

ALIBAMONS

Ouachita

River

Arkansas Post

Black Warrior River

Cahawba River

Coosa River

Fort Toulouse

River

Yazoo River

N A T C H E Z

CHICKASAW-CHOCTAW

Kaapa
(Cahawba)

TAENSA

Fort St. Pierre

Fort
Tombecbe

Tallapoosa

River

CADDO CONFEDERACY

Red River

Natchitoches

C H O C T A W

Tombigbee River

Alabama River

Mississippi River

POINTE COUPÉE

Natchez
Fort Rosalie

Pearl River

Amite River

Perdido River

Escambia River

Opelousas

Sabine River

Calcasieu River

Atchafalaya River

Baton Rouge

Bayou
Manchac

Lake Maurepas

Lake Pontchartrain

Fort Maurepas

Mobile
Fort
Condé

Pensacola
(San Carlos
de Austria)
(Spanish)

Attakapas Post

ACADIAN COAST

CÔTE DES ALLEMANDS
(German Coast)

ISLE OF ORLEANS

Lake
Salvador

New Orleans

Biloxi

Dauphine Island
(Massacre)

Lake Borgne

Balize

G U L F   O F   M E X I C O

MILES
25   0   50   100

Drawn under the supervision of WALTER PRICHARD

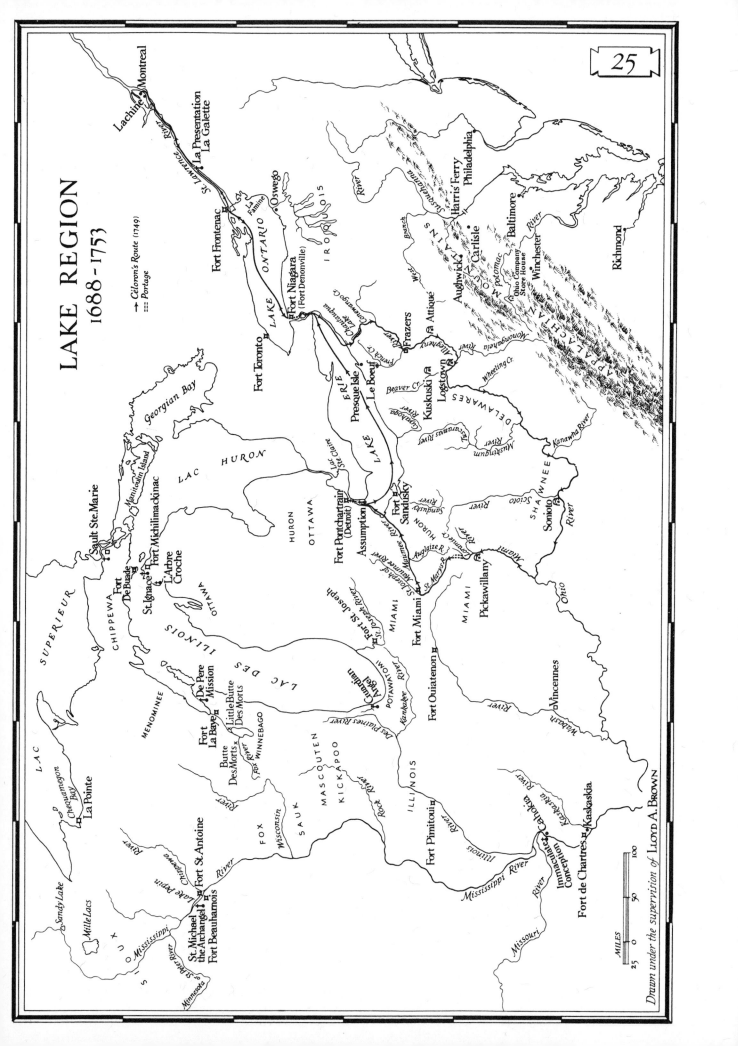

25

LAKE REGION
1688–1753

→ Céloron's Route (1749)
::: Portage

Montreal
Lachine
La Presentation La Galette
St. Lawrence River
Oswego
La Famine
Fort Frontenac
LAKE ONTARIO
IROQUOIS
Susquehanna River
Harris' Ferry
Philadelphia
Carlisle
Aughwick
Baltimore
Richmond
Fort Niagara
(Fort Denonville)
Chautauqua Lake
Conewango Cr.
Potomac River
Winchester
Ohio Company Store House
APPALACHIAN
Fort Toronto
Frazers
Attiqué
French Cr.
West Branch
Presque Isle
LAKE ERIE
Le Boeuf
Logstown
Kuskuski
Beaver Cr.
DELAWARES
Wheeling Cr.
Monongahela River
Allegheny River
Georgian Bay
Cuyahoga River
Tuscarawas River
Muskingum River
Kanawha River
Lac Ste. Claire
Manitoulin Island
LAC HURON
HURON
OTTAWA
Fort Pontchartrain
(Detroit)
Assumption
Fort Sandusky
HURON
Sandusky River
Scioto River
SHAWNEE
Sonioto River
Sault Ste. Marie
Fort De Buade
St. Ignace
L'Arbre Croche
Fort Michilimackinac
Maumee River
St. Joseph River
Auglaize R.
St. Marys River
Ohio River
LAC SUPERIEUR
CHIPPEWA
OTTAWA
ILLINOIS
LAC DES ILLINOIS
St. Joseph River
Fort St. Joseph
MIAMI
Fort Miami
Pickawillany
MIAMI
Miami River
De Pere Mission
Fort La Baye
Little Butte
Des Morts
Butte Des Morts
Fox River
WINNEBAGO
MENOMINEE
MASCOUTEN
KICKAPOO
SAUK
Wisconsin River
FOX
Rock River
Fox River
Des Plaines River
Canadian Angel
POTAWATOMI
Kankakee River
Iroquois River
Fort Ouiatenon
Fort Pimitoui
ILLINOIS
Illinois River
Vincennes
Wabash River
Sandy Lake
Mille Lacs
La Pointe
Chequamegon Bay
LAC
St. Peters River
St. Croix River
Mississippi River
Lake Pepin
St. Michael the Archangel
Fort Beauharnois
Fort St. Antoine
Minnesota River
Chippewa River
SIOUX
Immaculate Conception
Fort de Chartres
Kaskaskia
Kaskaskia River
Cahokia River
Mississippi River
Missouri River

MILES
25 0 50 100

Drawn under the supervision of LLOYD A. BROWN

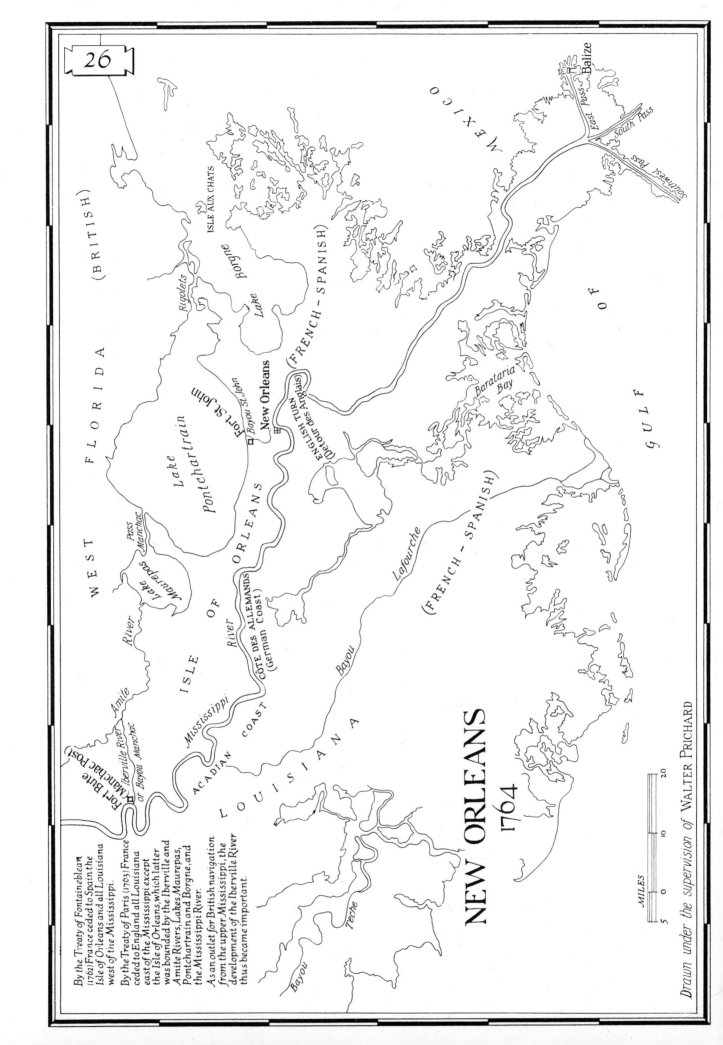

26

Balize

East Pass

South Pass

Southwest Pass

M E X I C O

G U L F   O F

ISLE AUX CHATS

Lake Borgne

Rigolets

(BRITISH)

F L O R I D A

W E S T

Pass Manchac

Lake Maurepas

Amite River

Iberville River or Bayou Manchac

Fort Bute (Manchac Post)

Lake Pontchartrain

Fort St. John

Bayou St. John

New Orleans

ENGLISH TURN (Detour des Anglais)

(FRENCH – SPANISH)

Baratarta Bay

I S L E   O F   O R L E A N S

Mississippi River

CÔTE DES ALLEMANDS (German Coast)

A C A D I A N   C O A S T

Bayou Lafourche

(FRENCH – SPANISH)

L O U I S I A N A

Teche

Bayou

By the Treaty of Fontainebleau (1762) France ceded to Spain the Isle of Orleans and all Louisiana west of the Mississippi.

By the Treaty of Paris (1763) France ceded to England all Louisiana east of the Mississippi except the Isle of Orleans, which latter was bounded by the Iberville and Amite Rivers, Lakes Maurepas, Pontchartrain and Borgne, and the Mississippi River.

As an outlet for British navigation from the upper Mississippi, the development of the Iberville River thus became important.

NEW ORLEANS
1764

MILES

5   0   10   20

Drawn under the supervision of WALTER PRICHARD

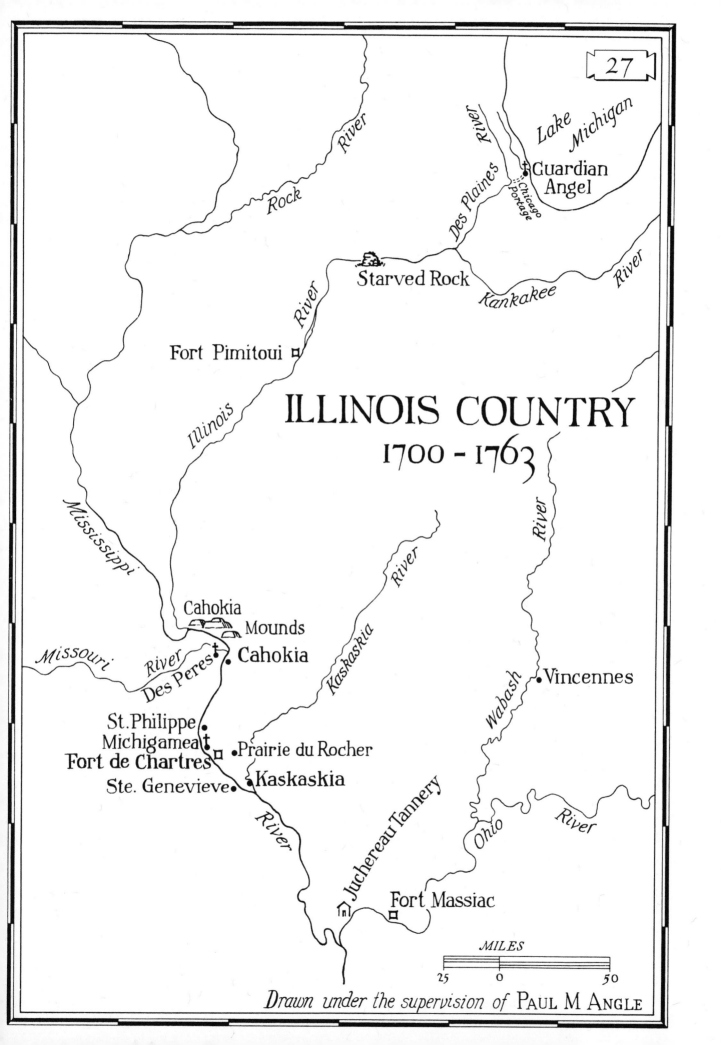

27

Lake Michigan

Rock River

Des Plaines River

Guardian Angel

Chicago Portage

Starved Rock

Kankakee River

Fort Pimitoui

Illinois River

ILLINOIS COUNTRY
1700 - 1763

Mississippi

River

Missouri River

Des Peres

Cahokia

Mounds

Cahokia

Kaskaskia River

Wabash

Vincennes

St.Philippe

Michigamea

Fort de Chartres

Prairie du Rocher

Ste. Genevieve

Kaskaskia

River

Juchereau Tannery

Ohio River

Fort Massiac

MILES

25   0   50

Drawn under the supervision of PAUL M ANGLE

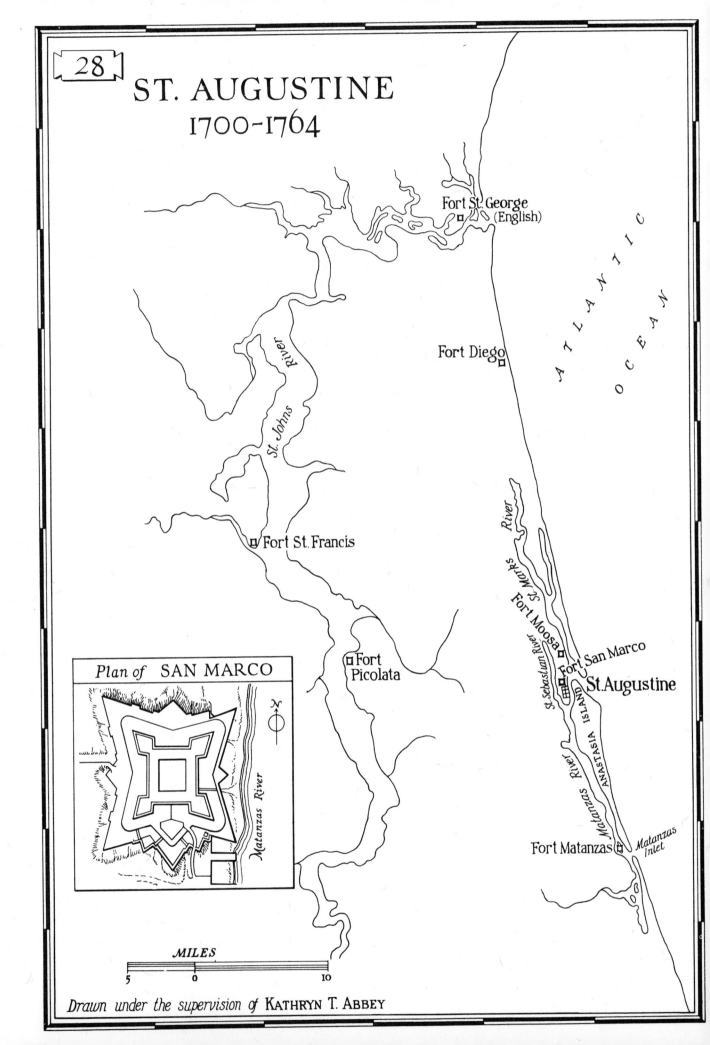

28

ST. AUGUSTINE
1700–1764

Fort St. George
(English)

ATLANTIC OCEAN

Fort Diego

St. Johns River

St. Marks River

Fort Moosa

Fort St. Francis

Fort San Marco

St. Sebastian River

St. Augustine

Fort Picolata

ANASTASIA ISLAND

Matanzas River

Fort Matanzas

Matanzas Inlet

Plan of SAN MARCO

N

Matanzas River

MILES

5   0   10

Drawn under the supervision of KATHRYN T. ABBEY

III LAND GRANTS AND SETTLEMENT OF THE THIRTEEN COLONIES

30

ROANOKE ISLAND COLONIES
1584-1591

CHAWANOAC

(Chowan River)

WEAPEMEOC

(ALBEMARLE SOUND)

ROANOKE

English Settlement

HATORASCK

MORATUC

DASAMONQUEPEUC

ISLAND

Moratuc (Roanoke) River

SECOTAN

AQUASEOGOC

CROATOAN

(Pamlico River)

WOCOCON

(PAMLICO SOUND)

ATLANTIC

OCEAN

(Neuse River)

MILES

5   0   10   20

Drawn under the supervision of C. C. CRITTENDEN

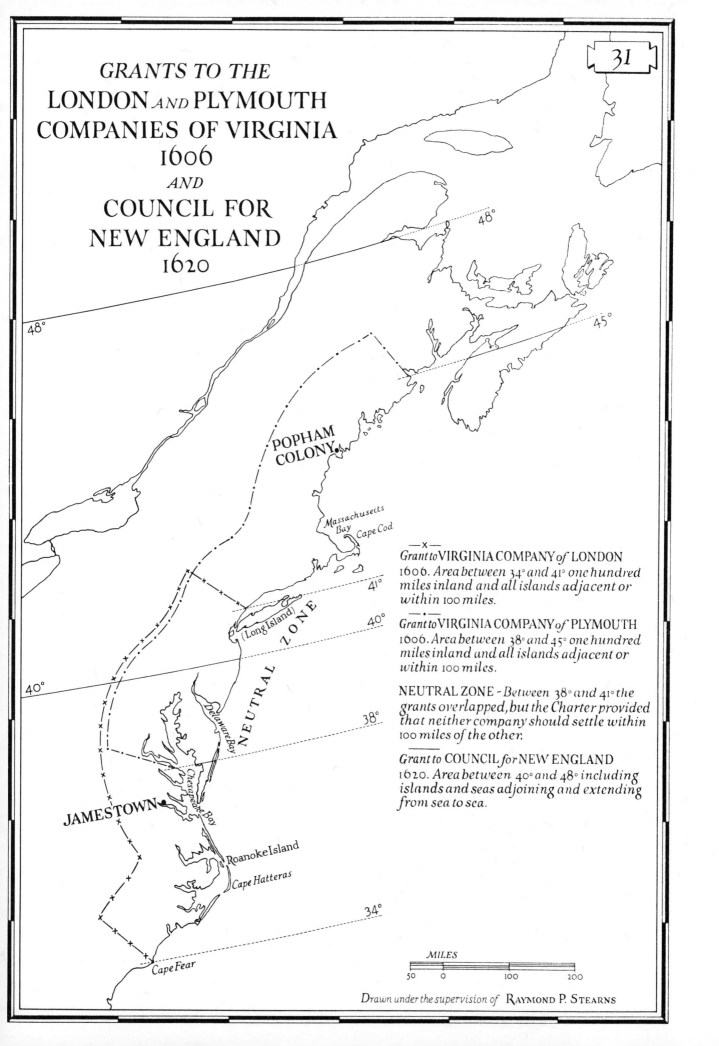

GRANTS TO THE
LONDON AND PLYMOUTH
COMPANIES OF VIRGINIA
1606
AND
COUNCIL FOR
NEW ENGLAND
1620

POPHAM
COLONY.

Massachusetts
Bay
Cape Cod

(Long Island)

NEUTRAL ZONE

Delaware Bay

Chesapeake Bay

JAMESTOWN

Roanoke Island
Cape Hatteras

Cape Fear

48°
45°
48°
41°
40°
40°
38°
34°

— × —
Grant to VIRGINIA COMPANY *of* LONDON
1606. *Area between 34° and 41° one hundred
miles inland and all islands adjacent or
within 100 miles.*

— • —
Grant to VIRGINIA COMPANY *of* PLYMOUTH
1606. *Area between 38° and 45° one hundred
miles inland and all islands adjacent or
within 100 miles.*

NEUTRAL ZONE - *Between 38° and 41° the
grants overlapped, but the Charter provided
that neither company should settle within
100 miles of the other.*

Grant to COUNCIL *for* NEW ENGLAND
1620. *Area between 40° and 48° including
islands and seas adjoining and extending
from sea to sea.*

MILES
50   0   100   200

Drawn under the supervision of RAYMOND P. STEARNS

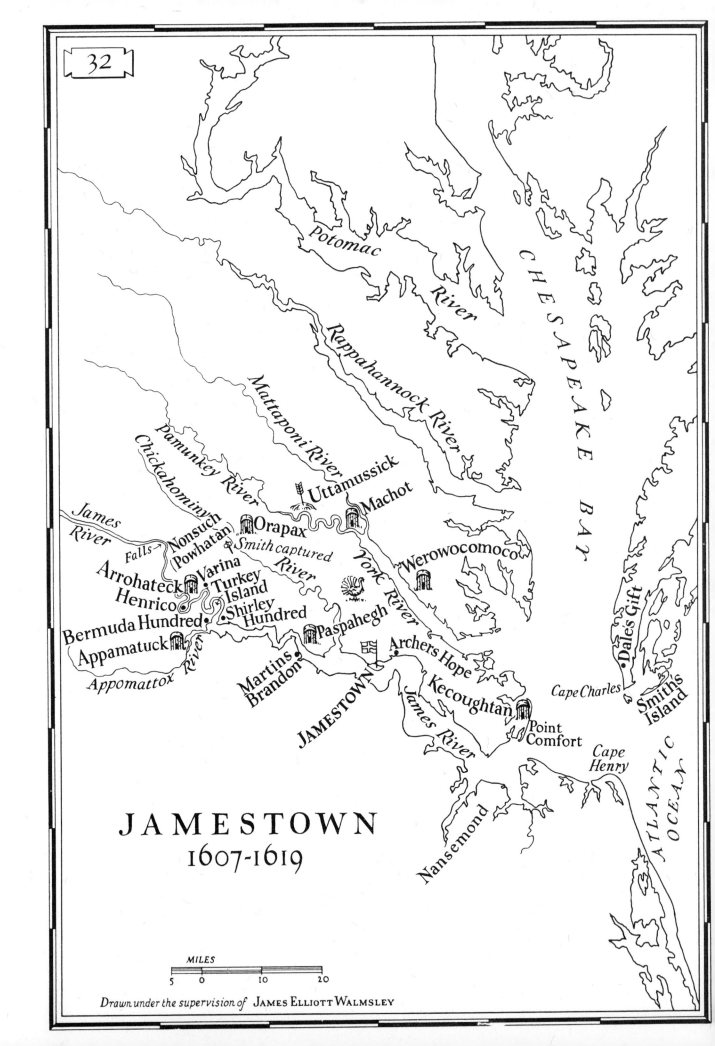

32

Potomac
River

Rappahannock River

C H E S A P E A K E B A Y

Mattaponi River

Pamunkey River

Chickahominy

James
River

Falls

Uttamussick

Machot

Nonsuch
(Powhatan)

Orapax

Smith captured

River

York River

Werowocomoco

Arrohateck

Varina

Turkey
Island

Henrico

Shirley
Hundred

Bermuda Hundred

Paspahegh

Appamatuck

Appomattox River

Martins
Brandon

JAMESTOWN

Archers Hope

Kecoughtan

James River

Dale's Gift

Cape Charles

Smiths
Island

Point
Comfort

Cape
Henry

Nansemond

ATLANTIC OCEAN

JAMESTOWN
1607-1619

MILES

5   0   10   20

Drawn under the supervision of JAMES ELLIOTT WALMSLEY

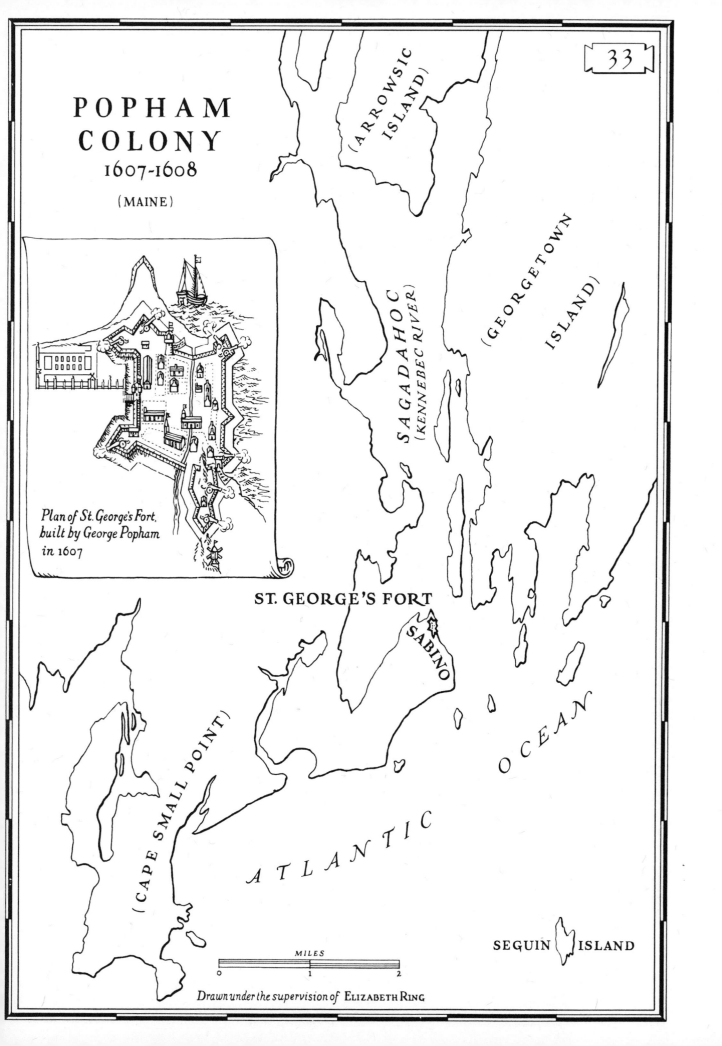

POPHAM COLONY
1607-1608
(MAINE)

Plan of St. George's Fort, built by George Popham in 1607

(ARROWSIC ISLAND)

(GEORGETOWN ISLAND)

SAGADAHOC (KENNEBEC RIVER)

ST. GEORGE'S FORT

SABINO

(CAPE SMALL POINT)

ATLANTIC OCEAN

SEGUIN ISLAND

MILES

0   1   2

Drawn under the supervision of ELIZABETH RING

33

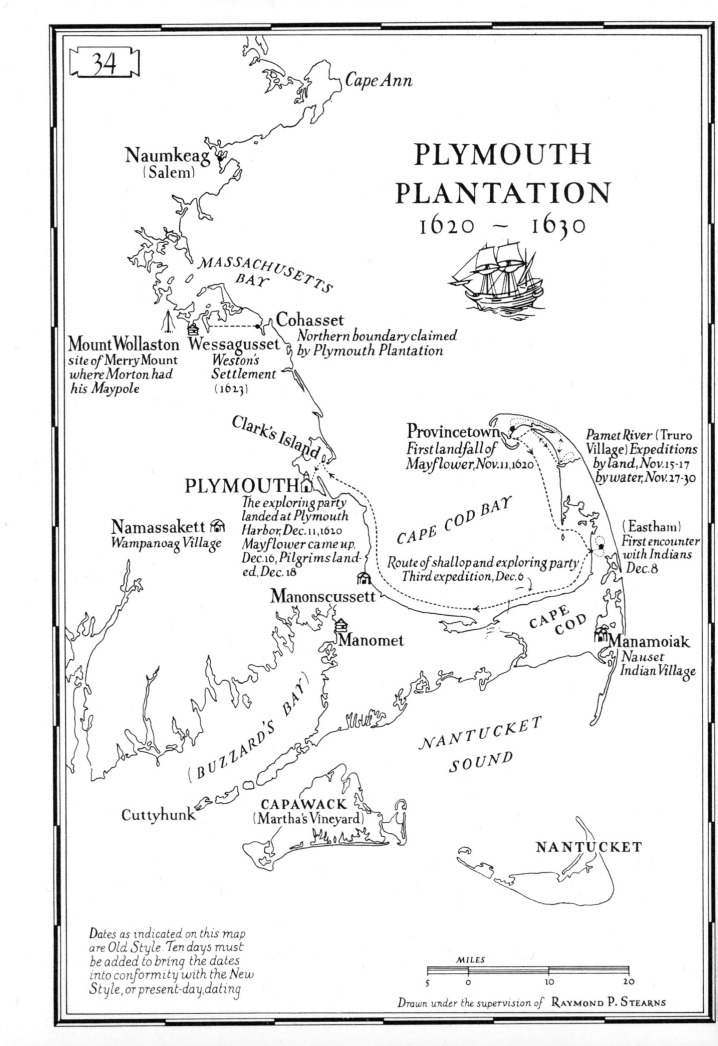

34

Cape Ann

Naumkeag
(Salem)

*MASSACHUSETTS
BAY*

PLYMOUTH
PLANTATION
1620 ~ 1630

Cohasset
*Northern boundary claimed
by Plymouth Plantation*

MountWollaston
*site of Merry Mount
where Morton had
his Maypole*

Wessagusset
*Weston's
Settlement
(1623)*

Clark's Island

Provincetown
*First landfall of
Mayflower,Nov.11,1620*

*Pamet River (Truro
Village) Expeditions
by land, Nov.15-17
by water,Nov.27-30*

PLYMOUTH

*The exploring party
landed at Plymouth
Harbor, Dec.11,1620
Mayflower came up,
Dec.16, Pilgrims land-
ed, Dec.18*

CAPE COD BAY

Namassakett
Wampanoag Village

(Eastham)
*First encounter
with Indians
Dec.8*

*Route of shallop and exploring party
Third expedition, Dec.6*

Manonscussett

Manomet

*CAPE
COD*

Manamoiak
*Nauset
Indian Village*

BUZZARD'S BAY

*NANTUCKET
SOUND*

Cuttyhunk

CAPAWACK
(Martha's Vineyard)

NANTUCKET

*Dates as indicated on this map
are Old Style. Ten days must
be added to bring the dates
into conformity with the New
Style, or present-day dating*

MILES
5   0   10   20

Drawn under the supervision of RAYMOND P. STEARNS

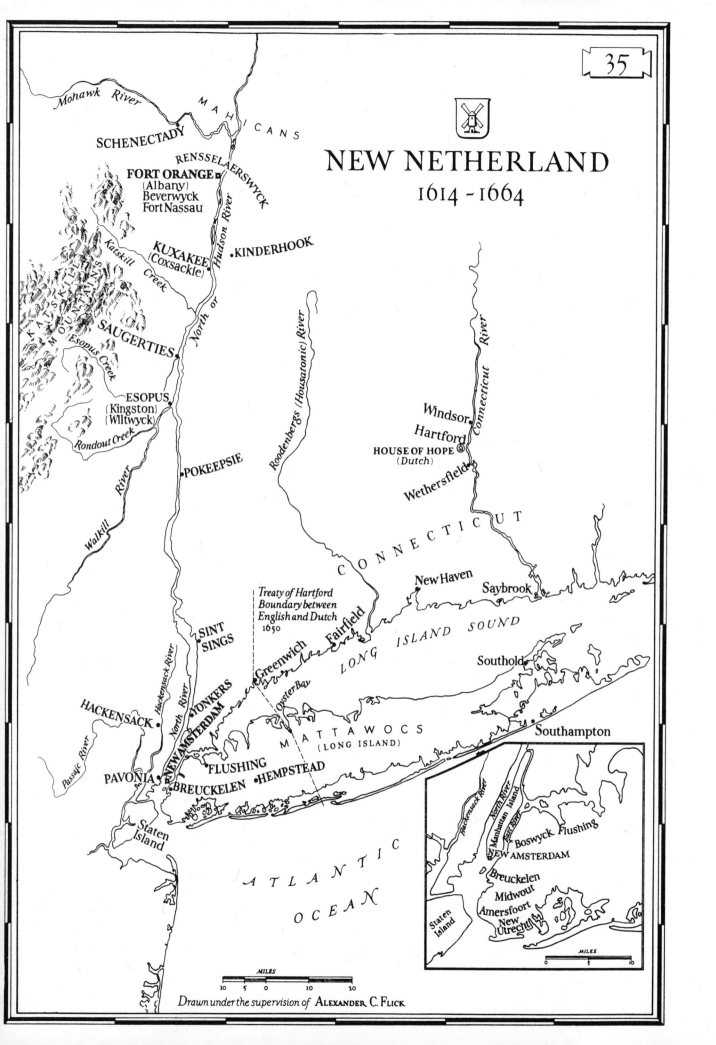

35

NEW NETHERLAND
1614-1664

Mohawk River

M A H I C A N S

SCHENECTADY

RENSSELAERSWYCK

FORT ORANGE (Albany)
Beverwyck
Fort Nassau

KUXAKEE (Coxsackie) • KINDERHOOK

Katskill Creek

Hudson River

KATSKILL MOUNTAINS

SAUGERTIES

Esopus Creek

ESOPUS (Kingston) (Wiltwyck)

Rondout Creek

North or Hudson River

Roodenbergs (Housatonic) River

Connecticut River

Windsor
Hartford
HOUSE OF HOPE (Dutch)

Wethersfield

POKEEPSIE

Walkill River

C O N N E C T I C U T

New Haven
Saybrook

Treaty of Hartford
Boundary between
English and Dutch
1650

Fairfield

L O N G I S L A N D S O U N D

Greenwich

Southold

SINT SINGS

Hackensack River

North River

YONKERS

Oyster Bay

HACKENSACK

M A T T A W O C S (LONG ISLAND)

Southampton

Passaic River

NEW AMSTERDAM
FLUSHING
• HEMPSTEAD

PAVONIA
BREUCKELEN

Staten Island

A T L A N T I C
O C E A N

Hackensack River
North River
East River
Manhattan Island
Boswyck Flushing
NEW AMSTERDAM
Breuckelen
Midwout
Amersfoort
New Utrecht
Staten Island

MILES
0   5   10

MILES
10 5 0   10   20

Drawn under the supervision of ALEXANDER C. FLICK

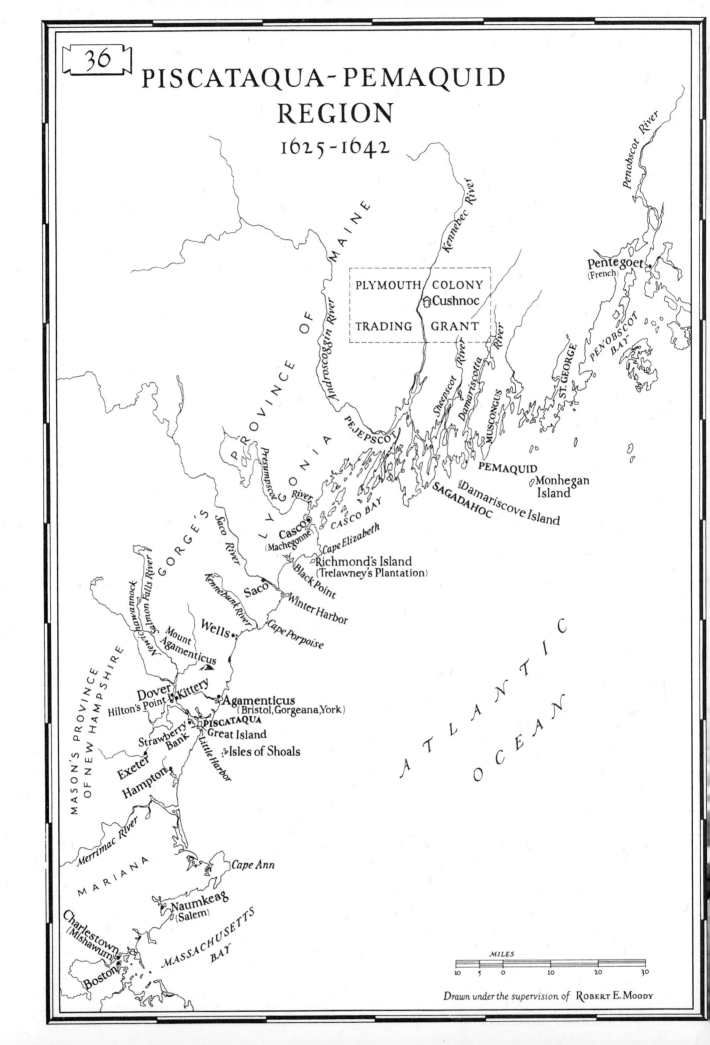

PISCATAQUA-PEMAQUID REGION
1625-1642

PLYMOUTH COLONY
Cushnoc
TRADING GRANT

Penobscot River

Kennebec River

Pentegoet
(French)

Androscoggin River

PROVINCE OF MAINE

PEJEPSCOT

Sheepscot River

Damariscotta River

Muscongus River

ST. GEORGE

PENOBSCOT BAY

Presumpscot River

LYGONIA

CASCO BAY

PEMAQUID

Monhegan
Island

GORGE'S

Saco River

Casco
(Machegonne)

SAGADAHOC

Damariscove Island

Cape Elizabeth

Richmond's Island
(Trelawney's Plantation)

Black Point

Newichawannock River

Salmon Falls River

Kennebunk River

Saco

Winter Harbor

Wells

Mount
Agamenticus

Cape Porpoise

A T L A N T I C

Dover
Hilton's Point

Kittery

Agamenticus
(Bristol, Gorgeana, York)

MASON'S PROVINCE OF NEW HAMPSHIRE

PISCATAQUA
Great Island

Strawberry
Bank

Little Harbor

Exeter

Isles of Shoals

O C E A N

Hampton

Merrimac River

MARIANA

Cape Ann

Naumkeag
(Salem)

Charlestown
(Mishawum)

MASSACHUSETTS
BAY

Boston

MILES

10   5   0   10   20   30

Drawn under the supervision of ROBERT E. MOODY

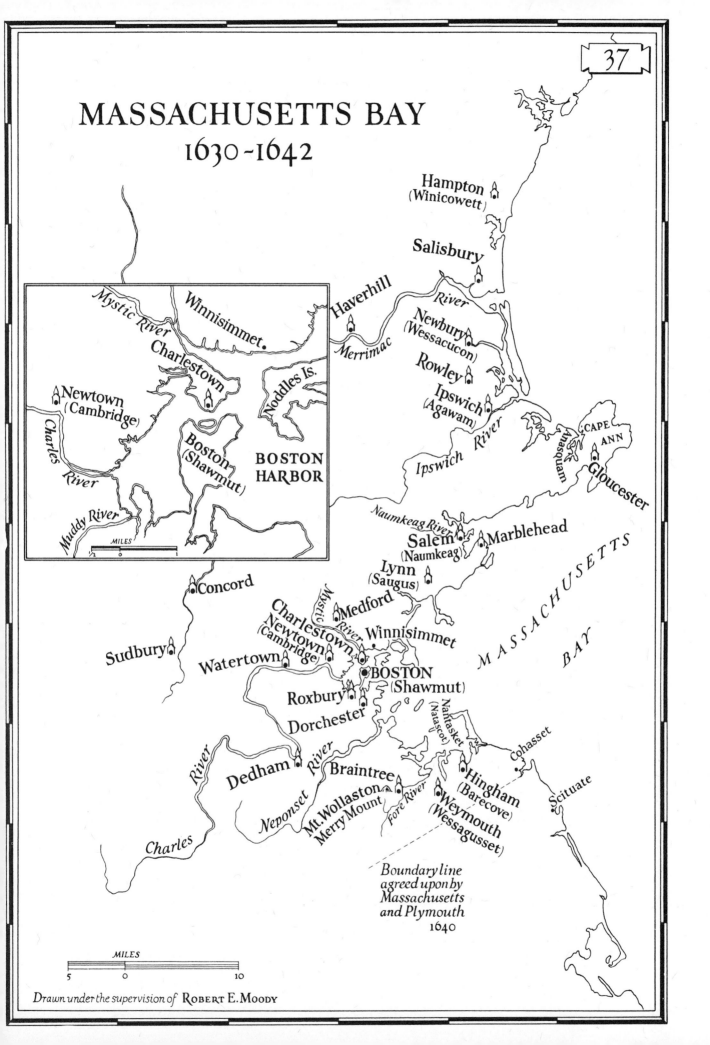

MASSACHUSETTS BAY
1630~1642

Hampton
(Winicowett)

Salisbury

Haverhill

River

Newbury
(Wessacucon)

Merrimac

Rowley

Ipswich
(Agawam)

Ipswich River

Annisquam

CAPE
ANN

Gloucester

Naumkeag River

Salem
(Naumkeag)

Marblehead

Lynn
(Saugus)

MASSACHUSETTS

BAY

Concord

Medford

Mystic River

Winnisimmet

Charlestown
Newtown
(Cambridge)

Sudbury

Watertown

BOSTON
(Shawmut)

Roxbury

Dorchester

Nantasket
(Natascot)

Cohasset

River

Dedham

River

Braintree

Hingham
(Barecove)

Scituate

Charles

Neponset

Mt. Wollaston
Merry Mount

Fore River

Weymouth
(Wessagusset)

Boundary line
agreed upon by
Massachusetts
and Plymouth
1640

MILES

5   0   10

Drawn under the supervision of ROBERT E. MOODY

Inset

Mystic River

Winnisimmet.

Charlestown

Noddles Is.

Newtown
(Cambridge)

Charles River

Boston
(Shawmut)

BOSTON
HARBOR

Muddy River

MILES

½   0   1

CONNECTICUT AND NEW HAVEN COLONIES
1635 – 1660

MASSACHUSETTS

WARANOKE
(Westfield)

SPRINGFIELD
(Agawam)

River

Windsor

PLYMOUTH TRADING POST

Hartford
DUTCH HOUSE OF HOPE

CONNECTICUT

Farmington
(Tunxis)

Wethersfield

COLONY

Connecticut

Quinebaug River

Middletown
(Mattabesec)

Norwich
(Mohegan)

Housatonic River

Naugatuck River

NEW HAVEN

River

New London
(Nameaug)

Mystic River

Pequot Forts

CONNECTICUT

COLONY

PAUGASSET
(Derby)

NEW HAVEN
(Quinnipiac)

Saybrook

Pequot

Fishers Island

Treaty of Hartford Boundary
between English
and Dutch, 1650

Stratford
(Cupheag)

BRANFORD
(Totoket)

GUILFORD

SOUND

Fairfield
Norwalk

Pequannock

MILFORD
(Wepawaug)

L O N G   I S L A N D

SOUTHOLD
(Yennycock)

Rippowam

STAMFORD

GREENWICH

East Hampton

Oyster
Bay

Setauket
(Brookhaven)

Huntington

Southampton

L O N G   I S L A N D
(MATTAWOCS)

MILES
5   0   10   20

Drawn under the supervision of MARJORIE E. CASE

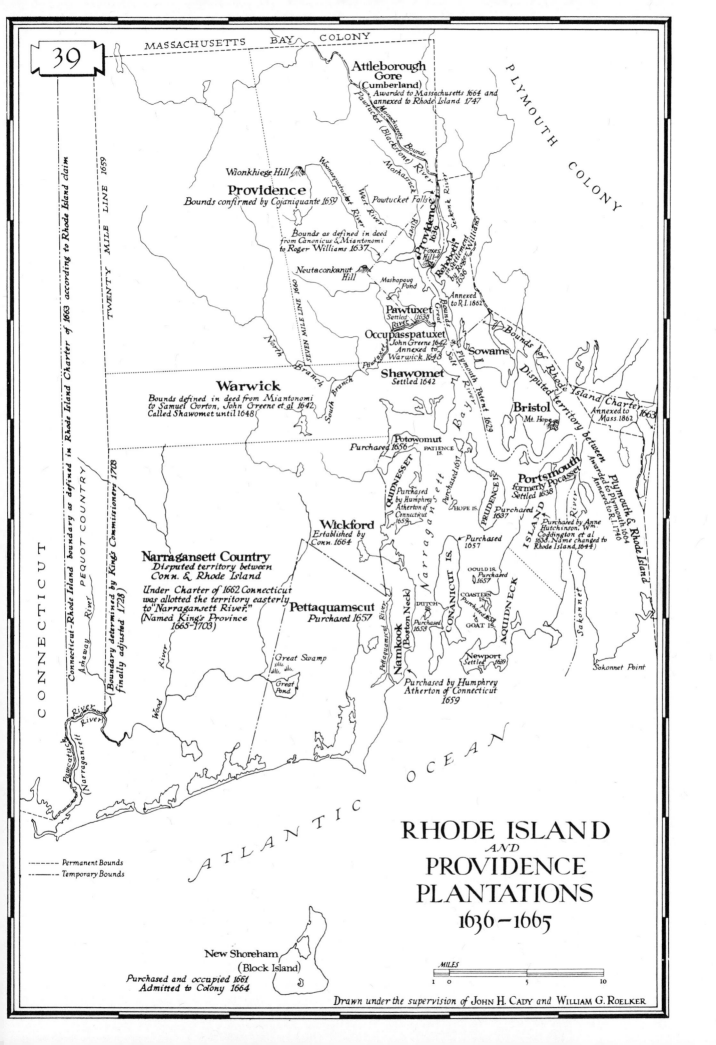

MASSACHUSETTS BAY COLONY

PLYMOUTH COLONY

39

Attleborough
Gore
(Cumberland)
Awarded to Massachusetts 1664 and
annexed to Rhode Island 1747

Wionkhiege Hill

Providence
Bounds confirmed by Cojaniquante 1659

Pawtucket Falls

Bounds as defined in deed
from Canonicus & Miantonomi
to Roger Williams 1637

Providence 1636

Rehoboth First settlement
by Roger Williams 1636

Foxes
Hill

Neutaconkanut
Hill

Mashapaug
Pond

Annexed
to R.I. 1862

Pawtuxet
Settled 1638

Occupasspatuxet
John Greene 1642
Annexed to
Warwick 1648

Sowams

Shawomet
Settled 1642

Disputed Territory between

Warwick
Bounds defined in deed from Miantonomi
to Samuel Gorton, John Greene et al 1642
Called Shawomet until 1648

Bristol
Mt. Hope
Annexed to
Mass. 1862

Bounds of Rhode Island Charter 1663

Potowomut
Purchased 1656

PATIENCE IS.

QUIDNESSET

Purchased
by Humphrey
Atherton of
Connecticut
1659

HOPE IS.

PRUDENCE IS.

Portsmouth
formerly Pocasset
Settled 1638

Purchased
1637

Plymouth & Rhode Island
Awarded to Plymouth 1664
Annexed to R.I. 1746

Wickford
Established by
Conn. 1664

Purchased
1657

Purchased by Anne
Hutchinson, Wm.
Coddington et al
1638. Name changed to
Rhode Island, 1644)

Narragansett Country
Disputed territory between
Conn. & Rhode Island

GOULD IS.
Purchased
1657

Under Charter of 1662 Connecticut
was allotted the territory easterly
to "Narragansett River."
(Named King's Province
1665-1703)

Pettaquamscut
Purchased 1657

Namkook
(Boston Neck)

DUTCH
IS.
Purchased
1658

CONANICUT IS.

COASTERS
IS.
Purchased 1658
GOAT IS.

AQUIDNECK

SAKONNET

Newport
Settled 1639

Sakonnet Point

Great Swamp

Great
Pond

Purchased by Humphrey
Atherton of Connecticut
1659

TWENTY MILE LINE 1659

Connecticut-Rhode Island boundary as defined in Rhode Island Charter of 1663 according to Rhode Island claim

PEQUOT COUNTRY

(Boundary determined by King's Commissioners 1703
finally adjusted 1728)

SEVEN MILE LINE 1660

North Branch

South Branch

Pawtuxet River

Pocasset River

Woonasquatucket River

West River

Moshassuck River

Massachusetts (Blackstone) River

Pawtucket (Blackstone) River

Seekonk River

Providence River

Narragansett Bay

Salt River

Ashaway River

Wood River

Pawcatuck (Narragansett) River

CONNECTICUT

ATLANTIC OCEAN

- - - - - Permanent Bounds
— - — Temporary Bounds

RHODE ISLAND
AND
PROVIDENCE
PLANTATIONS
1636–1665

New Shoreham
(Block Island)
Purchased and occupied 1661
Admitted to Colony 1664

MILES
1 0   5   10

Drawn under the supervision of JOHN H. CADY *and* WILLIAM G. ROELKER

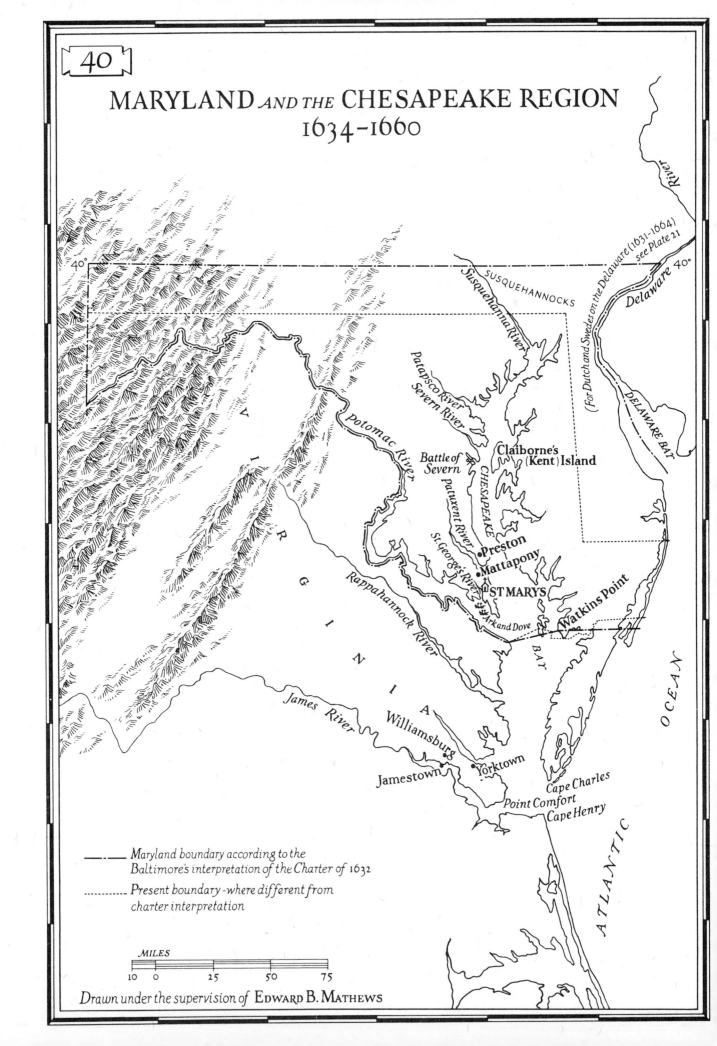

40

MARYLAND *AND THE* CHESAPEAKE REGION
1634-1660

40°

SUSQUEHANNOCKS

Susquehanna River

(For Dutch and Swedes on the Delaware (1631-1664) see Plate 21

Delaware River

40°

Delaware

DELAWARE BAY

Patapsco River

Severn River

Battle of Severn

Claiborne's (Kent) Island

V I R G I N I A

Potomac River

CHESAPEAKE

Patuxent River

St. George's River

Preston

Mattapony

ST MARYS

Rappahannock River

Ark and Dove

BAY

Watkins Point

ATLANTIC OCEAN

James River

Williamsburg

Yorktown

Jamestown

Cape Charles

Point Comfort

Cape Henry

ATLANTIC

—·—·— Maryland boundary according to the
Baltimore's interpretation of the Charter of 1632

············ Present boundary - where different from
charter interpretation

MILES

10 0   25   50   75

Drawn under the supervision of EDWARD B. MATHEWS

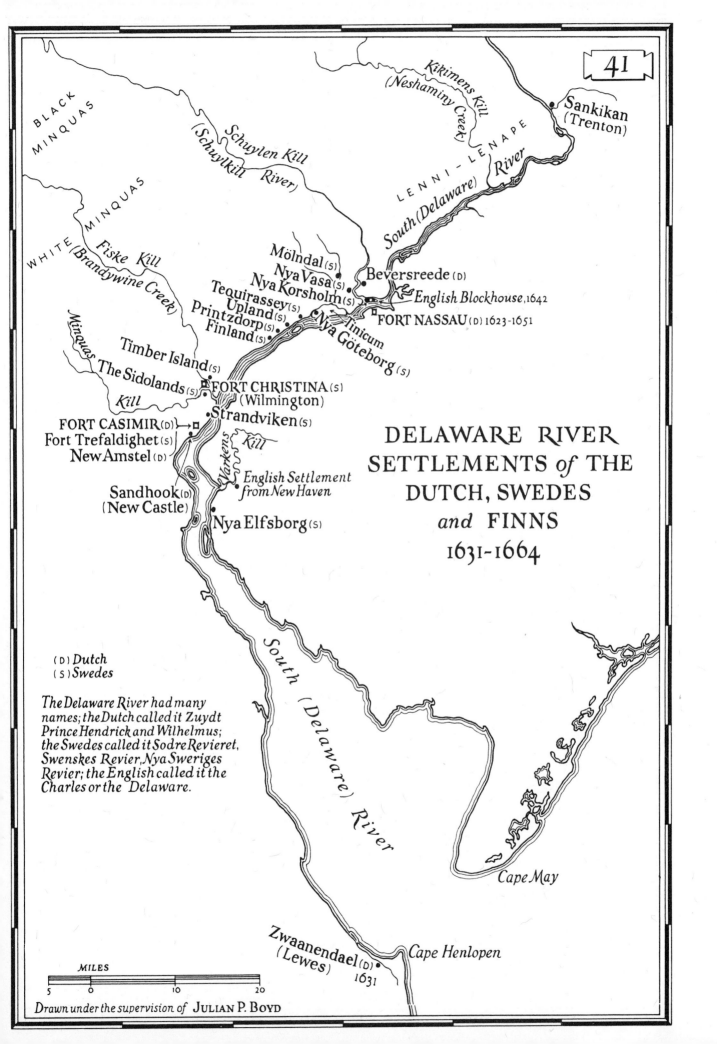

BLACK MINQUAS

WHITE MINQUAS

Kikimens Kill (Neshaminy Creek)

Schuylen Kill (Schuylkill River)

LENNI-LENAPE

Sankikan (Trenton)

South (Delaware) River

Fiske Kill (Brandywine Creek)

Mölndal (S)
Nya Vasa (S)
Nya Korsholm (S)
Tequirassey (S)
Upland (S)
Printzdorp (S)
Finland (S)

Beversreede (D)
English Blockhouse, 1642
Tinicum
Nya Göteborg (S)

FORT NASSAU (D) 1623-1651

Minquas Kill

Timber Island (S)
The Sidolands (S)

FORT CHRISTINA (S)
(Wilmington)

FORT CASIMIR (D)
Fort Trefaldighet (S)
New Amstel (D)

Strandviken (S)

Varkens Kill

English Settlement from New Haven

Sandhook (D)
(New Castle)

Nya Elfsborg (S)

DELAWARE RIVER
SETTLEMENTS of THE
DUTCH, SWEDES
and FINNS
1631-1664

(D) *Dutch*
(S) *Swedes*

*The Delaware River had many
names; the Dutch called it Zuydt
Prince Hendrick and Wilhelmus;
the Swedes called it Sodre Revieret,
Swenskes Revier, Nya Sweriges
Revier; the English called it the
Charles or the Delaware.*

South (Delaware) River

Cape May

Zwaanendael (D)
(Lewes)
1631

Cape Henlopen

MILES
5   0   10   20

Drawn under the supervision of JULIAN P. BOYD

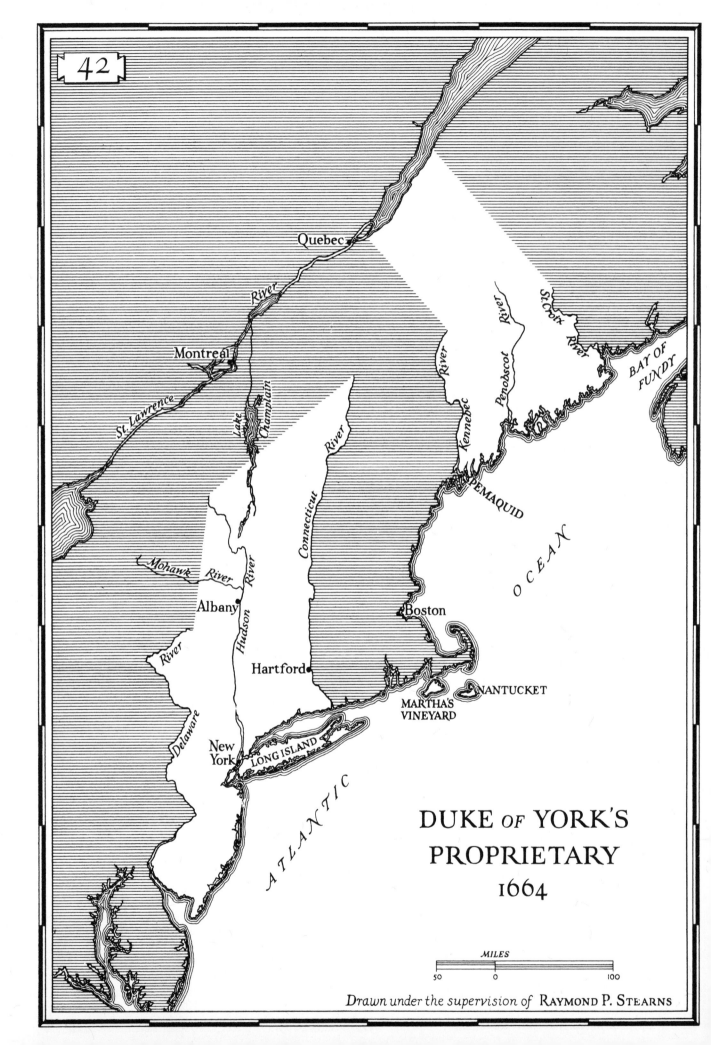

42

Quebec

Montreal

St. Lawrence

Lake Champlain

St. Croix River

Penobscot River

Kennebec River

River

BAY OF FUNDY

PEMAQUID

Mohawk River

Connecticut River

Hudson River

Albany

OCEAN

Boston

Hartford

River

NANTUCKET

MARTHA'S VINEYARD

Delaware

New York

LONG ISLAND

ATLANTIC

DUKE OF YORK'S
PROPRIETARY
1664

MILES

50   0   100

Drawn under the supervision of RAYMOND P. STEARNS

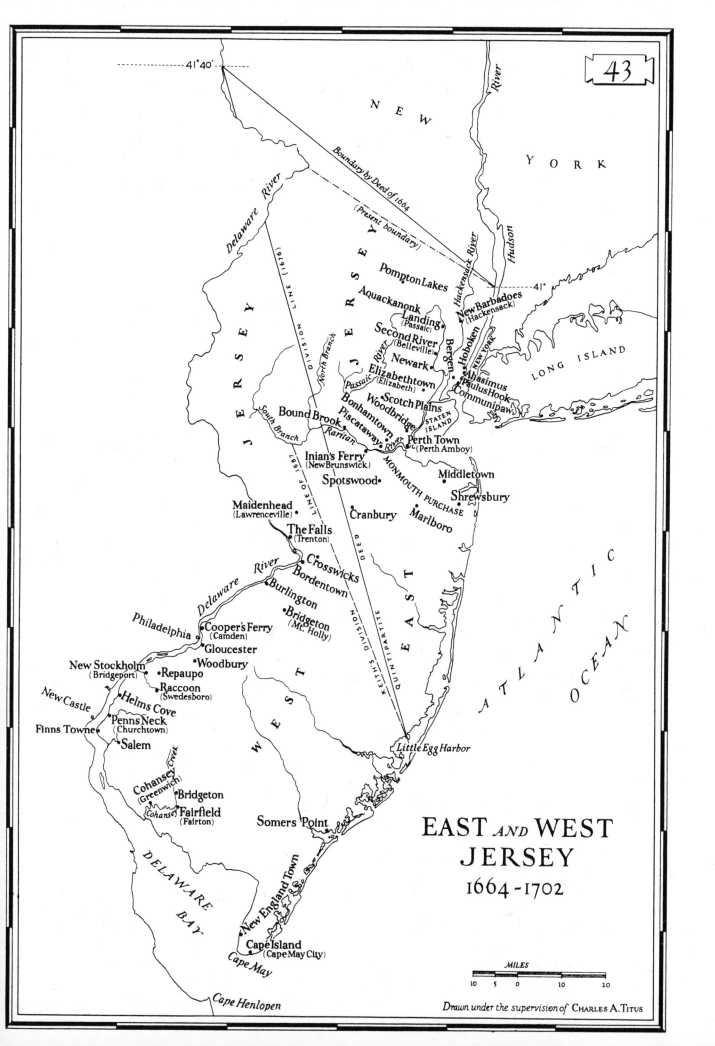

41°40'

NEW

YORK

Boundary by Deed of 1664

(Present boundary)

41°

Hackensack River

Hudson

Delaware River

DIVISION LINE (1676)

North Branch

South Branch

Raritan

Pompton Lakes

Aquackanonk Landing (Passaic)

Second River (Belleville)

Newark

Elizabethtown (Elizabeth)

Passaic

Scotch Plains

Bonhamtown

Woodbridge

Bound Brook

Piscataway

Raritan

Perth Town (Perth Amboy)

River

New Barbadoes (Hackensack)

Bergen

Hoboken

Ahasimus

Paulus Hook

Communipaw

NEW YORK

STATEN ISLAND

LONG ISLAND

Inian's Ferry (New Brunswick)

Spotswood

Cranbury

Middletown

Shrewsbury

Marlboro

MONMOUTH PURCHASE

Maidenhead (Lawrenceville)

The Falls (Trenton)

Crosswicks

Bordentown

Burlington

Bridgeton (Mt. Holly)

Cooper's Ferry (Camden)

Gloucester

Woodbury

Philadelphia

New Stockholm (Bridgeport)

Repaupo

Raccoon (Swedesboro)

Helms Cove

New Castle

Penns Neck (Churchtown)

Finns Towne

Salem

Cohansey Creek

Bridgeton

Greenwich (Cohansey)

Fairfield (Fairton)

Somers Point

New England Town

Cape Island (Cape May City)

Cape May

DELAWARE BAY

Cape Henlopen

LINE OF 1687

DEED DIVISION

KEITH'S DIVISION

QUINTIPARTITE

EAST

WEST

JERSEY

JERSEY

ATLANTIC OCEAN

Little Egg Harbor

Delaware River

EAST AND WEST JERSEY 1664-1702

MILES

10 5 0   10   20

Drawn under the supervision of CHARLES A. TITUS

43

44

WEST JERSEY
Cape May
LOWER COUNTIES OF DELAWARE

MARYLAND
Potomac River
Western boundary of the Fairfax Proprietary
Rappahannock River
FAIRFAX PROPRIETARY (Northern Neck)
Germanna
Route of Spotswood's Expedition
Shenandoah River

VIRGINIA

WILLIAMSBURG
James River
Fort Henry
Yorktown
Norfolk
Northern Boundary of Carolina under Charter of 1665 36° 30'
Currituck
Northern Boundary of Carolina under Charter of 1663 36°
Roanoke River
Chowan River
ALBEMARLE
Edenton
35° 34'

GRANVILLE (GRANT)

NORTH CAROLINA
Nease River
Fort Nohoroco
New Berne
TUSCARORA
Pamlico Sound

Cape Fear River
CLARENDON
Brunswick
Cape Fear

CHEROKEE

CATAWBA
Broad River
Saluda River
Wateree River
Peedee River

SOUTH CAROLINA
Santee River
Jamestown
ST. JOHN'S BERKELEY
The Orange Quarter
CHARLESTON
Edisto River
Ashley River
Cooper River
YAMASEE

Savannah River
Ogeechee River
Oconee River
Ocmulgee River

CREEK

Coweta Town
Savacola (Spanish)
Chattahoochee River
(Flint River)

Beaufort
Stuart's Town
Port Royal

Altamaha River
Fort King George
31°

Southern Boundary of Carolina under Charter of 1663

Santa Cruz de Savacola (Spanish)
AYUBALE
San Luis (Spanish)
Ochlockonee River
APALACHE
Apalachicola River

St. Mary's River

St. Johns River

St. Augustine (Spanish)

Southern Boundary of Carolina under Charter of 1665 29°

CAROLINAS
AND VIRGINIA
1663-1729

MILES
25   0   50   100

Drawn under the supervision of E. MERTON COULTER

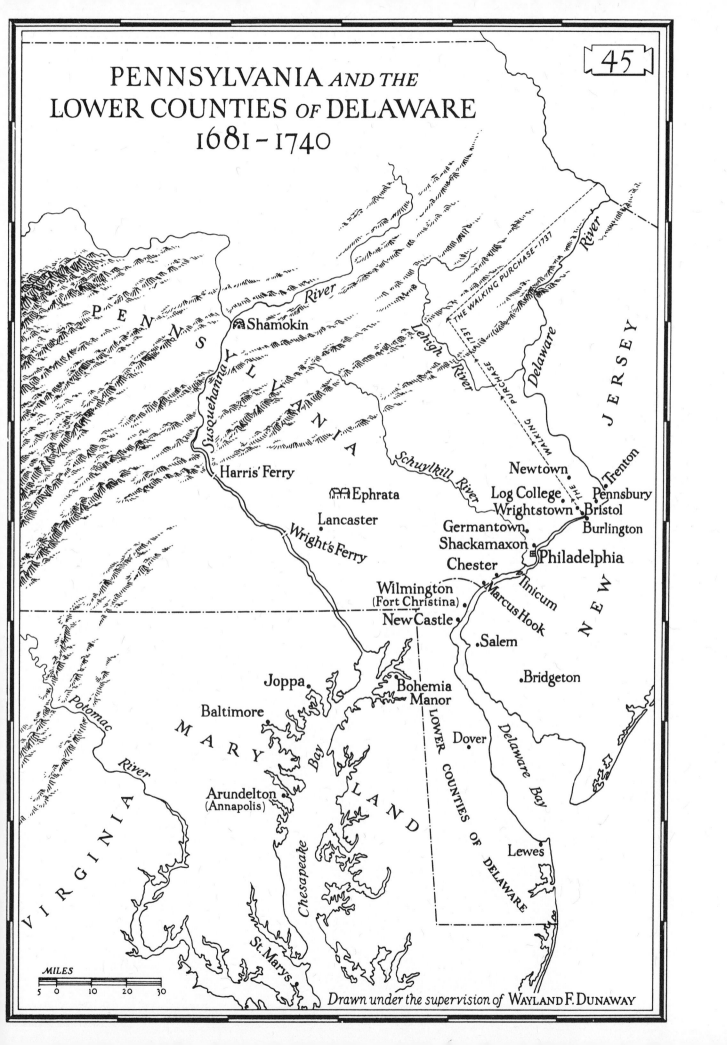

PENNSYLVANIA *AND THE*
LOWER COUNTIES *OF* DELAWARE
1681 – 1740

45

THE WALKING PURCHASE – 1737

River

Shamokin

Lehigh River

Susquehanna River

LEHIGH WALKING PURCHASE

Delaware River

J E R S E Y

P E N N S Y L V A N I A

Harris' Ferry

Schuylkill River

Newtown

Ephrata

Log College

Trenton

Lancaster

Wrightstown

Pennsbury

Bristol

Germantown

Wright's Ferry

Shackamaxon

Burlington

Chester

Philadelphia

Tinicum

N E W

Wilmington
(Fort Christina)

Marcus Hook

New Castle

Salem

Bridgeton

Joppa

Bohemia
Manor

Potomac

Baltimore

M A R Y

Dover

Delaware Bay

River

L A N D

LOWER COUNTIES OF DELAWARE

Arundelton
(Annapolis)

V I R G I N I A

Chesapeake Bay

Lewes

St. Marys

MILES

5   0   10   20   30

Drawn under the supervision of WAYLAND F. DUNAWAY

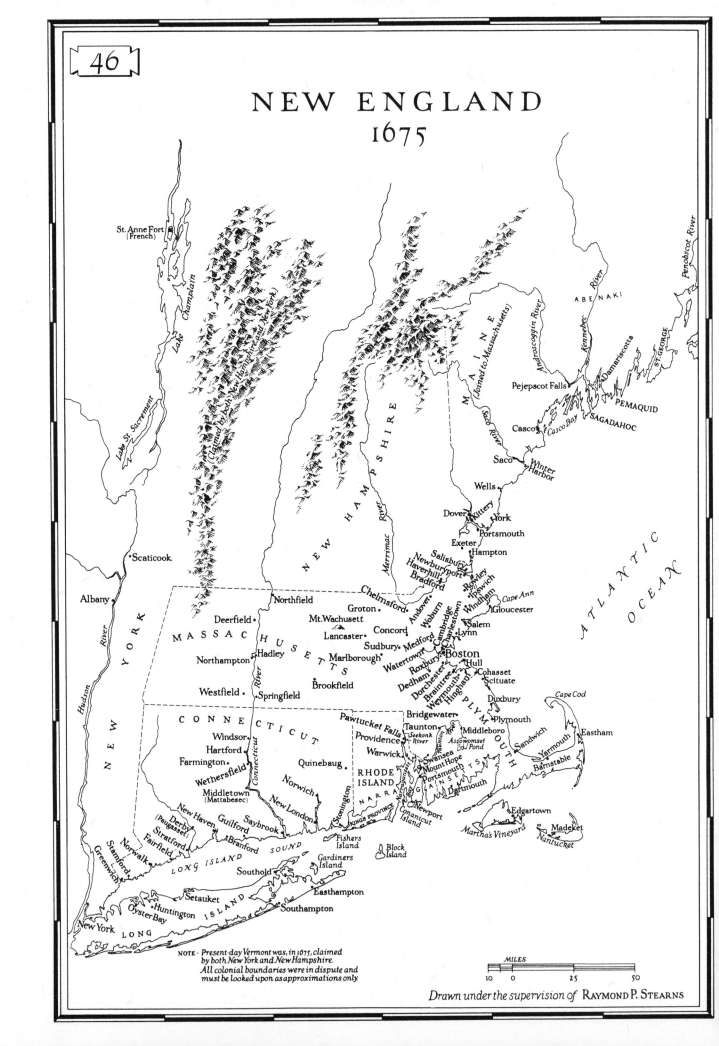

46

NEW ENGLAND
1675

St.Anne Fort ⚑
(French)

Lake Champlain

Lake St Sacrement

(Claimed by both New Hampshire and New York)

M A I N E
(Joined to Massachusetts)

A B E N A K I

Androscoggin River

Kennebec River

Damariscotta

ST. GEORGE

Penobscot River

Pejepscot Falls

PEMAQUID

Casco · *Casco Bay* · *SAGADAHOC*

Saco · Winter Harbor

Saco River

Wells

Dover · Kittery · York

Portsmouth

Exeter · Hampton

Salisbury

Newburyport

Haverhill · Rowley · Ipswich

Bradford · Windham · *Cape Ann*

Gloucester

· Scaticook

Albany ·

N E W   H A M P S H I R E

Merrimac River

Chelmsford ·

Northfield

Groton · Andover · Woburn · Cambridge · Charlestown · Salem

Deerfield · Mt.Wachusett · Concord · Medford · Lynn

M A S S A C H U S E T T S

Lancaster · Sudbury · Watertown · Boston

Northampton · Hadley · Marlborough · Roxbury · Hull

Dorchester · Cohasset

Dedham · Braintree · Scituate

Brookfield · Weymouth · Hingham

Westfield · Springfield

Duxbury · *Cape Cod*

Connecticut River

N E W   Y O R K

Hudson River

Bridgewater · Plymouth

C O N N E C T I C U T

Pawtucket Falls

Taunton · Middleboro

Providence · *Seekonk River* · Assowomset Pond · Sandwich · Eastham

Windsor · Warwick · *Taunton River* · Yarmouth

Hartford · Quinebaug · Swansea · Barnstable

Farmington · *RHODE ISLAND* · Mount Hope

Wethersfield · Norwich · Portsmouth · Dartmouth

Middletown · New London · *NARRA...GANSETTS*

(Mattabesec) · Newport

KINGS PROVINCE · Conanicut Island

New Haven · Guilford · Saybrook · Stonington

Derby · Branford · Fishers Island · Block Island · Edgartown

(Paugasset) · *P L Y M O U T H*

Stratford · Fairfield · Gardiners Island · Madeket

Stamford · Norwalk · *L O N G   I S L A N D   S O U N D* · *Martha's Vineyard* · Nantucket

Greenwich · Southold

Setauket · Easthampton

New York · Huntington · Southampton

Oyster Bay · *L O N G   I S L A N D*

A T L A N T I C   O C E A N

NOTE - *Present-day Vermont was, in 1675, claimed
by both New York and New Hampshire.
All colonial boundaries were in dispute and
must be looked upon as approximations only.*

MILES
10   0   25   50

Drawn under the supervision of RAYMOND P. STEARNS

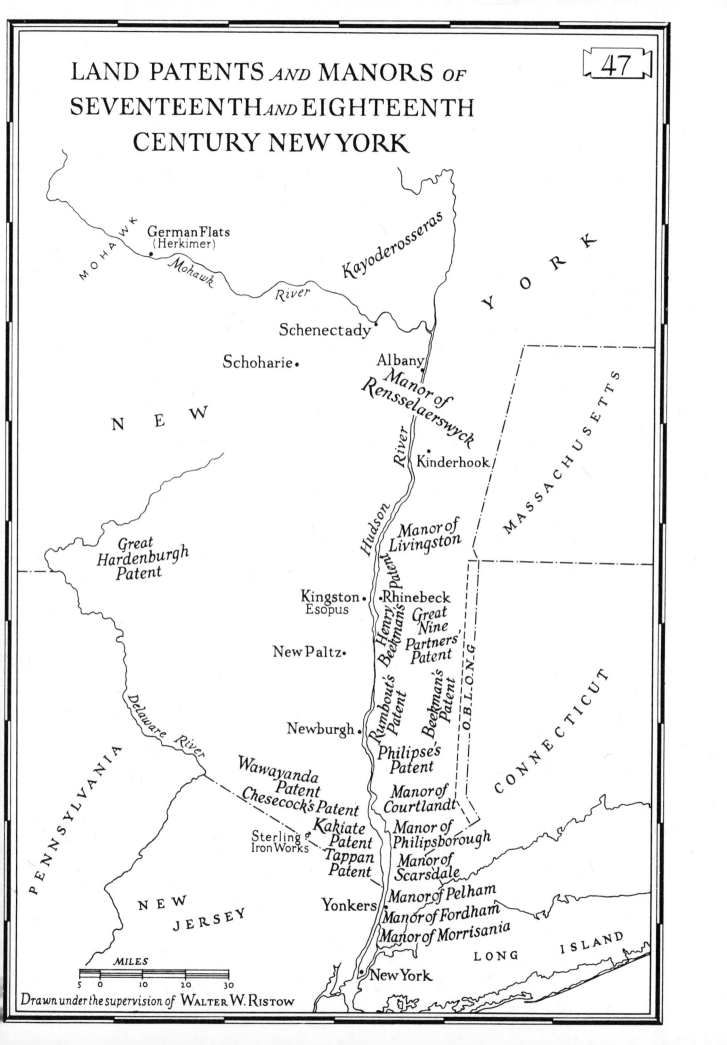

LAND PATENTS AND MANORS OF
SEVENTEENTH AND EIGHTEENTH
CENTURY NEW YORK

47

German Flats
(Herkimer)

MOHAWK

Mohawk River

Kayoderosseras

YORK

Schenectady

Schoharie

Albany

Manor of
Rensselaerswyck

NEW

Kinderhook

MASSACHUSETTS

Hudson River

Manor of
Livingston

Great
Hardenburgh
Patent

Kingston
Esopus

Rhinebeck

Great
Nine
Partners'
Patent

New Paltz

Henry Beekman's Patent

OBLONG

Delaware River

Newburgh

Rumbout's Patent

Beekman's Patent

CONNECTICUT

PENNSYLVANIA

Wawayanda
Patent

Chesecock's Patent

Sterling
Iron Works

Kakiate
Patent

Tappan
Patent

Philipse's
Patent

Manor of
Courtlandt

Manor of
Philipsborough

Manor of
Scarsdale

NEW

JERSEY

Yonkers

Manor of Pelham

Manor of Fordham

Manor of Morrisania

LONG ISLAND

MILES
5 0 10 20 30

New York

Drawn under the supervision of WALTER W. RISTOW

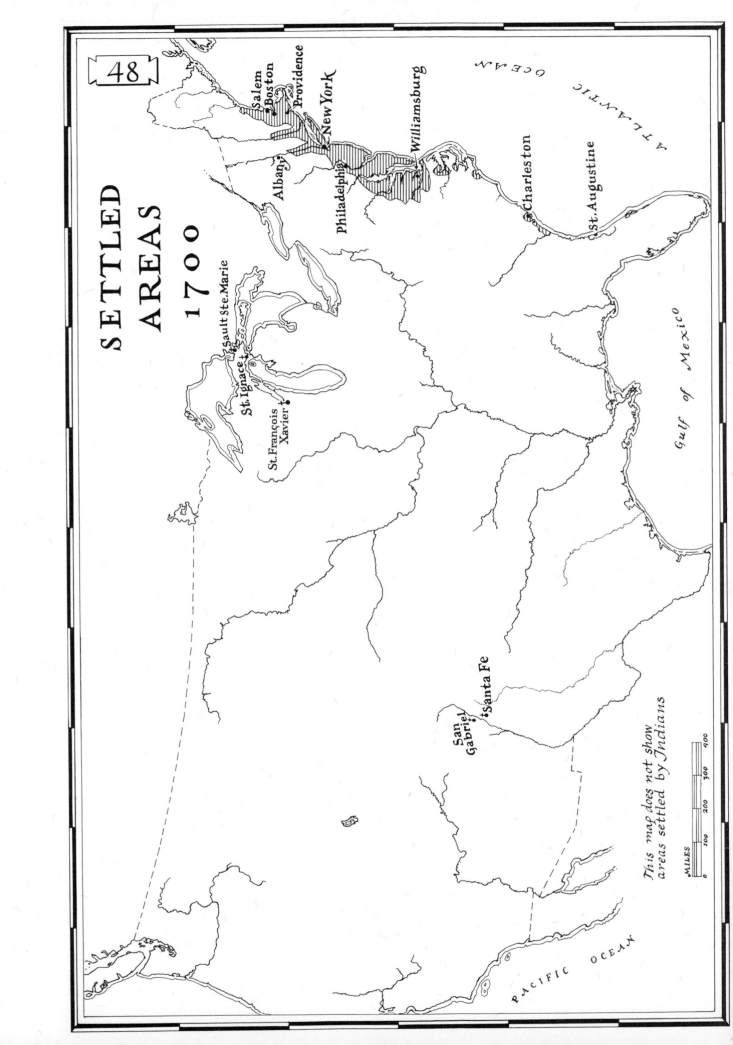

SETTLED AREAS 1700

48

Salem
Boston
Providence
New York
Albany
Philadelphia
Williamsburg
Charleston
St. Augustine

Sault Ste. Marie
St. Ignace
St. François Xavier

Santa Fe
San Gabriel

ATLANTIC OCEAN

Gulf of Mexico

PACIFIC OCEAN

This map does not show
areas settled by Indians

MILES
0   100   200   300   400

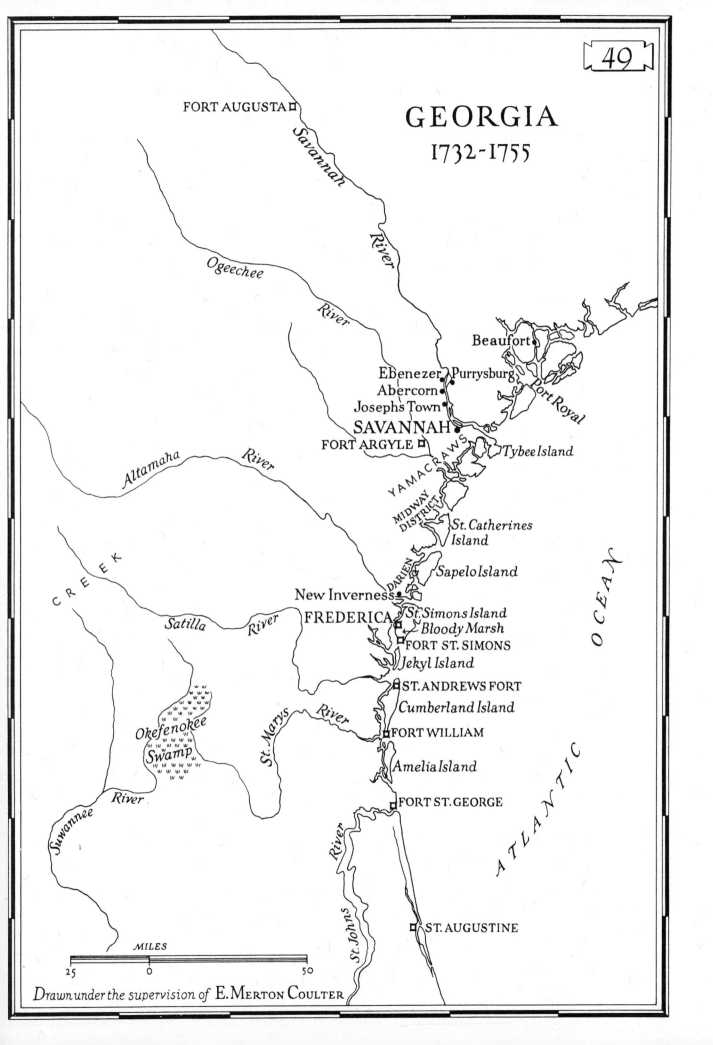

49

GEORGIA
1732-1755

FORT AUGUSTA ◻

Savannah

River

Ogeechee

River

Beaufort •

Ebenezer • Purrysburg

Abercorn •

Josephs Town •

SAVANNAH •

FORT ARGYLE ◻

Port Royal

Tybee Island

Altamaha   *River*

YAMACRAWS

MIDWAY
DISTRICT

*St. Catherines
Island*

Sapelo Island

C R E E K

DARIEN

New Inverness •

FREDERICA

Satilla   *River*

St. Simons Island

Bloody Marsh

FORT ST. SIMONS ◻

Jekyl Island

◻ ST. ANDREWS FORT

Cumberland Island

*Okefenokee
Swamp*

St. Marys   *River*

◻ FORT WILLIAM

Amelia Island

Suwannee   *River*

◻ FORT ST. GEORGE

O C E A N

A T L A N T I C

River

St. Johns

◻ ST. AUGUSTINE

MILES

25   0   50

Drawn under the supervision of E. MERTON COULTER

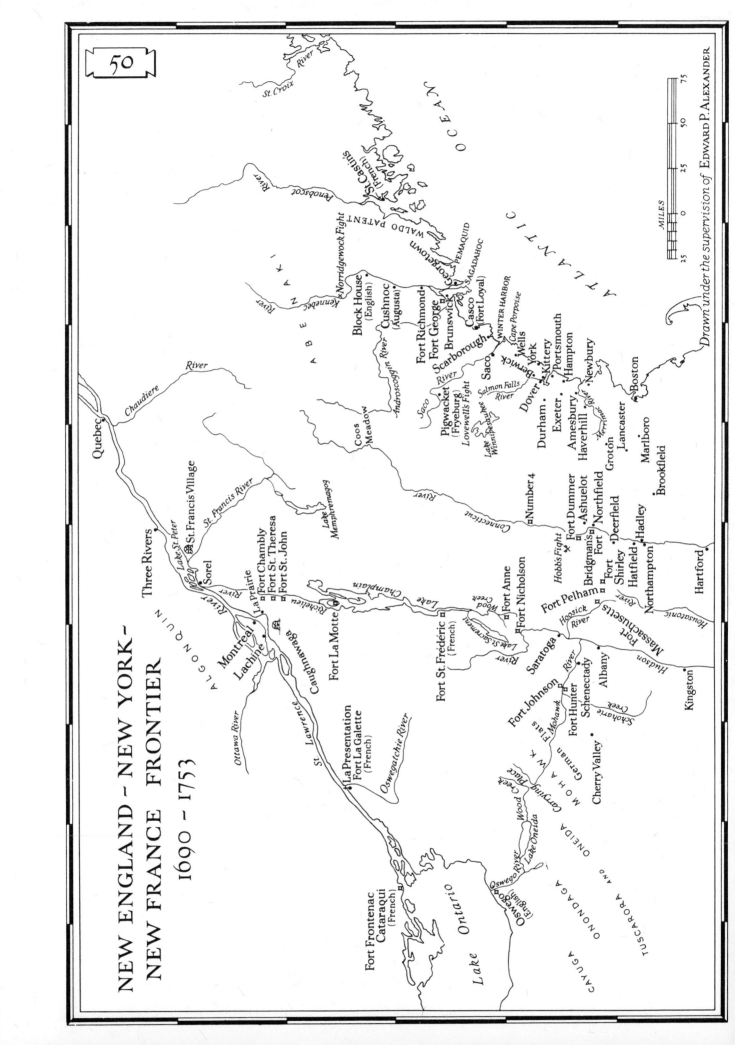

NEW ENGLAND ~ NEW YORK ~
NEW FRANCE FRONTIER
1690 ~ 1753

50

Drawn under the supervision of EDWARD P. ALEXANDER

MILES
25   0   25   50   75

ATLANTIC OCEAN

St. Croix River

Penobscot River

St. Castins (French)

WALDO PATENT

ABENAKI

Kennebec River

Norridgewock Fight

Block House (English)

Cushnoc (Augusta)

Georgetown
PEMAQUID
SAGADAHOC

Fort Richmond
Fort George
Brunswick
Casco (Fort Loyal)
WINTER HARBOR
Cape Porpoise
Wells
York
Portsmouth
Hampton
Newbury

Scarborough
Saco River
Saco
Berwick
Kittery
Dover
Durham
Exeter
Amesbury
Haverhill
Merrimac River
Lancaster
Marlboro
Boston
Groton
Brookfield

Androscoggin River

Pigwacket (Fryeburg)
Lovewell's Fight
Salmon Falls River
Lake Winnipesaukee

Chaudiere River

Quebec

Coos Meadow

Connecticut River

Number 4

Fort Dummer
Ashuelot
Northfield
Deerfield
Hatfield
Hadley
Northampton
Hartford

Hobbs Fight
Bridgman's Fort
Fort Shirley
Fort Pelham

Houssatonic River

St. Francis Village
St. Francis River
Lake Memphremagog

Three Rivers
Lake St. Peter
Sorel

La Prairie
Fort Chambly
Fort St. Theresa
Fort St. John

Richelieu River

Fort La Motte

Lake Champlain

Fort Anne
Wood Creek
Fort Nicholson

Fort St. Frédéric (French)
Lake St. Sacrement

Saratoga
Hoosick River
Fort Massachusetts

ALGONQUIN

Montreal
Lachine
Caughnawaga

St. Lawrence River

Ottawa River

La Presentation
Fort La Galette (French)

Oswegatchie River

Fort Frontenac
Cataraqui (French)

Lake Ontario

Oswego (English)
Oswego River
Lake Oneida
Wood Creek
Carrying Place

ONONDAGA

CAYUGA

TUSCARORA

ONEIDA

MOHAWK

Fort Johnson
Fort Hunter
Schenectady
Albany
Kingston

Mohawk River
German Flats
Schoharie Creek
Cherry Valley

Hudson River

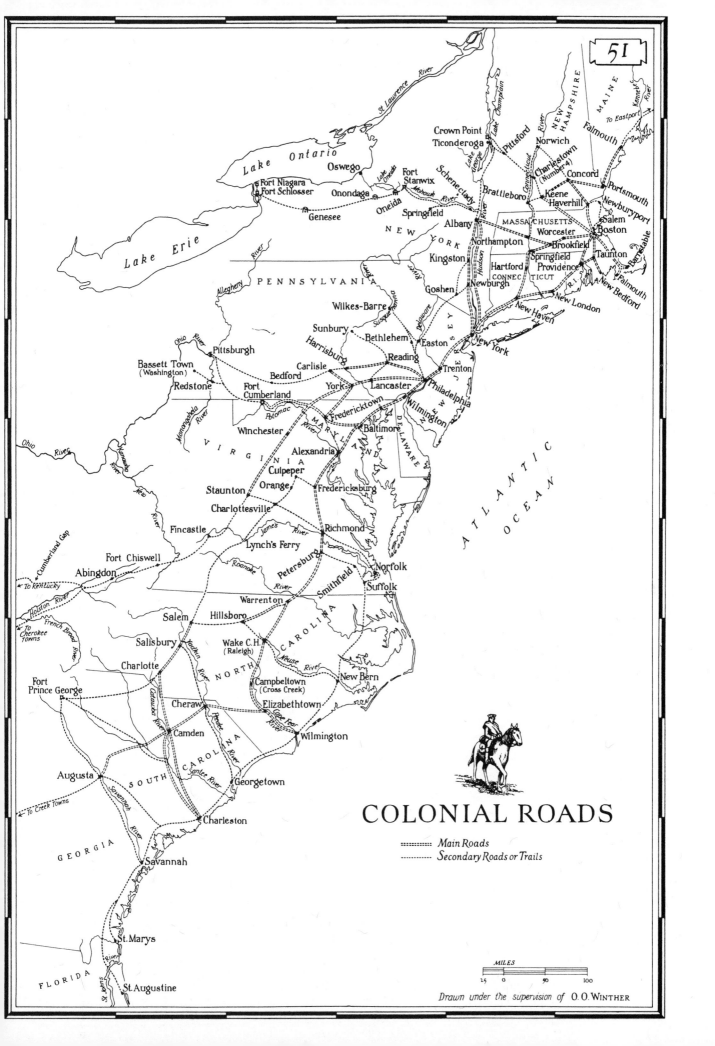

51

COLONIAL ROADS

············· *Main Roads*
------- *Secondary Roads or Trails*

MILES
25 0   50   100

Drawn under the supervision of O.O.WINTHER

Lake Ontario
Lake Erie
St. Lawrence River
Lake Champlain
Lake George
Lake Oneida
Mohawk River
Connecticut River
Kennebec River

MAINE
To Eastport
NEW HAMPSHIRE
Falmouth
Portsmouth
Newburyport
Salem
Boston
Barnstable
Taunton
Falmouth
New Bedford
R.I.
New London
Providence
Springfield
Hartford
CONNECTICUT
New Haven
Brookfield
Worcester
MASSACHUSETTS
Concord
Keene
Haverhill
Charlestown (Number 4)
Brattleboro
Northampton
Pittsford
Norwich
Crown Point
Ticonderoga
Schenectady
Albany
Kingston
Goshen
Newburgh
New York
NEW YORK
NEW JERSEY
Oswego
Fort Niagara
Fort Schlosser
Onondaga
Genesee
Oneida
Fort Stanwix
Springfield
Wilkes-Barre
Sunbury
Bethlehem
Easton
Reading
Trenton
Philadelphia
Wilmington
PENNSYLVANIA
Allegheny River
Ohio River
Pittsburgh
Bassett Town (Washington)
Redstone
Monongahela River
Fort Cumberland
Bedford
Carlisle
Harrisburg
York
Lancaster
Frederickton
Baltimore
Winchester
Potomac River
MARYLAND
DELAWARE
Alexandria
Culpeper
Orange
Staunton
Charlottesville
Fincastle
VIRGINIA
Ohio River
New River
Kanawha River
James River
Lynch's Ferry
Richmond
Fredericksburg
Fort Chiswell
Abingdon
Cumberland Gap
To Kentucky
Holston River
French Broad River
To Cherokee Towns
Petersburg
Roanoke River
Warrenton
Norfolk
Smithfield
Suffolk
Hillsboro
Salem
NORTH CAROLINA
Salisbury
Yadkin River
Wake C.H. (Raleigh)
Neuse River
New Bern
Charlotte
Catawba River
Fort Prince George
Cheraw
Campbeltown (Cross Creek)
Elizabethtown
Cape Fear River
Camden
Pedee River
Wilmington
SOUTH CAROLINA
Santee River
Augusta
To Creek Towns
Savannah River
Georgetown
Charleston
GEORGIA
Savannah
St. Marys
St. Johns River
FLORIDA
St. Augustine
ATLANTIC OCEAN
Susquehanna River
Delaware River
Hudson River

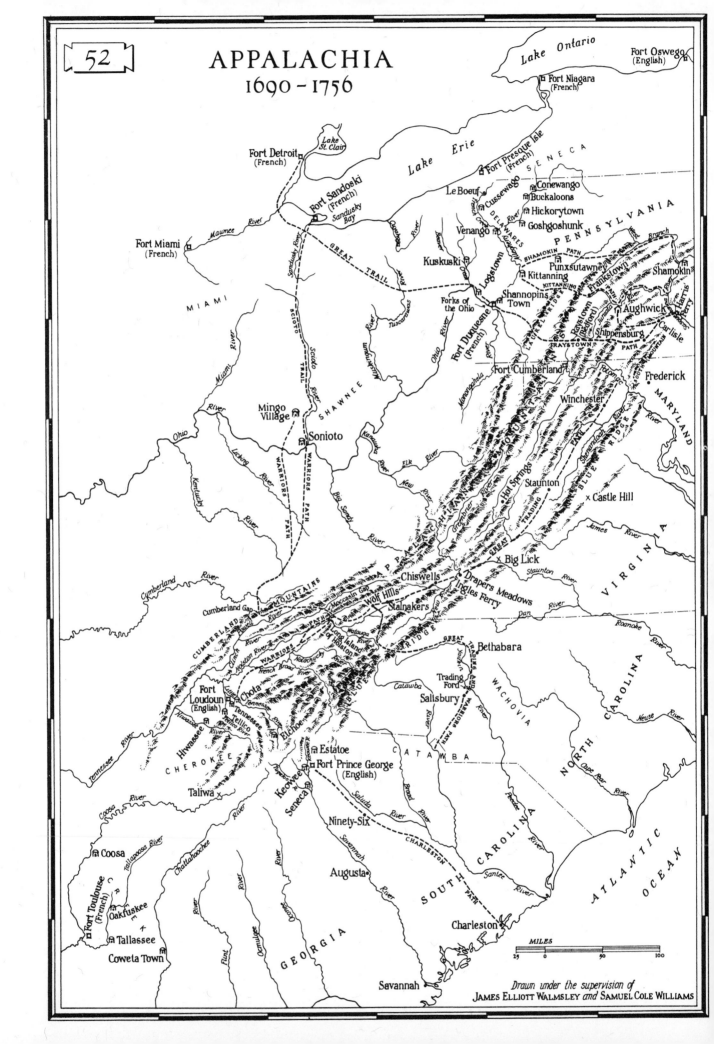

APPALACHIA
1690–1756

Lake Ontario

Fort Oswego
(English)

Fort Niagara
(French)

Lake Erie

Fort Detroit
(French)

Lake
St. Clair

Fort Presque Isle
(French)

SENECA

Le Boeuf

Cussewago   Conewango
Buckaloons
Hickorytown
Goshgoshunk

Fort Sandoski
(French)

Sandusky
Bay

Maumee River

Fort Miami
(French)

MIAMI

GREAT TRAIL

Venango

PENNSYLVANIA

Kuskuski

SHAMOKIN PATH

Punxsutawney
Frankstown   Shamokin

Logstown

Kittanning

Shannopins
Town

Aughwick

Forks of
the Ohio

Fort Duquesne
(French)

Carlisle
Shippensburg

TRAYSTOWN PATH

Fort Cumberland

Frederick

MARYLAND

Winchester

Mingo
Village

Sonioto

SHAWNEE

WARRIORS PATH

Hot Springs

Staunton

BLUE RIDGE

× Castle Hill

VIRGINIA

× Big Lick

Chiswells   Drapers Meadows
Ingles Ferry

Wolf Hills
Stalnakers

Cumberland Gap

APPALACHIAN MOUNTAINS

Bethabara

Trading
Ford

GREAT TRADING PATH

Salisbury

WACHOVIA

NORTH
CAROLINA

Fort
Loudoun
(English)

Chota

Tellico

CHEROKEE

Estatoe

CATAWBA

Taliwa ×

Keowee

Fort Prince George
(English)

Seneca

Ninety-Six

SOUTH
CAROLINA

Coosa

Fort Toulouse
(French)

Oakfuskee

Augusta

CHARLESTON PATH

ATLANTIC
OCEAN

Tallassee

GEORGIA

Coweta Town

Savannah

Charleston

Drawn under the supervision of
JAMES ELLIOTT WALMSLEY *and* SAMUEL COLE WILLIAMS

MILES
25   0   50   100

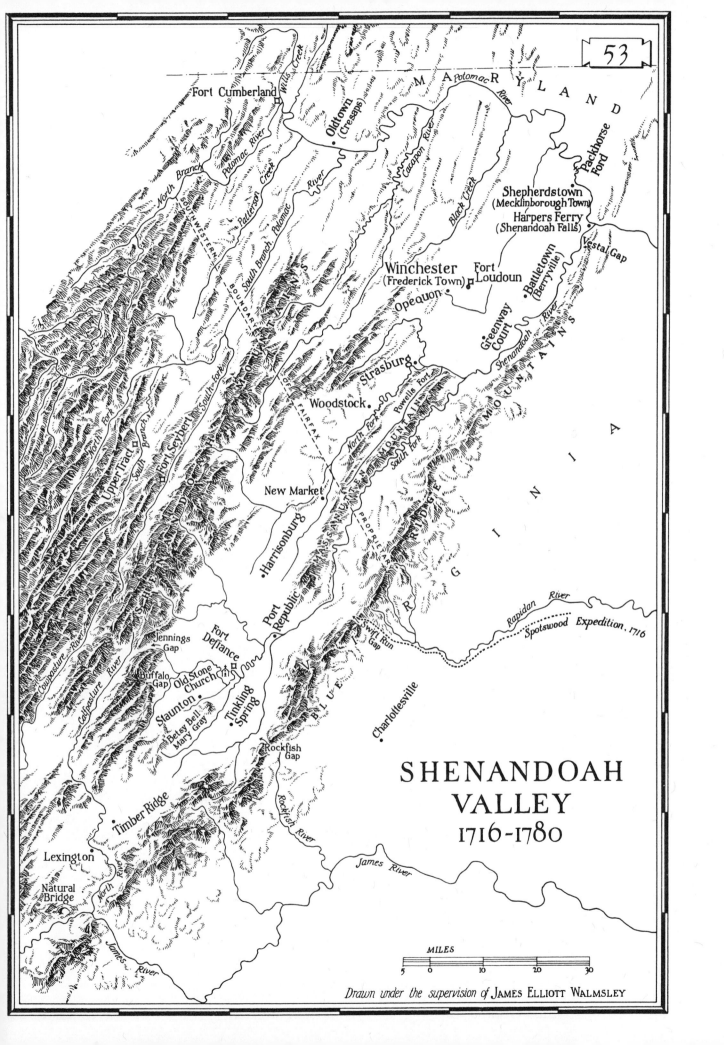

MARYLAND

Fort Cumberland

Oldtown
(Cresaps)

Potomac River

Packhorse
Ford

Shepherdstown
(Mecklinborough Town)

Harpers Ferry
(Shenandoah Falls)

Vestal Gap

Wills Creek

North Branch

Patterson Creek

Potomac River

South Branch Potomac

SOUTHWESTERN

BOUNDARY

Cacapon River

Black Creek

Winchester
(Frederick Town)

Fort
Loudoun

Battletown
(Berryville)

Opequon

Greenway
Court

Shenandoah River

BLUE

MOUNTAINS

Strasburg

Woodstock

Powells Fort

North Fork

South Fork

FAIRFAX

North Fork South Fork

Fort Seybert

Upper Tract

North Fork

South Branch

MASSANUTTEN MOUNTAINS

PROPRIETARY

RIDGE

MOUNTAINS

New Market

Harrisonburg

V I R G I N I A

Port
Republic

Swift
Run
Gap

Rapidan River

Spotswood Expedition, 1716

Jennings
Gap

Fort
Defiance

Buffalo
Gap

Old Stone
Church

Calpasture River

Cowpasture River

Staunton

Betsy Bell
Mary Gray

Tinkling
Spring

Charlottesville

Rockfish
Gap

BLUE

Timber Ridge

Rockfish River

Lexington

North River

Natural
Bridge

James River

James River

SHENANDOAH
VALLEY
1716-1780

MILES

5 0 10 20 30

Drawn under the supervision of JAMES ELLIOTT WALMSLEY

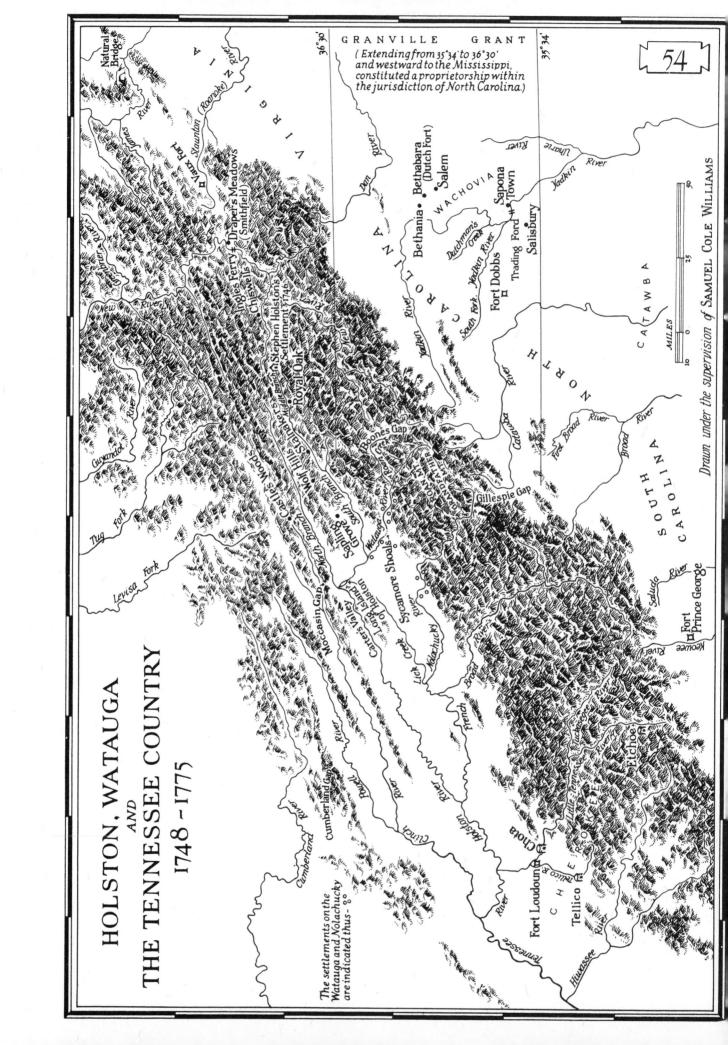

HOLSTON, WATAUGA
AND
THE TENNESSEE COUNTRY
1748 – 1775

The settlements on the
Watauga and Nolachucky
are indicated thus – °

GRANVILLE GRANT
(Extending from 35°34' to 36°30'
and westward to the Mississippi,
constituted a proprietorship within
the jurisdiction of North Carolina.)

54

Drawn under the supervision of SAMUEL COLE WILLIAMS

Natural
Bridge
VIRGINIA
James River
Staunton (Roanoke) River
Vaux Fort
Drapers Meadows
(Smithfield)
Ingles Ferry
Chiswells
New River
Stephen Holstons
Settlement 1746
Reed Creek
Royal Oak
Castles Woods
Wolf Hills
North Fork
Moccasin Gap
Sapling Grove
Smith River
Boones Gap
Walnut
Watauga Creek
Sycamore Shoals
Lick Creek
Nolachucky
Carters Valley
Long Island
Holston
Guyandot
Tug Fork
Levisa Fork
Cumberland Gap
Cumberland River
Powell River
Clinch River
Holston River
French Broad River
Chota
Fort Loudoun
Tellico
Tellico R.
Little Tennessee River
CHEROKEE
Tuckasegee River
Elchoe
Hiwassee River
Tennessee River

Don River
Yadkin River
Uharie River
Bethania
Bethabara
(Dutch Fort)
Salem
WACHOVIA
Sapona
Town
Salisbury
Trading Ford
Dutchman's Creek
South Fork Yadkin River
Fort Dobbs
NORTH CAROLINA
Catawba River
First Broad River
Broad River
SOUTH CAROLINA
CATAWBA
Saluda River
Fort
Prince George
Keowee River
Gillespie Gap
ROAN MTS.
UNAKA MTS.
GREAT SMOKY MTS.

MILES
10   25   50

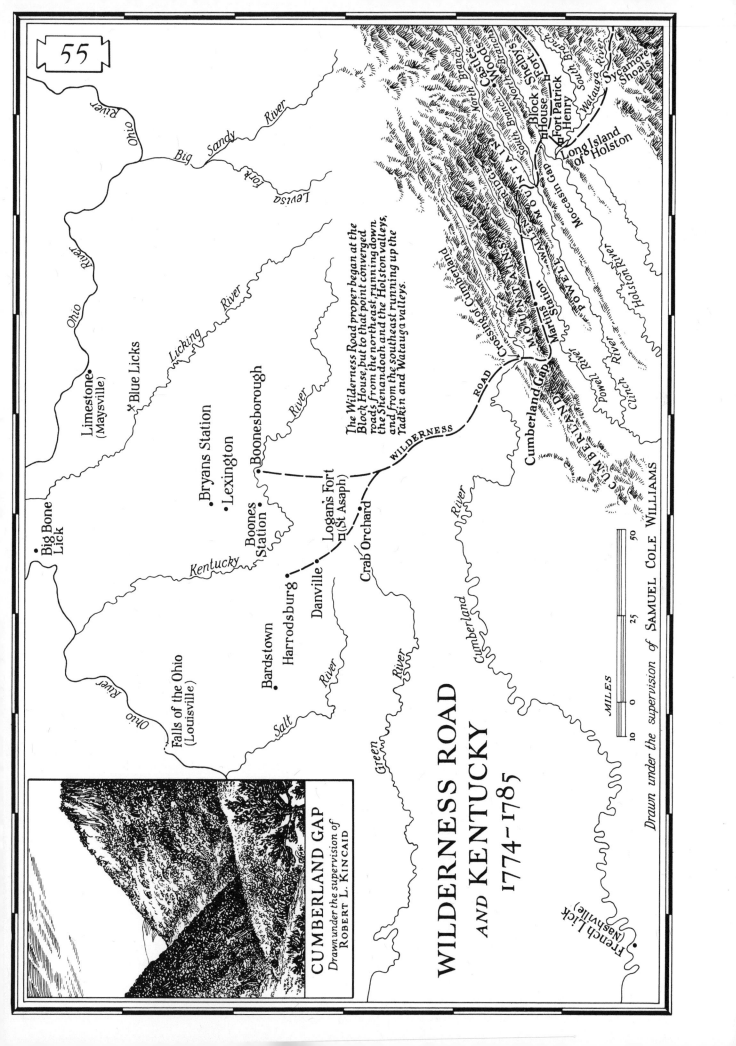

55

Ohio River

Big Sandy River

Levisa Fork

Ohio River

Licking River

Limestone (Maysville)

× Blue Licks

Bryans Station
• Lexington
• Boones Station
• Boonesborough

Big Bone Lick

Kentucky River

Logan's Fort (St Asaph)

Crab Orchard

Bardstown
• Harrodsburg
• Danville

Salt River

Falls of the Ohio (Louisville)

Ohio River

Green River

Cumberland River

French Lick (Nashville)

WILDERNESS ROAD

The Wilderness Road proper began at the Block House, but to that point converged roads from the northeast, running down the Shenandoah and the Holston valleys, and from the southeast running up the Yadkin and Watauga valleys.

Cumberland Gap

Crossing of Cumberland

Martin's Station

CUMBERLAND MOUNTAIN

POWELL

BLUE RIDGE MOUNTAINS

North Branch
South Branch
Castle's Woods
Block House
Fort Shelby's
Fort Patrick Henry
Long Island of Holston
Sycamore Shoals
Watauga River
South Fork
Moccasin Gap

Powell River

Clinch River

Holston River

MILES

0   10   25   50

Drawn under the supervision of SAMUEL COLE WILLIAMS

WILDERNESS ROAD
AND KENTUCKY
1774–1785

CUMBERLAND GAP
Drawn under the supervision of
ROBERT L. KINCAID

IV COLONIAL WARS OF THE INDIANS, FRENCH AND BRITISH

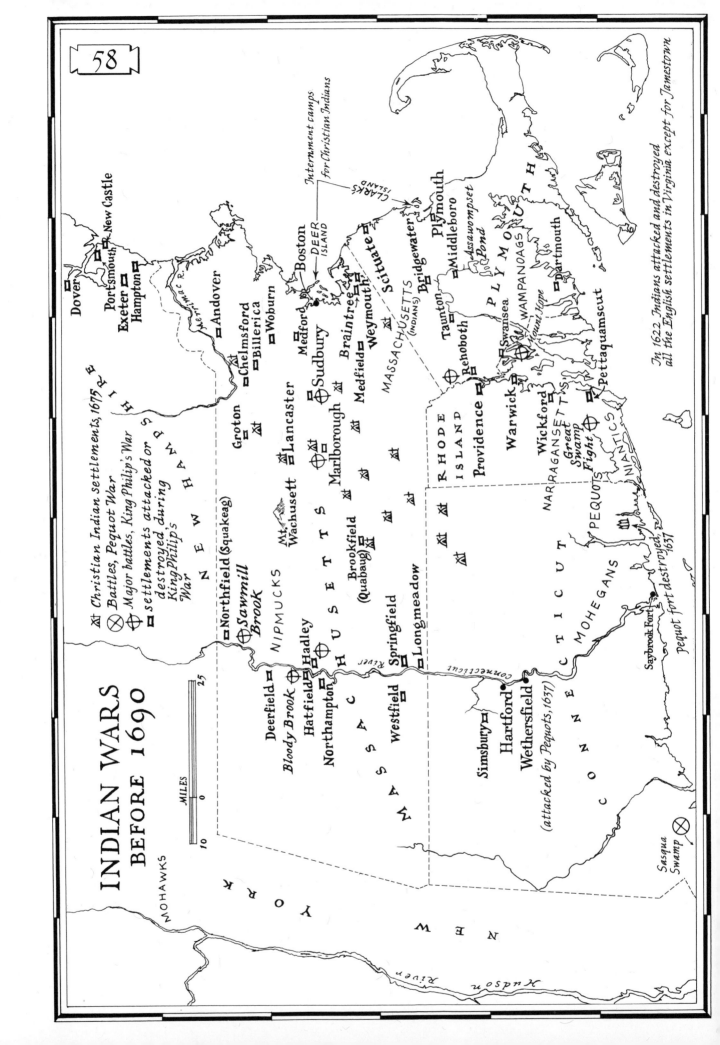

58

INDIAN WARS BEFORE 1690

Christian Indian settlements, 1675
Battles, Pequot War
Major battles, King Philip's War
settlements attacked or destroyed during King Philip's War

MILES
10   0   25

MOHAWKS

NEW YORK

NEW HAMPSHIRE

Dover
Portsmouth New Castle
Exeter
Hampton
Andover
Chelmsford
Billerica
Woburn
Medford
Boston
Sudbury
Braintree
Weymouth
Medfield
Scituate
Groton
Lancaster
Marlborough
MASSACHUSETTS (INDIANS)
Taunton
Rehoboth
Bridgewater
Middleboro
Plymouth
Assawompset Pond
PLYMOUTH
Swansea
Mount Hope
WAMPANOAGS
Dartmouth

Interment camps for Christian Indians
CLARK'S ISLAND
DEER ISLAND

Northfield (Squakeag)
Sawmill Brook
NIPMUCKS
Mt. Wachusett
Brookfield (Quabaug)
Deerfield
Bloody Brook
Hatfield
Hadley
Northampton
MASSACHUSETTS
Westfield
Springfield
Longmeadow
Connecticut River

RHODE ISLAND
Providence
Warwick
Wickford
Great Swamp Fight
NARRAGANSETTS
NIANTICS
PEQUOTS
Pettaquamscut

Simsbury
Hartford
Wethersfield
(attacked by Pequots, 1637)
CONNECTICUT
MOHEGANS
Saybrook Fort
Pequot fort destroyed 1637

Sasqua Swamp

In 1622 Indians attacked and destroyed all the English settlements in Virginia except for Jamestown

Hudson River

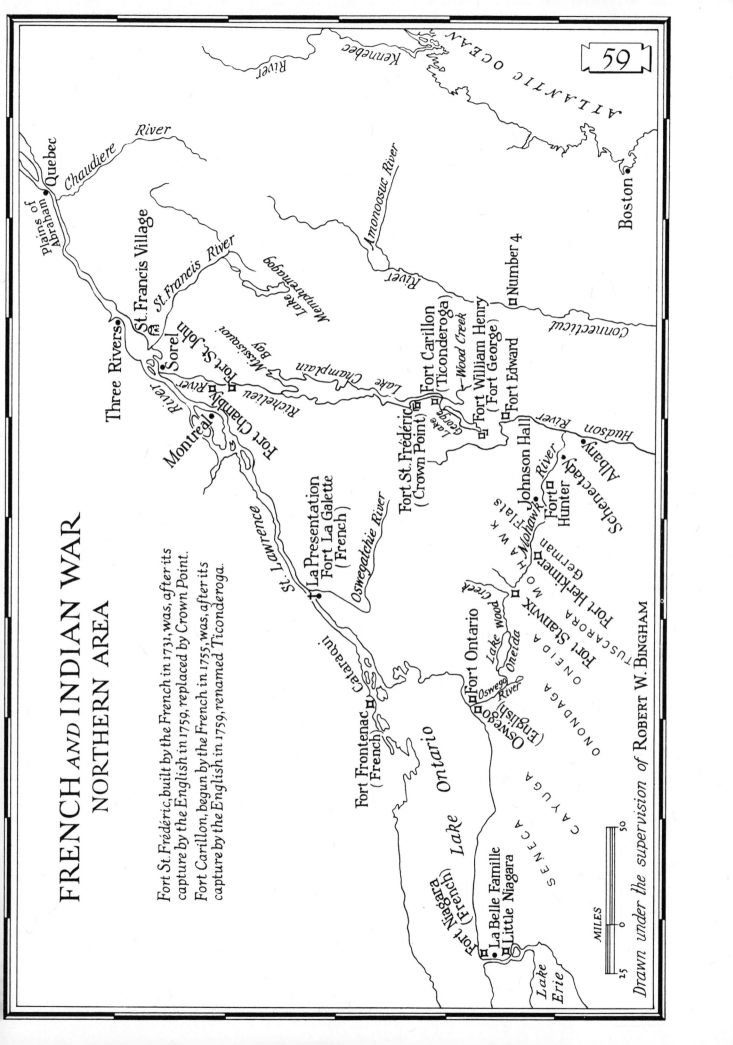

FRENCH AND INDIAN WAR
NORTHERN AREA

Fort St. Frédéric, built by the French in 1731, was, after its capture by the English in 1759, replaced by Crown Point.

Fort Carillon, begun by the French in 1755, was, after its capture by the English in 1759, renamed Ticonderoga.

Drawn under the supervision of ROBERT W. BINGHAM.

MILES
25   0   50

59

ATLANTIC OCEAN

Kennebec River

Boston

Chaudiere River

Quebec

Plains of Abraham

River

Amonoosuc River

River

Connecticut

Number 4

St. Francis Village

St. Francis River

Lake Memphremagog

Three Rivers

Sorel

Fort St. John

Missisquoi Bay

Richelieu River

Fort Chambly

River

Lake Champlain

Fort Carillon (Ticonderoga)

Wood Creek

Fort William Henry (Fort George)

Fort Edward

Montreal

St. Lawrence River

La Presentation Fort La Galette (French)

Oswegatchie River

Fort St. Frédéric (Crown Point)

Lake George

Hudson River

Johnson Hall

Mohawk River

Schenectady

Albany

Fort Hunter

German Flats

Fort Herkimer

MOHAWK

Cataraqui

Fort Frontenac (French)

Fort Ontario

Fort Stanwix

TUSCARORA

ONEIDA

ONONDAGA

Lake wood

Oneida

Oswego River

Oswego (English)

Lake Ontario

CAYUGA

SENECA

Fort Niagara (French)

La Belle Famille

Little Niagara

Lake Erie

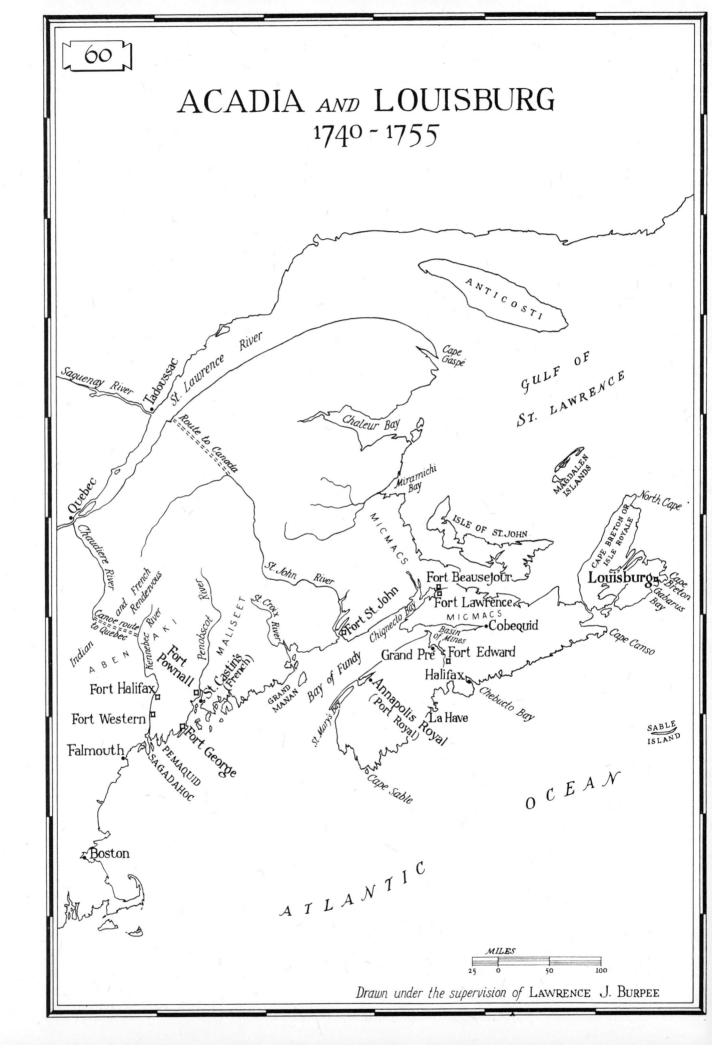

ACADIA AND LOUISBURG
1740 - 1755

60

ANTICOSTI

GULF OF ST. LAWRENCE

Saguenay River

Tadoussac

St. Lawrence River

Cape Gaspé

Route to Canada

Chaleur Bay

Quebec

Miramichi Bay

MAGDALEN ISLANDS

ISLE OF ST. JOHN

North Cape

Chaudière River

MICMACS

CAPE BRETON OR ISLE ROYALE

Canoe route to Quebec

Indian

French and Rendezvous

St. John River

Louisburg

Cape Breton

Penobscot River

St. Croix River

Fort St. John

Fort Beausejour

Gabarus Bay

ABEN AKI

MALISEET

Chignecto Bay

Fort Lawrence

Cobequid

MICMACS

Cape Canso

Fort Pownall

St. Castin's (French)

GRAND MANAN

Bay of Fundy

Basin of Mines

Grand Pré

Fort Edward

Fort Halifax

Halifax

Kennebec River

Chebucto Bay

Fort Western

Fort George

Annapolis Royal (Port Royal)

La Have

SABLE ISLAND

Falmouth

PEMAQUID

SAGADAHOC

St. Mary's Bay

Cape Sable

OCEAN

Boston

A T L A N T I C

MILES

25 0 50 100

Drawn under the supervision of LAWRENCE J. BURPEE

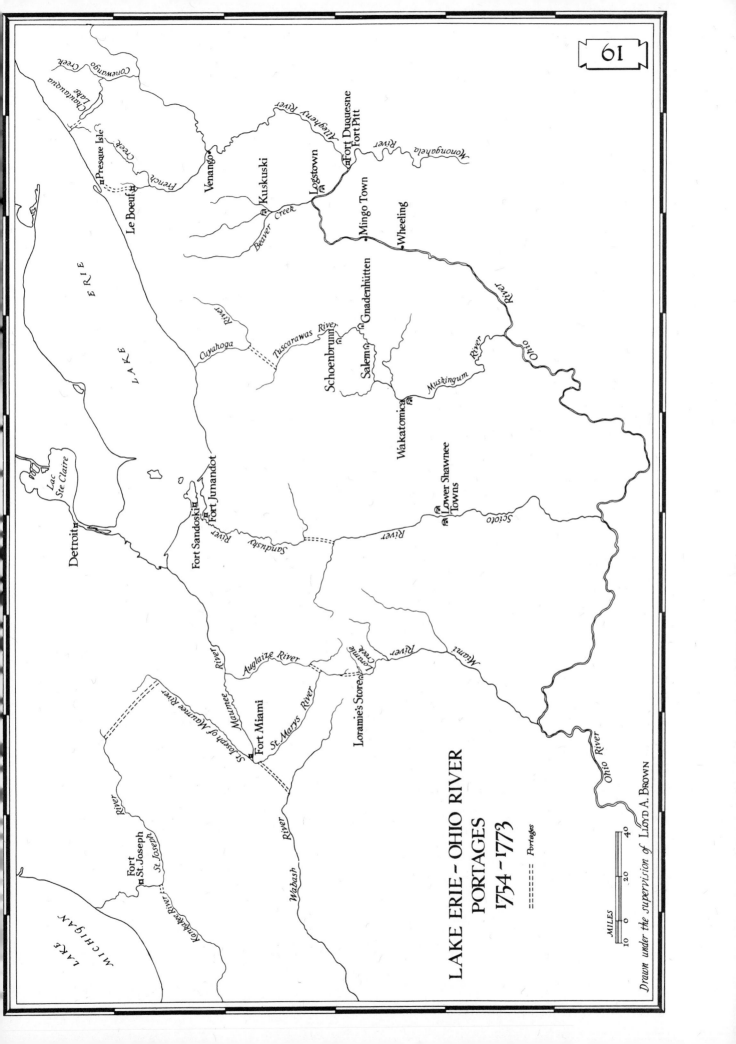

LAKE ERIE ~ OHIO RIVER
PORTAGES
1754 ~ 1773

------- Portages

MILES

Drawn under the supervision of LLOYD A. BROWN

LAKE ERIE

LAKE MICHIGAN

Lac Ste. Claire

Detroit

Chautauqua Lake

Conewango Creek

Presque Isle

Le Boeuf

French Creek

Venango

Kuskuski

Beaver Creek

Logstown

Allegheny River

Fort Duquesne
Fort Pitt

Monongahela River

Mingo Town

Wheeling

Cuyahoga River

Tuscarawas River

Schoenbrunn

Salem

Gnadenhütten

Muskingum River

Wakatomica

Ohio River

Fort Sandoski

Fort Junandot

Sandusky River

Lower Shawnee Towns

Scioto River

River

Maumee River

Auglaize River

St. Joseph of Maumee River

Fort Miami

St. Marys River

Loramie's Store

Loramie Creek

River

Miami River

Fort
St. Joseph

St. Joseph River

Wabash River

Kankakee River

Ohio River

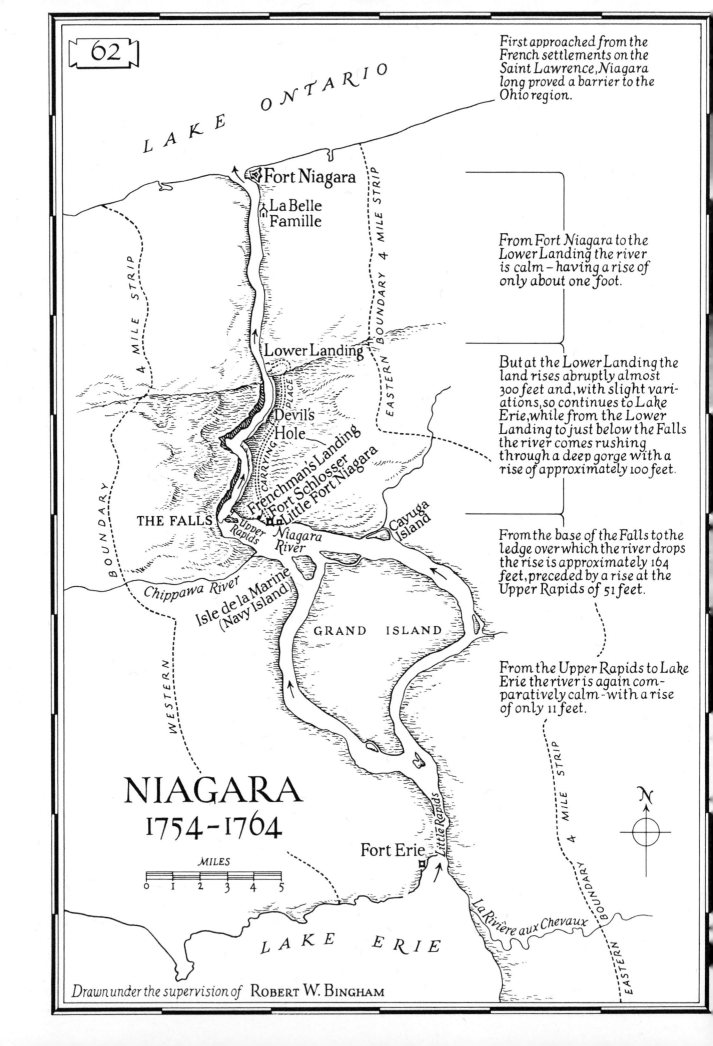

62

LAKE ONTARIO

First approached from the French settlements on the Saint Lawrence, Niagara long proved a barrier to the Ohio region.

Fort Niagara

La Belle Famille

From Fort Niagara to the Lower Landing the river is calm – having a rise of only about one foot.

Lower Landing

Devil's Hole

Frenchman's Landing
Fort Schlosser
Little Fort Niagara

But at the Lower Landing the land rises abruptly almost 300 feet and, with slight variations, so continues to Lake Erie, while from the Lower Landing to just below the Falls the river comes rushing through a deep gorge with a rise of approximately 100 feet.

THE FALLS

Upper Rapids

Niagara River

Cayuga Island

From the base of the Falls to the ledge over which the river drops the rise is approximately 164 feet, preceded by a rise at the Upper Rapids of 51 feet.

Chippawa River

Isle de la Marine (Navy Island)

GRAND ISLAND

From the Upper Rapids to Lake Erie the river is again comparatively calm – with a rise of only 11 feet.

NIAGARA
1754–1764

MILES
0 1 2 3 4 5

Fort Erie

Little Rapids

La Rivière aux Chevaux

WESTERN BOUNDARY

EASTERN BOUNDARY 4 MILE STRIP

4 MILE STRIP

N

LAKE ERIE

Drawn under the supervision of ROBERT W. BINGHAM

Lake Ontario

63

SENECA

⊡ Fort Niagara
• La Belle Famille
⊡ Little Niagara

Lake Erie

FORKS OF THE OHIO
1754-1759

Chautauqua Lake

Conewango Creek

Conewango River

⊡ Presque Isle

French Creek

Le Boeuf ⊡

DELAWARES

Allegheny River

DELAWARES

West Branch

Venango
⊡ Fort Machault

SHAWNEE

Kuskuski

Murthering Town

Connoquenessing Creek

Kittanning ⊞

Beaver Creek

Sawcunk

Ohio

Logstown

Allegheny River

Kiskiminetas River

Penn Creek

Penn Creek Massacre ✕

⊡ Fort Augusta

River

Susquehanna

River

Little Juniata

Juniata

Raystown Branch

MOUNTAINS

Braddock's Defeat

⊡ Fort Duquesne (Fort Pitt)

Turtle Cr.

Loyalhanna Creek

Conemaugh River

FORBES

Catfish Camp (Washington)

Youghiogheny River

CHESTNUT RIDGE

Loyal Hannon (Ligonier)

LAUREL RIDGE

ROAD

ALLEGHENY

Aughwick
Fort Shirley

Carlisle •

Harris Ferry

Redstone Old Fort
Fort Burd ⊡

Gist's ✕

Fort Necessity

GREAT MEADOWS

Monongahela

BRADDOCK'S ROAD

Raystown (Bedford)

WILLS MOUNTAIN

Wills Creek

TUSSEY MOUNTAIN

SIDELING MOUNTAIN

Fort Littleton

TUSCARORA MOUNTAIN

⊞ Fort Loudon

Shippensburg •

SOUTH MOUNTAIN

York

Fort Cumberland ⊡

Oldtown (Cresaps)

Potomac River

Potomac River

Baltimore

Winchester •

MILES
10 5 0   25   50

Drawn under the supervision of ALFRED P. JAMES

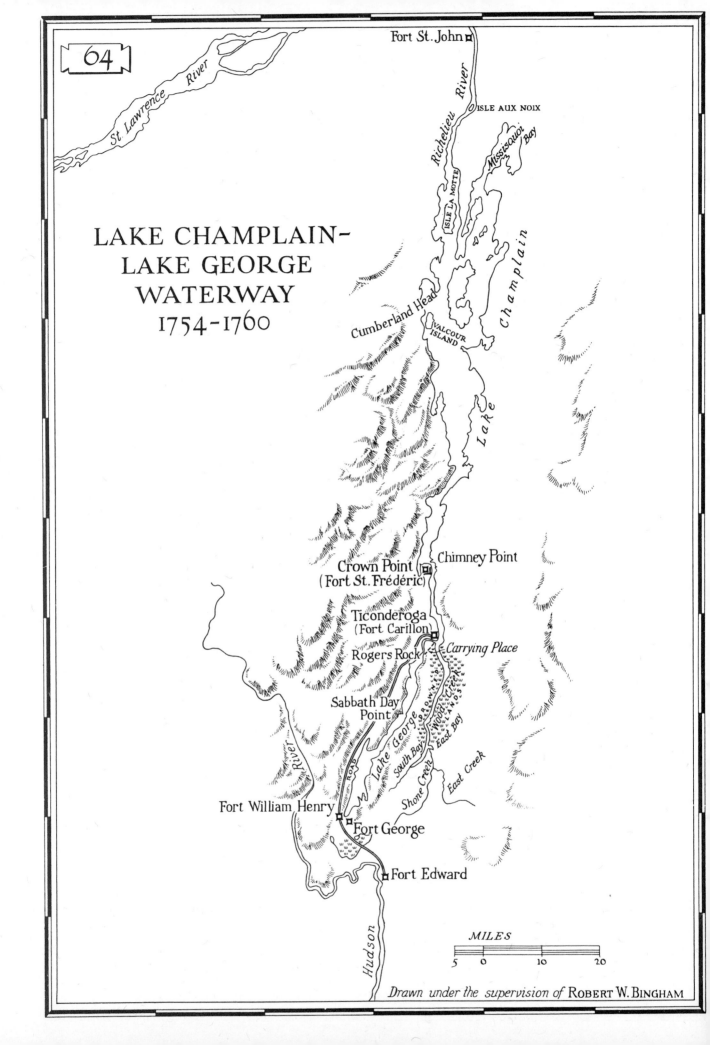

64

LAKE CHAMPLAIN-
LAKE GEORGE
WATERWAY
1754-1760

St. Lawrence River

Fort St. John

Richelieu River

ISLE AUX NOIX

Missisquoi Bay

ISLE LA MOTTE

Lake Champlain

Cumberland Head

VALCOUR ISLAND

Crown Point
(Fort St. Frédéric)

Chimney Point

Ticonderoga
(Fort Carillon)

Carrying Place

Rogers Rock

DROWNED LANDS

Wood Creek

Sabbath Day
Point

Lake George

South Bay

East Bay

Stone Creek

East Creek

ROAD

River

Fort William Henry

Fort George

Fort Edward

Hudson

MILES

5   0   10   20

Drawn under the supervision of ROBERT W. BINGHAM

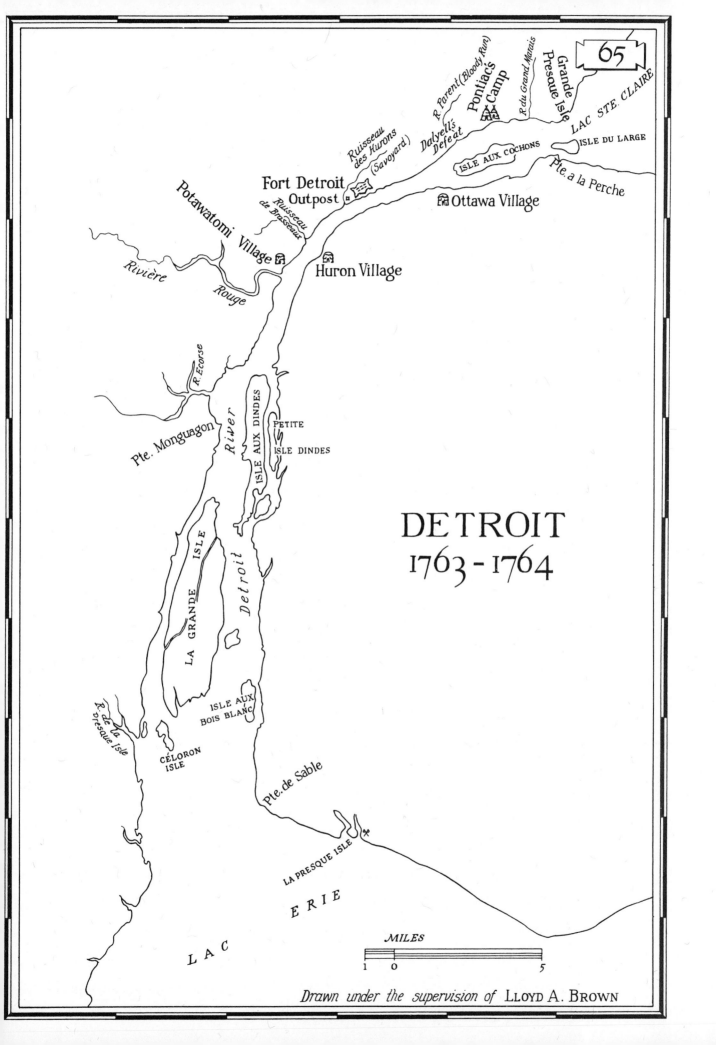

65

R. Parent (Bloody Run)

Dalyell's Defeat

Pontiac's Camp

R. du Grand Marais

Grande Presque Isle

LAC STE. CLAIRE

ISLE DU LARGE

Ruisseau des Hurons (Savoyard)

ISLE AUX COCHONS

Pte. a la Perche

Fort Detroit

Outpost

Ruisseau de Brosseaux

Ottawa Village

Potawatomi Village

Rivière Rouge

Huron Village

R. Ecorse

Pte. Monguagon

River

ISLE AUX DINDES

PETITE ISLE DINDES

Detroit

DETROIT
1763 - 1764

LA GRANDE ISLE

R. de la Presque Isle

ISLE AUX BOIS BLANC

CÉLORON ISLE

Pte. de Sable

LA PRESQUE ISLE

LAC   ERIE

MILES

1   0   5

Drawn under the supervision of LLOYD A. BROWN

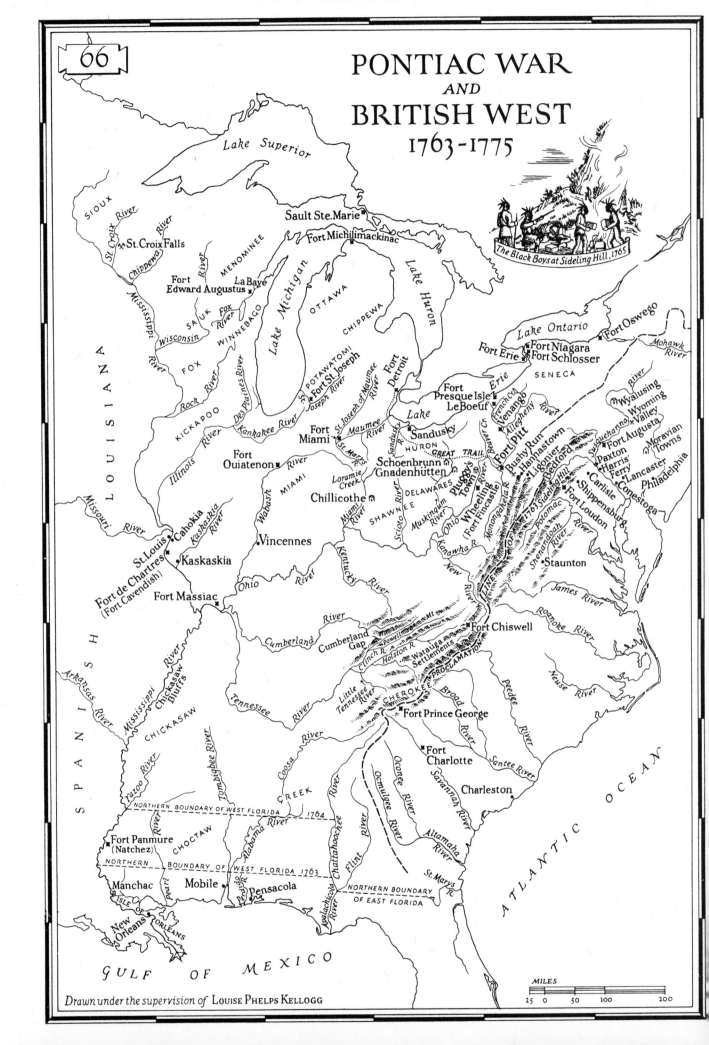

66

PONTIAC WAR
AND
BRITISH WEST
1763-1775

The Black Boys at Sideling Hill, 1765

Lake Superior

SIOUX River

St. Croix River

✕ St. Croix Falls

Chippewa River

MENOMINEE

Sault Ste.Marie

Fort Michilimackinac

Fort Edward Augustus

La Baye

SAUK River

Fox River

Wisconsin River

WINNEBAGO

FOX

Mississippi River

Rock River

KICKAPOO

Des Plaines River

Kankakee River

POTAWATOMI

Lake Michigan

OTTAWA

CHIPPEWA

Lake Huron

Lake Ontario

Fort Oswego

Fort Erie

Fort Niagara
Fort Schlosser

Mohawk River

SENECA

Erie

Fort Presque Isle
LeBoeuf

French Cr.

Venango

Allegheny River

Wyalusing

Wyoming ✕ Valley

Fort St. Joseph

St. Joseph River

St. Joseph of Maumee River

Fort Detroit

Lake Erie

Sandusky

Sandusky

HURON

Fort Miami

Maumee River

St. Marys R.

GREAT TRAIL

Beaver Cr.

Fort Pitt

Bushy Run

Hannastown

Ligonier

Bedford

Fort Augusta

Moravian Towns

Paxton

Harris Ferry

Lancaster

Conestoga

Philadelphia

Fort Ouiatenon

Miami River

Loramie Creek

Schoenbrunn
Gnadenhütten

Pluggy's Town

DELAWARES

Muskingum R.

Wheeling

(Fort Fincastle)

OF 1763 Sideling Hill

LINE

Potomac River

Shippensburg

Carlisle

Fort Loudon

ILLINOIS River

Wabash River

MIAMI

Chillicothe

Scioto River

SHAWNEE

Monongahela R.

Ohio River

Kanawha R.

New River

Shenandoah River

Staunton

James River

Missouri River

Kaskaskia River

Cahokia

St. Louis
Fort de Chartres
(Fort Cavendish)

Kaskaskia

Vincennes

Kentucky River

Licking River

Roanoke River

Fort Massiac

Ohio River

Cumberland River

Cumberland Gap

Powell Mt.

Powell R.

Clinch R.

Holston R.

Watauga Settlements

CHEROKEE PROCLAMATION

Fort Chiswell

Broad River

Peedee River

Neuse River

Arkansas River

Mississippi River

Chickasaw Bluffs

CHICKASAW

Tennessee River

Little Tennessee River

Fort Prince George

Fort Charlotte

Santee River

Charleston

LOUISIANA

S P A N I S H

Yazoo River

Tombigbee River

CHOCTAW

COOSA River

CREEK

Flint River

Chattahoochee River

Oconee River

Ocmulgee River

Savannah River

Altamaha River

St. Marys R.

ATLANTIC OCEAN

NORTHERN BOUNDARY OF WEST FLORIDA 1764

Alabama River

Fort Panmure
(Natchez)

NORTHERN BOUNDARY OF WEST FLORIDA 1763

Manchac

Pearl R.

Mobile

Pedro R.

Pensacola

Apalachicola River

NORTHERN BOUNDARY OF EAST FLORIDA

New Orleans

ISLE OF ORLEANS

G U L F   O F   M E X I C O

Drawn under the supervision of LOUISE PHELPS KELLOGG

MILES
25 0   50   100   200

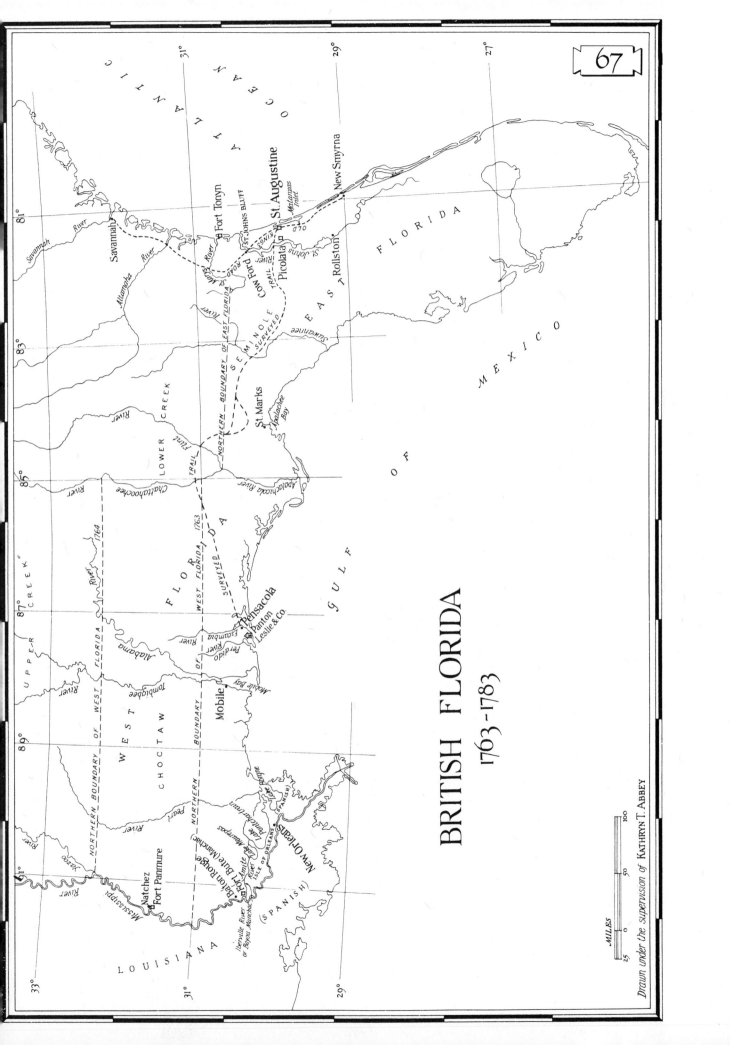

BRITISH FLORIDA
1763-1783

Drawn under the supervision of KATHRYN T. ABBEY

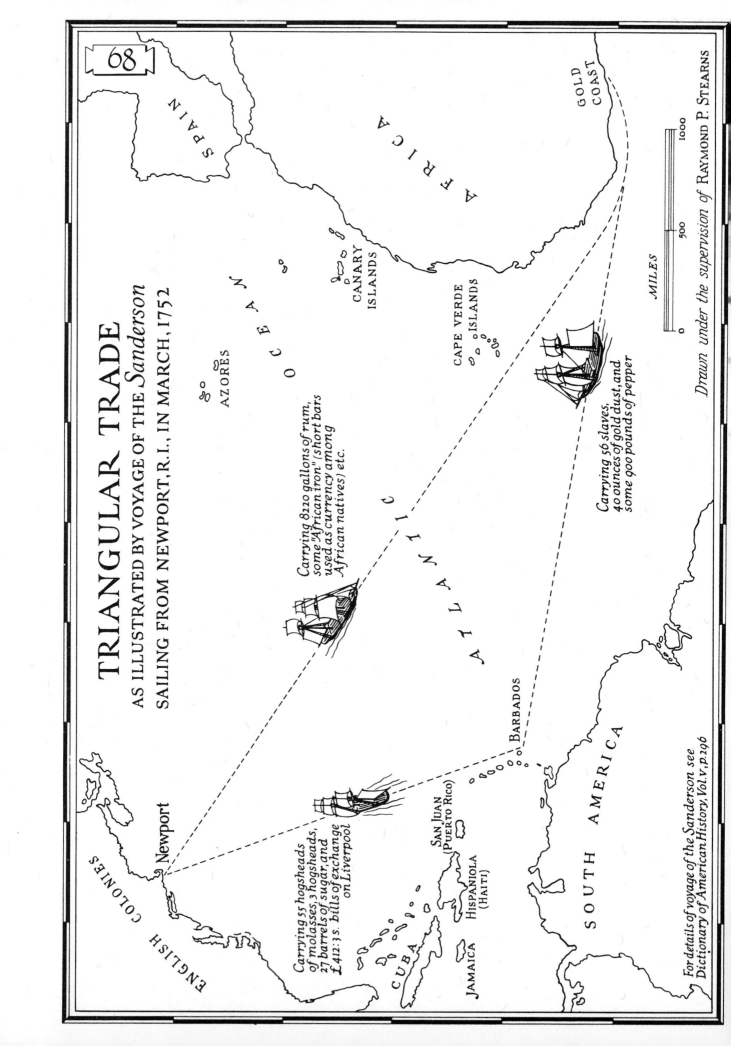

68

TRIANGULAR TRADE

AS ILLUSTRATED BY VOYAGE OF THE *Sanderson*
SAILING FROM NEWPORT, R.I., IN MARCH, 1752

ENGLISH COLONIES

SPAIN

Newport

AZORES

OCEAN

AFRICA

Carrying 55 hogsheads of molasses, 3 hogsheads, 27 barrels of sugar, and £412:3s. bills of exchange on Liverpool

Carrying 8210 gallons of rum, some "African iron" (short bars used as currency among African natives) etc.

CUBA

JAMAICA

HISPANIOLA (HAITI)

SAN JUAN (PUERTO RICO)

BARBADOS

ATLANTIC

CANARY ISLANDS

CAPE VERDE ISLANDS

GOLD COAST

Carrying 56 slaves, 40 ounces of gold dust, and some 900 pounds of pepper

SOUTH AMERICA

MILES

0   500   1000

Drawn under the supervision of RAYMOND P. STEARNS

For details of voyage of the Sanderson see
Dictionary of American History, Vol. v, p. 296

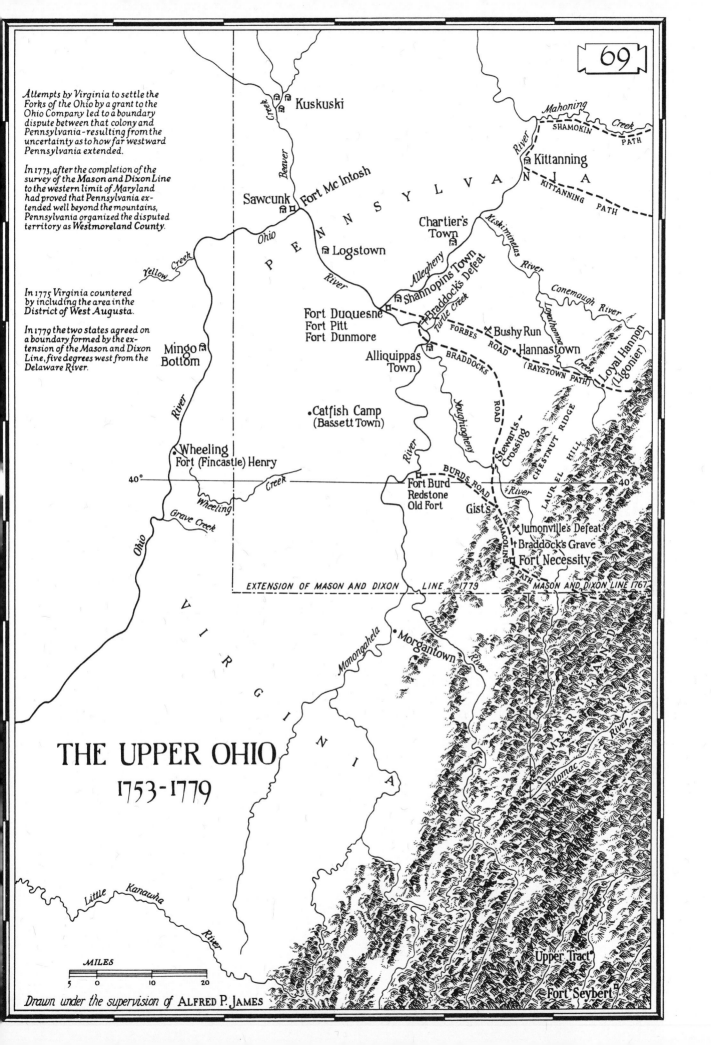

69

Attempts by Virginia to settle the
Forks of the Ohio by a grant to the
Ohio Company led to a boundary
dispute between that colony and
Pennsylvania—resulting from the
uncertainty as to how far westward
Pennsylvania extended.

In 1773, after the completion of the
survey of the Mason and Dixon Line
to the western limit of Maryland
had proved that Pennsylvania extended well beyond the mountains,
Pennsylvania organized the disputed
territory as Westmoreland County.

In 1775 Virginia countered
by including the area in the
District of West Augusta.

In 1779 the two states agreed on
a boundary formed by the extension of the Mason and Dixon
Line, five degrees west from the
Delaware River.

Kuskuski

Creek

Beaver

Mahoning
Creek
SHAMOKIN
PATH

Kittanning

Fort Mc Intosh

KITTANNING
PATH

Sawcunk

PENNSYLVANIA

Ohio

Logstown

River

Yellow Creek

Chartier's
Town

Allegheny

Kiskiminetas River

Shannopins Town

Braddock's Defeat

Conemaugh River

Fort Duquesne
Fort Pitt
Fort Dunmore

Turtle Creek

FORBES

ROAD

Bushy Run

Hannastown

Loyalhanna Creek

Loyal Hannon
(Ligonier)

Mingo
Bottom

Alliquippas
Town

BRADDOCKS

(RAYSTOWN PATH)

River

ROAD

CHESTNUT RIDGE

Catfish Camp
(Bassett Town)

Youghiogheny

Stewarts
Crossing

LAUREL HILL

Wheeling
Fort (Fincastle) Henry

River

BURDS ROAD

River

40°

Creek

40°

Wheeling

Fort Burd
Redstone
Old Fort

Gist's

NEMACOLINS

Grave Creek

Jumonville's Defeat
Braddock's Grave
Fort Necessity

Ohio

PATH

MARYLAND

EXTENSION OF MASON AND DIXON LINE 1779

MASON AND DIXON LINE 1767

V
I
R
G
I
N
I
A

Monongahela

Morgantown

Cheat River

Polomac River

THE UPPER OHIO
1753-1779

Little Kanawha River

Upper Tract

MILES
5   0   10   20

Fort Seybert

Drawn under the supervision of ALFRED P. JAMES

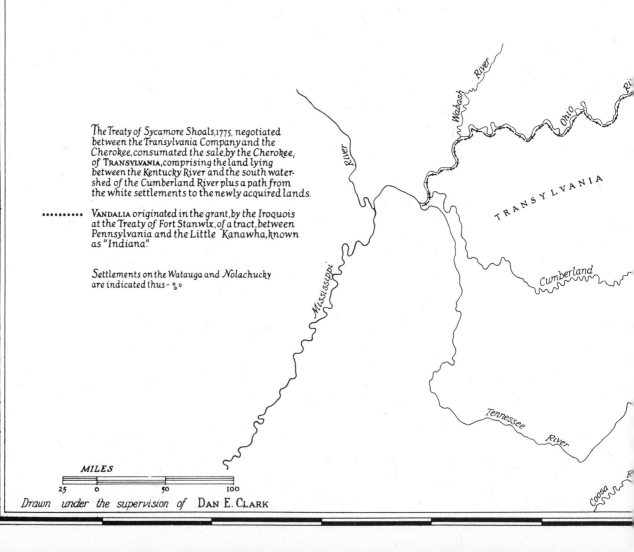

PROCLAMATION LINE OF 1763
INDIAN CESSIONS
AND THE LAND COMPANIES

— — — The Proclamation of 1763 forbade the purchase or settlement of Indian lands westerly of a line running through the heads of the rivers which fell into the Atlantic from the west or northwest.

—x—x— Tryon's Line, 1767, (by agreement with the Cherokee) directed that no white settlement should be made westerly of a line running from a point where Reedy River was intersected by the then North Carolina-South Carolina boundary, to Tryon's Mountain and thence to Fort Chiswell.

—+—+— The Treaty of Fort Stanwix, 1768, (with the Iroquois) extinguished Iroquois claims to the lands southeasterly of a line running from Fort Stanwix to Fort Pitt, and thence along the southern bank of the Ohio to the mouth of the Tennessee (Cherokee) River.

—o—o— The Treaty of Hard Labor, 1768, (with the Cherokee) confirmed Tryon's Line
—x—x— of 1767 and extended it from Fort Chiswell to the mouth of the Kanawha River.

—•—•— The Treaty of Lochaber, 1770, (with the Cherokee) moved the northern part of the line established at the Treaty of Hard Labor westerly to run from six miles east of Long Island of Holston directly to the mouth of the Kanawha River. Lochaber was the name of the plantation of Alexander Cameron, Assistant Commissioner of Indian Affairs for the Southern Provinces.

—••—••— Donelson's Line. When Col. Donelson acting for Virginia, and Chief Attakullakulla and Alex. Cameron, acting for the Cherokee, came to run the Lochaber Line, some agreement was entered into by which it was turned westward and made to run with the Kentucky (Louisa) River.

The Treaty of Sycamore Shoals, 1775, negotiated between the Transylvania Company and the Cherokee, consumated the sale, by the Cherokee, of TRANSYLVANIA, comprising the land lying between the Kentucky River and the south watershed of the Cumberland River plus a path from the white settlements to the newly acquired lands.

••••••••• VANDALIA originated in the grant, by the Iroquois at the Treaty of Fort Stanwix, of a tract, between Pennsylvania and the Little Kanawha, known as "Indiana."

Settlements on the Watauga and Nolachucky are indicated thus - ⸰⸰

MILES

25   0   50   100

Drawn under the supervision of DAN E. CLARK

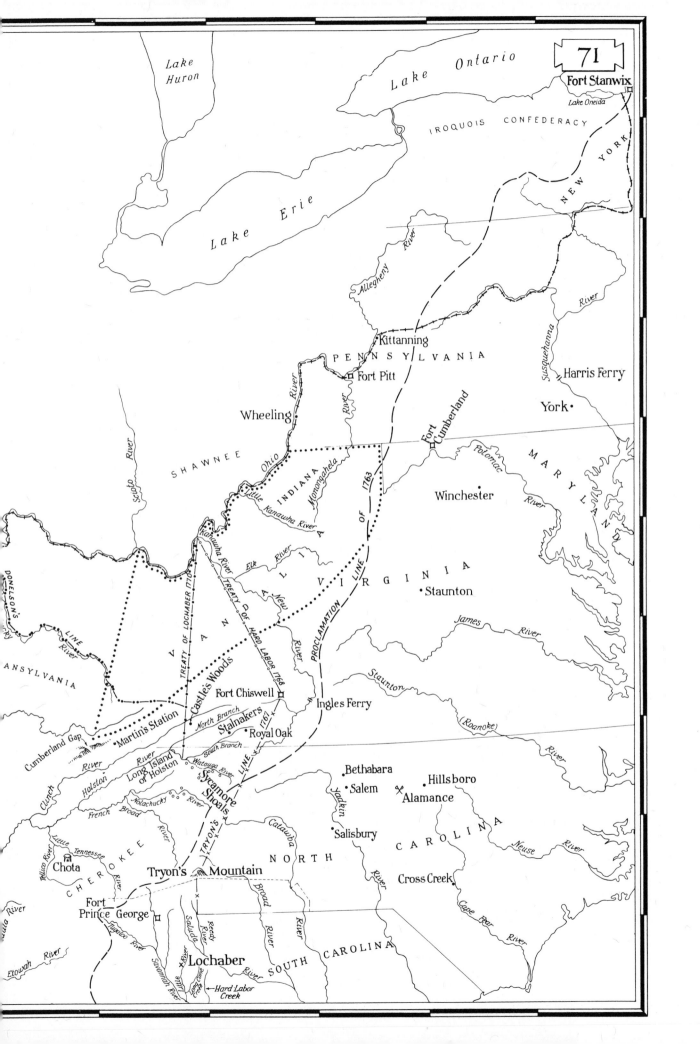

Lake Huron

Lake Ontario

Fort Stanwix

Lake Oneida

I R O Q U O I S   C O N F E D E R A C Y

Lake Erie

NEW YORK

Allegheny River

River

Susquehanna

•Kittanning

P E N N S Y L V A N I A

□Fort Pitt

Harris Ferry

River

York•

Wheeling

Ohio River

River

Fort Cumberland

M A R Y L A N D

Potomac River

S H A W N E E

INDIANA

Little Kanawha River

Monongahela River

Winchester

Scioto River

Elk River

River

V A N D A L I A

V I R G I N I A

•Staunton

Kanawha River TREATY 1770

New River

James River

□ONELSON'S River

LINE

River

TREATY OF LOCHABER

TREATY OF HARD LABOR 1768

PROCLAMATION LINE OF 1763

Staunton River

ANSYLVANIA

Castle's Woods

Fort Chiswell□

Ingles Ferry

(*Roanoke*)

Cumberland Gap

•Martin's Station

North Branch

Stalnakers•

•Royal Oak

River

LINE 1761

River

River

Long Island of Holston

South Branch

Watauga River

Bethabara•

•Salem

Hillsboro•

✗Alamance

Holston River

Clinch River

French Broad River

Nolachucky River

Sycamore Shoals

River

TRYON'S

Catawba River

N O R T H

Yadkin River

•Salisbury

C A R O L I N A

Neuse River

Little Tennessee River

Pellico River

C H E R O K E E

Tennessee River

□Chota

Tryon's ✗ Mountain

LINE

Cross Creek•

River

Broad River

Cape Fear River

Fort Prince George □

Etowah River

Tugaloo River

Saluda River

Reedy River

River

S O U T H   C A R O L I N A

✗ Lochaber

Savannah River

Little River

Long Cane Creek

← Hard Labor Creek

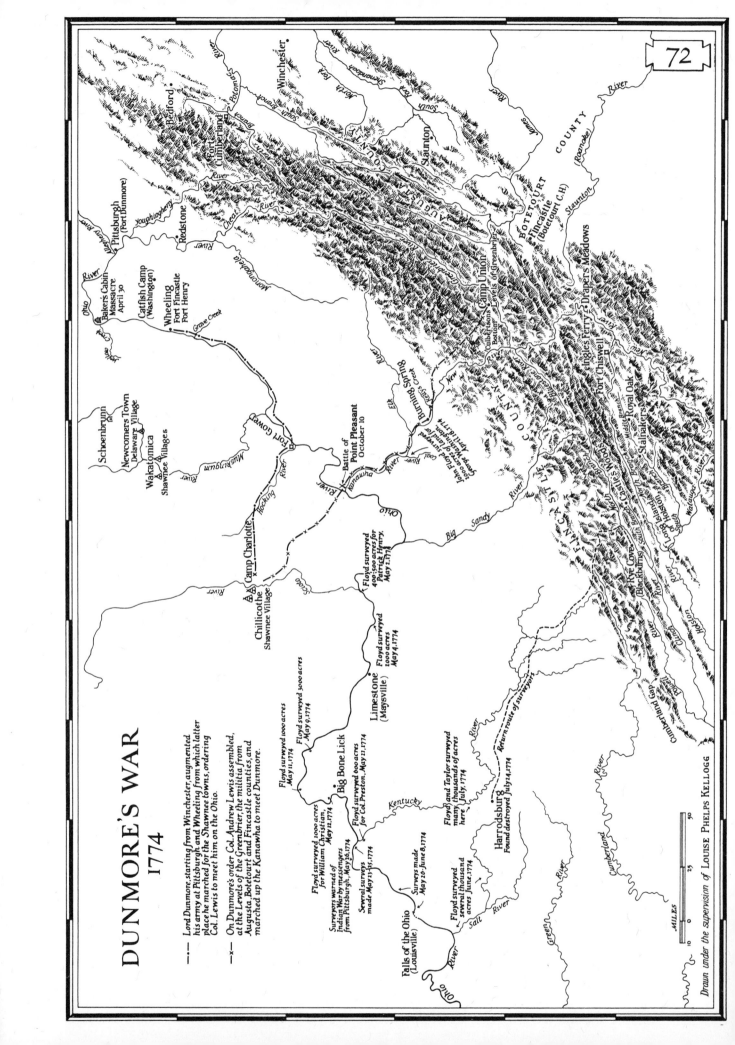

DUNMORE'S WAR
1774

-·-·- Lord Dunmore, starting from Winchester, augmented his army at Pittsburgh and Wheeling from which latter place he marched for the Shawnee towns, ordering Col. Lewis to meet him on the Ohio.

-×- On Dunmore's order Col. Andrew Lewis assembled, at the Levels of the Greenbrier, the militia from Augusta, Botetourt and Fincastle counties, and marched up the Kanawha to meet Dunmore.

72

Bedford

Winchester

Fort Cumberland

Pittsburgh (Fort Dunmore)

Staunton

BOTETOURT

Fincastle
Boteteurt C.H.

Drapers Meadows

AUGUSTA COUNTY

Redstone

Baker's Cabin Massacre April 30

Catfish Camp (Washington)

Wheeling
Fort Fincastle
Fort Henry

Grave Creek

Camp Union
Levels of Greenbrier

Culbertsons Bottom

Ingles Ferry

Fort Chiswell

Royal Oak

Stalnakers

Bulling Spring

FINCASTLE COUNTY

Schoenbrun

Newcomers Town
Delaware Village

Wakatomica
Shawnee Villages

Fort Gower

Battle of
Point Pleasant
October 10

John Floyd surveyed 2000 acres of land for
George Washington
April 19, 1774

Castle's Woods

Rye Cove

Blackmores

Floyd surveyed
400,500 acres for
Patrick Henry,
May 1, 1774

Camp Charlotte

Chillicothe
Shawnee Village

Floyd surveyed 1000 acres
May 4, 1774

Floyd surveyed 1000 acres
May 11, 1774

Floyd surveyed 2000 acres
May 9, 1774

Limestone
(Maysville)

Big Bone Lick

Floyd surveyed 1000 acres
for Col. Preston, May 11, 1774

Floyd and Taylor surveyed
many thousands of acres
here, July, 1774

Return route of surveyors

Harrodsburg
Found destroyed July 14, 1774

Floyd surveyed 1000 acres
for William Christian,
May 20, 1774

Surveyors warned of
Indian War by messengers
from Pittsburgh, May 20, 1774

Several surveys
made May 23-25, 1774

Surveys made
May 20-June 8, 1774

Floyd surveyed
several thousand
acres June, 1774

Falls of the Ohio
(Louisville)

Salt River

Kentucky River

Green River

Cumberland River

Cumberland Gap

MILES
0   25   50

Drawn under the supervision of LOUISE PHELPS KELLOGG

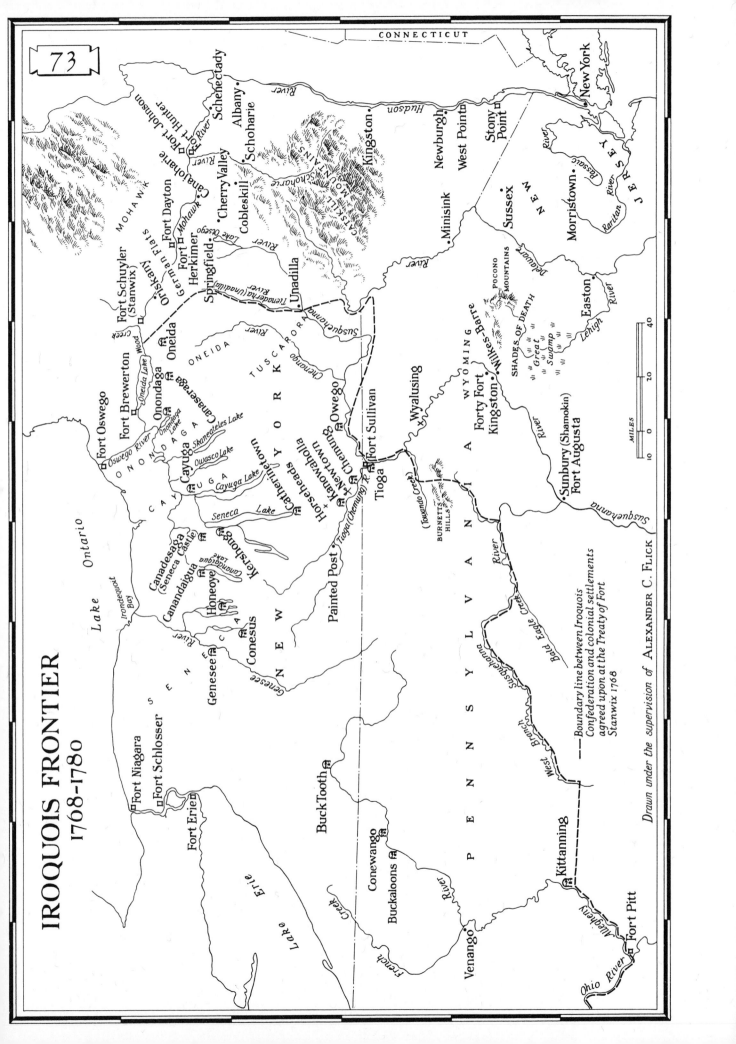

IROQUOIS FRONTIER
1768-1780

73

CONNECTICUT

New York

Schenectady
Albany
Schoharie
Kingston
Newburgh
West Point
Stony Point
JERSEY
NEW
Morristown
Sussex
Minisink
Easton
Raritan River
Passaic River

CATSKILL MOUNTAINS
Schoharie River

Fort Johnson
Fort Hunter
Canajoharie River
Cherry Valley
Cobleskill
MOHAWK
Fort Dayton
Fort Herkimer
German Flats
Fort Mohawk
Lake Otsego
Springfield
Oriskany
Fort Schuyler (Stanwix)
Wood Creek
Oneida
ONEIDA
Unadilla
Tienaderha (Unadilla) River
Susquehanna River

POCONO MOUNTAINS
SHADES OF DEATH
Great Swamp
Lehigh River
Delaware River

WYOMING
Forty Fort
Wilkes-Barre
Kingston
Wyalusing
Susquehanna River

Fort Oswego
Fort Brewerton
Oswego River
Oneida Lake
Onondaga
Onondaga Lake
Canaseraga
ONONDAGA
Skaneateles Lake
Owasco Lake
Cayuga
CAYUGA
Cayuga Lake
Seneca Lake
Catherinetown
Kanawholla
Horseheads
Newtown
Chemung
Owego
Chenango River
Fort Sullivan
Tioga (Fort Sullivan)
Tioga (Chemung) R.
Painted Post
TUSCARORA
NEW YORK

Sunbury (Shamokin)
Fort Augusta
(Towando Creek)
BURNETT'S HILLS
River
Bad Eagle Creek

Lake Ontario
Irondequoit Bay
Kershons
Canadesaga (Seneca Castle)
Canandaigua
Canandaigua Lake
Honeye
Conesus
Genesee
Genesee River
SENECA

PENNSYLVANIA
Susquehanna
West Branch
River

Fort Niagara
Fort Schlosser
Fort Erie
Lake Erie

BuckTooth

Conewango
Buckaloons
French Creek
River

Venango
Kittanning
Allegheny
Ohio River
Fort Pitt

MILES
10 0 10 20 40

— — Boundary line between Iroquois
Confederation and colonial settlements
agreed upon at the Treaty of Fort
Stanwix 1768

Drawn under the supervision of ALEXANDER C. FLICK

V THE AMERICAN REVOLUTION

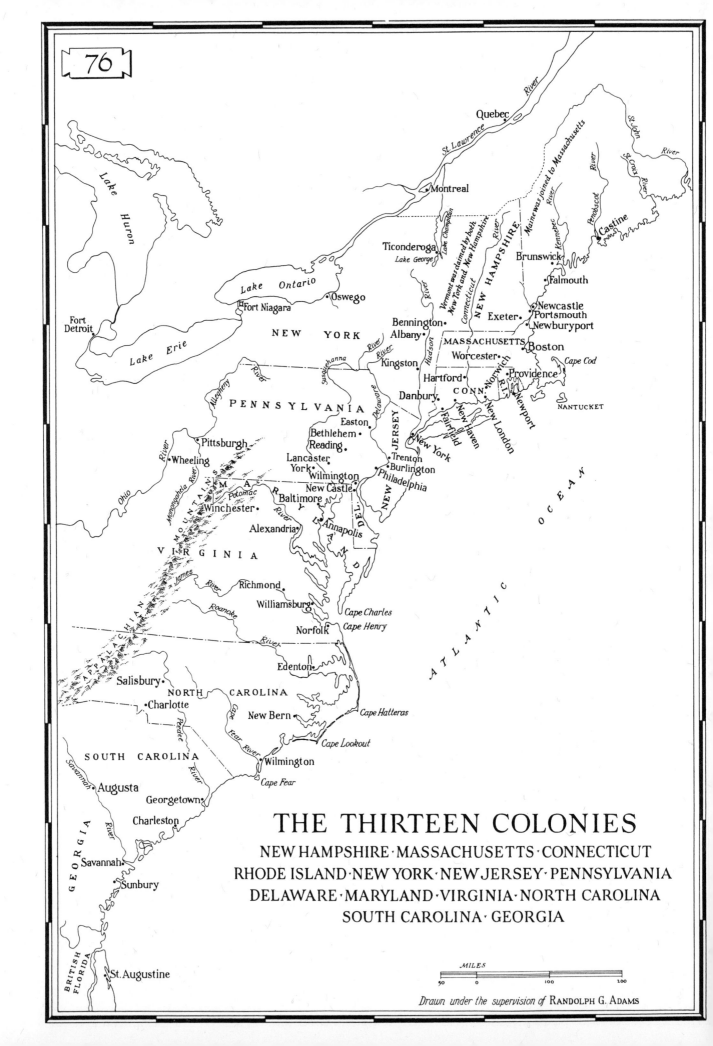

76

Quebec

Lake Huron

St. Lawrence River

Montreal

St. John River

St. Croix River

Penobscot River

Kennebec River

Castine

NEW HAMPSHIRE

Ticonderoga

Lake George

Lake Champlain

Vermont was claimed by both New York and New Hampshire

Maine was joined to Massachusetts

Brunswick

Falmouth

Lake Ontario

Oswego

Fort Niagara

NEW YORK

Connecticut River

Exeter

Newcastle
Portsmouth
Newburyport

Fort Detroit

Lake Erie

Bennington

Albany

Hudson River

MASSACHUSETTS

Worcester

Boston

Cape Cod

Susquehanna River

Kingston

Hartford

Providence

Norwich

R.I.

ALLEGHANY River

PENNSYLVANIA

Danbury

CONN.

New Haven

New London

Newport

NANTUCKET

Delaware River

Easton

NEW JERSEY

Fairfield

New York

Pittsburgh

Bethlehem

Reading

Ohio River

Wheeling

Lancaster

York

Trenton

Burlington

Monongahela River

MOUNTAINS

Wilmington

New Castle

Philadelphia

MARYLAND

DEL.

Potomac River

Baltimore

Winchester

Annapolis

Alexandria

VIRGINIA

James River

Richmond

Roanoke River

Williamsburg

Cape Charles

Cape Henry

Norfolk

ATLANTIC OCEAN

APPALACHIAN MOUNTAINS

Edenton

Salisbury

NORTH CAROLINA

Charlotte

New Bern

Cape Hatteras

Pedee River

Cape Fear River

Cape Lookout

SOUTH CAROLINA

Wilmington

Savannah River

Augusta

Cape Fear

Georgetown

Charleston

GEORGIA

Savannah

Sunbury

BRITISH FLORIDA

St. Augustine

THE THIRTEEN COLONIES

NEW HAMPSHIRE · MASSACHUSETTS · CONNECTICUT
RHODE ISLAND · NEW YORK · NEW JERSEY · PENNSYLVANIA
DELAWARE · MARYLAND · VIRGINIA · NORTH CAROLINA
SOUTH CAROLINA · GEORGIA

MILES

50   0   100   100

Drawn under the supervision of RANDOLPH G. ADAMS

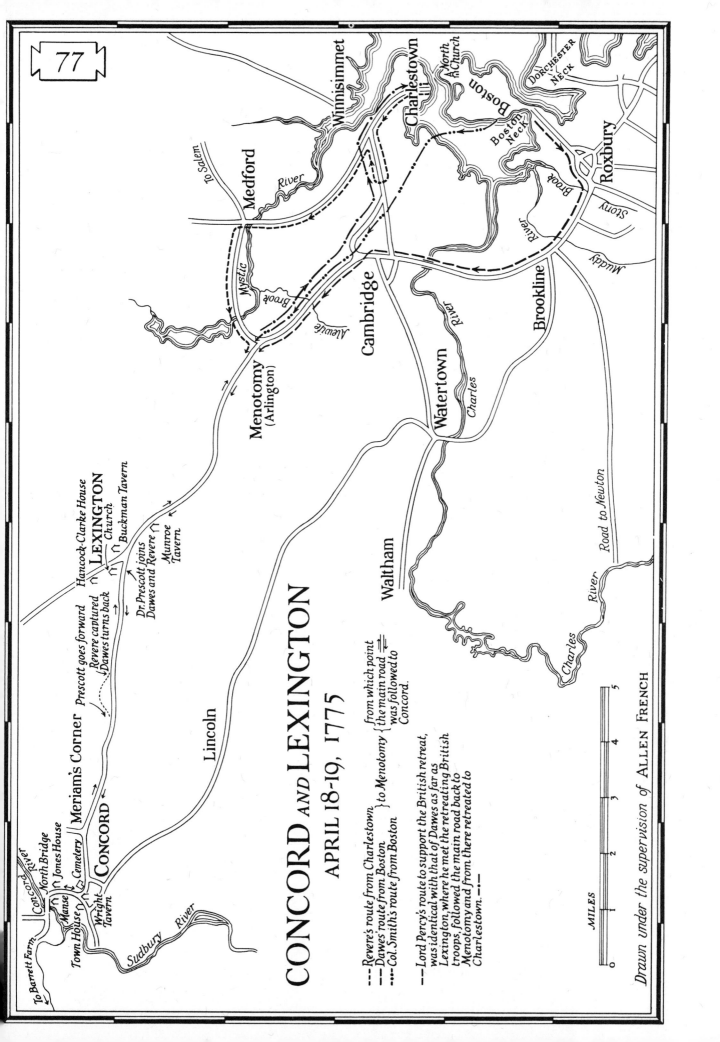

CONCORD AND LEXINGTON
APRIL 18-19, 1775

Winnisimmet

To Salem

Medford

River

Mystic

Brook

Mystic

Menotomy
(Arlington)

Alewife

Brook

Charlestown

North A Church

Boston

Boston Neck

Stony Brook

Roxbury

Dorchester Neck

Cambridge

Watertown

Charles River

Brookline

Muddy River

Waltham

Charles River

Road to Newton

Lincoln

Sudbury River

Buckman Tavern

LEXINGTON Church

Munroe Tavern

Dr. Prescott joins Dawes and Revere

Revere captured Dawes turns back

Prescott goes forward

Hancock-Clarke House

Meriam's Corner

CONCORD

Wright Tavern

Town House

Manse

Cemetery

Jones House

North Bridge

Concord River

To Barrett Farm

--- Revere's route from Charlestown ⎱ from which point
-- Dawes route from Boston ⎰ to Menotomy ⎱ the main road
— Col. Smith's route from Boston ⎰ was followed to Concord.

—Lord Percy's route to support the British retreat, was identical with that of Dawes as far as Lexington, where he met the retreating British troops, followed the main road back to Menotomy and from there retreated to Charlestown. —·—

MILES
0 1 2 3 4 5

Drawn under the supervision of ALLEN FRENCH

77

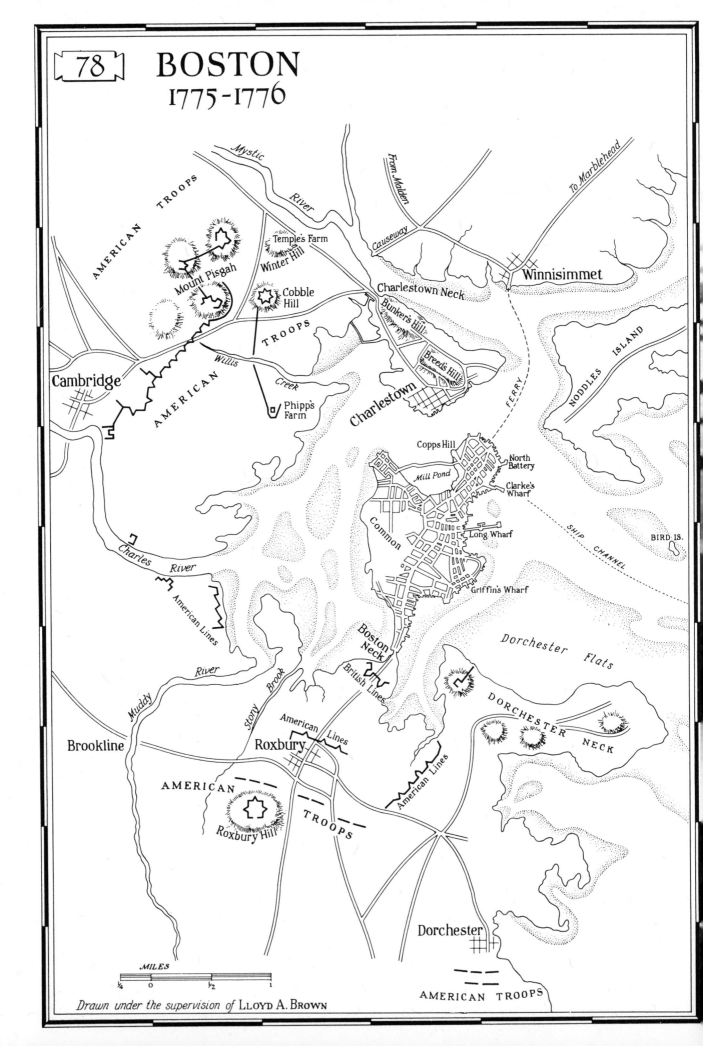

78 BOSTON
1775-1776

Mystic River

From Malden

To Marblehead

AMERICAN TROOPS

Temple's Farm

Mount Pisgah

Winter Hill

Cobble Hill

Causeway

Charlestown Neck

Winnisimmet

Bunker's Hill

Breed's Hill

NODDLES ISLAND

TROOPS

Willis

Cambridge

Creek

AMERICAN

Phipps Farm

Charlestown

FERRY

Copps Hill

North Battery

Mill Pond

Clarke's Wharf

Common

SHIP CHANNEL

BIRD IS.

Long Wharf

Charles River

American Lines

Griffin's Wharf

River

Muddy

Dorchester Flats

Boston Neck

British Lines

DORCHESTER NECK

Story Brook

American Lines

Brookline

Roxbury

American Lines

AMERICAN

American Lines

Roxbury Hill

TROOPS

Dorchester

MILES

¼ 0 ½ 1

Drawn under the supervision of LLOYD A. BROWN

AMERICAN TROOPS

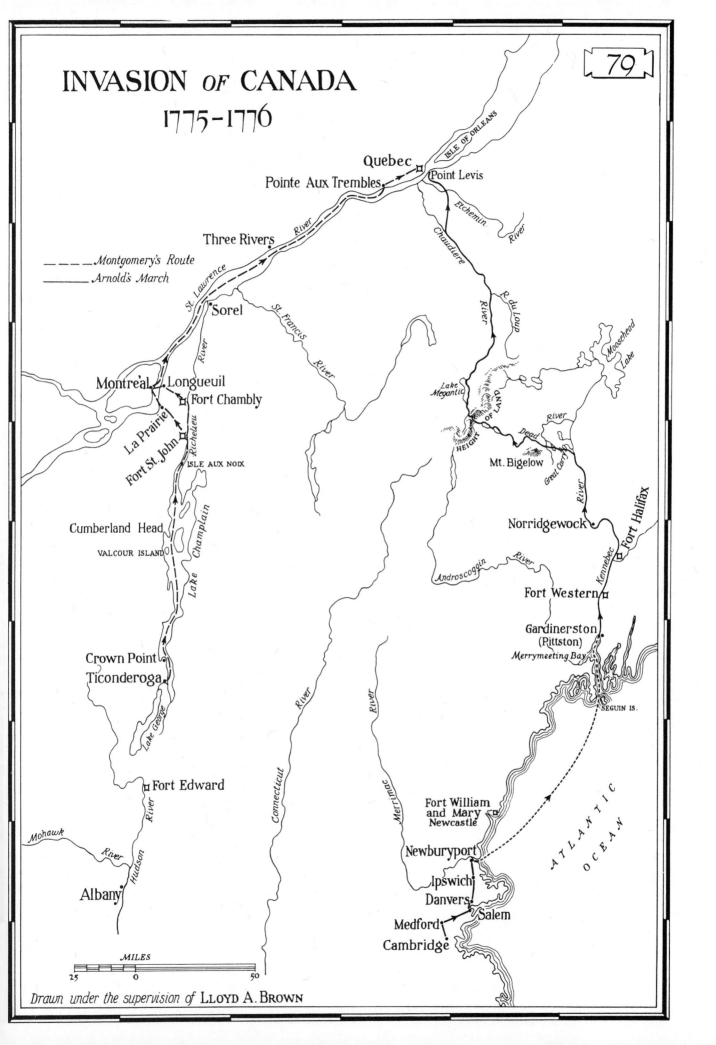

INVASION *of* CANADA
1775–1776

ISLE OF ORLEANS

Quebec
Point Levis
Pointe Aux Trembles

Etchemin River

Three Rivers

Chaudiere River

R. du Loup

Moosehead Lake

– – – – *Montgomery's Route*
———— *Arnold's March*

St. Lawrence River

Sorel

St. Francis River

Lake Megantic

Montréal
Longueuil
Fort Chambly

Richelieu River

HEIGHT OF LAND

Dead River

La Prairie
Fort St. John

Mt. Bigelow

Great Carry

ISLE AUX NOIX

Cumberland Head

Lake Champlain

Norridgewock

Fort Halifax

VALCOUR ISLAND

Androscoggin River

Kennebec River

Fort Western

Crown Point

Gardinerston
(Pittston)

Ticonderoga

Merrymeeting Bay

Lake George

SEGUIN IS.

Connecticut River

River

Fort Edward

Hudson River

Merrimac River

Fort William
and Mary
Newcastle

Mohawk River

Newburyport

ATLANTIC OCEAN

Ipswich
Danvers

Albany

Salem

Medford
Cambridge

MILES
25   0   50

Drawn under the supervision of LLOYD A. BROWN

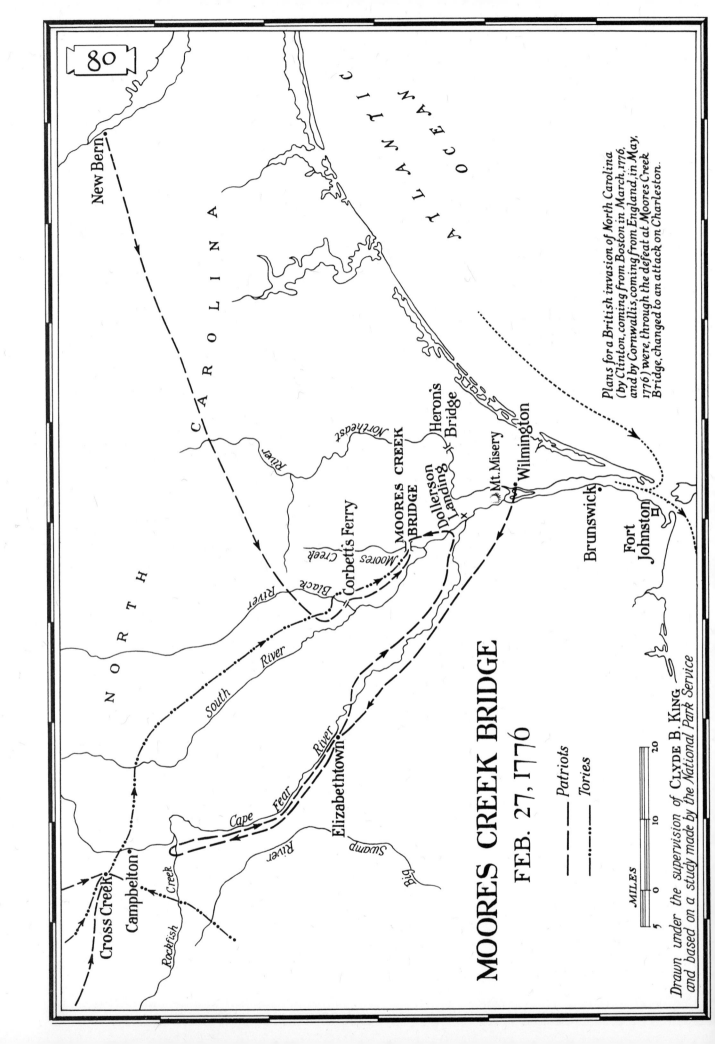

80

ATLANTIC OCEAN

New Bern

NORTH CAROLINA

River

Northeast

Heron's Bridge
MOORES CREEK BRIDGE
Dollerson Landing
Corbett's Ferry
Black Creek
Moores Creek
Mt. Misery
Wilmington

Brunswick

Fort Johnston

River
South River
Cape Fear River
River
Campbelton
Cross Creek
Rockfish Creek
Elizabethtown
Swamp
Big

Plans for a British invasion of North Carolina (by Clinton, coming from Boston in March, 1776, and by Cornwallis, coming from England, in May, 1776) were, through the defeat at Moores Creek Bridge, changed to an attack on Charleston.

MOORES CREEK BRIDGE
FEB. 27, 1776

——— Patriots
—·—·— Tories

MILES
5   0   10   20

Drawn under the supervision of CLYDE B. KING and based on a study made by the National Park Service

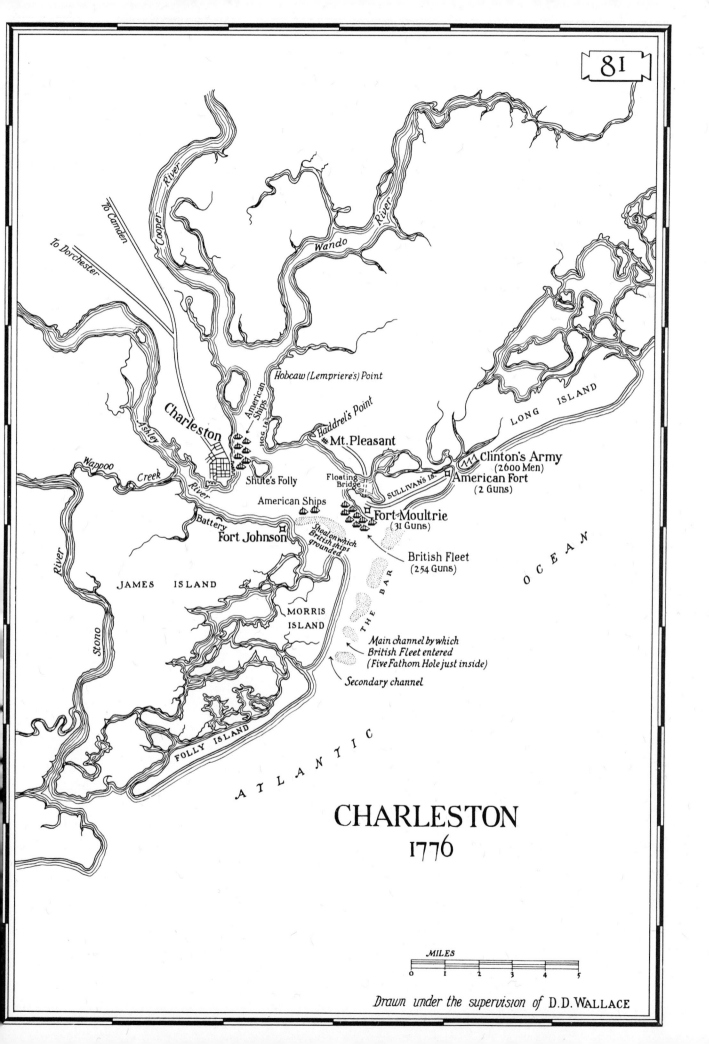

To Camden

To Dorchester

Cooper River

Wando River

Ashley River

Wappoo Creek

Stono River

Hobcaw (Lempriere's) Point

Haddrel's Point

Charleston

American Ships

HOG IS.

Mt. Pleasant

Shute's Folly

Floating Bridge

SULLIVAN'S IS.

LONG ISLAND

Clinton's Army
(2600 Men)

American Fort
(2 Guns)

American Ships

Fort Moultrie
(31 Guns)

Battery

Fort Johnson

Shoal on which
British ships
grounded

British Fleet
(254 Guns)

OCEAN

JAMES ISLAND

MORRIS ISLAND

THE BAR

Main channel by which
British Fleet entered
(Five Fathom Hole just inside)

Secondary channel

FOLLY ISLAND

ATLANTIC

CHARLESTON
1776

MILES

0 1 2 3 4 5

Drawn under the supervision of D.D. WALLACE

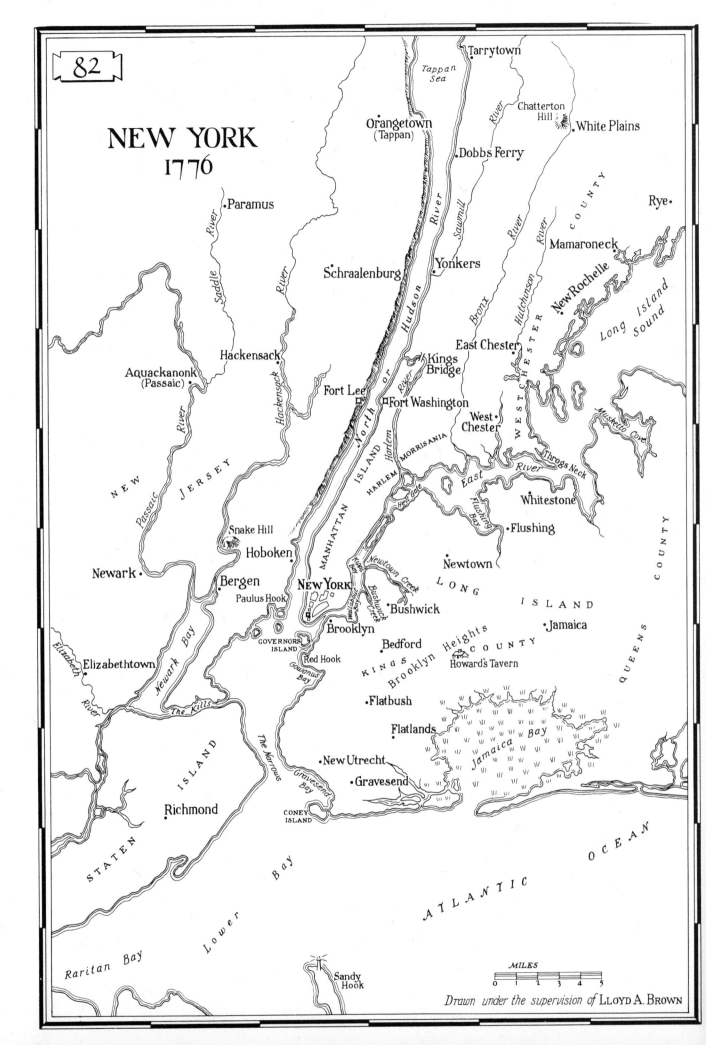

82

NEW YORK
1776

Tarrytown

Tappan Sea

Orangetown
(Tappan)

River

Chatterton
Hill
• White Plains

•Dobbs Ferry

•Paramus

Saddle River

River

Schraalenburg

•Yonkers

Sawmill River

Bronx River

Hutchinson River

W E S T C H E S T E R   C O U N T Y

• Rye

Mamaroneck

New Rochelle

Long Island Sound

Hackensack

Aquackanonk
(Passaic) •

Hackensack River

Passaic River

Fort Lee

East Chester

Kings
Bridge

Harlem River

Fort Washington

West •
Chester

Muskello Cove.

Throgs Neck

MANHATTAN ISLAND

Harlem

MORRISANIA

Hell Gate

East River

Whitestone

Flushing Bay

•Flushing

N E W   J E R S E Y

Snake Hill

Hoboken

Newtown

L O N G

I S L A N D

Q U E E N S   C O U N T Y

Newark •

Bergen

Paulus Hook

NEW YORK

Kings Bay

Newtown Creek

Wallabout Bay

Bushwick Creek

•Bushwick

Brooklyn

Bedford

Howard's Tavern

Jamaica

K I N G S   C O U N T Y

Brooklyn Heights

Elizabethtown •

Elizabeth River

Newark Bay

GOVERNORS
ISLAND

Red Hook

*Gowanus
Bay*

The Kills

•Flatbush

•Flatlands

Jamaica   Bay

Richmond •

S T A T E N   I S L A N D

The Narrows

•New Utrecht

•Gravesend

Gravesend Bay

CONEY
ISLAND

A T L A N T I C

O C E A N

Lower   Bay

Raritan Bay

Sandy
Hook

MILES
0 1 2 3 4 5

Drawn under the supervision of LLOYD A. BROWN

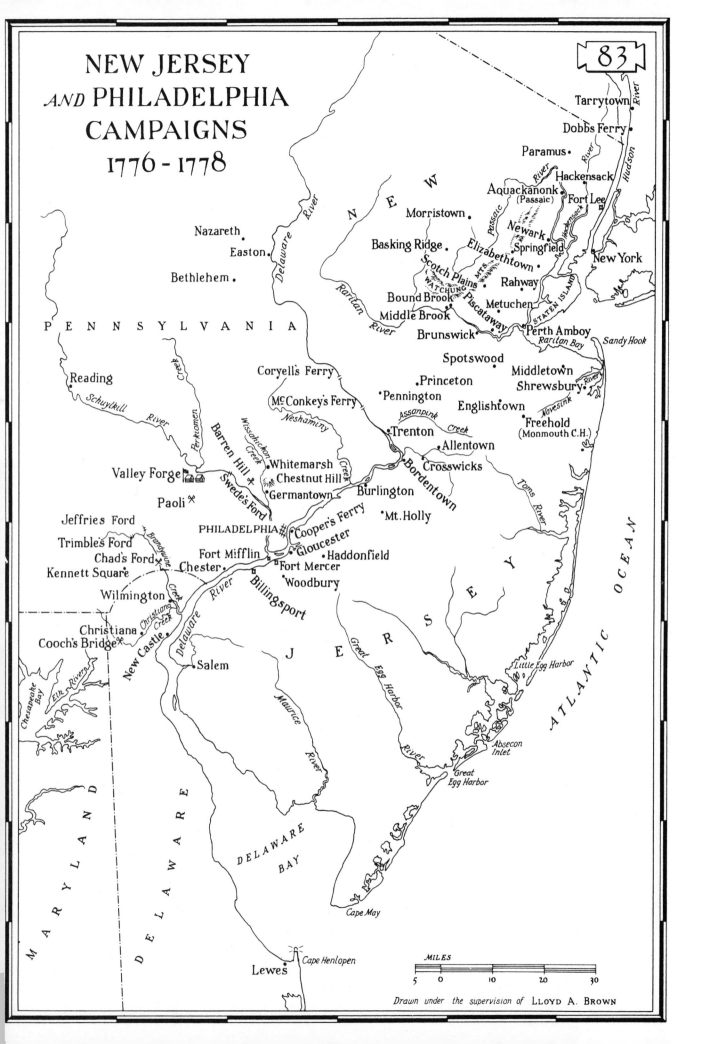

NEW JERSEY
AND PHILADELPHIA
CAMPAIGNS
1776 - 1778

83

Tarrytown
Dobbs Ferry
Paramus
Hudson River
Hackensack
Aquackanonk (Passaic)
Fort Lee
N E W
Morristown
Newark
Springfield
Basking Ridge
Elizabethtown
New York
Scotch Plains
Rahway
WATCHUNG MTS.
Bound Brook
Piscataway
Metuchen
STATEN ISLAND
Middle Brook
Nazareth
Easton
Delaware River
Raritan River
Brunswick
Perth Amboy
Bethlehem
Raritan Bay
Sandy Hook

P E N N S Y L V A N I A
Spotswood
Creek
Middletown
Princeton
Shrewsbury
Reading
Coryell's Ferry
Pennington
Englishtown
Navesink River
Schuylkill River
McConkey's Ferry
Assanpink Creek
Freehold (Monmouth C.H.)
Perkiomen
Neshaminy
Trenton
Barren Hill
Wissahickon Creek
Allentown
Valley Forge
Whitemarsh
Crosswicks
Paoli
Swede's Ford
Chestnut Hill
Bordentown
Germantown
Burlington
Jeffries Ford
PHILADELPHIA
Cooper's Ferry
Mt. Holly
Toms River
Trimble's Ford
Gloucester
Chad's Ford
Fort Mifflin
Haddonfield
Kennett Square
Chester
Fort Mercer
Brandywine Creek
Woodbury
Billingsport
J E R S E Y
Wilmington
Delaware River
Christiana Creek
Christiana
New Castle
Cooch's Bridge
Salem
Chesapeake Bay
Elk River
Great Egg Harbor
Little Egg Harbor
M A R Y L A N D
Maurice River
Absecon Inlet
D E L A W A R E
Great Egg Harbor
Great Egg Harbor River
A T L A N T I C   O C E A N
D E L A W A R E   B A Y
Cape May
Lewes
Cape Henlopen

MILES
5   0   10   20   30

Drawn under the supervision of LLOYD A. BROWN

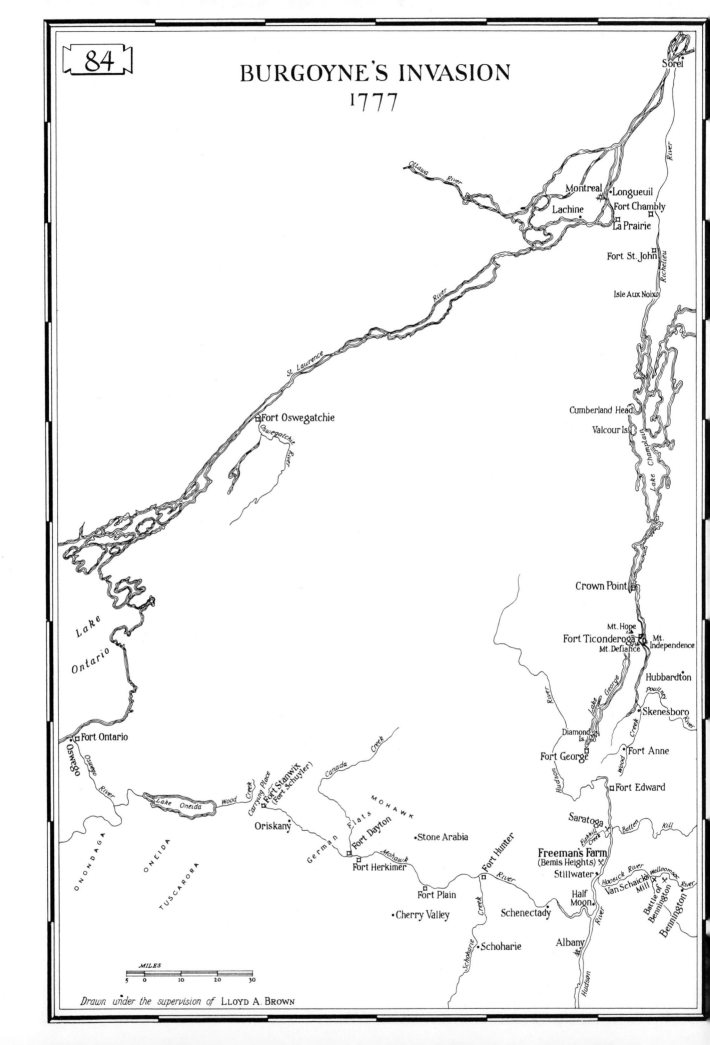

BURGOYNE'S INVASION
1777

84

Sorel

Ottawa River

Montreal · Longueuil
Lachine · Fort Chambly
La Prairie

Fort St. John

Isle Aux Noix

River

St. Lawrence

Fort Oswegatchie

Oswegatchie River

Cumberland Head
Valcour Is.

Lake Champlain

Crown Point

Mt. Hope
Fort Ticonderoga · Mt. Independence
Mt. Defiance

Hubbardton

Lake George

Poultney River

Skenesboro

Lake Ontario

Diamond Is.

Fort George · Fort Anne

Wood Creek

Fort Ontario

Oswego

Oswego River

Carrying Place
Fort Stanwix (Fort Schuyler)

Canada Creek

Hudson River

Fort Edward

Lake Oneida

Wood Creek

MOHAWK

German Flats

Saratoga

Batten Kill

Oriskany

Fort Dayton

· Stone Arabia

Fishkill Creek

Freeman's Farm
(Bemis Heights) ✕

Fort Hunter

Stillwater ·

Hoosick River

Walloomsac River

ONONDAGA

ONEIDA

Mohawk River

Fort Herkimer

Fort Plain

Van Schaick's Mill

Battle of Bennington +

TUSCARORA

Creek

Half Moon

Schenectady ·

Bennington

· Cherry Valley

Schoharie Creek

· Schoharie

Albany

Hudson

MILES
5 0   10   20   30

Drawn under the supervision of LLOYD A. BROWN

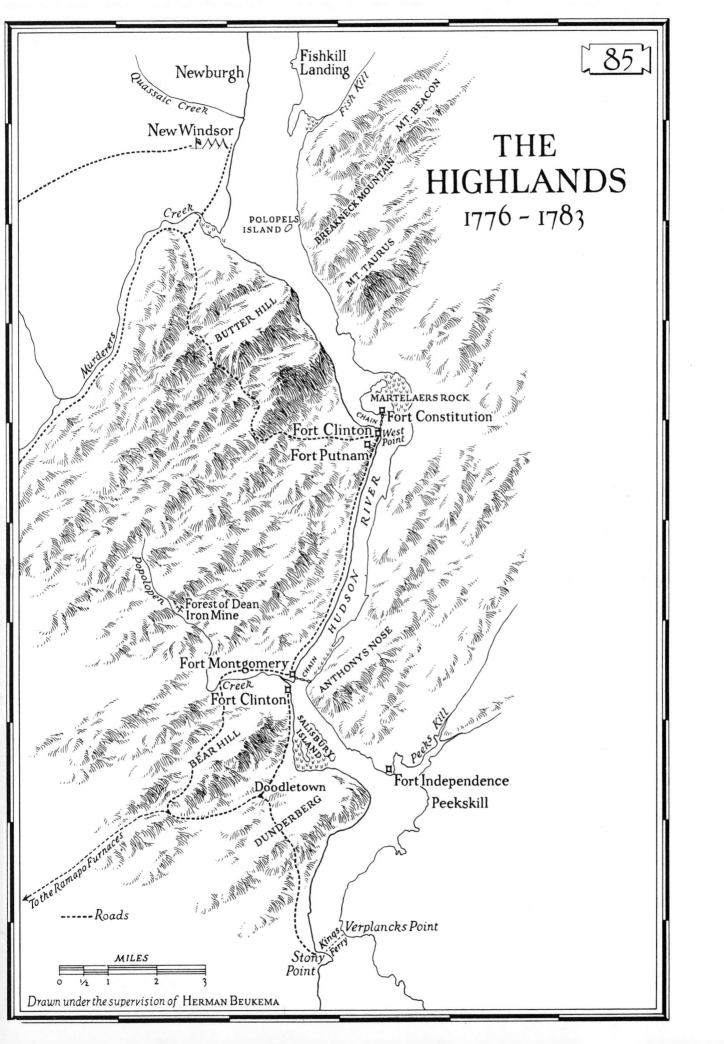

Newburgh

Quassaic Creek

Fishkill Landing

Fish Kill

MT. BEACON

85

THE HIGHLANDS
1776 – 1783

New Windsor

Creek

POLOPELS ISLAND

BREAKNECK MOUNTAIN

MT. TAURUS

BUTTER HILL

Murderers

MARTELAERS ROCK

CHAIN

Fort Constitution

Fort Clinton

West Point

Fort Putnam

HUDSON RIVER

Popolopen

Forest of Dean Iron Mine

ANTHONYS NOSE

Fort Montgomery

CHAIN

Creek

Fort Clinton

Peeks Kill

BEAR HILL

SALISBURY ISLAND

Fort Independence

Peekskill

Doodletown

DUNDERBERG

To the Ramapo Furnaces

----- Roads

MILES

0   ½   1   2   3

Kings Ferry

Verplancks Point

Stony Point

Drawn under the supervision of HERMAN BEUKEMA

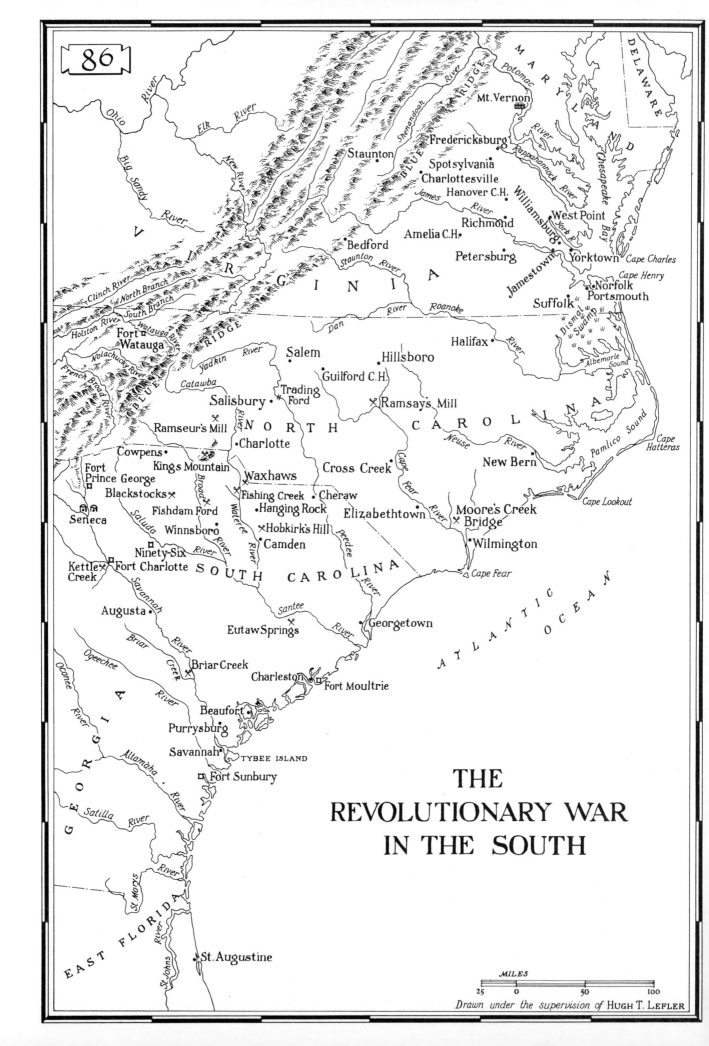

86

THE
REVOLUTIONARY WAR
IN THE SOUTH

MILES
25   0   50   100

Drawn under the supervision of HUGH T. LEFLER

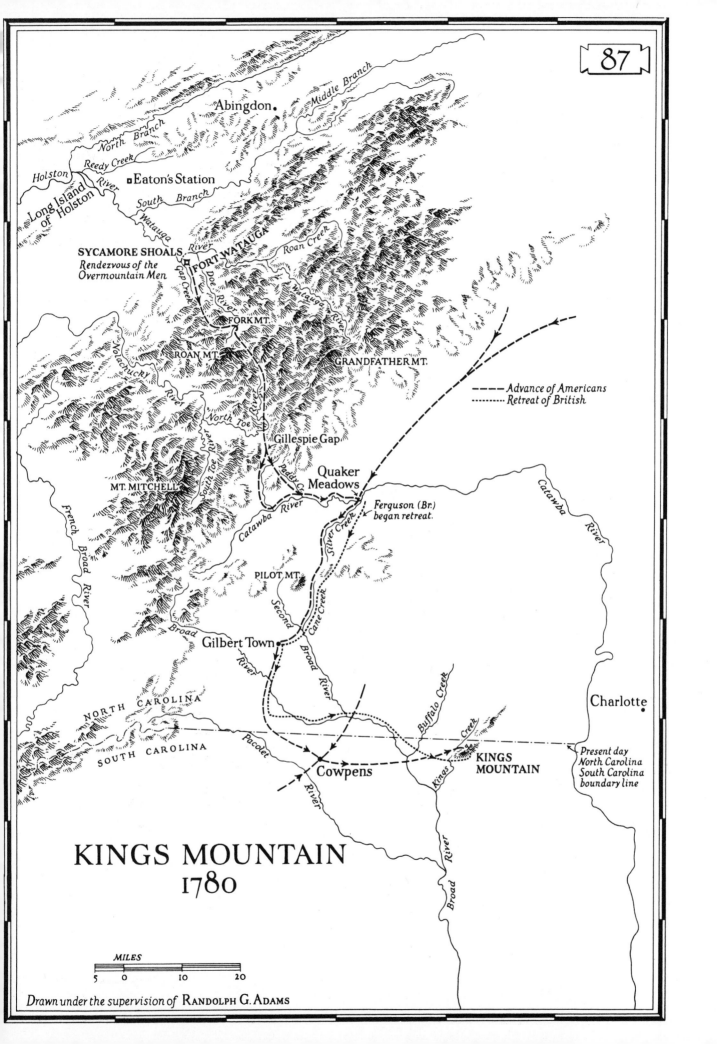

87

Abingdon.

Middle Branch

North Branch

Reedy Creek

Holston

Long Island of Holston

Eaton's Station

South Branch

Watauga River

SYCAMORE SHOALS
*Rendezvous of the
Overmountain Men*

FORT WATAUGA

Roan Creek

Doe River

Watauga River

Gap Creek

FORK MT.

ROAN MT.

GRANDFATHER MT.

Nolachucky River

North Toe River

—————— *Advance of Americans*
··········· *Retreat of British*

Gillespie Gap

Quaker Meadows

Ferguson (Br.)
began retreat.

MT. MITCHELL

South Toe River

Paddy C.

Catawba River

Silver Creek

Catawba River

French Broad River

PILOT MT.

Cane Creek

Second Broad River

Gilbert Town

NORTH CAROLINA

Broad River

Buffalo Creek

Charlotte.

Pacolet

SOUTH CAROLINA

Cowpens

Kings Creek

KINGS MOUNTAIN

*Present day
North Carolina
South Carolina
boundary line*

River

Broad River

KINGS MOUNTAIN
1780

MILES

5   0   10   20

Drawn under the supervision of RANDOLPH G. ADAMS

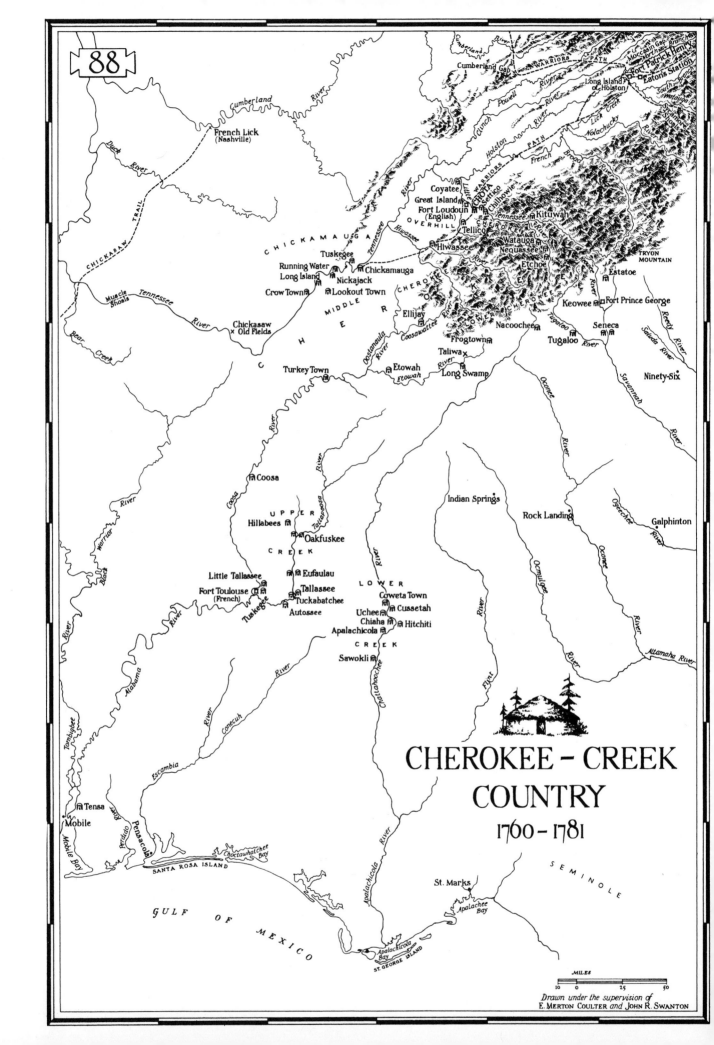

CHEROKEE – CREEK COUNTRY 1760 – 1781

Drawn under the supervision of
E. MERTON COULTER *and* JOHN R. SWANTON

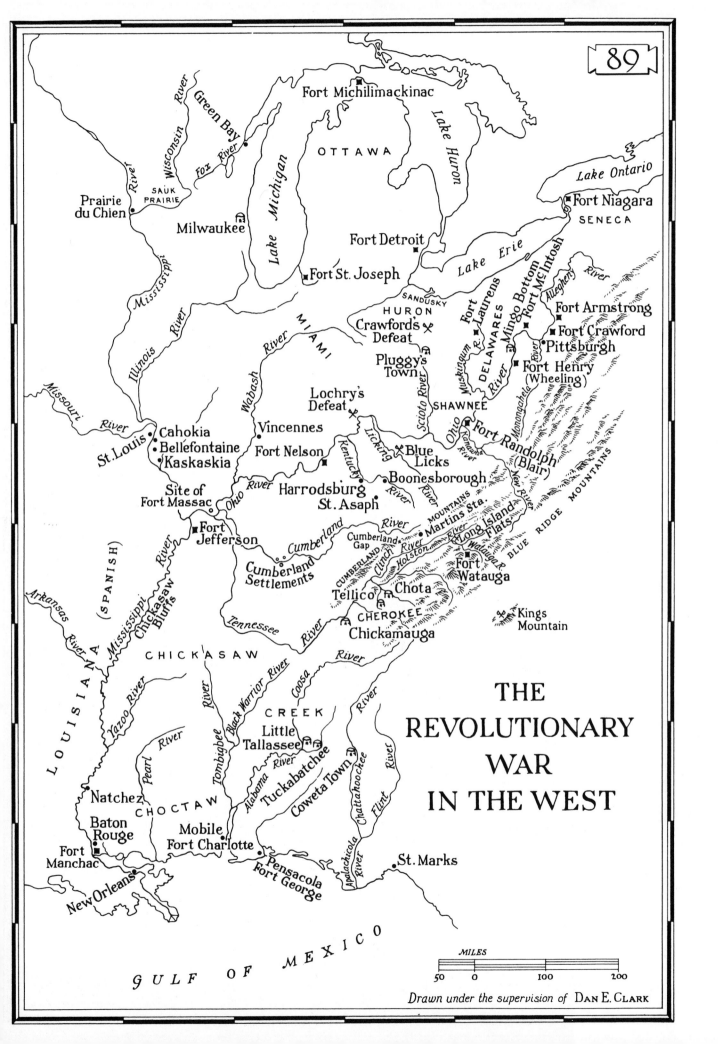

THE REVOLUTIONARY WAR IN THE WEST

MILES
50   0   100   200

Drawn under the supervision of DAN E. CLARK

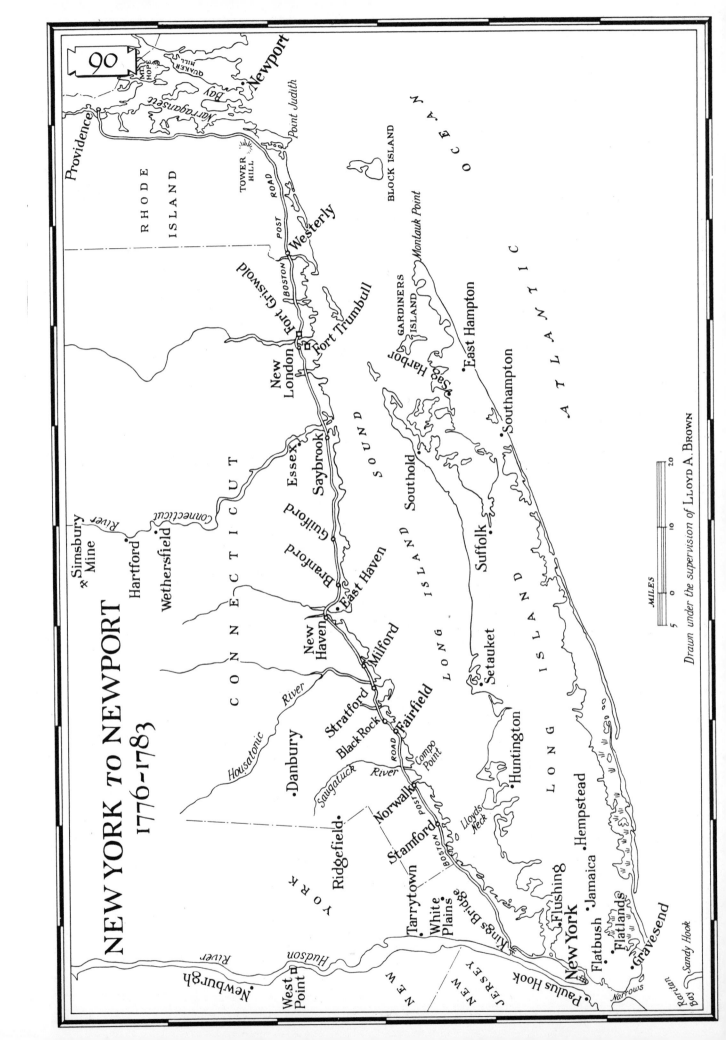

NEW YORK *to* NEWPORT
1776–1783

Drawn under the supervision of LLOYD A. BROWN

MILES

90

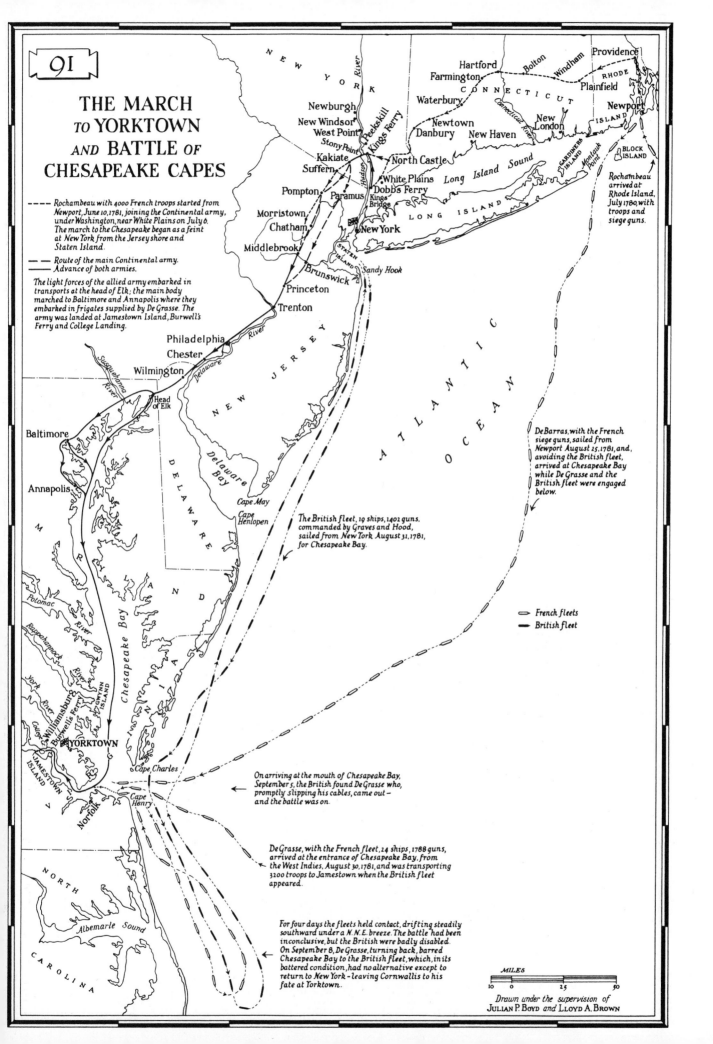

91

THE MARCH
TO YORKTOWN
AND BATTLE OF
CHESAPEAKE CAPES

- - - - *Rochambeau with 4000 French troops started from Newport, June 10, 1781, joining the Continental army, under Washington, near White Plains on July 6. The march to the Chesapeake began as a feint at New York from the Jersey shore and Staten Island.*

– – – *Route of the main Continental army.*

———— *Advance of both armies.*

The light forces of the allied army embarked in transports at the head of Elk; the main body marched to Baltimore and Annapolis where they embarked in frigates supplied by De Grasse. The army was landed at Jamestown Island, Burwell's Ferry and College Landing.

Rochambeau arrived at Rhode Island, July 1780, with troops and siege guns.

De Barras, with the French siege guns, sailed from Newport August 25, 1781, and, avoiding the British fleet, arrived at Chesapeake Bay while De Grasse and the British fleet were engaged below.

The British fleet, 19 ships, 1402 guns, commanded by Graves and Hood, sailed from New York August 31, 1781, for Chesapeake Bay.

⊏⊐ *French fleets*
▬▬ *British fleet*

On arriving at the mouth of Chesapeake Bay, September 5, the British found De Grasse who, promptly slipping his cables, came out – and the battle was on.

De Grasse, with the French fleet, 24 ships, 1788 guns, arrived at the entrance of Chesapeake Bay, from the West Indies, August 30, 1781, and was transporting 3200 troops to Jamestown when the British fleet appeared.

For four days the fleets held contact, drifting steadily southward under a N.N.E. breeze. The battle had been inconclusive, but the British were badly disabled. On September 8, De Grasse, turning back, barred Chesapeake Bay to the British fleet, which, in its battered condition, had no alternative except to return to New York – leaving Cornwallis to his fate at Yorktown.

MILES
10 0   25   50

Drawn under the supervision of
JULIAN P. BOYD *and* LLOYD A. BROWN

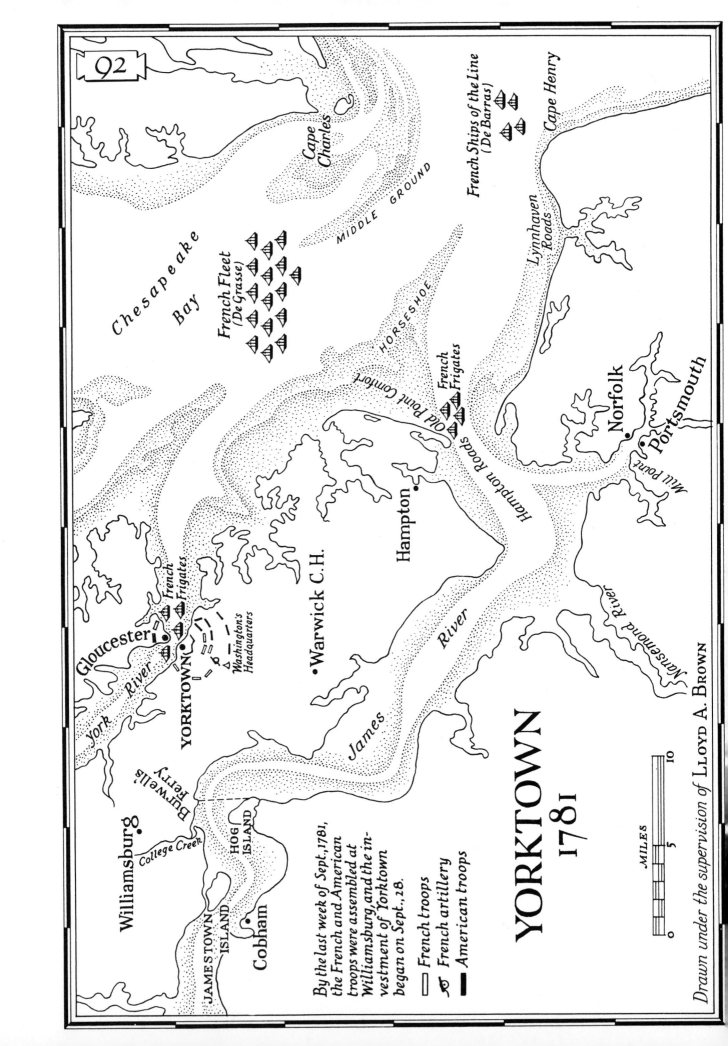

92

Cape Charles

Cape Henry

French Ships of the Line
(De Barras)

Lynnhaven Roads

MIDDLE GROUND

Chesapeake
Bay

French Fleet
(De Grasse)

HORSESHOE

Hampton Roads

French
Frigates

Norfolk

Portsmouth

Mill Point

Old Point Comfort

Hampton

Nansemond River

French Frigates

Gloucester

York River

YORKTOWN

Washington's
Headquarters

Warwick C.H.

James River

Williamsburg

Burwell's Ferry

College Creek

JAMESTOWN ISLAND

HOG ISLAND

Cobham

By the last week of Sept.,1781,
the French and American
troops were assembled at
Williamsburg, and the in-
vestment of Yorktown
began on Sept.,28.

☐ French troops
⚔ French artillery
▬ American troops

YORKTOWN
1781

MILES
0   5   10

Drawn under the supervision of LLOYD A. BROWN

VI THE NEW NATION

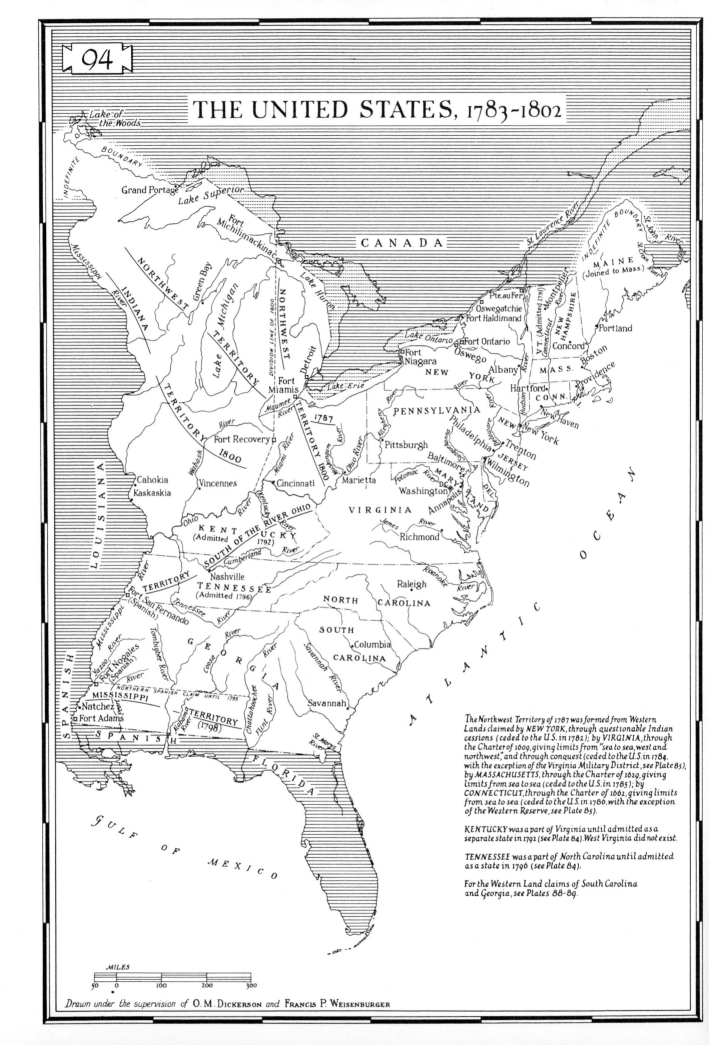

THE UNITED STATES, 1783-1802

Lake of the Woods

INDEFINITE BOUNDARY

Grand Portage • Lake Superior

CANADA

St Lawrence River

INDEFINITE BOUNDARY

St. John River

Fort Michilimackinac

MAINE
(Joined to Mass.)

St. Croix River

NORTHWEST

INDIANA

Green Bay

Lake Michigan

NORTHWEST TERRITORY

DIVISION LINE OF 1800

Pte. au Fer
Oswegatchie
Fort Haldimand

V.T. (Admitted 1791)
Montpelier
Connecticut River
NEW HAMPSHIRE

Portland

Mississippi River

Detroit

Lake Huron

Lake Erie

Fort Miamis

Maumee River

Lake Ontario
Fort Ontario
Oswego
Fort Niagara

Concord

NEW YORK

Albany
Mohawk River

Boston

MASS.

Providence

TERRITORY

1800

Fort Recovery

1787

TERRITORY 1800

Muskingum River

Hudson River

Hartford
CONN.

R.I.

New Haven

New York

Cahokia
Kaskaskia

Vincennes

Kentucky River
Cincinnati

Miami River

Ohio River
Marietta

Pittsburgh

Allegheny River

PENNSYLVANIA

Susquehanna River

Philadelphia
Trenton
NEW JERSEY
Wilmington
DEL.

LOUISIANA

Wabash River

Ohio River

KENT UCKY
(Admitted 1792)

SOUTH OF THE RIVER OHIO

Cumberland River

Potomac River
Washington
MARY LAND
D.C.
Annapolis

Baltimore

VIRGINIA

James River

Richmond

ATLANTIC OCEAN

TERRITORY

Fort San Fernando
(Spanish)

Nashville

TENNESSEE
(Admitted 1796)

Tennessee River

Roanoke River

Raleigh

NORTH CAROLINA

SPANISH

Mississippi River

Yazoo River
Fort Nogales
(Spanish)

Tombigbee River

GEORGIA

Coosa River

Savannah River

Columbia

SOUTH CAROLINA

NORTHERN SPANISH CLAIM UNTIL 1795

MISSISSIPPI
Natchez
Fort Adams

Alabama River

TERRITORY
(1798)

Chattahoochee River

Flint River

Savannah

SPANISH

St. Mary's River

FLORIDA

GULF OF MEXICO

The Northwest Territory of 1787 was formed from Western Lands claimed by NEW YORK, through questionable Indian cessions (ceded to the U.S. in 1781); by VIRGINIA, through the Charter of 1609, giving limits from "sea to sea, west and northwest," and through conquest (ceded to the U.S. in 1784, with the exception of the Virginia Military District, see Plate 85), by MASSACHUSETTS, through the Charter of 1629, giving limits from sea to sea (ceded to the U.S. in 1785); by CONNECTICUT, through the Charter of 1662, giving limits from sea to sea (ceded to the U.S. in 1786, with the exception of the Western Reserve, see Plate 85).

KENTUCKY was a part of Virginia until admitted as a separate state in 1792 (see Plate 84). West Virginia did not exist.

TENNESSEE was a part of North Carolina until admitted as a state in 1796 (see Plate 84).

For the Western Land claims of South Carolina and Georgia, see Plates 88-89.

MILES
50 0   100   200   300

Drawn under the supervision of O. M. DICKERSON *and* FRANCIS P. WEISENBURGER

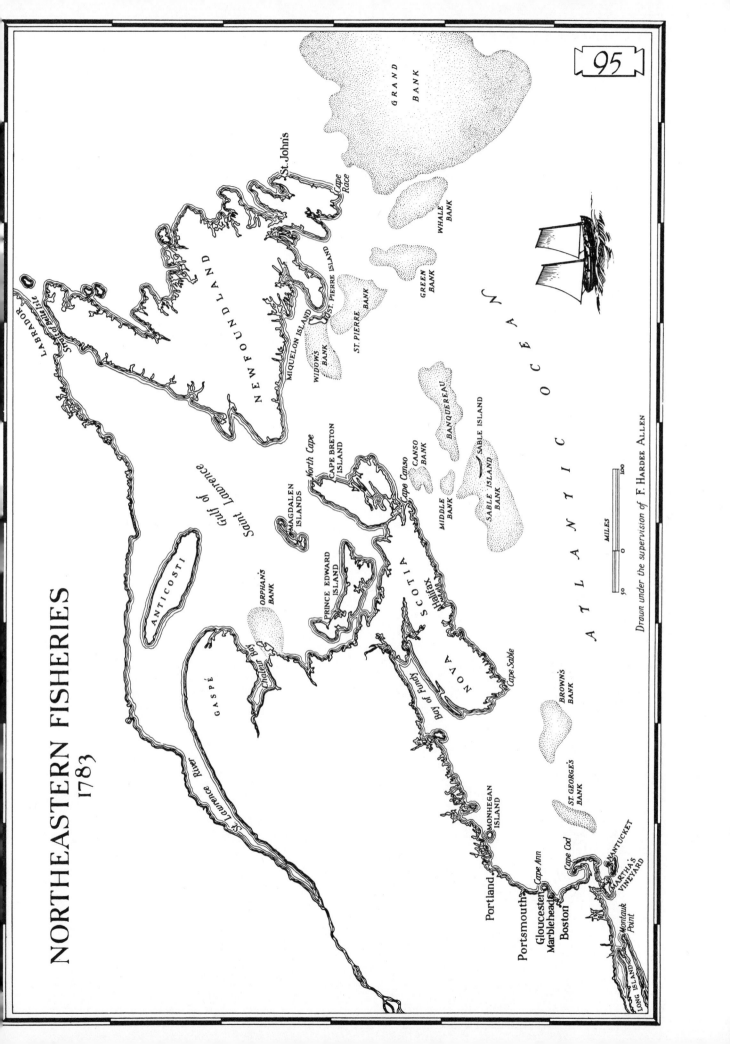

NORTHEASTERN FISHERIES
1783

95

GRAND BANK

St. John's

Cape Race

WHALE BANK

GREEN BANK

LABRADOR

Strait of Belle Isle

NEWFOUNDLAND

MIQUELON ISLAND

ST. PIERRE ISLAND

ST. PIERRE BANK

WIDOW'S BANK

BANQUEREAU

SABLE ISLAND BANK

CANSO BANK

MIDDLE BANK

ATLANTIC OCEAN

Gulf of Saint Lawrence

ANTICOSTI

Lawrence River

GASPÉ

MAGDALEN ISLANDS

North Cape

CAPE BRETON ISLAND

Cape Canso

SABLE ISLAND

ORPHAN'S BANK

Chaleur Bay

PRINCE EDWARD ISLAND

NOVA SCOTIA

Halifax

Bay of Fundy

Cape Sable

BROWN'S BANK

MONHEGAN ISLAND

ST. GEORGE'S BANK

Portland

Portsmouth
Gloucester
Marblehead
Boston

Cape Ann

Cape Cod

NANTUCKET

MARTHA'S VINEYARD

Montauk Point

LONG ISLAND

MILES
0   50   100

Drawn under the supervision of F. Hardee Allen

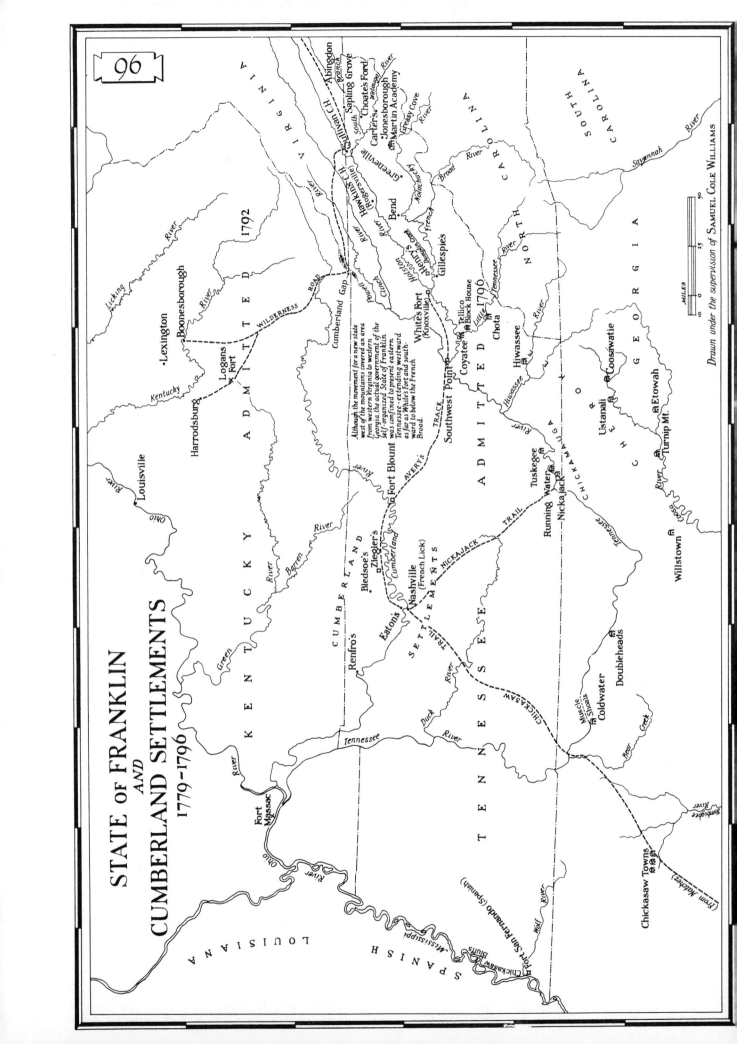

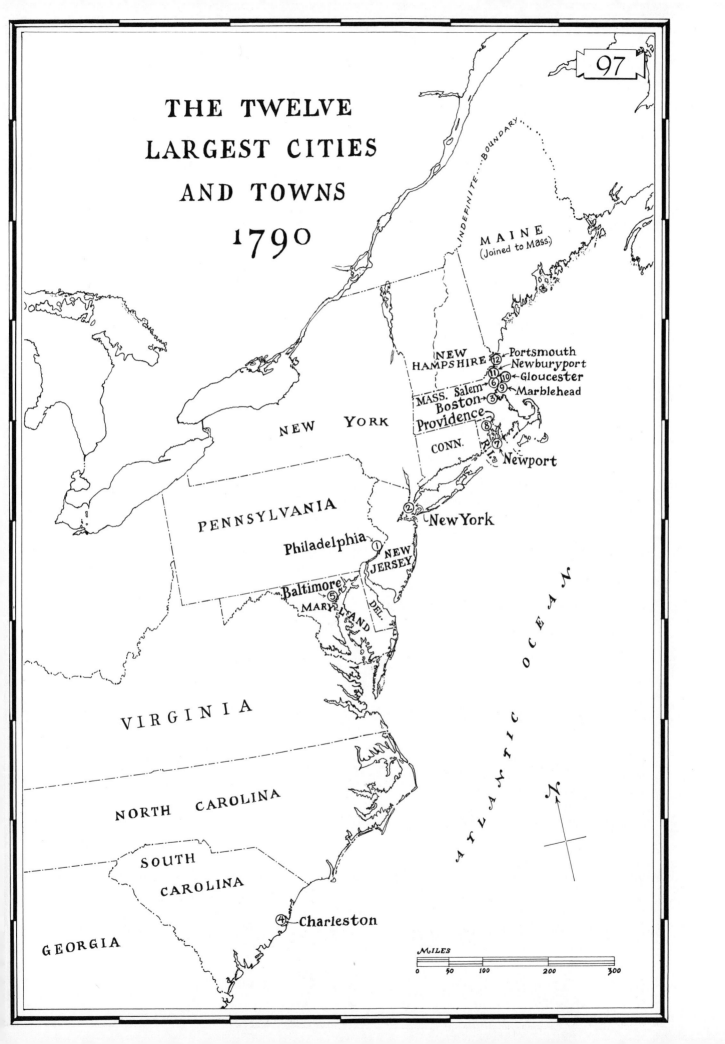

THE TWELVE
LARGEST CITIES
AND TOWNS
1790

MAINE
(Joined to Mass.)

INDEFINITE BOUNDARY

NEW
HAMPSHIRE

Portsmouth
Newburyport
Gloucester

MASS. Salem
Boston
Providence
Marblehead

Newport

NEW YORK

New York

PENNSYLVANIA

Philadelphia

NEW
JERSEY

Baltimore

MARYLAND

DEL.

CONN.

R.I.

VIRGINIA

ATLANTIC OCEAN

N

NORTH CAROLINA

SOUTH
CAROLINA

Charleston

GEORGIA

MILES
0   50   100   200   300

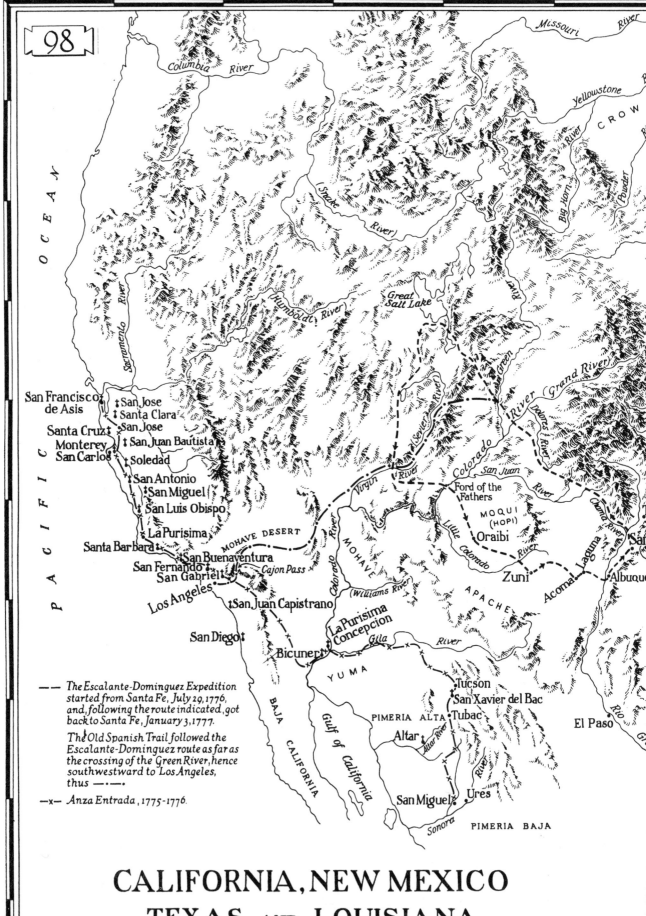

OCEAN

Columbia River

Missouri River

Yellowstone R.

CROW

Big Horn R.

Powder R.

(Snake River)

Sacramento River

Great Salt Lake

(Humboldt River)

San Francisco de Asis
San Jose
Santa Clara
San Jose
Santa Cruz
Monterey
San Carlos
San Juan Bautista
Soledad
San Antonio
San Miguel
San Luis Obispo
La Purisima
Santa Barbara
San Buenaventura
San Fernando
San Gabriel
Los Angeles
San Juan Capistrano
San Diego

PACIFIC

Virgin River

Sevier River

Green River

River (Grand River)

Dolores River

San Juan River

Colorado

Ford of the Fathers

MOQUI (HOPI)

Oraibi

Little Colorado River

Chama River

San

Zuni

Acoma Laguna

Albuque

MOHAVE DESERT

Colorado River

MOHAVE

(Williams River)

APACHE

La Purisima Concepcion

Gila River

Bicuner

Cajon Pass

YUMA

Tucson
San Xavier del Bac
Tubac

PIMERIA ALTA

El Paso

Rio Gra

Altar

Altar River

BAJA CALIFORNIA

Gulf of California

San Miguel

Ures

Sonora

PIMERIA BAJA

--- The Escalante-Dominguez Expedition
started from Santa Fe, July 29, 1776,
and, following the route indicated, got
back to Santa Fe, January 3, 1777.

The Old Spanish Trail followed the
Escalante-Dominguez route as far as
the crossing of the Green River, hence
southwestward to Los Angeles,
thus —·—.

—x— Anza Entrada, 1775-1776.

CALIFORNIA, NEW MEXICO
TEXAS AND LOUISIANA
1763-1802

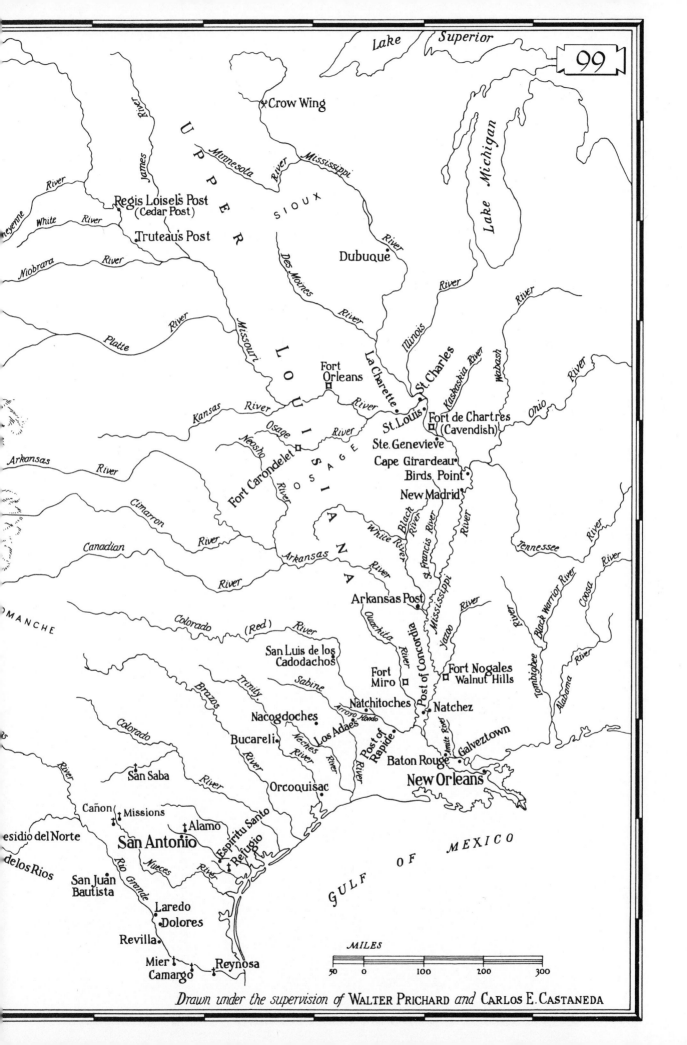

99

Lake Superior

Crow Wing

U P P E R

Lake Michigan

River
James River
Minnesota River
Mississippi River
SIOUX
Cheyenne
White River
River
Niobrara River
Des Moines River
Regis Loisel's Post (Cedar Post)
Truteau's Post

Dubuque

River

River

L O U I S I A N A

Platte
River
Kansas River
Missouri
Osage River
La Charette
River
Illinois
St. Charles

Fort Orleans

Fort Carondelet
Neosho
Osage River
O S A G E

St. Louis
Fort de Chartres (Cavendish)
Kaskaskia River
Wabash
Ohio River

Ste. Genevieve
Cape Girardeau
Birds Point
New Madrid

Arkansas River
Cimarron River
Canadian River
Arkansas River

White River
Black River
St. Francis River
River
Tennessee River
River

COMANCHE

Colorado (Red) River
San Luis de los Cadodachos

Arkansas Post
Ouachita River
Post of Concordia
Mississippi River
Yazoo River
Fort Nogales Walnut Hills
Black Warrior River
Coosa River

Fort Miro
Natchez
Tombigbee River
Alabama River

Trinity River
Sabine River
Natchitoches
Nacogdoches
Arroyo Hondo
Los Adaes
Neches River
Brazos
Colorado
River
Bucareli
San Saba
Post of Rapide
Baton Rouge
Amite River
Galveztown
New Orleans

Orcoquisac

Cañon ┼ Missions
┼ Alamo
San Antonio
Espiritu Santo
Refugio
Nueces River

Presidio del Norte
de los Rios
San Juan Bautista
Rio Grande

Laredo
Dolores

Revilla

Mier
Camargo
Reynosa

G U L F   O F   M E X I C O

MILES
50   0   100   200   300

Drawn under the supervision of WALTER PRICHARD and CARLOS E. CASTANEDA

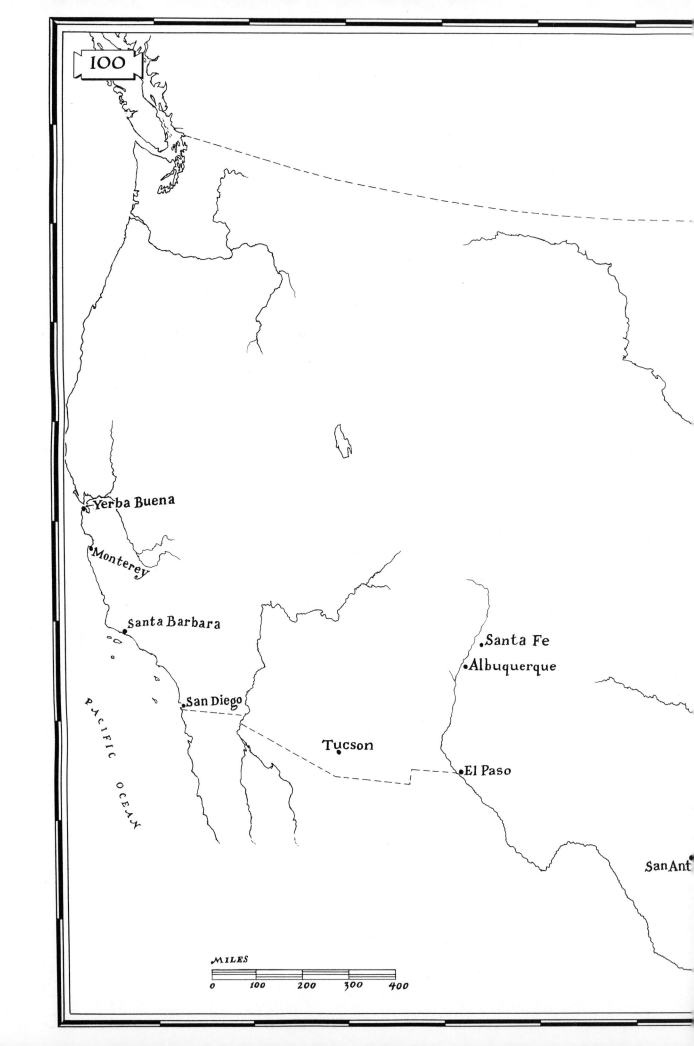

100

Yerba Buena

Monterey

Santa Barbara

Santa Fe
Albuquerque

San Diego

Tucson

El Paso

PACIFIC OCEAN

San Ant

MILES

0   100   200   300   400

SETTLED AREAS 1800

This map does not show areas settled by Indians. The western settlements were very small.

Portland

Salem
Boston
Worcester
New Bedford
Providence

Albany

Ft. Detroit

Brooklyn
New York

Lancaster
Wilmington
Philadelphia
Pittsburgh
Baltimore
Cumberland
Washington
Chillicothe
Cincinnati
Staunton
Louisville
Lexington
Richmond
Williamsburg

Ft. Orleans
St. Louis

Raleigh

Charlotte

Fort Prudhomme

Augusta
Charleston

Arkansas Post

Savannah

chitoches
Natchez

cogdoches

St. Augustine

New Orleans
Pensacola

ATLANTIC OCEAN

Gulf of Mexico

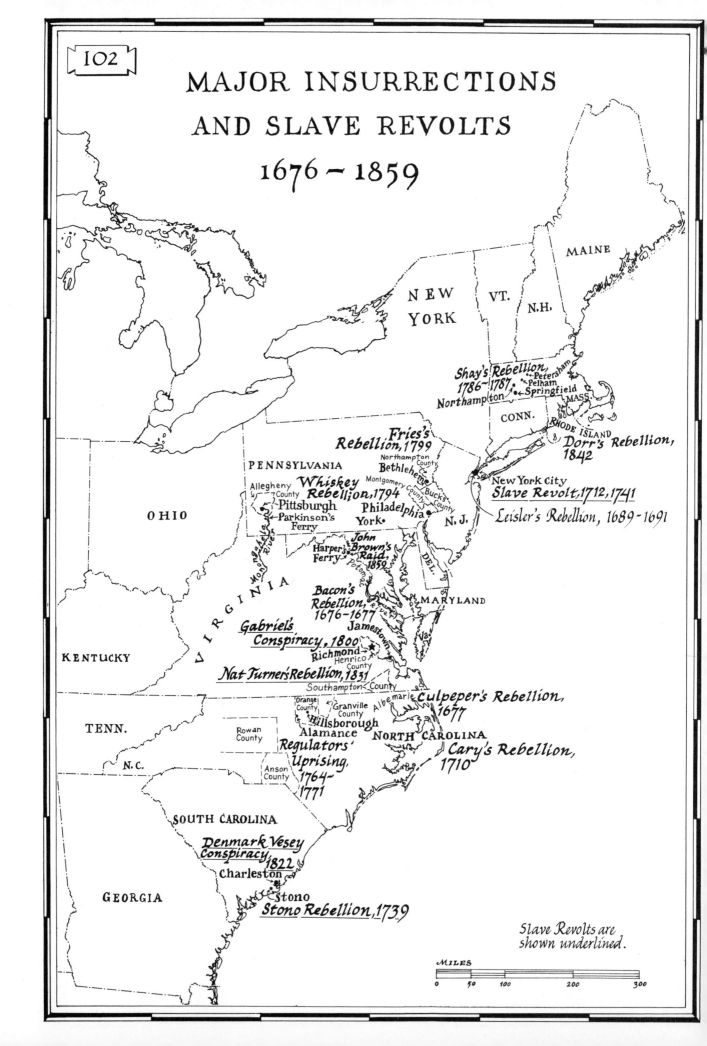

MAJOR INSURRECTIONS AND SLAVE REVOLTS

1676 – 1859

MAINE

NEW YORK

VT.

N.H.

Shay's Rebellion, 1786~1787
Northampton
Petersham
Pelham
Springfield

CONN.

MASS.

RHODE ISLAND

Dorr's Rebellion, 1842

Fries's Rebellion, 1799

PENNSYLVANIA

Northampton County
Bethlehem
Montgomery County
Bucks County

Whiskey Rebellion, 1794

Allegheny County

Pittsburgh
Parkinson's Ferry

Philadelphia
York

New York City
Slave Revolt, 1712, 1741

Leisler's Rebellion, 1689-1691

N. J.

DEL.

OHIO

VIRGINIA

Monongahela River

Harper's Ferry

John Brown's Raid, 1859

Potomac River

Bacon's Rebellion, 1676-1677

Gabriel's Conspiracy, 1800

MARYLAND

Va.

Jamestown

Richmond
Henrico County

Nat Turner's Rebellion, 1831

Southampton County

KENTUCKY

Albemarle

Culpeper's Rebellion, 1677

TENN.

Orange County
Granville County

Hillsborough

Alamance

Rowan County

Regulators' Uprising, 1764~1771

NORTH CAROLINA

Cary's Rebellion, 1710

N.C.

Anson County

SOUTH CAROLINA

Denmark Vesey Conspiracy, 1822

Charleston

GEORGIA

Stono

Stono Rebellion, 1739

Slave Revolts are shown underlined.

MILES

0   50   100   200   300

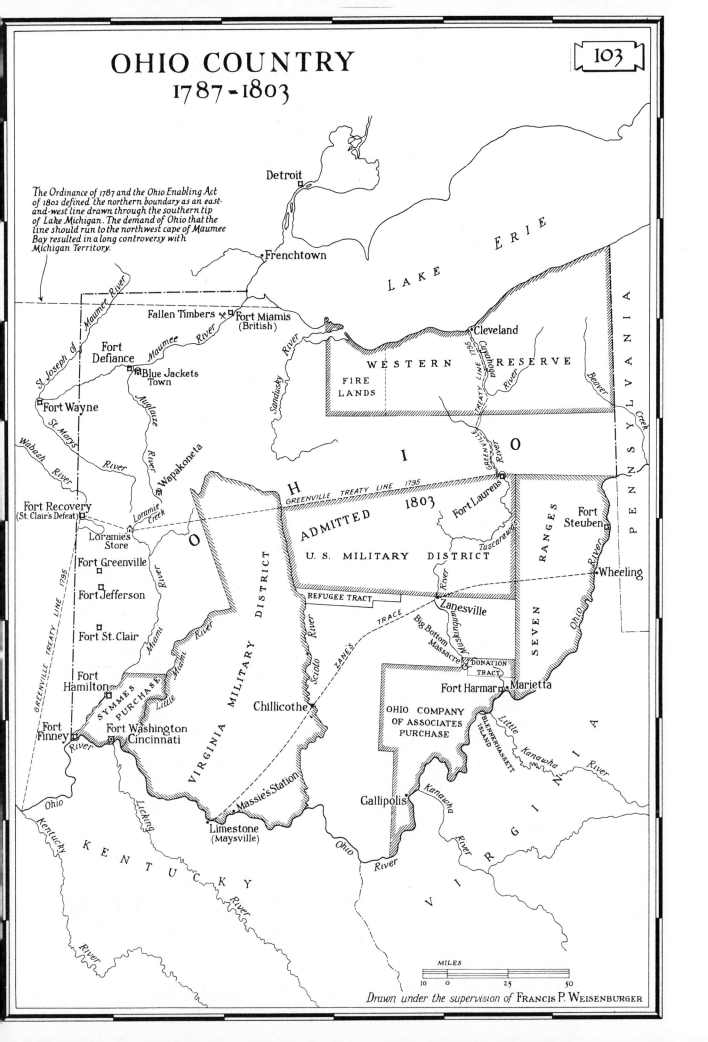

OHIO COUNTRY
1787-1803

103

The Ordinance of 1787 and the Ohio Enabling Act of 1802 defined the northern boundary as an east-and-west line drawn through the southern tip of Lake Michigan. The demand of Ohio that the line should run to the northwest cape of Maumee Bay resulted in a long controversy with Michigan Territory.

Detroit

• Frenchtown

LAKE ERIE

Fallen Timbers ✗ ☐ Fort Miamis (British)

Sandusky River

•Cleveland

WESTERN RESERVE

Cuyahoga River

Greenville Treaty Line 1795

Beaver Creek

PENNSYLVANIA

Fort Defiance ☐
☐ Blue Jackets Town

Maumee River

St. Joseph of

FIRE LANDS

Auglaize River

Fort Wayne ☐

St. Marys River

H   I   O

Wabash River

Wapakoneta •

Loramie Creek

Greenville Treaty Line 1795

1803

Fort Laurens

Tuscarawas River

Fort Steuben

SEVEN RANGES

Fort Recovery ☐
(St. Clair's Defeat)

Loramie's Store •

O

ADMITTED

Muskingum River

U. S. MILITARY   DISTRICT

Ohio River

GREENVILLE TREATY LINE 1795

Fort Greenville ☐

Miami River

VIRGINIA   MILITARY   DISTRICT

•Wheeling

Fort Jefferson ☐

REFUGEE TRACT

Zanesville •

Fort St. Clair ☐

ZANE'S TRACE

Big Bottom Massacre

Scioto River

DONATION TRACT

Fort Hamilton ☐

Little Miami River

SYMMES PURCHASE

Fort Harmar ☐ • Marietta

BLENNERHASSETT ISLAND

Fort Finney ☐

Fort Washington ☐ • Cincinnati

Chillicothe •

OHIO COMPANY OF ASSOCIATES PURCHASE

Little Kanawha River

River

V   I   R   G   I   N   I   A

Ohio River

Licking River

Massie's Station •

Gallipolis •

Kanawha River

• Limestone (Maysville)

K   E   N   T   U   C   K   Y

Ohio River

Kentucky River

River

River

MILES

10   0   25   50

Drawn under the supervision of FRANCIS P. WEISENBURGER

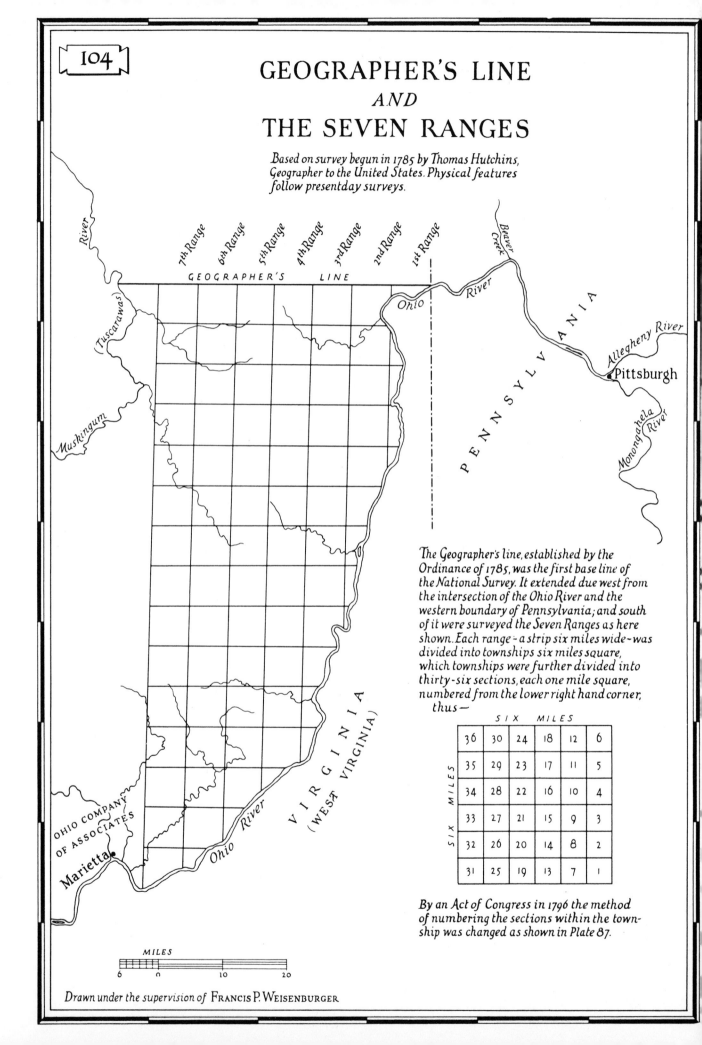

GEOGRAPHER'S LINE
AND
THE SEVEN RANGES

Based on survey begun in 1785 by Thomas Hutchins,
Geographer to the United States. Physical features
follow presentday surveys.

7th Range · 6th Range · 5th Range · 4th Range · 3rd Range · 2nd Range · 1st Range

GEOGRAPHER'S LINE

Beaver Creek

River (Tuscarawas)

Ohio River

Muskingum

PENNSYLVANIA

Allegheny River

Pittsburgh

Monongahela River

The Geographer's line, established by the
Ordinance of 1785, was the first base line of
the National Survey. It extended due west from
the intersection of the Ohio River and the
western boundary of Pennsylvania; and south
of it were surveyed the Seven Ranges as here
shown. Each range ~ a strip six miles wide ~ was
divided into townships six miles square,
which townships were further divided into
thirty-six sections, each one mile square,
numbered from the lower right hand corner,
thus ~

SIX MILES

	SIX MILES				
36	30	24	18	12	6
35	29	23	17	11	5
34	28	22	16	10	4
33	27	21	15	9	3
32	26	20	14	8	2
31	25	19	13	7	1

SIX MILES

By an Act of Congress in 1796 the method
of numbering the sections within the township was changed as shown in Plate 87.

VIRGINIA (WEST VIRGINIA)

OHIO COMPANY OF ASSOCIATES

Marietta

Ohio River

MILES

6   0   10   20

Drawn under the supervision of FRANCIS P. WEISENBURGER

THE SURVEY *OF THE* PUBLIC DOMAIN

THE SURVEY *OF THE* PUBLIC DOMAIN

is based upon the Ordinance of 1785. Beginning with the Seven Ranges (see Plate 86), this survey was continued across the country, although there still remains, in the mountainous sections of the Far West, over one hundred million acres of unsurveyed land. However, with a few local exceptions, the survey applies in every state in the Union, except in the Thirteen Colonies and in Maine, Vermont, Kentucky, Tennessee, West Virginia, and Texas. From arbitrarily selected east-and-west Base Lines and north-and-south Meridians, the land is surveyed into Ranges of Townships, lying north and south of the Base Lines, and east and west of the Meridians. The Ranges are numbered east and west from the Meridians. The Townships, each six miles square, are numbered north and south from the Base Lines. The diagrams below illustrate the actual survey east of the Sixth Principal Meridian and south of a Base Line located on 40° north latitude.

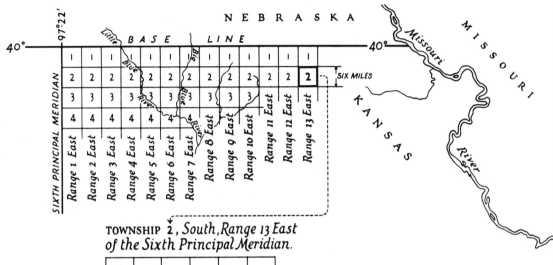

TOWNSHIP 2, South, Range 13 East of the Sixth Principal Meridian.

In 1796 Congress directed that the method of numbering the sections should be as here shown, thus discarding the method followed in the Seven Ranges, (see Plate 86). This method of numbering has prevailed in all surveys subsequent to that date.

SECTION 25, Township 2, South, Range 13 East of the Sixth Principal Meridian.

A Section contains 640 acres

NORTHEAST ONE-FOURTH of Section 25, Township 2, South, Range 13 East of the Sixth Principal Meridian,

A Quarter Section contains 160 acres

which, by this description, can be instantly located as lying in an exact place in northeastern Kansas.

Drawn under the supervision of
PAUL WALLACE GATES

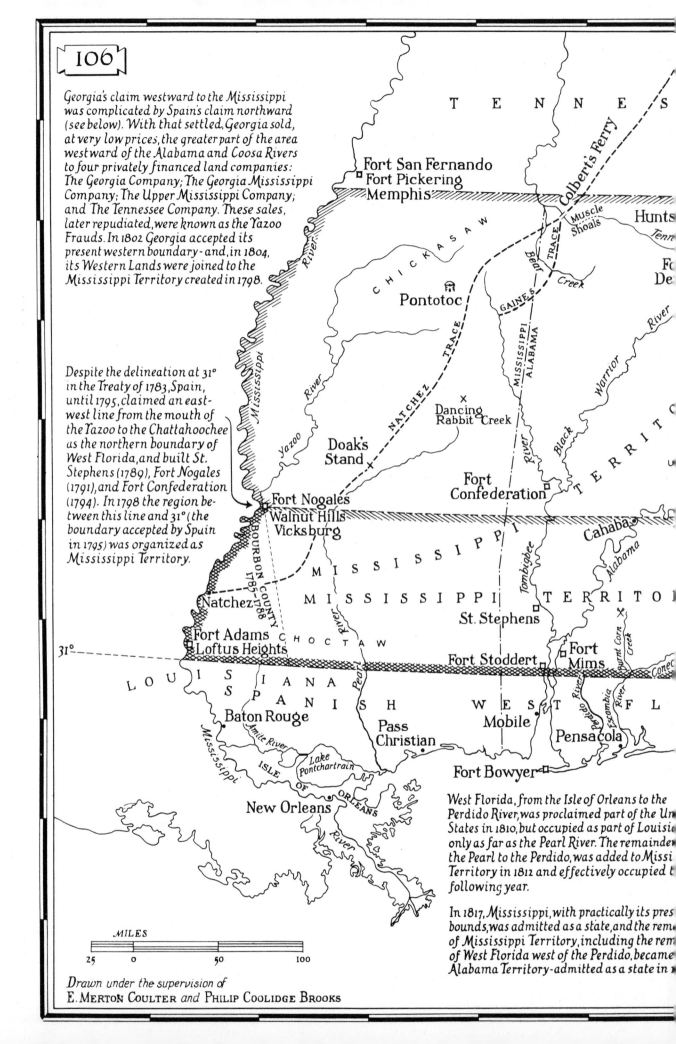

106

Georgia's claim westward to the Mississippi
was complicated by Spain's claim northward
(see below). With that settled, Georgia sold,
at very low prices, the greater part of the area
westward of the Alabama and Coosa Rivers
to four privately financed land companies:
The Georgia Company; The Georgia Mississippi
Company; The Upper Mississippi Company;
and The Tennessee Company. These sales,
later repudiated, were known as the Yazoo
Frauds. In 1802 Georgia accepted its
present western boundary—and, in 1804,
its Western Lands were joined to the
Mississippi Territory created in 1798.

Despite the delineation at 31°
in the Treaty of 1783, Spain,
until 1795, claimed an east-
west line from the mouth of
the Yazoo to the Chattahoochee
as the northern boundary of
West Florida, and built St.
Stephens (1789), Fort Nogales
(1791), and Fort Confederation
(1794). In 1798 the region between this line and 31° (the
boundary accepted by Spain
in 1795) was organized as
Mississippi Territory.

T E N N E S S

Fort San Fernando
Fort Pickering
Memphis

Colbert's Ferry

Hunts

Tenn

Muscle
Shoals

C H I C K A S A W

River

Fo
De

Pontotoc

N A T C H E Z   T R A C E

G A I N E S   T R A C E

Bear   Creek

MISSISSIPPI
ALABAMA

Warrior

River

Dancing
Rabbit Creek ×

Doak's
Stand

Fort
Confederation

River

Black

T E R R I T O

Fort Nogales
Walnut Hills
Vicksburg

M I S S I S S I P P I

Cahaba

Alabama

River

BOURBON COUNTY
1785-1788

Natchez

M I S S I S S I P P I   T E R R I T O R

Tombigbee

River

St. Stephens

Burnt Corn Creek ×

Fort Adams
Loftus Heights

C H O C T A W

Pearl River

31°

Fort Stoddert

Fort
Mims

Conec

L O U I S I A N A

S P A N I S H

W E S T

F L

Perdido River

Escambia River

Baton Rouge

Amite River

Pass
Christian

Mobile

Pensacola

ISLE OF

Lake
Pontchartrain

Mississippi

Fort Bowyer

New Orleans

OF   ORLEANS

River

MILES

25   0   50   100

Drawn under the supervision of
E. Merton Coulter and Philip Coolidge Brooks

West Florida, from the Isle of Orleans to the
Perdido River, was proclaimed part of the Un
States in 1810, but occupied as part of Louisie
only as far as the Pearl River. The remainder
the Pearl to the Perdido, was added to Missi
Territory in 1812 and effectively occupied t
following year.

In 1817, Mississippi, with practically its pres
bounds, was admitted as a state, and the rem
of Mississippi Territory, including the rem
of West Florida west of the Perdido, became
Alabama Territory—admitted as a state in

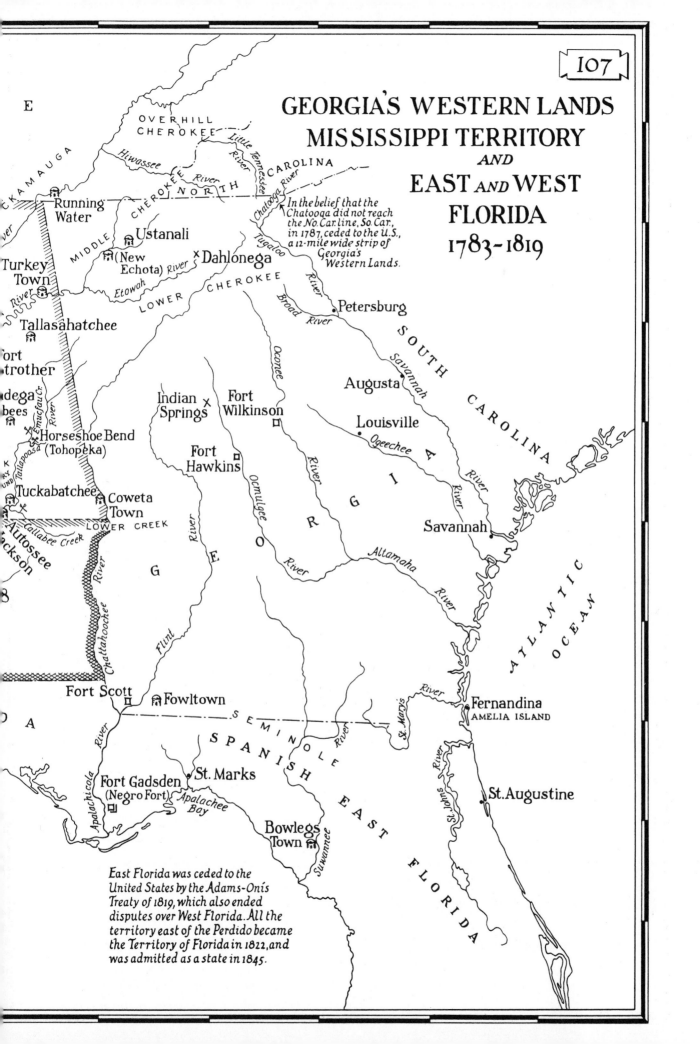

GEORGIA'S WESTERN LANDS
MISSISSIPPI TERRITORY
AND
EAST AND WEST
FLORIDA
1783-1819

E

OVERHILL
CHEROKEE

Little Tennessee River

NORTH CAROLINA

In the belief that the Chatooga did not reach the No. Car. line, So. Car., in 1787, ceded to the U.S., a 12-mile wide strip of Georgia's Western Lands.

CKAMAUGA

Hiwassee River

CHEROKEE

Chatooga River

Running Water

MIDDLE

Ustanali

(New Echota)

Etowah River

× Dahlonega

LOWER CHEROKEE

Tugaloo River

Broad River

• Petersburg

Turkey Town

River

Tallasahatchee

Fort trother

Emuckfau Cr.

Talapoosa River

dega bees

× Horseshoe Bend (Tohopeka)

Tuckabatchee

Coweta Town

LOWER CREEK

Callabee Creek

Autossee

Jackson

Indian Springs ×

Fort Wilkinson

Fort Hawkins

SOUTH

Savannah

Augusta

Louisville

Ogeechee

River

CAROLINA

G

E

O

R

G

I

A

River

Ocmulgee River

Oconee River

Flint

Chattahoochee River

Savannah

Altamaha River

ATLANTIC OCEAN

Fort Scott

Fowltown

SEMINOLE

St. Mary's River

Fernandina
AMELIA ISLAND

DA

Apalachicola River

Fort Gadsden (Negro Fort)

St. Marks

Apalachee Bay

SPANISH

EAST

FLORIDA

St. Johns River

St. Augustine

Bowlegs Town

Suwannee River

East Florida was ceded to the United States by the Adams-Onis Treaty of 1819, which also ended disputes over West Florida. All the territory east of the Perdido became the Territory of Florida in 1822, and was admitted as a state in 1845.

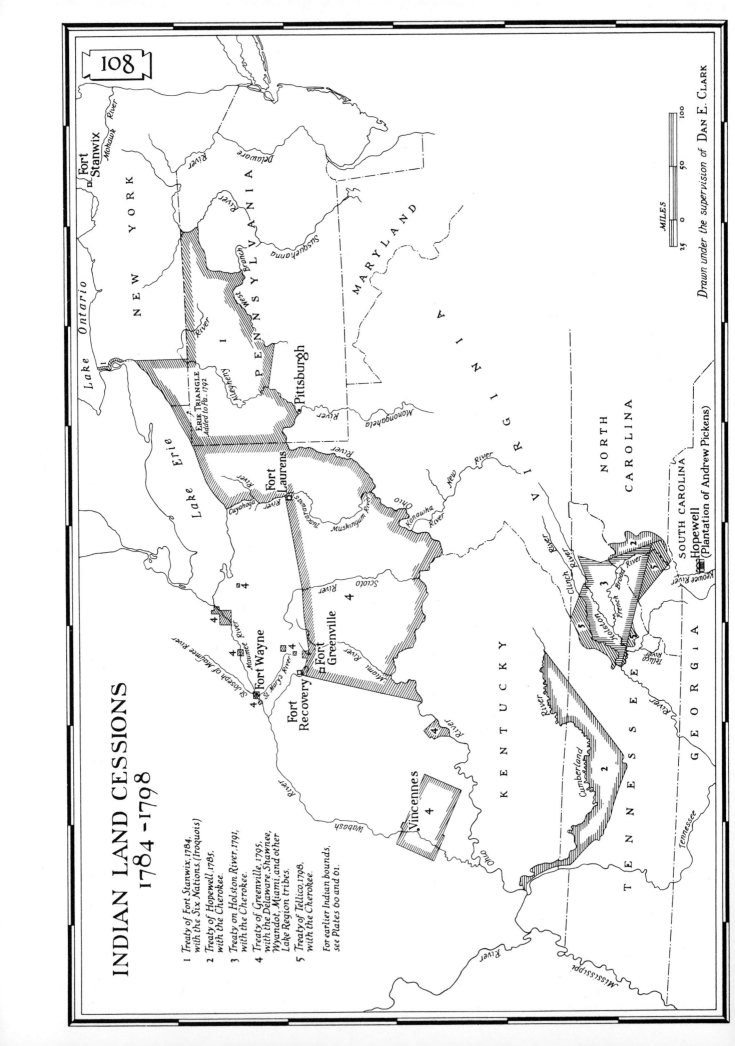

108

INDIAN LAND CESSIONS
1784–1798

1 *Treaty of Fort Stanwix, 1784, with the Six Nations. (Iroquois)*

2 *Treaty of Hopewell, 1785, with the Cherokee.*

3 *Treaty on Holston River, 1791, with the Cherokee.*

4 *Treaty of Greenville, 1795, with the Delaware, Shawnee, Wyandot, Miami, and other Lake Region tribes.*

5 *Treaty of Tellico, 1798, with the Cherokee.*

For earlier Indian bounds, see Plates 60 and 61.

Drawn under the supervision of DAN E. CLARK

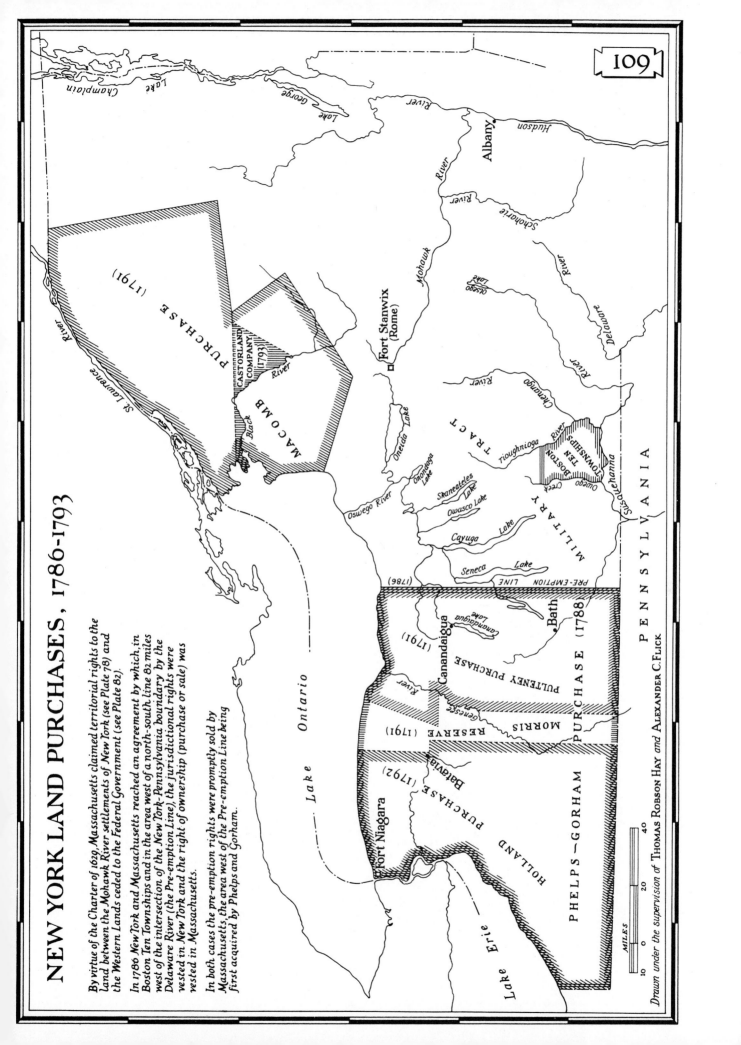

NEW YORK LAND PURCHASES, 1786-1793

By virtue of the Charter of 1629, Massachusetts claimed territorial rights to the land between the Mohawk River settlements of New York (see Plate 78) and the Western Lands ceded to the Federal Government (see Plate 82).

In 1786 New York and Massachusetts reached an agreement by which, in Boston Ten Townships and in the area west of a north-south line 82 miles west of the intersection of the New York-Pennsylvania boundary by the Delaware River (the Pre-emption Line), the jurisdictional rights were vested in New York and the right of ownership (purchase or sale) was vested in Massachusetts.

In both cases the pre-emption rights were promptly sold by Massachusetts, the area west of the Pre-emption Line being first acquired by Phelps and Gorham.

109

Drawn under the supervision of THOMAS ROBSON HAY and ALEXANDER C. FLICK

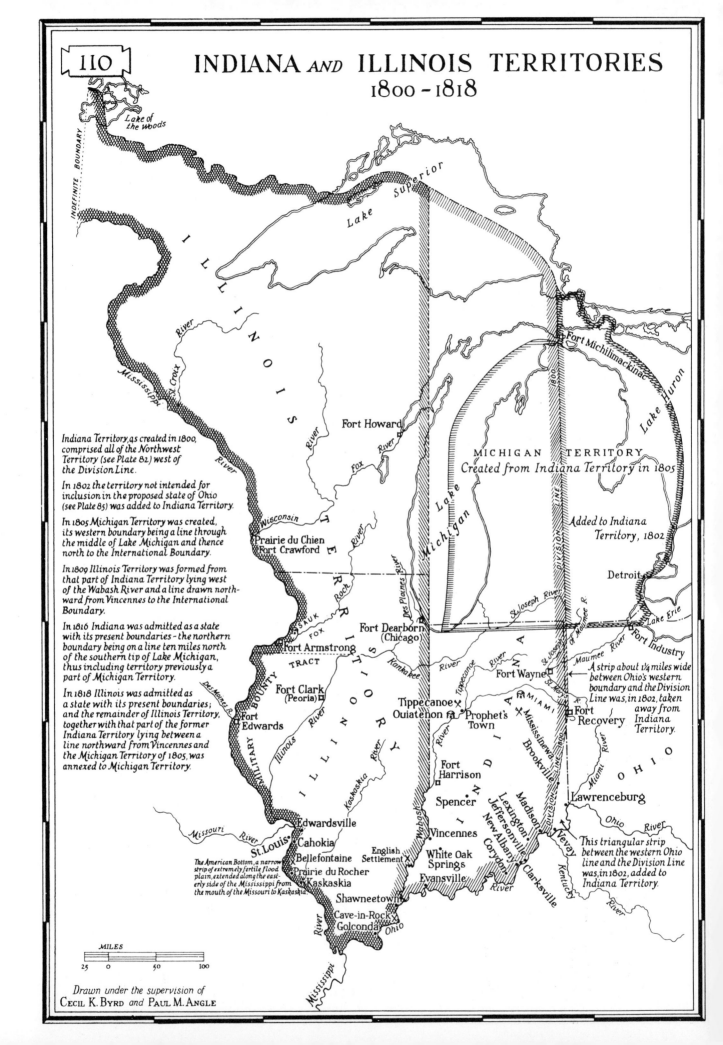

INDIANA AND ILLINOIS TERRITORIES
1800-1818

110

Lake of the Woods

INDEFINITE BOUNDARY

ILLINOIS

Lake Superior

Lake Huron

Fort Michilimackinac

MICHIGAN TERRITORY
Created from Indiana Territory in 1805

Added to Indiana Territory, 1802

Lake Michigan

Mississippi River

St. Croix River

River

Fox River

Wisconsin River

Prairie du Chien
Fort Crawford

Rock River

SAUK

FOX

TRACT

BOUNTY

MILITARY

TERRITORY

Fort Howard

Fox River

Des Plaines River

Fort Dearborn
(Chicago)

Kankakee River

Fort Armstrong

Fort Clark
(Peoria)

Fort Edwards

Illinois River

Kaskaskia River

ILLINOIS

Des Moines R.

Indiana Territory, as created in 1800, comprised all of the Northwest Territory (see Plate 82) west of the Division Line.

In 1802 the territory not intended for inclusion in the proposed state of Ohio (see Plate 85) was added to Indiana Territory.

In 1805 Michigan Territory was created, its western boundary being a line through the middle of Lake Michigan and thence north to the International Boundary.

In 1809 Illinois Territory was formed from that part of Indiana Territory lying west of the Wabash River and a line drawn northward from Vincennes to the International Boundary.

In 1816 Indiana was admitted as a state with its present boundaries - the northern boundary being on a line ten miles north of the southern tip of Lake Michigan, thus including territory previously a part of Michigan Territory.

In 1818 Illinois was admitted as a state with its present boundaries; and the remainder of Illinois Territory, together with that part of the former Indiana Territory lying between a line northward from Vincennes and the Michigan Territory of 1805, was annexed to Michigan Territory.

DIVISION LINE

1800

St. Joseph River

Detroit

Lake Erie

Fort Industry

Maumee River

St. Joseph of Maumee R.

Fort Wayne

Tippecanoe River

St. Mary's R.

Fort Recovery

A strip about 1¼ miles wide between Ohio's western boundary and the Division Line was, in 1802, taken away from Indiana Territory.

MIAMI

Mississinewa River

Brookville

Tippecanoe
Ouiatenon
Prophet's Town

INDIANA

DIVISION LINE 1809

Miami River

OHIO

Fort Harrison

Spencer

Madison
Lexington
Jeffersonville
New Albany
Corydon
Clarksville

Lawrenceburg

Ohio River

This triangular strip between the western Ohio line and the Division Line was, in 1802, added to Indiana Territory.

Edwardsville
Cahokia
St. Louis
Bellefontaine
Prairie du Rocher
Kaskaskia

Missouri River

The American Bottom, a narrow strip of extremely fertile flood plain, extended along the easterly side of the Mississippi from the mouth of the Missouri to Kaskaskia.

English Settlement

Vincennes

White Oak Springs

Evansville

Nevay

Kentucky River

Wabash River

Shawneetown

Cave-in-Rock
Golconda

Ohio

Mississippi

MILES
25 0 50 100

Drawn under the supervision of
CECIL K. BYRD and PAUL M. ANGLE

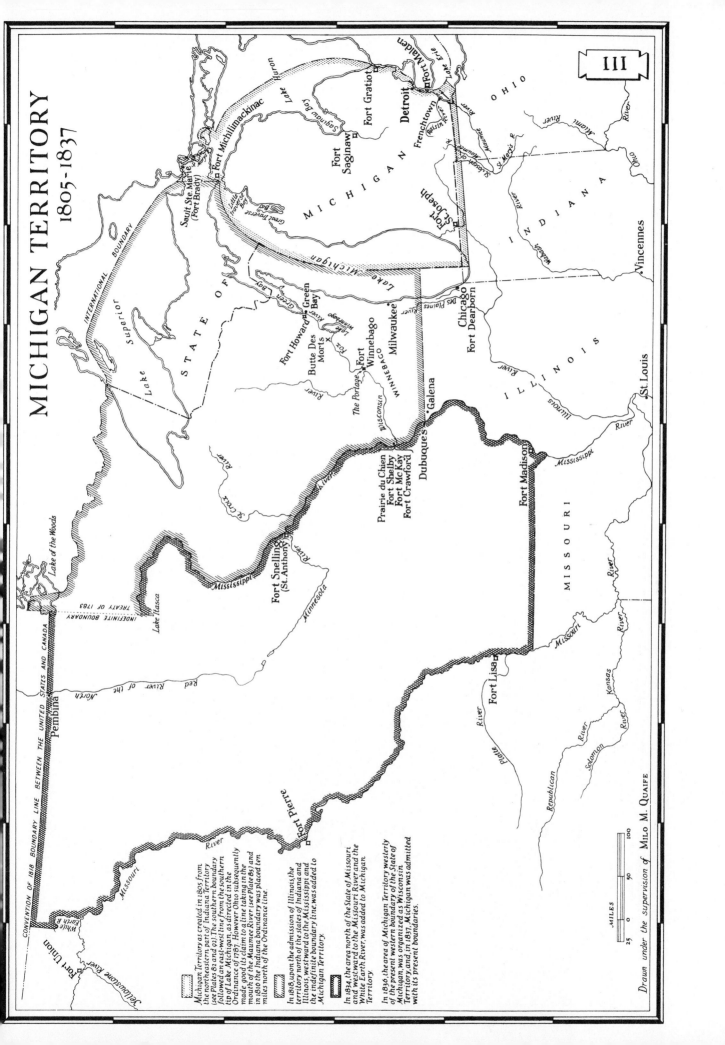

MICHIGAN TERRITORY 1805-1837

III

Michigan Territory as created in 1805 from the northeastern part of Indiana Territory (see Plates 81 and 92). The southern boundary followed an east-west line from the southern tip of Lake Michigan, as directed in the Ordinance of 1787. However Ohio subsequently made good its claim to a line taking in the mouth of the Maumee River (see Plate 85) and in 1810 the Indiana boundary was placed ten miles north of the Ordinance line.

In 1818, upon the admission of Illinois, the territory north of the states of Indiana and Illinois, westward to the Mississippi and the indefinite boundary line, was added to Michigan Territory.

In 1834, the area north of the State of Missouri and westward to the Missouri River and the White Earth River, was organized as Wisconsin Territory.

In 1836, the area of Michigan Territory westerly of the present western boundary of the State of Michigan, was organized as Wisconsin Territory, and, in 1837, Michigan was admitted with its present boundaries.

Drawn under the supervision of MILO M. QUAIFE

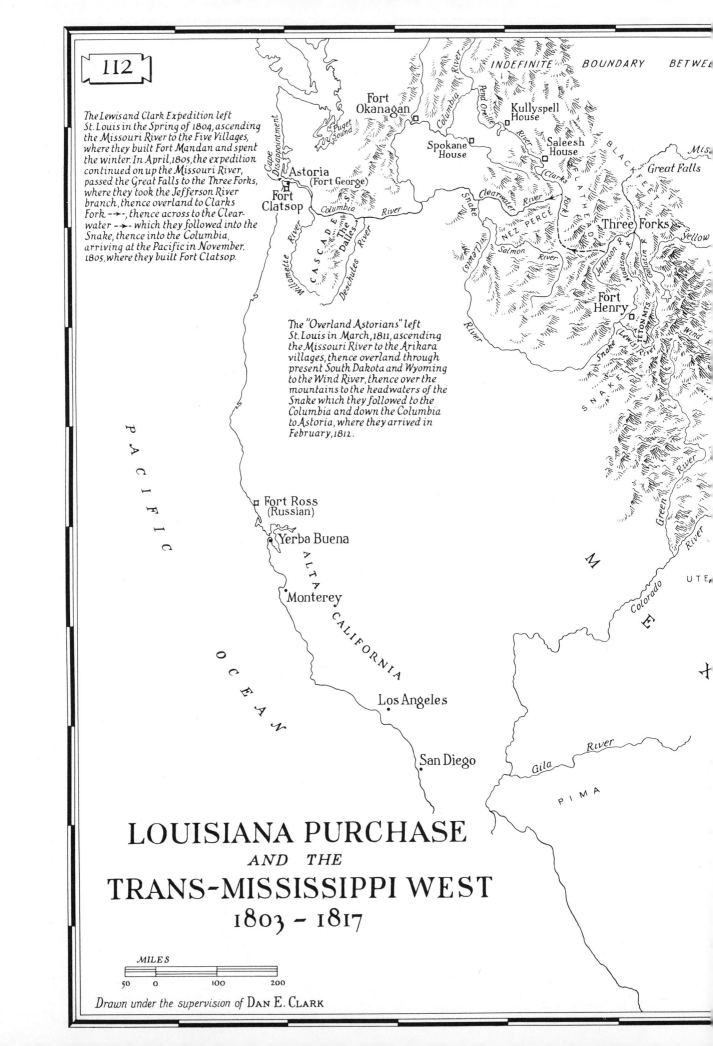

112

The Lewis and Clark Expedition left
St. Louis in the Spring of 1804, ascending
the Missouri River to the Five Villages,
where they built Fort Mandan and spent
the winter. In April, 1805, the expedition
continued on up the Missouri River,
passed the Great Falls to the Three Forks,
where they took the Jefferson River
branch, thence overland to Clarks
Fork -→-, thence across to the Clearwater -→- which they followed into the
Snake, thence into the Columbia,
arriving at the Pacific in November,
1805, where they built Fort Clatsop.

The "Overland Astorians" left
St. Louis in March, 1811, ascending
the Missouri River to the Arikara
villages, thence overland through
present South Dakota and Wyoming
to the Wind River, thence over the
mountains to the headwaters of the
Snake which they followed to the
Columbia and down the Columbia
to Astoria, where they arrived in
February, 1812.

INDEFINITE   BOUNDARY   BETWE

Fort
Okanagan

Kullyspell
House

Pend Oreille

Columbia River

Spokane
House

Saleesh
House

Mis.

Great Falls

Astoria
(Fort George)

Cape
Disappointment

Clarks

Clearwater River

BLACKFEET

Fort
Clatsop

Columbia

River

Snake

Clearwater

Fork

Three Forks

Yellow

Willamette River

CASCADES

The
Dalles

Deschutes River

NEZ PERCE

(Salmon)

Salmon

River

Madison R.

Jefferson

Gallatin R.

PACIFIC

Fort
Henry

TETONAMIS

(Lewis) River

Wind

River

SNAKE

Snake

Green

River

OCEAN

Fort Ross
(Russian)

Yerba Buena

ALTA

M

River

UTE

Monterey

CALIFORNIA

E

Colorado

Los Angeles

H

San Diego

Gila

River

PIMA

LOUISIANA PURCHASE
AND THE
TRANS-MISSISSIPPI WEST
1803 – 1817

MILES

50   0   100   200

Drawn under the supervision of DAN E. CLARK

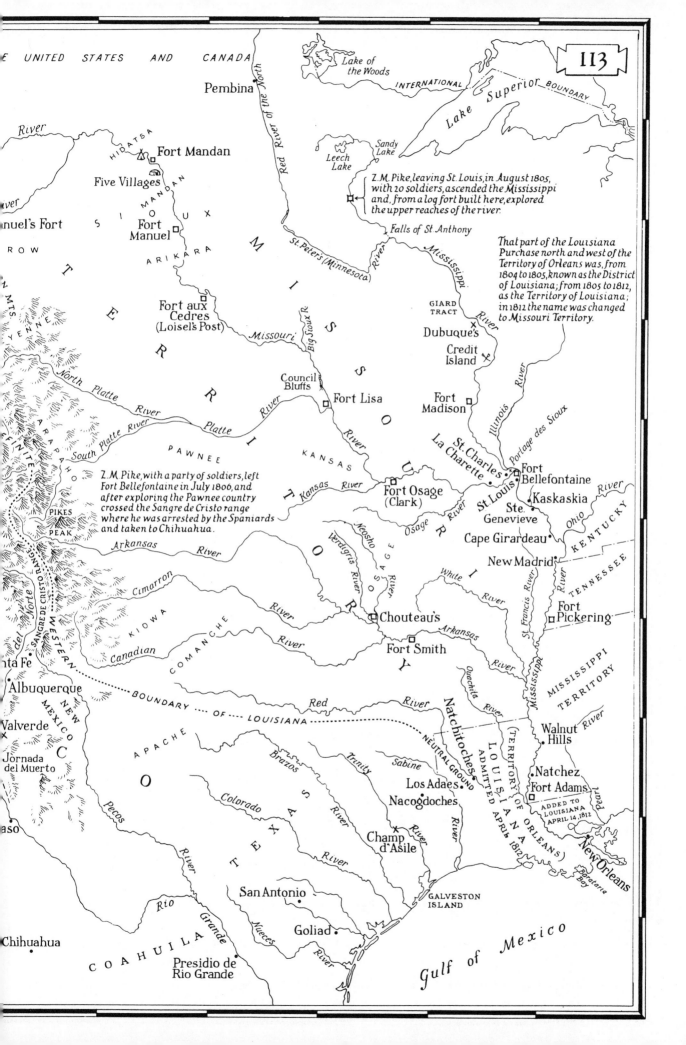

E UNITED STATES AND CANADA

Lake of the Woods

INTERNATIONAL BOUNDARY

Lake Superior

Pembina

Red River of the North

Sandy Lake

Leech Lake

HIDATSA

Fort Mandan

Five Villages

MANDAN

Z. M. Pike, leaving St. Louis, in August 1805, with 20 soldiers, ascended the Mississippi and, from a log fort built here, explored the upper reaches of the river.

River

nuel's Fort

Fort Manuel

S I O U X

Falls of St. Anthony

St. Peters (Minnesota) River

Mississippi

ROW

ARIKARA

T E R R

Missouri

North Platte River

South Platte River

That part of the Louisiana Purchase north and west of the Territory of Orleans was, from 1804 to 1805, known as the District of Louisiana; from 1805 to 1812, as the Territory of Louisiana; in 1812 the name was changed to Missouri Territory.

CYENNE

MTS.

Fort aux Cedres (Loisel's Post)

Big Sioux R.

GIARD TRACT

Dubuque's

Credit Island

ARAPAHO

Platte River

Council Bluffs

Fort Lisa

Fort Madison

Illinois River

St. Charles

La Charette

Portage des Sioux

Fort Bellefontaine

INFINITE

PIKES PEAK

PAWNEE

Platte River

Kansas River

KANSAS

I T O R

Fort Osage (Clark)

St. Louis

Kaskaskia

Ste. Genevieve

Z. M. Pike, with a party of soldiers, left Fort Bellefontaine in July 1806, and after exploring the Pawnee country crossed the Sangre de Cristo range where he was arrested by the Spaniards and taken to Chihuahua.

Kansas River

Osage River

Cape Girardeau

KENTUCKY

Arkansas River

Neosho River

Verdigris River

New Madrid

White River

St. Francis River

Ohio River

TENNESSEE

Cimarron River

KIOWA

Chouteau's

Arkansas

Fort Pickering

SANGRE DE CRISTO RANGE

WESTERN

del Norte

Canadian River

COMANCHE

Fort Smith

Ouachita River

Mississippi River

MISSISSIPPI TERRITORY

nta Fe

Albuquerque

NEW

BOUNDARY —— OF —— LOUISIANA

Red River

Natchitoches

Walnut Hills

Valverde

MEXICO

APACHE

Brazos River

Trinity River

NEUTRAL GROUND

(TERRITORY OF ORLEANS) ADMITTED APRIL 30, 1812

Natchez

Jornada del Muerto

C

Sabine River

Los Adaes

Fort Adams

Colorado River

Nacogdoches

Pecos River

O

T E X A S

River

ADDED TO LOUISIANA APRIL 14, 1812

Pearl River

aso

Rio Grande

Champ d'Asile

New Orleans

Barataria Bay

San Antonio

Nueces River

GALVESTON ISLAND

Chihuahua

COAHUILA

Goliad

Gulf of Mexico

Presidio de Rio Grande

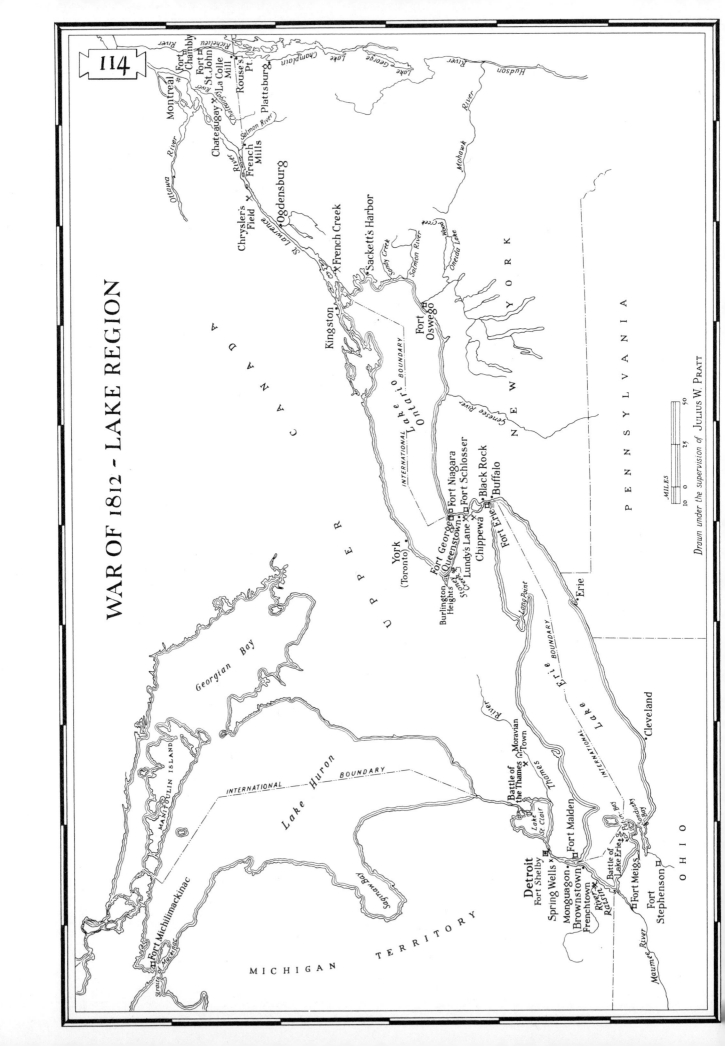

WAR OF 1812 - LAKE REGION

114

Drawn under the supervision of JULIUS W. PRATT

MILES

OHIO
PENNSYLVANIA
NEW YORK
MICHIGAN TERRITORY

CANADA
UPPER CANADA

Montreal
Fort Chambly
Fort St. John
La Colle Mill
Rouse's Pt.
Plattsburg
Chateaugay
French Mills
Chrysler's Field
Ogdensburg
French Creek
Sackett's Harbor
Fort Oswego
Kingston

Ottawa River
Richelieu River
Chateaugay River
Salmon River
St. Lawrence River
Lake Champlain
Lake George
Hudson River
Mohawk River
Sandy Creek
Salmon River
Oneida Lake
Wood Creek

York (Toronto)
Fort George
Queenstown
Lundy's Lane
Chippewa
Fort Schlosser
Black Rock
Buffalo
Fort Erie
Fort Niagara
Burlington Heights
Stoney Creek

Lake Ontario
INTERNATIONAL BOUNDARY
Genesee River

Erie
Long Point
Lake Erie
INTERNATIONAL BOUNDARY
Erie BOUNDARY
Cleveland

Georgian Bay
MANITOULIN ISLAND
Lake Huron
INTERNATIONAL BOUNDARY
Saginaw Bay
Fort Michillimackinac
Straits of Mackinac

Battle of the Thames
Moravian Town
Thames River
Lake St. Clair
Fort Malden
Detroit
Fort Shelby
Spring Wells
Monguagon
Brownstown
Frenchtown
River Raisin
Battle of Lake Erie
Fort Meigs
Fort Stephenson
Maumee River
Put-in Bay
Sandusky Bay

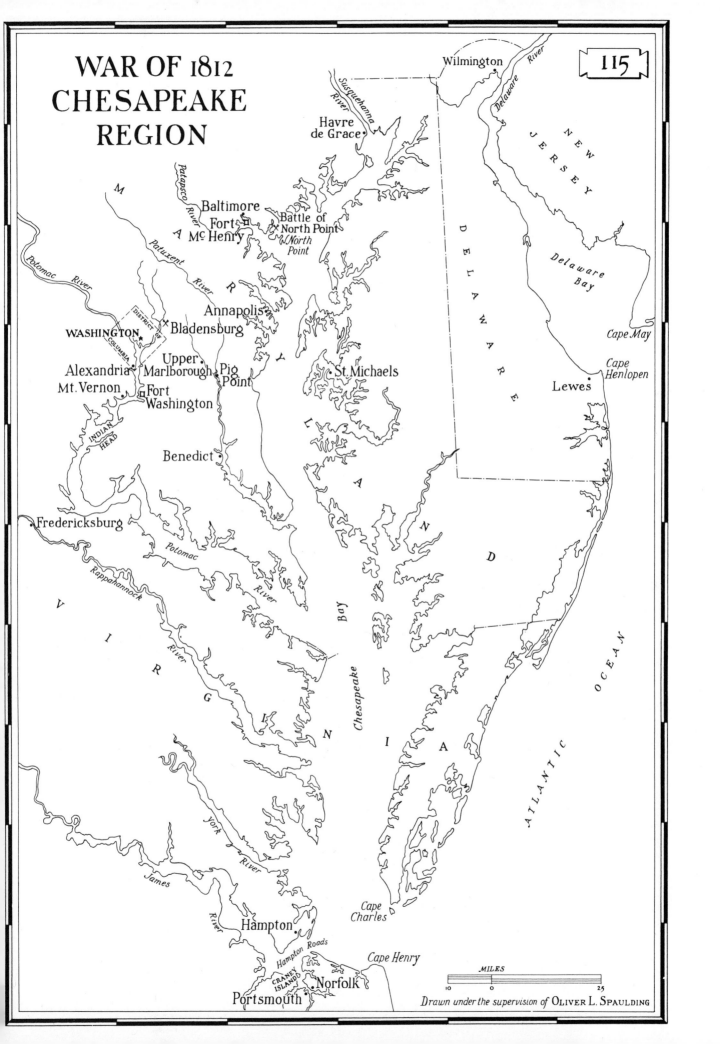

WAR OF 1812 CHESAPEAKE REGION

Wilmington

115

Susquehanna River

Havre de Grace

NEW JERSEY

Delaware River

Patapsco River

Baltimore
Fort McHenry
Battle of North Point
× North Point

DELAWARE

Delaware Bay

Patuxent River

Potomac River

M A R Y L A N D

Annapolis
× Bladensburg

Cape May

Cape Henlopen

WASHINGTON
DISTRICT OF COLUMBIA

Upper Marlborough
Pig Point

St. Michaels

Lewes

Alexandria
Mt. Vernon
Fort Washington

INDIAN HEAD

Benedict

Fredericksburg

Potomac River

Rappahannock River

V I R G I N I A

River

York River

James River

Chesapeake Bay

ATLANTIC OCEAN

Cape Charles

Hampton

Cape Henry

Hampton Roads
CRANEY ISLAND
Norfolk

Portsmouth

MILES
10   0   25

Drawn under the supervision of OLIVER L. SPAULDING

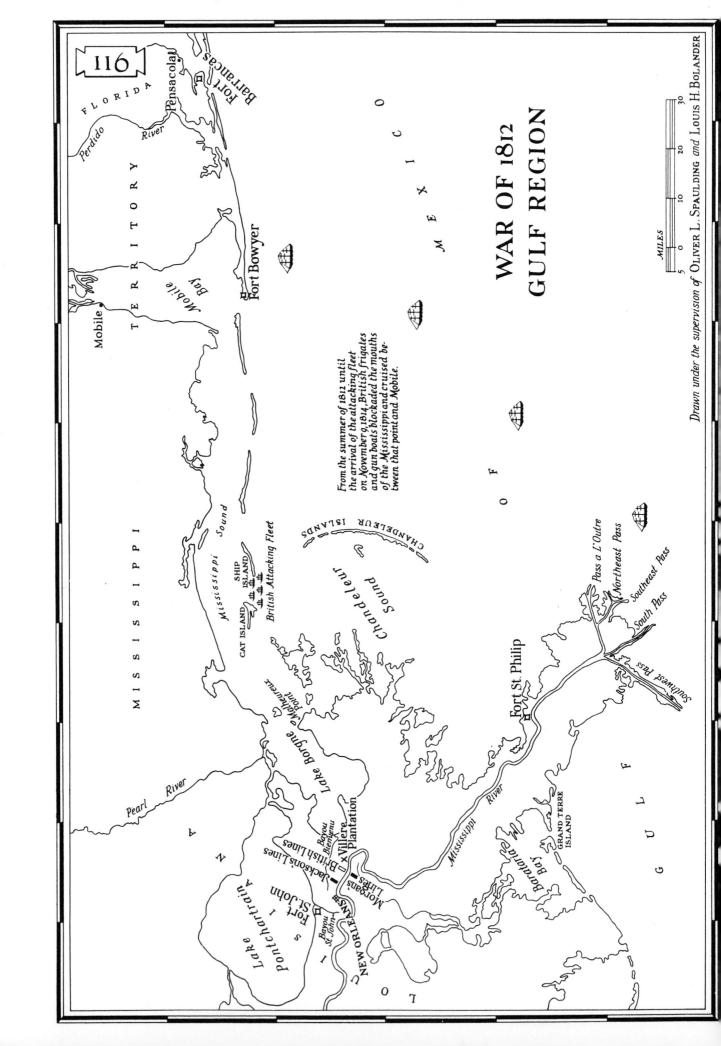

116

FLORIDA

Pensacola

Fort Barrancas

Perdido River

Fort Bowyer

Mobile Bay

Mobile

TERRITORY

MISSISSIPPI

Mississippi Sound

SHIP ISLAND

CAT ISLAND

British Attacking Fleet

CHANDELEUR ISLANDS

Chandeleur Sound

Pearl River

LOUISIANA

Lake Borgne

Pearl River

Bayou Bienvenu

Villeré Plantation

British Lines

Jackson's Lines

Morgan's Lines

Bayou St. John

Fort St. John

Lake Pontchartrain

NEW ORLEANS

Mississippi River

Fort St. Philip

Baratoria Bay

GRAND TERRE ISLAND

Pass a L'Outre

Northeast Pass

Southeast Pass

South Pass

Southwest Pass

GULF OF MEXICO

From the summer of 1812 until
the arrival of the attacking fleet
on November 9, 1814, British frigates
and gun boats blockaded the mouths
of the Mississippi and cruised between that point and Mobile.

WAR OF 1812
GULF REGION

MILES

5   0   10   20   30

Drawn under the supervision of OLIVER L. SPAULDING and LOUIS H. BOLANDER

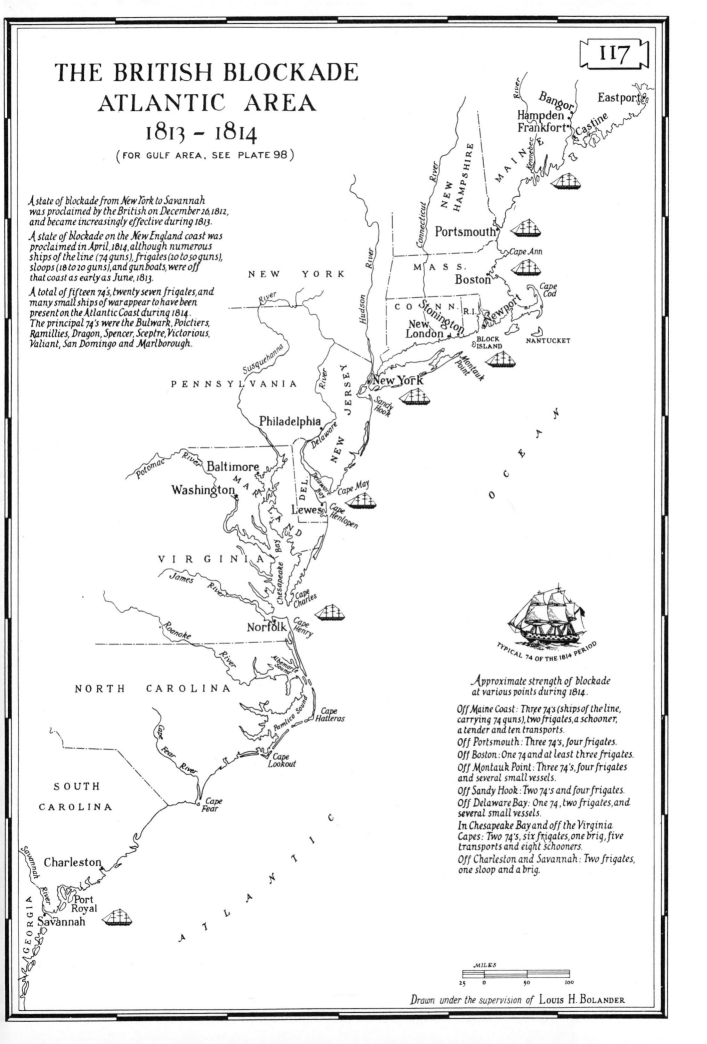

THE BRITISH BLOCKADE ATLANTIC AREA
1813 – 1814
(FOR GULF AREA, SEE PLATE 98)

117

A state of blockade from New York to Savannah was proclaimed by the British on December 26, 1812, and became increasingly effective during 1813.

A state of blockade on the New England coast was proclaimed in April, 1814, although numerous ships of the line (74 guns), frigates (20 to 50 guns), sloops (18 to 20 guns), and gun boats, were off that coast as early as June, 1813.

A total of fifteen 74's, twenty seven frigates, and many small ships of war appear to have been present on the Atlantic Coast during 1814. The principal 74's were the Bulwark, Poictiers, Ramillies, Dragon, Spencer, Sceptre, Victorious, Valiant, San Domingo and Marlborough.

TYPICAL 74 OF THE 1814 PERIOD

Approximate strength of blockade at various points during 1814.

Off Maine Coast: Three 74's (ships of the line, carrying 74 guns), two frigates, a schooner, a tender and ten transports.

Off Portsmouth: Three 74's, four frigates.

Off Boston: One 74 and at least three frigates.

Off Montauk Point: Three 74's, four frigates and several small vessels.

Off Sandy Hook: Two 74's and four frigates.

Off Delaware Bay: One 74, two frigates, and several small vessels.

In Chesapeake Bay and off the Virginia Capes: Two 74's, six frigates, one brig, five transports and eight schooners.

Off Charleston and Savannah: Two frigates, one sloop and a brig.

MILES
25 0   50   100

Drawn under the supervision of LOUIS H. BOLANDER

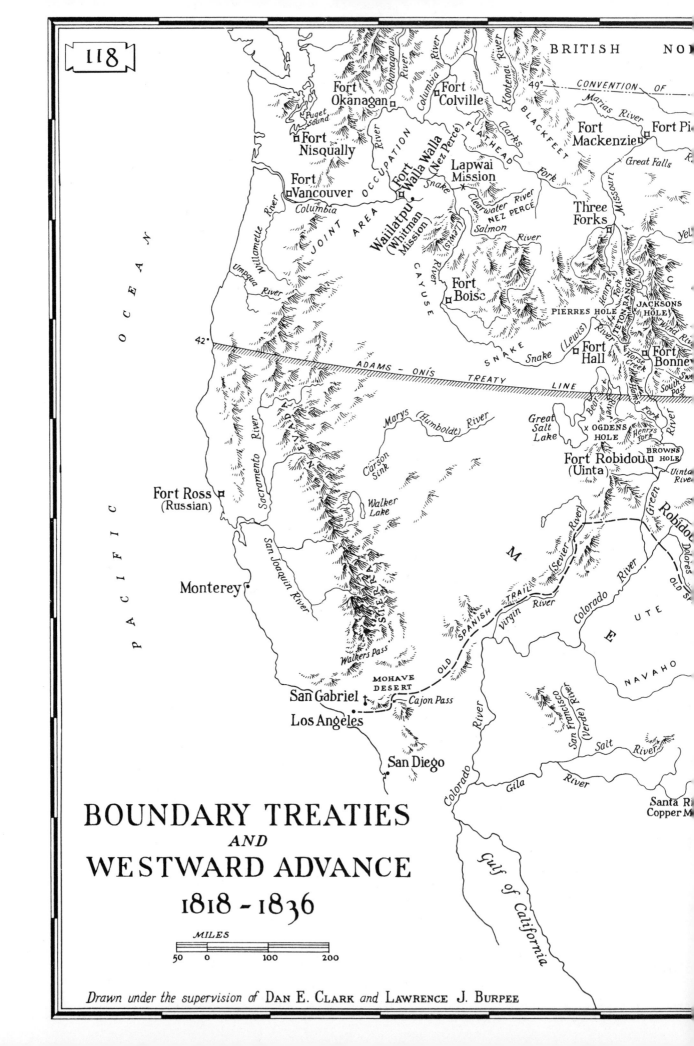

BOUNDARY TREATIES
AND
WESTWARD ADVANCE
1818 - 1836

MILES
50 0   100   200

Drawn under the supervision of DAN E. CLARK *and* LAWRENCE J. BURPEE

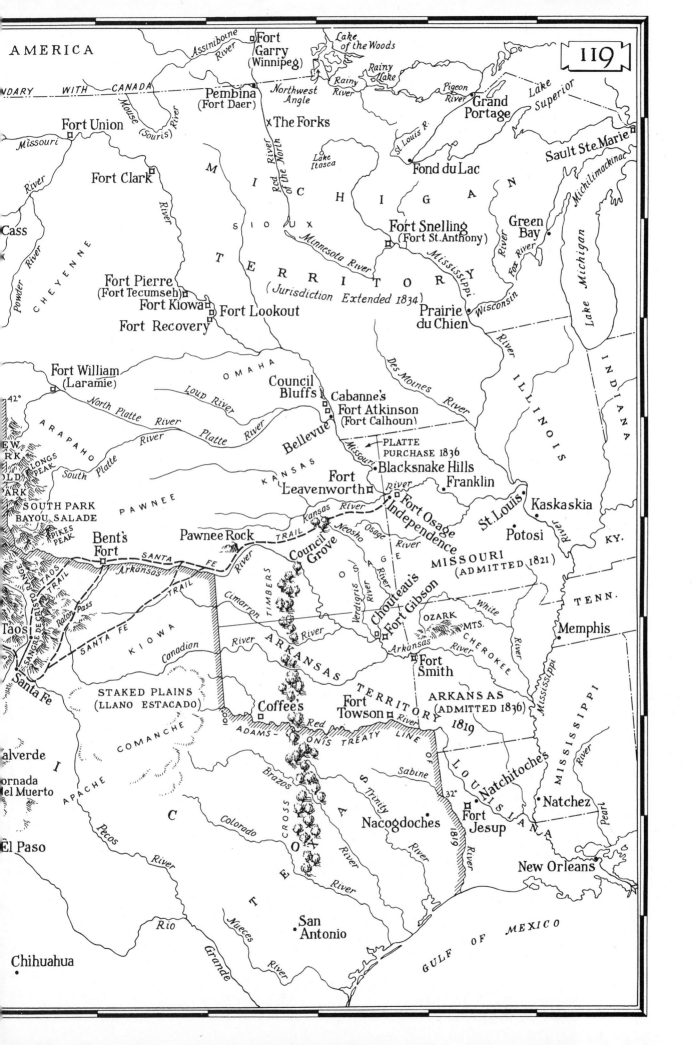

AMERICA

Assiniboine River

Fort Garry (Winnipeg)

Lake of the Woods

BOUNDARY WITH CANADA

Pembina (Fort Daer)

Northwest Angle

Rainy River

Rainy Lake

Pigeon River

Lake Superior

Mouse (Souris) River

Red River of the North

Grand Portage

Fort Union

Missouri River

Fort Clark

Lake Itasca

St. Louis R.

Sault Ste. Marie

Michilimackinac

Cass

Powder River

CHEYENNE

M I C H I G A N

Fond du Lac

Minnesota River

S I O U X

Fort Pierre (Fort Tecumseh)

Fort Kiowa

Fort Lookout

Fort Recovery

T E R R I T O R Y

(Jurisdiction Extended 1834)

Fort Snelling (Fort St. Anthony)

Green Bay

Fox River

Mississippi River

Wisconsin River

Lake Michigan

I N D I A N A

Prairie du Chien

Fort William (Laramie)

North Platte River

Loup River

O M A H A

Council Bluffs

Cabanne's

Fort Atkinson (Fort Calhoun)

Des Moines River

I L L I N O I S

42°

ARAPAHO

South Platte River

Platte River

KANSAS

Bellevue

Missouri River

PLATTE PURCHASE 1836

Blacksnake Hills

River

Franklin

Kaskaskia

NEW PARK OLD PARK

LONGS PEAK

PAWNEE

Fort Leavenworth

Kansas River

Fort Osage

Independence

St. Louis

Potosi

River

KY.

SOUTH PARK BAYOU SALADE

PIKES PEAK

Bent's Fort

Pawnee Rock

SANTA FE

Arkansas River

TRAIL

Council Grove

TIMBERS

Neosho

Osage River

Chouteau's

Fort Gibson

MISSOURI (ADMITTED 1821)

OZARK MTS.

White River

TENN.

Memphis

Taos

SANGRE DE CRISTO

Santa Fe

RANGE

Raton Pass

SANTA FE TRAIL

Cimarron River

KIOWA

Canadian River

A R K A N S A S

Verdigris River

CHEROKEE

Arkansas River

Fort Smith

River

STAKED PLAINS (LLANO ESTACADO)

Coffee's

COMANCHE

T E R R I T O R Y

Fort Towson

ARKANSAS (ADMITTED 1836)

1819

River

Calverde

Jornada del Muerto

APACHE

C O

Pecos River

Colorado River

CROSS

Red River

ADAMS-ONIS TREATY LINE OF 1819

Brazos River

Sabine River

LOUISIANA

Natchitoches

Natchez

MISSISSIPPI River

Pearl River

El Paso

I

Trinity River

Nacogdoches

32°

Fort Jesup

1819

New Orleans

Rio Grande

Nueces River

San Antonio

T E X A S

Colorado River

River

GULF OF MEXICO

Chihuahua

GULF OF MEXICO

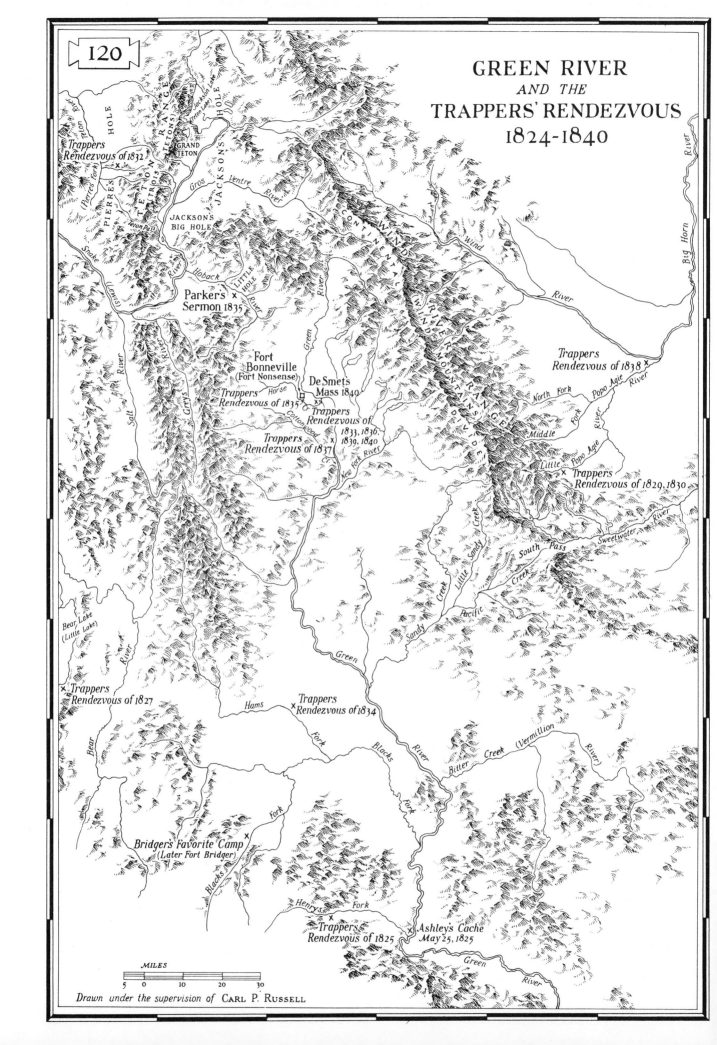

120

GREEN RIVER
AND THE
TRAPPERS' RENDEZVOUS
1824-1840

Teton River

Trappers
Rendezvous of 1832 ×

(Pierre's Fork)

TETONS

TETON RANGE

Jackson Lake

GRAND TETON

JACKSON'S HOLE

Gros Ventre River

JACKSON'S BIG HOLE

Teton Pass

CONTINENTAL

WIND

Wind River

Big Horn River

Snake (Lewis) River

Hoback River

LITTLE HOLE

Parkers ×
Sermon 1835

Green River

WIND RIVER RANGE DIVIDE

Fort
Bonneville
(Fort Nonsense)

Horse Cr.

De Smet's
Mass 1840

Trappers
Rendezvous of 1838 ×

Salt River

Greys River

Trappers
Rendezvous of 1835 ×

Cottonwood

Trappers
Rendezvous of
1833, 1836,
1839, 1840

North Fork

Popo Agie River

Trappers ×
Rendezvous of 1837

New Fork River

Middle Fork

Little Popo Agie River

Trappers ×
Rendezvous of 1829, 1830

Bear Lake
(Little Lake)

Bear Lake River

Sandy Creek

Little Sandy Creek

Pacific Creek

South Pass

Sweetwater River

× Trappers
Rendezvous of 1827

Green River

Hams Fork

Trappers ×
Rendezvous of 1834

Blacks River

Bitter Creek (Vermillion River)

Bear River

Fork

Blacks Fork

Bridger's Favorite Camp ×
(Later Fort Bridger)

Blacks Fork

Henrys Fork

Trappers ×
Rendezvous of 1825

Ashley's Cache ×
May 25, 1825

Green River

MILES

5 0 10 20 30

Drawn under the supervision of CARL P. RUSSELL

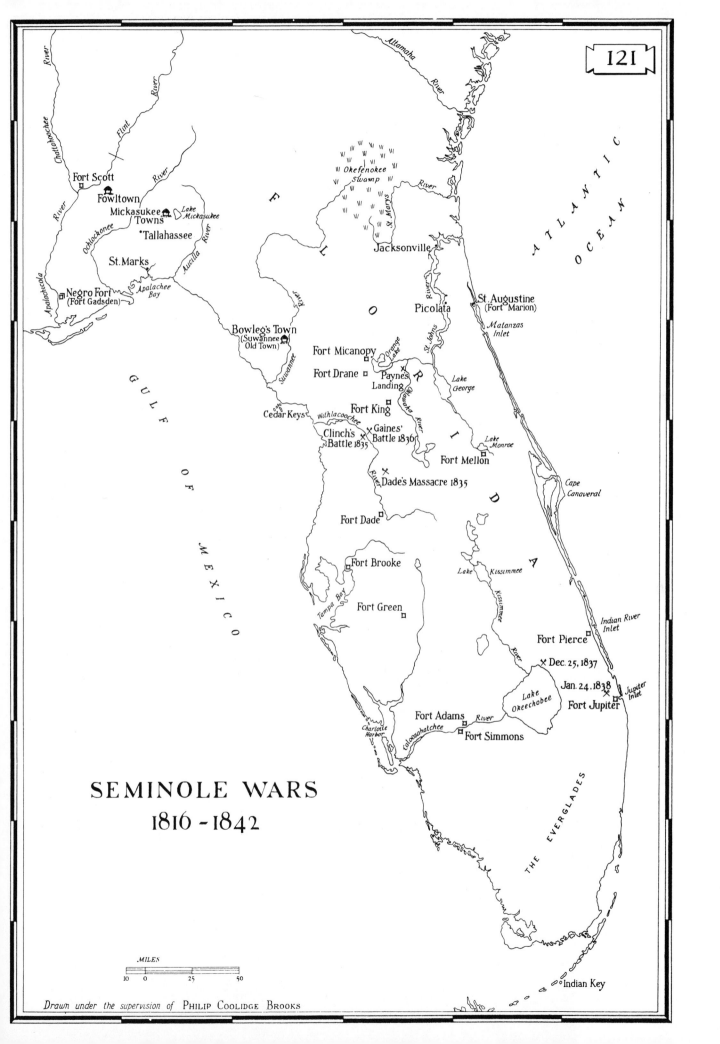

121

River (Altamaha)

River (Chattahoochee)

Flint River

River (Ochlockonee)

Fort Scott

Fowltown

Mickasukee Towns

Lake Mickasukee

•Tallahassee

St.Marks

Negro Fort (Fort Gadsden)

Apalachee Bay

Apalachicola

Ocilla River

St. Marys River

Okefenokee Swamp

Jacksonville

ATLANTIC OCEAN

F L O R I D A

St. Johns River

St. Augustine (Fort Marion)

Picolata

Matanzas Inlet

Bowleg's Town (Suwannee Old Town)

Suwannee River

Fort Micanopy

Orange Lake

Fort Drane

Paynes Landing

Ocklawaha River

Lake George

Fort King

Cedar Keys

Withlacoochee

Clinch's Battle 1835

Gaines' Battle 1836

River

Dade's Massacre 1835

Lake Monroe

Fort Mellon

Cape Canaveral

Fort Dade

GULF OF MEXICO

Fort Brooke

Tampa Bay

Fort Green

Lake Kissimmee

Kissimmee River

Indian River Inlet

Fort Pierce

✕ Dec. 25, 1837

Jan. 24. 1838 ✕

Jupiter Inlet

Fort Jupiter

Lake Okeechobee

Fort Adams

River

Caloosahatchee

Fort Simmons

Charlotte Harbor

THE EVERGLADES

SEMINOLE WARS
1816 - 1842

MILES

10   0   25   50

Indian Key

Drawn under the supervision of PHILIP COOLIDGE BROOKS

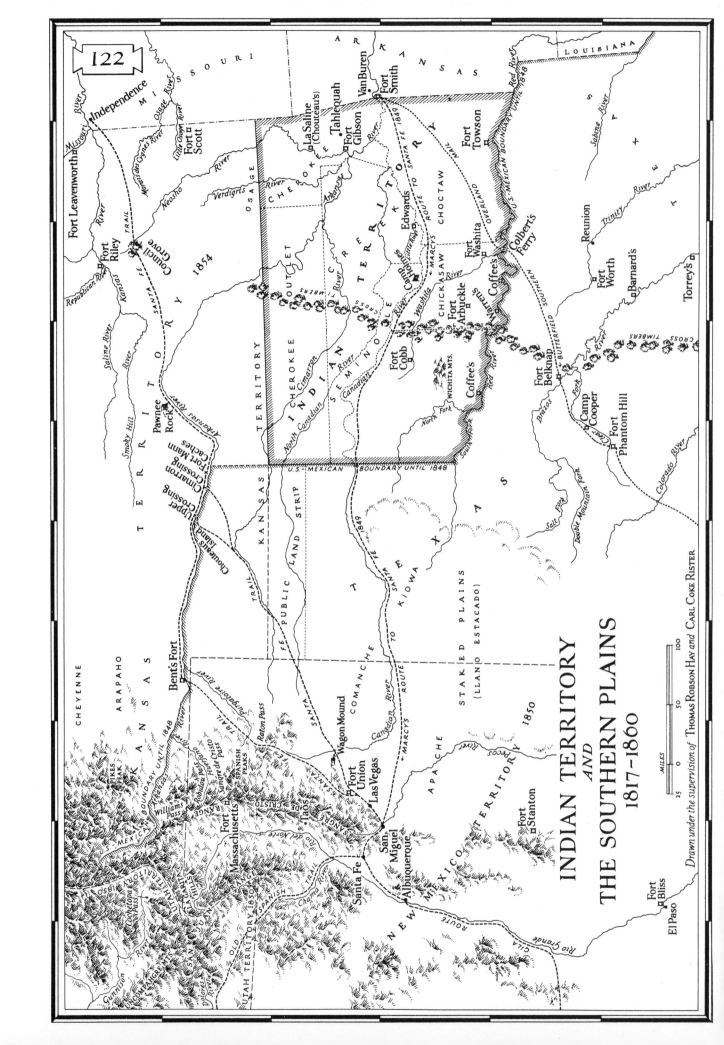

122

INDIAN TERRITORY
AND
THE SOUTHERN PLAINS
1817-1860

Drawn under the supervision of THOMAS ROBSON HAY *and* CARL COKE RISTER

MILES

100
50
25
0

MISSOURI

ARKANSAS

LOUISIANA

Independence
Osage River
Missouri River

Fort Leavenworth
SANTA FE TRAIL
Fort Riley
Council Grove
Kansas River
Republican River

Neosho River
Marais des Cygnes River
Little Osage River
Fort Scott

Verdigris River
OSAGE
CHEROKEE
La Saline (Chouteau's)
Tahlequah
Arkansas River
VanBuren
Fort Smith

Fort Gibson
CHEROKEE OUTLET
CREEK
SANTA FE 1849
SANTA FE
CHOCTAW MAIL
Fort Towson
Red River until 1848
U.S. MEXICAN BOUNDARY UNTIL

Saline River

Smoky Hill River

TERRITORY

1854

CHEROKEE TERRITORY
INDIAN TERRITORY
CROSS TIMBERS
Cimarron River
North Canadian River
Canadian River
SEMINOLE
CREEK
Edwards
Camp Holmes
Canadian River
Washita River
CHICKASAW
Fort Washita
OVERLAND
Colbert's Ferry
Coffee's
Fort Arbuckle
SOUTHERN
BUTTERFIELD
Reunion
Trinity River
Fort Worth
Barnard's
Torrey's

Pawnee Rock
Arkansas River
Fort Mann
Caches
Cimarron Crossing
Upper Crossing
Chouteau's Island
SANTA FE TRAIL

Fort Cobb
WICHITA MTS.
Coffee's
North Fork
Red River
South Fork
Fort Belknap
CROSS TIMBERS
Camp Cooper
Fort Phantom Hill
Brazos
Clear Fork

KANSAS TERRITORY
U.S. MEXICAN BOUNDARY UNTIL 1848

PUBLIC LAND STRIP

SANTA FE 1849
TEXAS
SANTA FE TO
KIOWA
MARCY'S ROUTE
Salt Fork
Double Mountain Fork
Colorado River

CHEYENNE
ARAPAHO
KANSAS
Smoky Hill River

Bent's Fort
Purgatoire River
Arkansas River
SANTA FE TRAIL

COMANCHE
STAKED PLAINS (LLANO ESTACADO)
1850

PIKES PEAK
SPANISH PEAKS
Williams Pass
Robidoux Pass
Raton Pass
Sangre de Cristo Pass
Huerfano River
Wagon Mound
Canadian River
MARCY'S ROUTE TO SANTA FE
APACHE
Pecos River

Gunnison River
UNCOMPAHGRE MTS.
SAN JUAN RIVER
Dolores River
UTAH TERRITORY 1850
COCHETOPA PASS
SAN LUIS VALLEY
SANGRE DE CRISTO RANGE
Fort Massachusetts
Fort
Taos
Rio del Norte
SANTA FE TRAIL
Fort Union
Las Vegas
San Miguel
Santa Fe
Albuquerque
NEW MEXICO TERRITORY 1850
SOUTHERN ROUTE
Fort Stanton
APACHE TERRITORY 1850

Chama River
Rio Grande
Gila River
El Paso
Fort Bliss

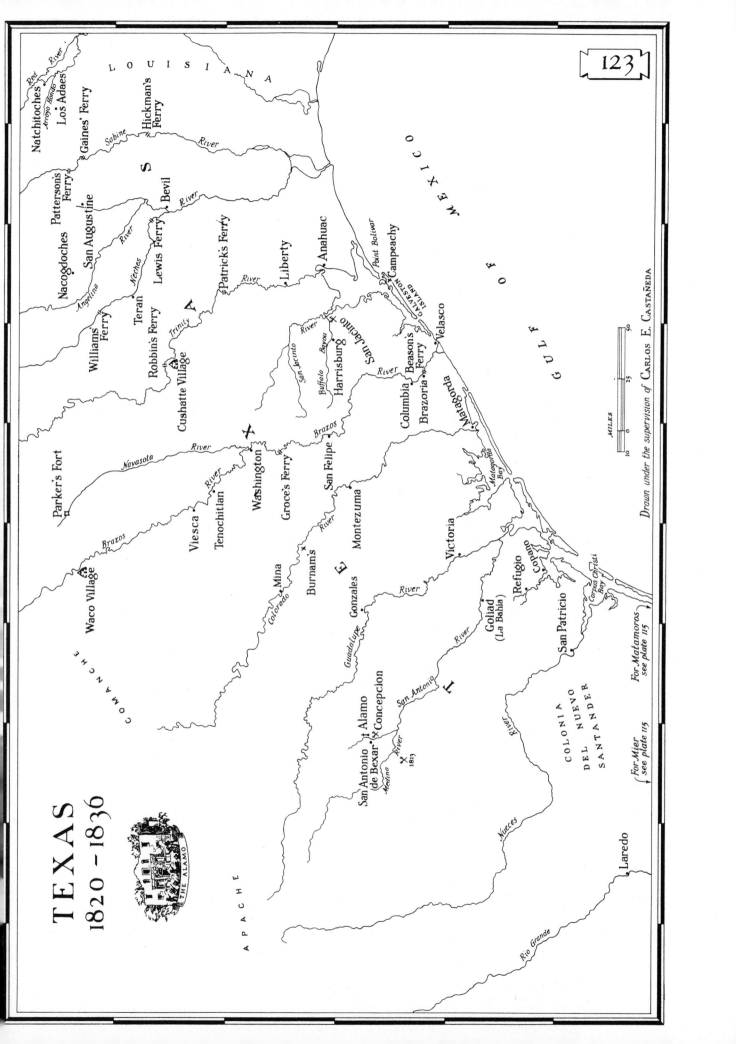

123

TEXAS
1820–1836

THE ALAMO

L O U I S I A N A

Red River

Natchitoches
Arroyo Hondo
Los Adaes?
Gaines' Ferry
Pattersons Ferry

Sabine River

Hickman's Ferry

S

Nacogdoches
San Augustine
Bevil

Neches River

Williams Ferry
Teran
Lewis Ferry
Robbins Ferry
Patrick's Ferry

Angelina

Trinity River

A

Liberty
Anahuac
Point Bolivar
Campeachy
GALVESTON ISLAND
Velasco

Cushatte Village

San Jacinto River

Buffalo Bayou
Harrisburg
San Jacinto

Columbia
Beason's Ferry
Brazoria
Matagorda

Parker's Fort

Navasota River

Washington
Groce's Ferry
San Felipe

Brazos River

M E X I C O

G U L F   O F

Viesca
Tenochtlan

Burnam's

E

Montezuma

Waco Village

Brazos

Mina

Colorado

Gonzales

Guadalupe

Victoria

Copano
Refugio
San Patricio

Corpus Christi Bay

C O M A N C H E

A P A C H E

San Antonio (de Bexar)
Alamo
Concepcion
1813

Medina River

San Antonio River

Goliad (La Bahia)

I

Nueces

COLONIA DEL NUEVO SANTANDER

For Matamoros see plate 115

For Mier see plate 115

Rio Grande

Laredo

MILES
10   0   25   50

Drawn under the supervision of CARLOS E. CASTAÑEDA

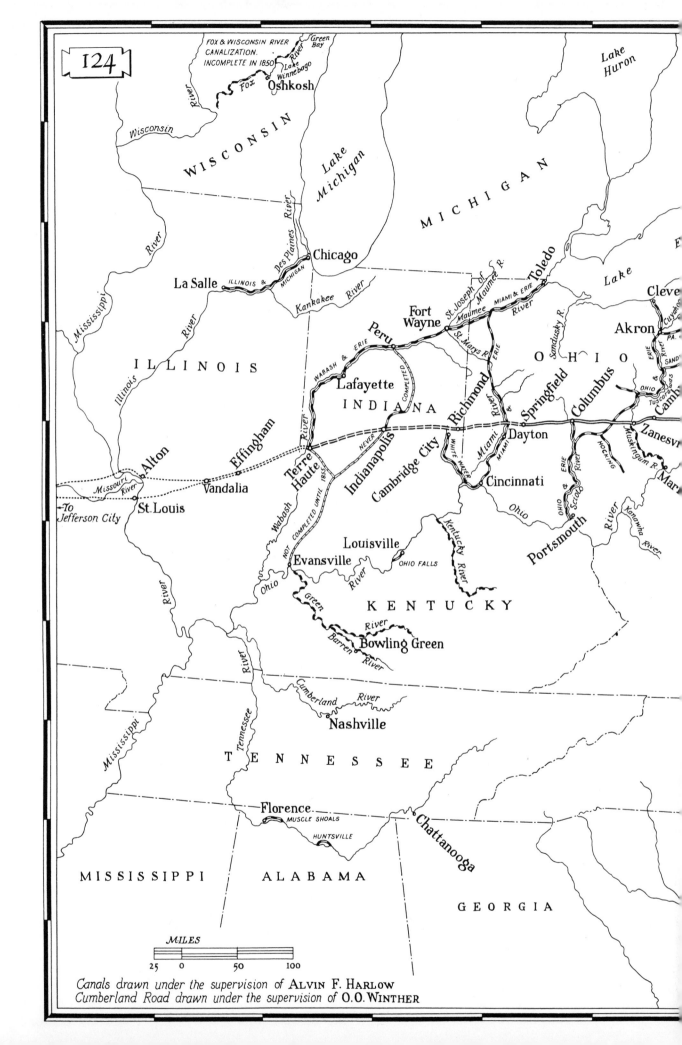

124

FOX & WISCONSIN RIVER
CANALIZATION.
INCOMPLETE IN 1850

Green
Bay

River

Lake
Winnebago

Oshkosh

Fox

Lake
Huron

Wisconsin

River

WISCONSIN

Lake
Michigan

MICHIGAN

Mississippi

River

River

Des Plaines River

Chicago

La Salle

ILLINOIS & MICHIGAN

Kankakee River

Illinois

River

ILLINOIS

River

Toledo

St. Joseph of Maumee

Maumee R.

MIAMI & ERIE

Maumee River

St. Marys R.

Lake

Cleve

PA.

Akron

ERIE

Cuyahoga

OHIO

Sandusky R.

ERIE

OHIO & TUSCORAWAS

SAND

Fort
Wayne

WABASH & ERIE

Peru

COMPLETED

Lafayette

INDIANA

Richmond

MIAMI & ERIE

Springfield

Columbus

Cambi

Zanesvi

River

Mar

Alton

Effingham

River

NEVER

NOT COMPLETED UNTIL 1855

Terre
Haute

Indianapolis

Cambridge City

WHITE WATER

Dayton

Miami River

MIAMI

OHIO & ERIE

HOCKING

Muskingum R.

Vandalia

Missouri

River

St. Louis

To
Jefferson City

WABASH

Louisville

OHIO FALLS

Cincinnati

Kentucky River

Ohio

ERIE

Scioto River

OHIO &

Portsmouth

River

Kanawha River

Evansville

Green

River

River

KENTUCKY

Ohio

River

Barren

River

Bowling Green

Mississippi

River

River

Cumberland

River

Nashville

TENNESSEE

Tennessee

River

T E N N E S S E E

Florence

MUSCLE SHOALS

HUNTSVILLE

Chattanooga

MISSISSIPPI

ALABAMA

GEORGIA

MILES

25   0   50   100

Canals drawn under the supervision of ALVIN F. HARLOW
Cumberland Road drawn under the supervision of O. O. WINTHER

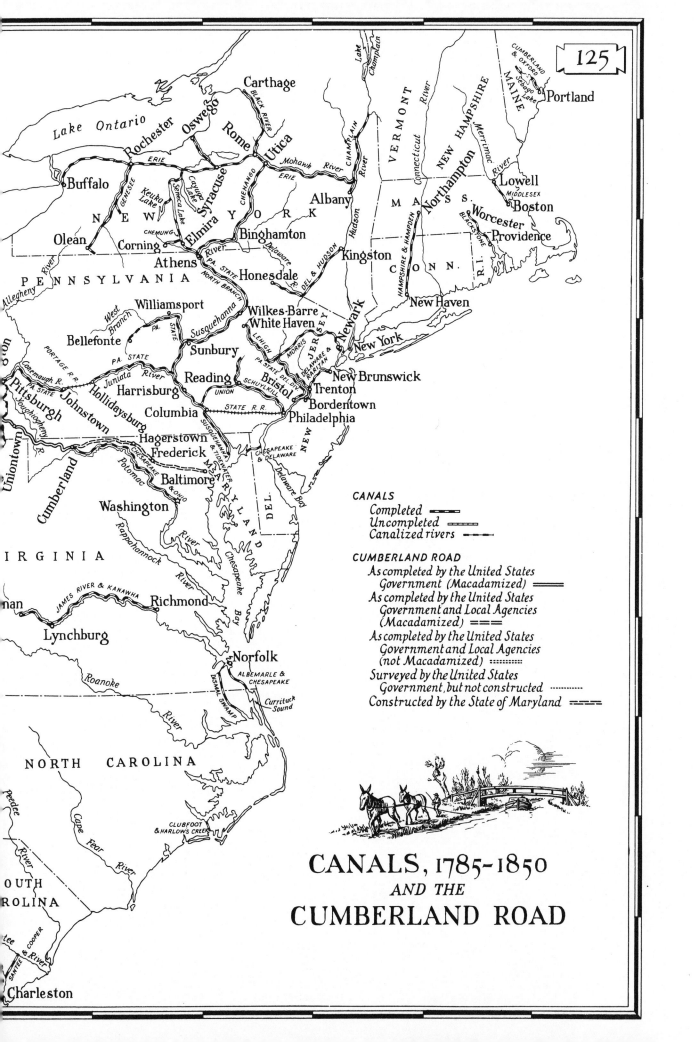

Lake Ontario

Carthage

Portland

CUMBERLAND & OXFORD

Sebago Lake

MAINE

VERMONT

NEW HAMPSHIRE

Lake Champlain

Champlain River

Connecticut River

Merrimac River

Northampton

Lowell

MIDDLESEX

Boston

Worcester

Providence

BLACKSTONE

MASS.

CONN.

R.I.

Rochester

Oswego

Rome

Utica

Mohawk River

ERIE

ERIE

GENESEE

Buffalo

Keuka Lake

Cayuga Lake

Seneca Lake

Syracuse

Albany

N E W   Y O R K

Olean

Corning

CHEMUNG

Elmira

Binghamton

PA. STATE

NORTH BRANCH

Kingston

New Haven

Allegheny River

Athens

Honesdale

DEL. & HUDSON

Delaware River

Hudson River

HAMPSHIRE & HAMPDEN

P E N N S Y L V A N I A

Williamsport

West Branch

Susquehanna River

Wilkes-Barre

White Haven

Newark

New York

Bellefonte

PA. STATE

Sunbury

LEHIGH

MORRIS

DELAWARE & RARITAN

New Brunswick

PA. STATE

PORTAGE R.R.

Conemaugh R.

PA. STATE

Reading

PA. STATE DEL. DIV.

SCHUYLKILL

Bristol

Trenton

N E W   J E R S E Y

Pittsburgh

Johnstown

Hollidaysburg

Juniata River

Harrisburg

UNION

Columbia

STATE R.R.

Bordentown

Philadelphia

Youghiogheny R.

Uniontown

Hagerstown

Frederick

SUSQUEHANNA & TIDEWATER

CHESAPEAKE & DELAWARE

D E L.

Cumberland

CHESAPEAKE & OHIO

Baltimore

M A R Y L A N D

Delaware Bay

Washington

Potomac River

V I R G I N I A

Rappahannock River

River

Chesapeake Bay

Richmond

JAMES RIVER & KANAWHA

Lynchburg

Roanoke River

Norfolk

ALBEMARLE & CHESAPEAKE

Currituck Sound

DISMAL SWAMP

N O R T H   C A R O L I N A

Peedee River

Cape Fear River

River

CLUBFOOT & HARLOWS CREEK

S O U T H   C A R O L I N A

Lee & Cooper River

SANTEE & COOPER RIVER

Charleston

CANALS

Completed ▬▬

Uncompleted ▭▭

Canalized rivers ▬·▬·

CUMBERLAND ROAD

As completed by the United States
Government (Macadamized) ▬▬

As completed by the United States
Government and Local Agencies
(Macadamized) ═══

As completed by the United States
Government and Local Agencies
(not Macadamized) ∷∷∷∷

Surveyed by the United States
Government, but not constructed ┈┈┈

Constructed by the State of Maryland ▭▭▭

CANALS, 1785–1850
AND THE
CUMBERLAND ROAD

RAILROADS, 1827-1850
WESTERN DIVISION

126

WISCONSIN

Lake Michigan

MICHIGAN

Kalamazoo Jackson Ann Arbor Pontiac

Elgin Chicago MICHIGAN CENTRAL Detroit

St.Charles

Aurora Coldwater MICHIGAN SOUTHERN Monroe

New Buffalo Adrian Toledo Sandusky Cleveland

Lake Erie

MISSISSIPPI River

ILLINOIS River INDIANA Springfield MAD RIVER & LAKE ERIE CIN CLEVELAND & COLUMBUS PENN.

Shelby

Mansfield Monongahela River

Springfield Naples Pendleton Knightstown OHIO Newark

Indianapolis Rushville COL & XEN. Columbus

MISSOURI River Shelbyville Xenia

MADISON & INDIAN'S LITTLE MIAMI

St.Louis Columbus Cincinnati Ohio River

Wabash River Madison

VIRGINIA

Frankfort

Louisville Lexington

Ohio River

KENTUCKY

Nashville

NORTH CAROLINA

Memphis La Grange TENNESSEE Tennessee River

Chattanooga

Tuscumbia SOUTH CAROLINA

Decatur Camden

Rome WESTERN & ATLANTIC Athens Columbia

MISSISSIPPI Atlanta Savannah Hamburg Branchville

Vicksburg Raymond Jackson ALABAMA MACON & WESTERN Warrenton GEORGIA Augusta SOUTH CAROLINA

VICK & JACKSON Brandon Macon CENTRAL Charleston

Opelika

Montgomery MONTG. & WEST POINT GEORGIA

Woodville Savannah

Clinton Flint River

Port Hudson Pearl River Mobile Perdido River Chattahoochee River ATLANTIC OCEAN

Bayou Sara Baton Rouge Pensacola FLORIDA

Carrollton LOUISIANA Proctorsville

New Orleans GULF OF MEXICO Apalachicola River

MILES
25 0 50 100

Drawn under the supervision of ALVIN F. HARLOW

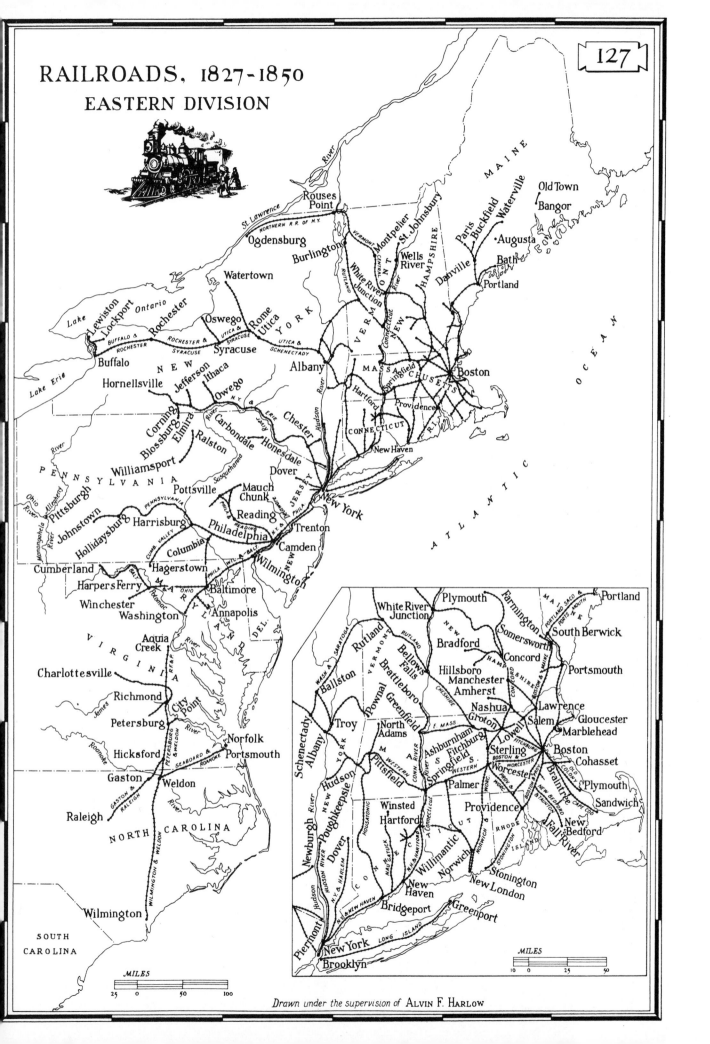

RAILROADS, 1827-1850
EASTERN DIVISION

127

Drawn under the supervision of ALVIN F. HARLOW

128

Ft. Nisqually

Ft. Vancouver

Whitman Mission

Portland

Ft. Walla Walla

Ft. Pierre

Ft. Laramie

Salt Lake City

Ft. Kearny

Sutter's Fort

San Francisco

Monterey

Santa Fe

Albuquerque

San Diego

Ft. Yuma

Ft. Worth

Tucson

El Paso

Aus

San Ant

Corp Chr

Lared

PACIFIC OCEAN

MILES

0   100   200   300   400

SETTLED AREAS 1850

This map does not show areas settled by Indians.

Sault Ste. Marie

Green Bay

Dubuque

Chicago

Ft. Des Moines

t. Leavenworth
Independence

St. Louis

Detroit

Indianapolis

Cincinnati

Louisville

Evansville

Lexington

Nashville

Knoxville

Chattanooga

Memphis

t. Smith   Little Rock

Atlanta

Augusta

Vicksburg

Montgomery

Savannah

Natchez

Mobile

New Orleans

Pensacola

St. Augustine

Cleveland

Buffalo

Albany

Harrisburg

Pittsburgh

Columbus

Baltimore

Washington

Richmond

Norfolk

Portland

Boston

Providence

Brooklyn
New York

Philadelphia
Wilmington

Charleston

ATLANTIC OCEAN

Gulf of Mexico

130

WISCONSIN

MINN.

IOWA

MILWAUKEE
Racine
(threshers)

MICHIGAN

Buffalo
(flour)

CHICAGO
(meat packing)

DETROIT

CLEVELAND
Youngstown

ILLINOIS

INDIANA

OHIO

Steubenville
Wheeling

PITTSBU

CINCINNATI
(meat packing)

ST.LOUIS

Ironton

Louisville
(cordage) **LEXINGTON**

MO.

KENTUCKY

VIRGINI

ARK.

TENNESSEE

NORTH CAR

MISS.

ALABAMA

GEORGIA

SOUTH CAROLINA
Graniteville

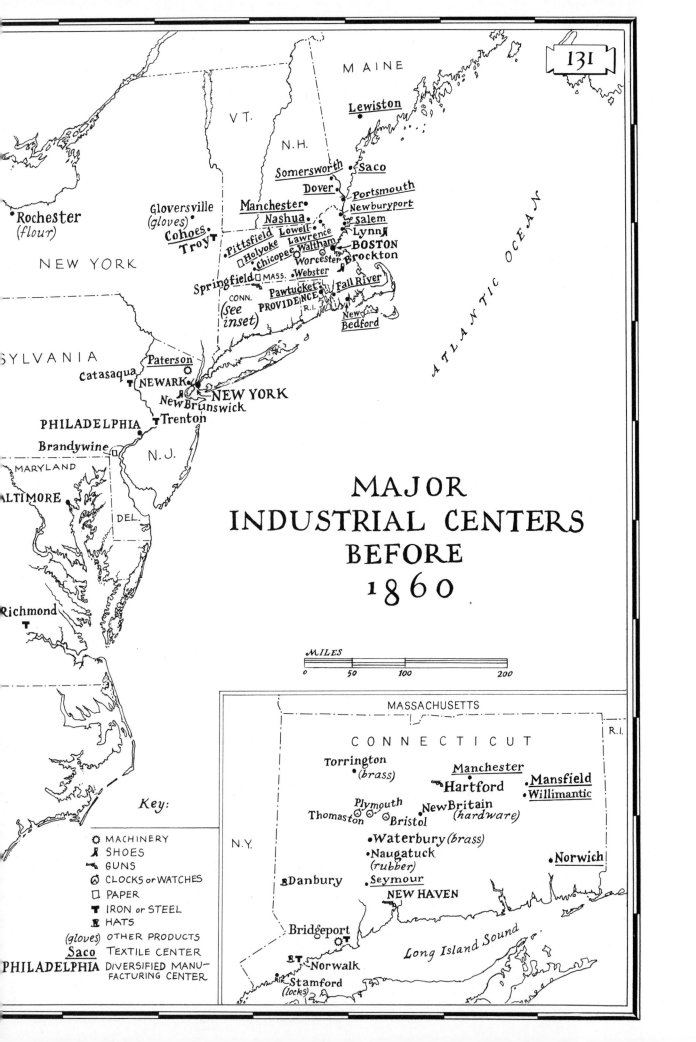

131

MAINE

Lewiston

VT.

N.H.

Rochester
(flour)

Somersworth • Saco
Dover
Portsmouth
Newburyport
Gloversville
(gloves)
Manchester•
Nashua •
Salem
Cohoes
Pittsfield Lowell Lynn
Troy Holyoke Lawrence BOSTON
Chicopee Waltham Brockton
Springfield □ MASS. • Webster Worcester
Pawtucket Fall River
CONN. PROVIDENCE New
(See R.I. Bedford
inset)

NEW YORK

ATLANTIC OCEAN

Paterson
Catasaqua
NEWARK
New Brunswick NEW YORK

SYLVANIA

PHILADELPHIA
Trenton
Brandywine

N.J.

MARYLAND

DEL.

ALTIMORE

Richmond

MAJOR
INDUSTRIAL CENTERS
BEFORE
1860

MILES
0   50   100   200

Key:

⚙ MACHINERY
👞 SHOES
🔫 GUNS
🕐 CLOCKS or WATCHES
□ PAPER
⊤ IRON or STEEL
🎩 HATS
(gloves) OTHER PRODUCTS
Saco TEXTILE CENTER
PHILADELPHIA DIVERSIFIED MANU-
FACTURING CENTER

MASSACHUSETTS

CONNECTICUT

R.I.

Torrington
(brass)
Manchester
Hartford
Mansfield
Willimantic

Plymouth NewBritain
Thomaston Bristol (hardware)

N.Y.

Waterbury (brass)
Naugatuck
(rubber)
Norwich
Danbury
Seymour
NEW HAVEN

Bridgeport

Norwalk
Stamford
(locks)

Long Island Sound

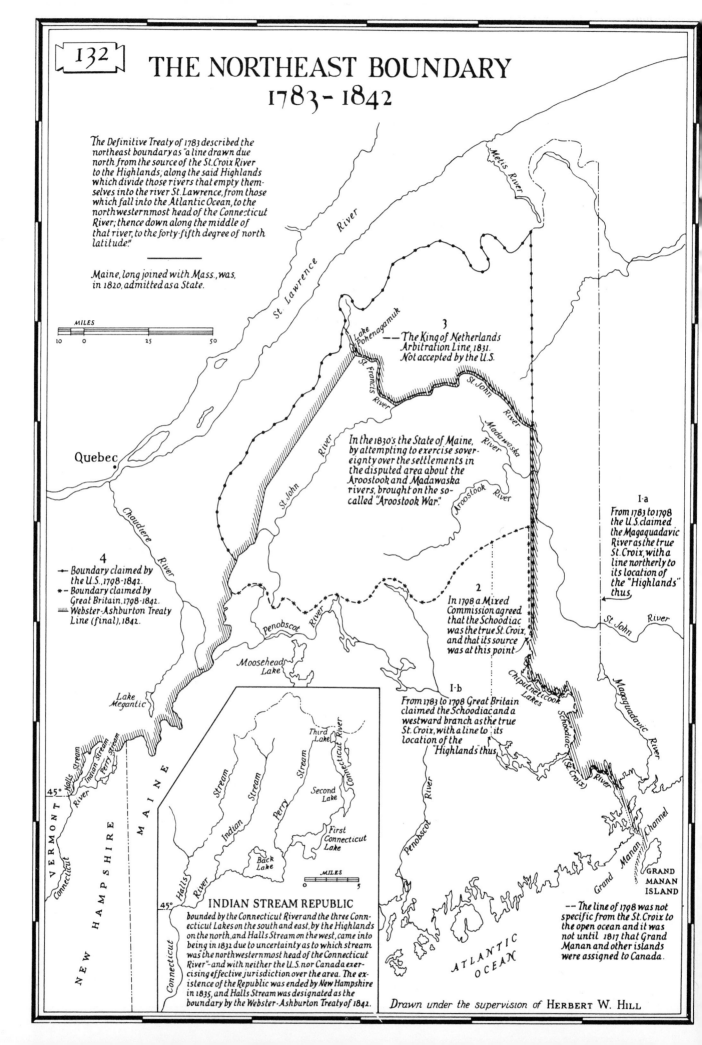

132

THE NORTHEAST BOUNDARY
1783-1842

The Definitive Treaty of 1783 described the northeast boundary as "a line drawn due north from the source of the St.Croix River to the Highlands; along the said Highlands which divide those rivers that empty themselves into the river St. Lawrence, from those which fall into the Atlantic Ocean, to the northwesternmost head of the Connecticut River; thence down along the middle of that river, to the forty-fifth degree of north latitude."

Maine, long joined with Mass., was, in 1820, admitted as a State.

MILES
10   0   25   50

3
— The King of Netherlands Arbitration Line, 1831. Not accepted by the U.S.

Quebec

In the 1830's the State of Maine, by attempting to exercise sovereignty over the settlements in the disputed area about the Aroostook and Madawaska rivers, brought on the so-called "Aroostook War".

I·a
From 1783 to 1798 the U.S. claimed the Magaquadavic River as the true St. Croix, with a line northerly to its location of the "Highlands" thus,

4
→ Boundary claimed by the U.S., 1798-1842.
✳ Boundary claimed by Great Britain, 1798-1842.
〰 Webster-Ashburton Treaty Line (final), 1842.

2
In 1798 a Mixed Commission agreed that the Schoodiac was the true St.Croix, and that its source was at this point

I·b
From 1783 to 1798 Great Britain claimed the Schoodiac and a westward branch as the true St. Croix, with a line to its location of the "Highlands" thus,

Mooshead Lake

Lake Megantic

Third Lake

Second Lake

First Connecticut Lake

Back Lake

VERMONT

NEW HAMPSHIRE

MAINE

45°

45°

MILES
0   5

INDIAN STREAM REPUBLIC
bounded by the Connecticut River and the three Connecticut Lakes on the south and east, by the Highlands on the north, and Halls Stream on the west, came into being in 1832 due to uncertainty as to which stream was the northwesternmost head of the Connecticut River"—and with neither the U.S. nor Canada exercising effective jurisdiction over the area. The existence of the Republic was ended by New Hampshire in 1835, and Halls Stream was designated as the boundary by the Webster-Ashburton Treaty of 1842.

GRAND MANAN ISLAND

-- The line of 1798 was not specific from the St. Croix to the open ocean and it was not until 1817 that Grand Manan and other islands were assigned to Canada.

ATLANTIC OCEAN

Drawn under the supervision of HERBERT W. HILL

St. Lawrence River

Metis River

Lake Pohenagamuk

St. Francis River

St. John River

St. John River

Madawaska River

Aroostook River

Chaudiere River

St. John River

Penobscot River

Chiputneticook Lakes

Schoodiac (St. Croix) River

Magaquadavic River

Grand Manan Channel

Connecticut River

Halls Stream

Indian Stream

Perry Stream

Penobscot River

Connecticut River

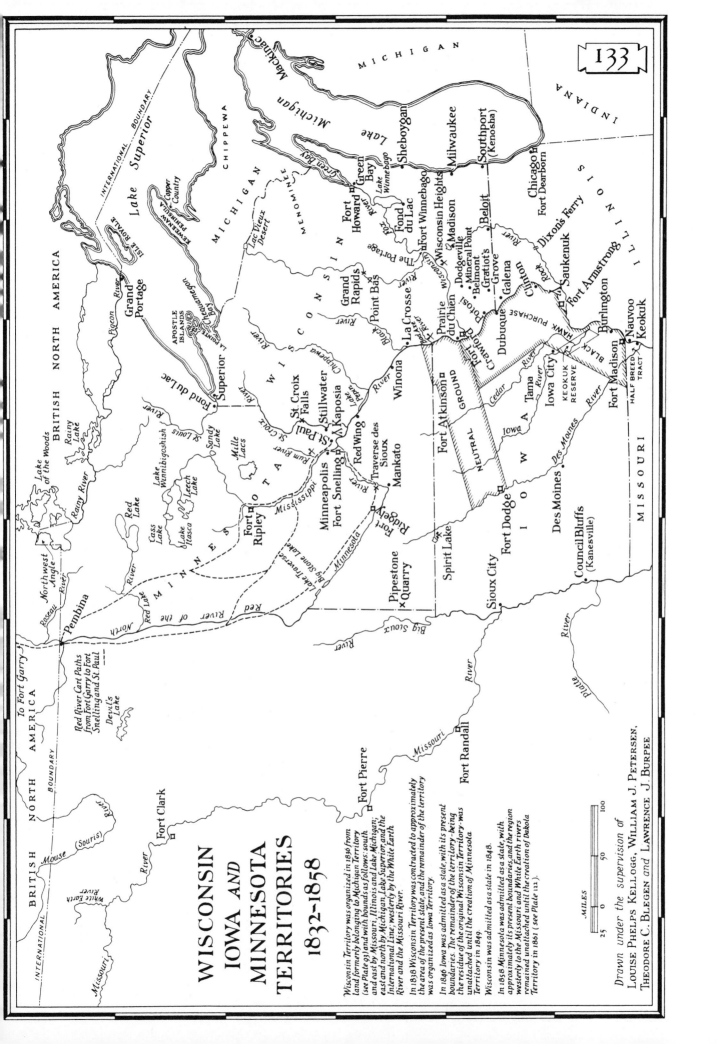

WISCONSIN IOWA AND MINNESOTA TERRITORIES 1832-1858

Wisconsin Territory was organized in 1836 from land formerly belonging to Michigan Territory (see Plate 93) and with bounds as follows: south and east by Missouri, Illinois and Lake Michigan; east and north by Michigan, Lake Superior, and the International Line; westerly by the White Earth River and the Missouri River.

In 1838 Wisconsin Territory was contracted to approximately the area of the present state, and the remainder of the territory was organized as Iowa Territory.

In 1846 Iowa was admitted as a state, with its present boundaries. The remainder of the territory—being the residue of the original Wisconsin Territory—was unattached until the creation of Minnesota Territory in 1849.

Wisconsin was admitted as a state in 1848.

In 1858 Minnesota was admitted as a state, with approximately its present boundaries, and the region westerly to the Missouri and White Earth rivers remained unattached until the creation of Dakota Territory in 1861 (see Plate 111).

MILES
25   0   50   100

Drawn under the supervision of
Louise Phelps Kellogg, William J. Petersen,
Theodore C. Blegen and Lawrence J. Burpee.

133

134

ALASKA

54°40 SOUTHERN RUSSIAN BOUNDARY

54°40'

N E W

C A L E D O N I A

QUEEN CHARLOTTE ISLANDS

Queen Charlotte Sound

Fraser River

Stuart River

BRITISH NOR

The definite boundary betwee
U.S. and Canada was carried th
by the Convention of 1818,
area to the west being uno
Joint Occupation until div
by the Treaty of 1846.

Nootka Sound

VANCOUVER ISLAND

49°

Strait of Juan de Fuca

Victoria

Puget Sound

Okanagan River

Columbia River

River

Kootenai

Clarks Fork

CONTINENTAL DIVIDE

BLACKFEET

Fort Colville

Spokane River

Coeur d'Alene

Fort Lewis

Miss

P A C I F I C   O C E A N

New Market • ☐ Fort Nisqually

Astoria •

Cowlitz River

Columbia

Fort Vancouver ☐

DES

Fort Walla Walla

Whitman Mission +

Snake

Clearwater River

Lapwai Mission

FLATHEAD

St.Marys

The Dalles

CASCADE MTS.

River

Umatilla R.

BLUE

Grande Ronde R.

Grande Ronde River

Salmon

NEZ PERCE

1848

Champoeg •
× Lee Mission

Willamette River

O R E G O N

T E R R I T O R Y

River

Snake

KE

PIERRES HOLE ×

JAC
HOL

☐ Fort Boise

S
N
A
K
E

OREGON

TRAIL

Fort Hall ☐

Soda Springs

Klamath

River

NORTHERN   MEXICAN   BOUNDARY   UNTIL   1848

Snake

CALIFORNIA

OGDENS HOLE ×

Fort Brid

Sacramento River

Marys (Humboldt) River

TO
Great Salt Lake

Bear

Fort Davy Cr

Salt Lake City •

MORMON TRAIL

U T E

Fort Robidou (Uinta)

Donner Tragedy ×

Green

Sutter's Fort ☐

MILES

50   0   100   200

Drawn under the supervision of DAN E. CLARK

THE UNORGANIZED TERRITORY
AND OREGON COUNTRY
1836-1848

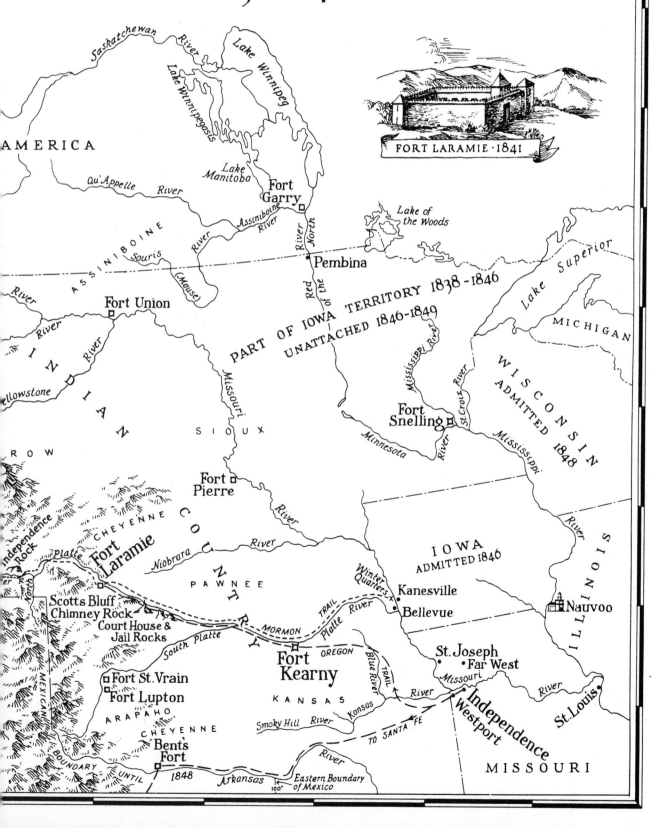

FORT LARAMIE · 1841

AMERICA

Saskatchewan River

Lake Winnipeg

Lake Winnipegosis

Lake Manitoba

Qu'Appelle River

Fort Garry

Assiniboine River

Lake of the Woods

ASSINIBOINE

Souris (Mouse) River

Pembina

Red River of the North

Lake Superior

PART OF IOWA TERRITORY 1838-1846

UNATTACHED 1846-1849

MICHIGAN

River

Fort Union

River

INDIAN

Missouri River

SIOUX

Mississippi River

St. Croix River

Fort Snelling

Minnesota River

WISCONSIN ADMITTED 1848

Mississippi

Yellowstone

ROW

Fort Pierre

River

River

Independence Rock

CHEYENNE

Fort Laramie

COUNTRY

Niobrara River

PAWNEE

IOWA ADMITTED 1846

River

ILLINOIS

Platte

Scotts Bluff
Chimney Rock
Court House &
Jail Rocks

South Platte

MORMON TRAIL

Platte River

Winter Quarters

Kanesville

Bellevue

Nauvoo

OREGON TRAIL

Fort Kearny

Blue River

KANSAS

Smoky Hill River

TRAIL

Kansas River

River

St. Joseph
Far West

Missouri River

St. Louis

River

Fort St. Vrain
Fort Lupton

ARAPAHO

MEXICAN

CHEYENNE

Bents' Fort

BOUNDARY UNTIL 1848

Arkansas River

TO SANTA FE

Independence
Westport

Eastern Boundary
of Mexico 100°

MISSOURI

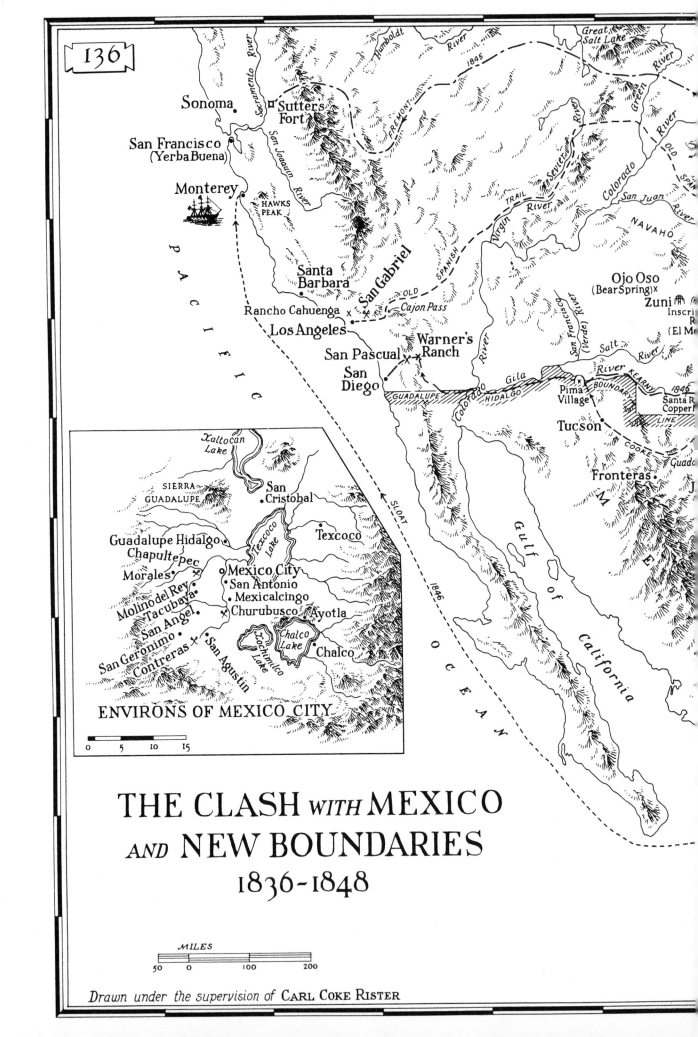

136

Sonoma
□ Sutters Fort
San Francisco
(Yerba Buena)
Monterey
HAWKS PEAK
Sacramento River
San Joaquin River

PACIFIC

FREMONT
1845
Humboldt River
Great Salt Lake
Green River
Sevier River
TRAIL
Virgin River
Colorado River
San Juan River
OLD SPANISH
NAVAHO

Santa Barbara
San Gabriel
Rancho Cahuenga ×
Los Angeles
San Pascual
San Diego
OLD SPANISH
Cajon Pass
Warner's Ranch
GUADALUPE
Colorado River
San Francisco (Verde) River
Salt River
Gila
HIDALGO
Pima Village
BOUNDARY
KEARNY
1846
Ojo Oso
(Bear Spring) ×
Zuni
Inscri R
(El M
Santa R
Copper

Gulf of California

Tucson
COOKE LINE
Fronteras
Guad
M E

SLOAT

1846

OCEAN

Xaltocan Lake
SIERRA GUADALUPE
San Cristobal
Texcoco Lake
Texcoco
Guadalupe Hidalgo
Chapultepec
Morales ×
Molino del Rey
Tacubaya
San Angel
San Geronimo
Contreras ×
San Agustin
Mexico City
San Antonio
Mexicalcingo
× Churubusco
Ayotla
Xochimilco Lake
Chalco Lake
Chalco

ENVIRONS OF MEXICO CITY

0   5   10   15

THE CLASH WITH MEXICO AND NEW BOUNDARIES
1836-1848

MILES
50   0   100   200

Drawn under the supervision of CARL COKE RISTER

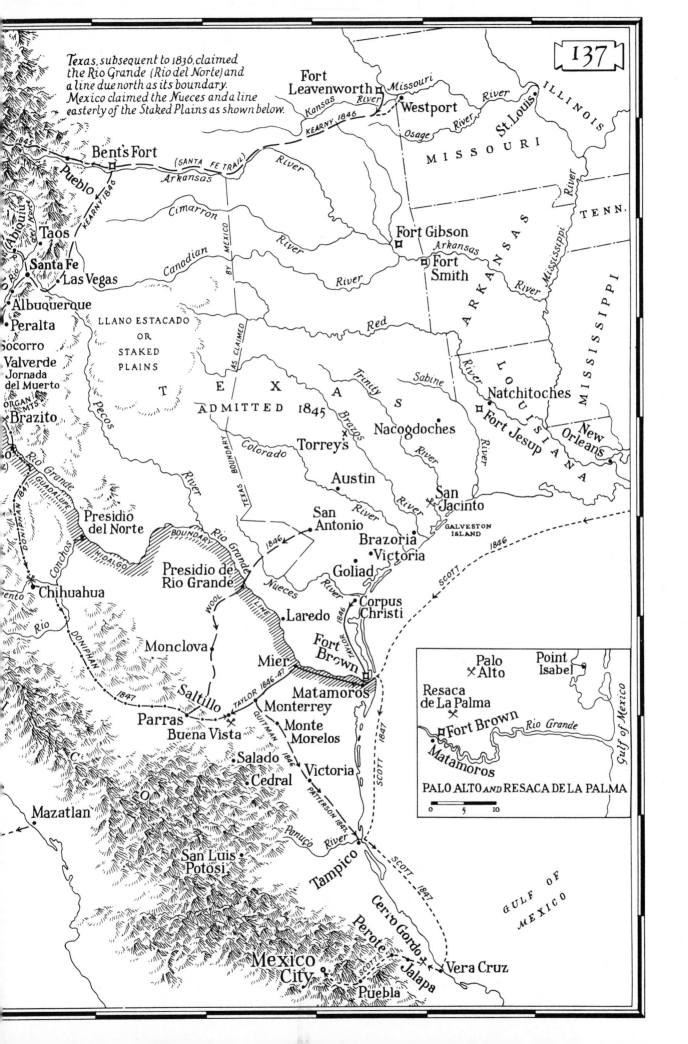

137

Texas, subsequent to 1836, claimed the Rio Grande (Rio del Norte) and a line due north as its boundary. Mexico claimed the Nueces and a line easterly of the Staked Plains as shown below.

Fort Leavenworth

Westport

St. Louis

MISSOURI

KEARNY 1846

Kansas River

Missouri River

Osage River

ILLINOIS

TENN.

Bent's Fort

Pueblo

KEARNY 1846

(SANTA FE TRAIL)

Arkansas River

Fort Gibson

Fort Smith

Arkansas River

Mississippi River

Cimarron River

1845

Taos

Santa Fe

Las Vegas

Abiquiu

Rio del Norte

Canadian River

BY MEXICO

Red River

ARKANSAS

LOUISIANA

Albuquerque

Peralta

Socorro

Valverde

Jornada del Muerto

ORGAN MTS

Brazito

LLANO ESTACADO OR STAKED PLAINS

Pecos

AS CLAIMED

T E X A S

ADMITTED 1845

Natchitoches

Fort Jesup

New Orleans

MISSISSIPPI

Trinity

Sabine River

Colorado River

Nacogdoches

Brazos River

Red River

Rio Grande

DONIPHAN 1841

GUADALUPE

Presidio del Norte

Conchos

HIDALGO

BOUNDARY

Rio Grande

TEXAS BOUNDARY

Torrey's

Austin

Brazos River

San Jacinto

GALVESTON ISLAND

1846

Chihuahua

Rio

DONIPHAN

Presidio de Rio Grande

WOOL

LIME

Nueces River

San Antonio

Brazoria

Victoria

Goliad

SCOTT 1846

Monclova

Laredo

Corpus Christi

Mier

Fort Brown

RIO GRANDE

1847

Saltillo

TAYLOR 1846-47

Matamoros

Parras

Buena Vista

QUITMAN 1846

Monterrey

Monte Morelos

SCOTT 1847

Salado

Cedral

Victoria

PATTERSON 1847

Mazatlan

Panuco River

San Luis Potosi

Tampico

SCOTT 1847

GULF OF MEXICO

Cerro Gordo

Perote

Jalapa

Vera Cruz

Mexico City

SCOTT 1847

Puebla

Palo Alto

Point Isabel

Resaca de La Palma

Fort Brown

Rio Grande

Gulf of Mexico

Matamoros

PALO ALTO AND RESACA DE LA PALMA

0   5   10

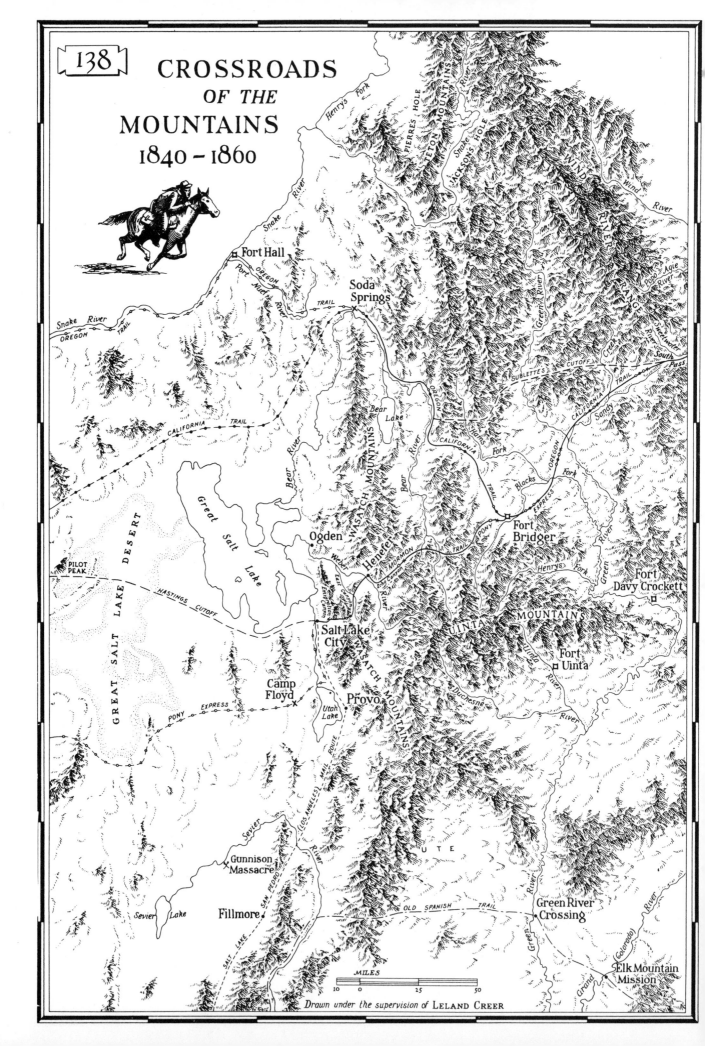

CROSSROADS
OF THE
MOUNTAINS
1840 – 1860

138

Fort Hall

Soda
Springs

Henrys Fork

PIERRES HOLE

TETON MOUNTAINS

JACKSON'S HOLE

Snake River

WIND RIVER RANGE

Wind River

Poo Agie River

Snake River

OREGON TRAIL

Port Neuf River

TRAIL

Bear
Lake

Green River

SUBLETTES CUTOFF

South Pass

Sandy Creek

Snake River

OREGON TRAIL

CALIFORNIA TRAIL

Bear River

WASATCH MOUNTAINS

Bear River

OREGON

CALIFORNIA

Smiths Fork

Blacks Fork

OREGON

Green River

Great Salt
Lake

Ogden

Henefer

Weber River

MORMON TRAIL

East Canyon

PONY EXPRESS

Fort
Bridger

Henrys Fork

Fort
Davy
Crockett

PILOT
PEAK

GREAT SALT LAKE DESERT

HASTINGS CUTOFF

Salt Lake
City

WASATCH MOUNTAINS

UINTA MOUNTAINS

Uinta River

Fort
Uinta

Camp
Floyd

PONY EXPRESS

Utah
Lake

Provo

ROUTE

MAIL

Duchesne River

(LOS ANGELES)

Green River

UTE

Sevier River

San Pedro River

Gunnison
Massacre

SALT LAKE

Sevier Lake

Fillmore

OLD SPANISH TRAIL

Green River
Crossing

Green River

Grand (Colorado) River

Elk Mountain
Mission

MILES
10   0   25   50

Drawn under the supervision of LELAND CREER

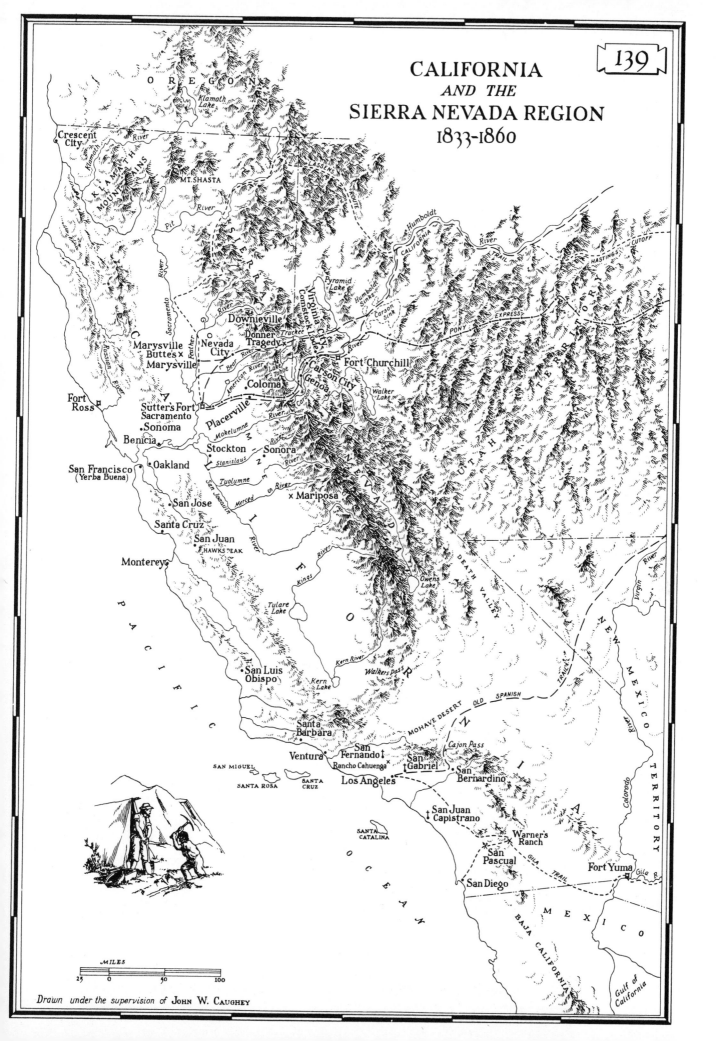

CALIFORNIA
AND THE
SIERRA NEVADA REGION
1833-1860

139

Drawn under the supervision of JOHN W. CAUGHEY

MILES
25 0 50 100

O R E G O N

Klamath
Lake

Crescent
City

Klamath *River*

KLAMATH MOUNTAINS

MT. SHASTA

LASSENS

Pit *River*

River

SIERRA

Sacramento *River*

Russian *River*

Fort
Ross

Marysville
Buttes ×
Marysville

Nevada
City

Feather *River*

Downieville

Donner
Tragedy ×

Pyramid
Lake

Humboldt
Sinks

Carson
Sink

Humboldt *River*

Virginia City
Comstock Lode

Bear *River*

Coloma

American River

Yuba *River*

Truckee *River*

Carson City
Genoa

Fort Churchill

Walker
Lake

CALIFORNIA TRAIL

HASTINGS
CUTOFF

PONY EXPRESS

U T A H   T E R R I T O R Y

Sutter's Fort
Sacramento
Sonoma

Benicia

Placerville

Mokelumne *River*

San Francisco
(Yerba Buena)

Oakland

Stockton

Stanislaus *River*

Sonora

Cosumnes *River*

San Joaquin *River*

Tuolumne *River*

Merced *River*

Mariposa ×

C A L I F O R N I A

San Jose

Santa Cruz

San Juan
HAWKS PEAK

Monterey

Kings *River*

Tulare
Lake

Owens
Lake

DEATH VALLEY

N E V A D A

S I E R R A

Kern River

Kern
Lake

Walkers Pass

San Luis
Obispo

P A C I F I C

SAN MIGUEL

SANTA ROSA

SANTA
CRUZ

Santa
Barbara

Ventura

San Miguel

OLD SPANISH TRAIL

MOHAVE DESERT

A R I Z O N A

Cajon Pass

San
Fernando
Rancho Cahuenga ×

San
Gabriel

San
Bernardino

Los Angeles

SANTA CATALINA

O C E A N

San Juan
Capistrano

Warner's
Ranch

San
Pascual

GILA TRAIL

Fort Yuma

Gila R.

Colorado *River*

Virgin *River*

N E W   M E X I C O   T E R R I T O R Y

San Diego

B A J A   C A L I F O R N I A

M E X I C O

Gulf of
California

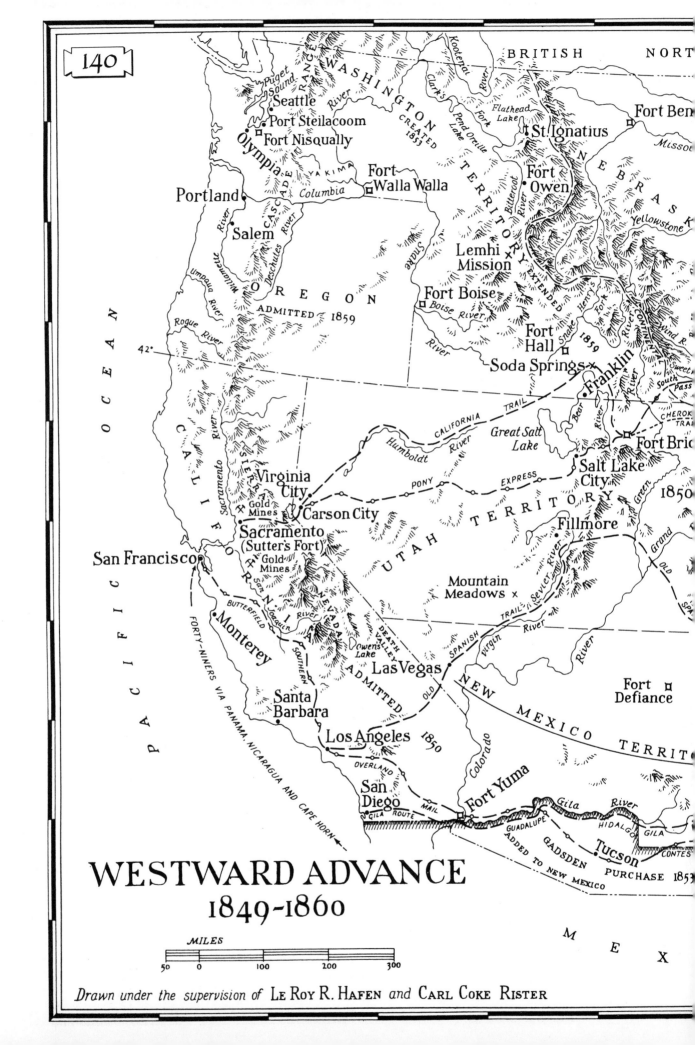

WESTWARD ADVANCE
1849-1860

MILES

50 0 100 200 300

Drawn under the supervision of Le Roy R. Hafen *and* Carl Coke Rister

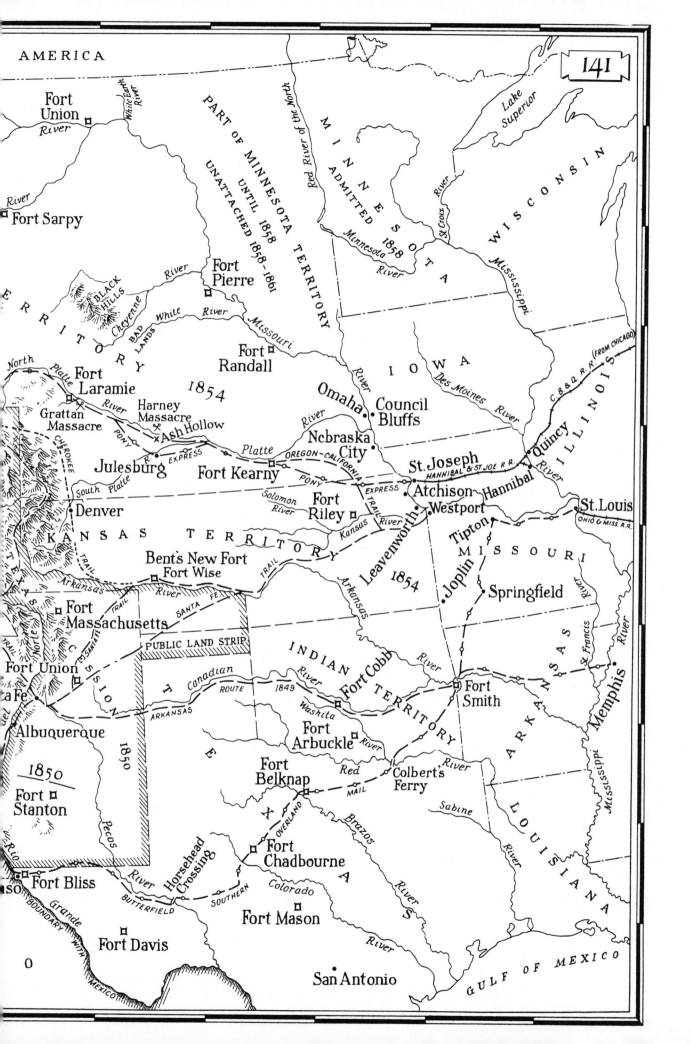

Fort
Union
River

White Earth River

River

Fort Sarpy

PART OF MINNESOTA TERRITORY
UNTIL 1858
UNATTACHED 1858-1861

Red River of the North

MINNESOTA
ADMITTED
1858

Minnesota
River

St Croix
River

Lake
Superior

WISCONSIN

Mississippi

River

TERRITORY

BLACK
HILLS

Cheyenne

BAD
LANDS

White

River

Missouri

Fort
Pierre

River

Fort
Randall

IOWA

River

Des Moines River

C. B. & Q. R. R. (FROM CHICAGO)

Fort
Laramie

1854

North
Platte

River

Harney
Massacre

Ash Hollow

PONY

Grattan
Massacre

CHEROKEE

Julesburg

PONY

R.

EXPRESS

South Platte

Platte

River

Platte

Omaha

Council
Bluffs

Nebraska
City

OREGON-CALIFORNIA

Fort Kearny

PONY

Solomon
River

Fort
Riley

EXPRESS

St. Joseph
HANNIBAL & ST JOE. R.R.

Atchison

Westport

Quincy

ILLINOIS

Hannibal

River

St. Louis

OHIO & MISS. R.R.

Denver

KANSAS

TERRITORY

Kansas

River

Leavenworth

1854

Tipton

MISSOURI

TEXAS

Bent's New Fort
Fort Wise

TRAIL

Arkansas

River

SANTA FE

Arkansas

Joplin

Springfield

River

St. Francis

River

Fort
Massachusetts

TRAIL

FLAGSTAFF

SANTA

PUBLIC LAND STRIP

INDIAN

River

Fort Cobb

River

Fort Smith

ARKANSAS

Memphis

Mississippi

Fort Union

CISION

ROUTE

ARKANSAS

Canadian

T

1850

1849

River

Washita

TERRITORY

a Fe

del

1850

Albuquerque

E

Fort
Arbuckle

River

Red

River

LOUISIANA

1850

Fort Stanton

Pecos

River

Fort
Belknap

River

Red

MAIL

Colbert's
Ferry

Sabine

River

Fort Bliss

so

BOUNDARY WITH

Grande

River

River

Horsehead Crossing

BUTTERFIELD

X

A

SOUTHERN

OVERLAND

Fort
Chadbourne

Brazos

Colorado

River

Fort Davis

MEXICO

Fort Mason

River

San Antonio

GULF OF MEXICO

0

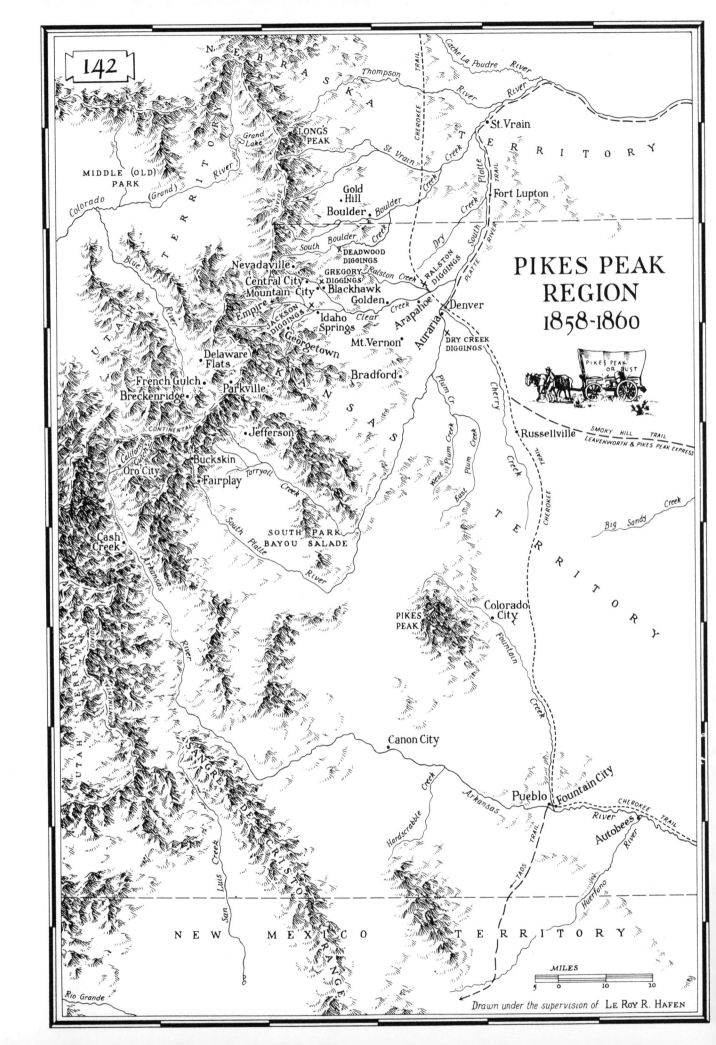

142

MIDDLE (OLD) PARK

NEBRASKA TERRITORY

N.

Thompson River

Cache La Poudre River

Grand Lake

LONG'S PEAK

St Vrain

Colorado River (Grand)

UTAH TERRITORY

DIVIDE

St Vrain Creek

CHEROKEE TRAIL

Platte River

• St.Vrain

TERRITORY

Gold Hill

Boulder

Boulder Creek

• Fort Lupton

South Boulder Creek

Dry Creek

South Platte River

Blue River

Nevadaville •

DEADWOOD DIGGINGS

GREGORY x DIGGINGS

Central City •

Mountain City •

Ralston Creek

RALSTON DIGGINGS

Blackhawk

Golden •

Clear Creek

Empire •

JACKSON DIGGINGS

Idaho Springs •

Arapahoe

x Denver

PIKES PEAK REGION 1858-1860

Georgetown

Mt.Vernon •

Auraria

x DRY CREEK DIGGINGS

ARKANSAS

Delaware Flats •

Bradford •

Cherry Creek

PIKES PEAK OR BUST

French Gulch •

Breckenridge •

Parkville •

Plum Cr.

West Plum Creek

East Plum Creek

CHEROKEE TRAIL

SMOKY HILL TRAIL

LEAVENWORTH & PIKES PEAK EXPRESS

CONTINENTAL

• Jefferson

• Russellville

California Gulch

Buckskin •

Oro City •

Tarryall Creek

TERRITORY

Big Sandy Creek

• Fairplay

SOUTH PARK BAYOU SALADE

South Platte River

Cash Creek •

Arkansas River

PIKES PEAK

Colorado • City

Fountain Creek

CONTINENTAL

SANGRE DE CRISTO RANGE

• Canon City

San Luis Creek

Hardscrabble Creek

Arkansas River

Pueblo • Fountain City

CHEROKEE TRAIL

Autobees

River

TAOS TRAIL

Huerfano River

Rio Grande

NEW MEXICO TERRITORY

MILES

5 0   10   20

Drawn under the supervision of LE ROY R. HAFEN

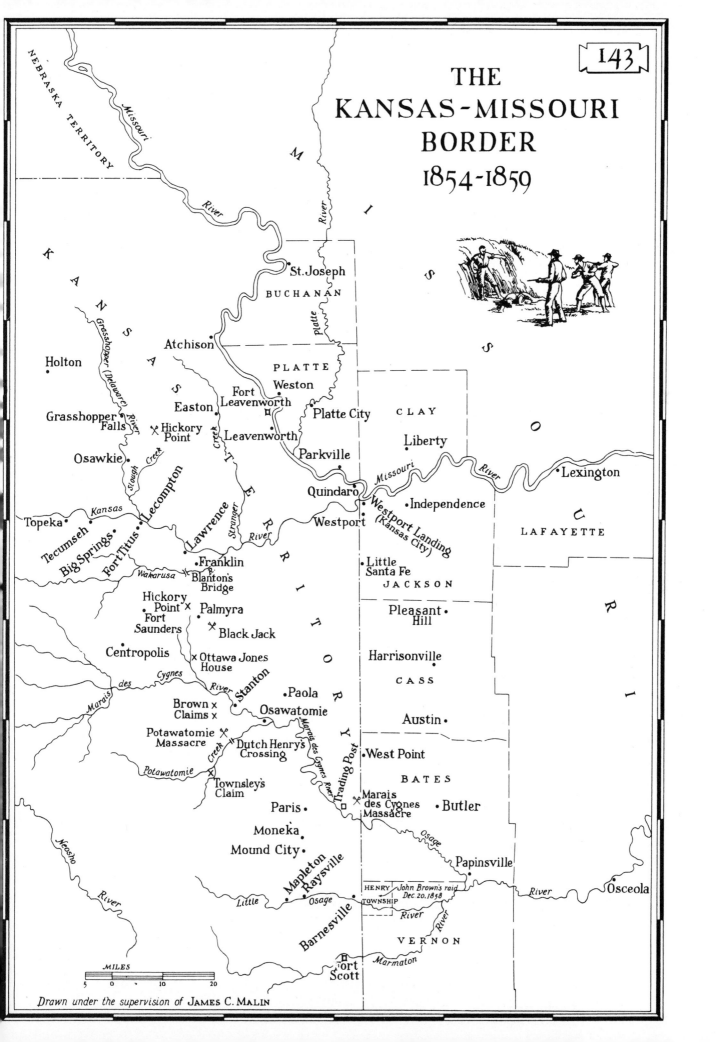

NEBRASKA TERRITORY

Missouri

River

M

I

S

S

O

U

R

I

143

THE
KANSAS-MISSOURI
BORDER
1854-1859

St. Joseph

BUCHANAN

Platte

River

K
A
N
S
A
S

Holton

Atchison

PLATTE

Weston

Fort
Leavenworth

Easton

Grasshopper
Falls

× Hickory
Point

Leavenworth

Platte City

CLAY

Osawkie

Parkville

Liberty

Grasshopper (Delaware) River

Slough

Creek

Lecompton

Quindaro

Missouri

River

Lexington

Topeka

Kansas

Tecumseh

Big Springs

Fort Titus

Lawrence

Stranger

River

Westport

Westport Landing
(Kansas City)

Independence

LAFAYETTE

T
E
R
R
I
T
O
R
Y

Franklin

Wakarusa

Blanton's
Bridge

Little
Santa Fe

JACKSON

Hickory
Point ×
Fort
Saunders

Palmyra

× Black Jack

Pleasant ·
Hill

Centropolis

× Ottawa Jones
House

Harrisonville

CASS

des

Cygnes

River

Stanton

· Paola

Brown ×
Claims ×

Osawatomie

Austin

Marais

Potawatomie ×
Massacre

Dutch Henry's
Crossing

Creek

Marais des Cygnes River

West Point

BATES

Potawatomie

× Townsley's
Claim

Trading Post

Marais
des Cygnes
Massacre

Paris ·

Butler

Moneka

Mound City

Osage

Papinsville

Neosho

River

Mapleton
Raysville

HENRY
TOWNSHIP

John Brown's raid
Dec. 20, 1858

River

River

Osceola

Little

Osage

Barnesville

VERNON

Marmaton

Fort
Scott

MILES

5   0   10   20

Drawn under the supervision of JAMES C. MALIN

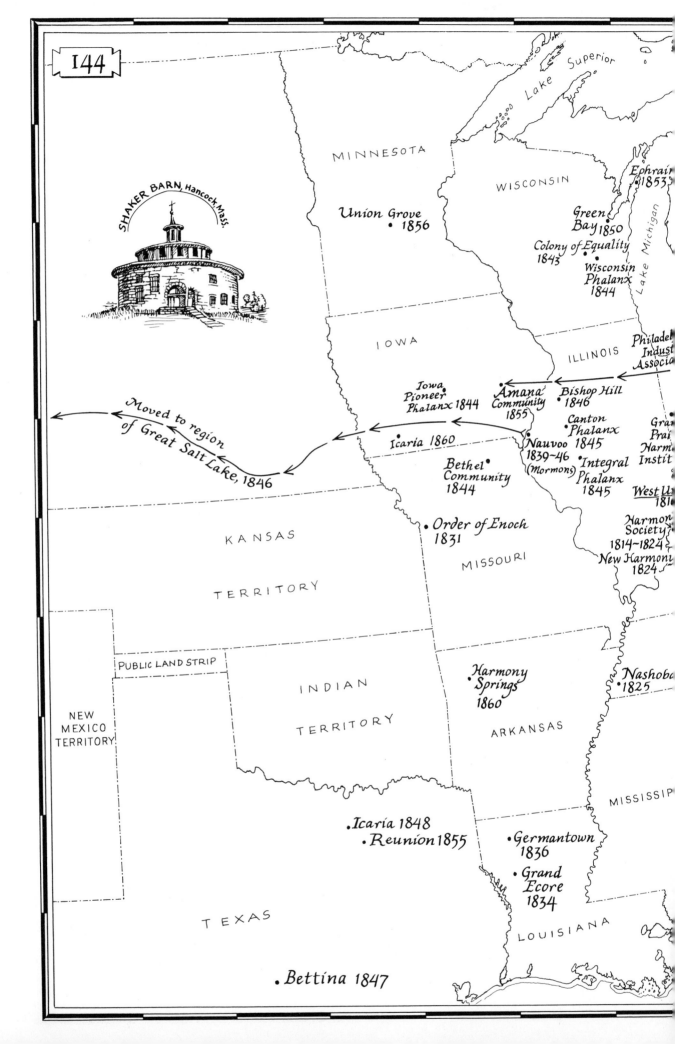

SHAKER BARN, Hancock, Mass.

MINNESOTA

WISCONSIN

Ephrai *1853*

Union Grove • 1856

Green Bay 1850

Colony of Equality 1843

Wisconsin Phalanx 1844

Lake Michigan

Lake Superior

IOWA

ILLINOIS

Philadel Indust Associa

Iowa Pioneer Phalanx 1844

Amana Community 1855

Bishop Hill • 1846

Moved to region of Great Salt Lake, 1846

Icaria 1860

Canton Phalanx 1845

Nauvoo 1839–46 (Mormons)

Integral Phalanx 1845

Gra Prai Harm Instit

Bethel Community 1844

West U 181

Order of Enoch 1831

Harmon Society 1814–1824

New Harmoni 1824

KANSAS

TERRITORY

MISSOURI

PUBLIC LAND STRIP

NEW MEXICO TERRITORY

INDIAN

TERRITORY

Harmony Springs 1860

Nashoba • 1825

ARKANSAS

MISSISSIP

Icaria 1848
• Reunion 1855

Germantown 1836

Grand Ecore 1834

TEXAS

LOUISIANA

• Bettina 1847

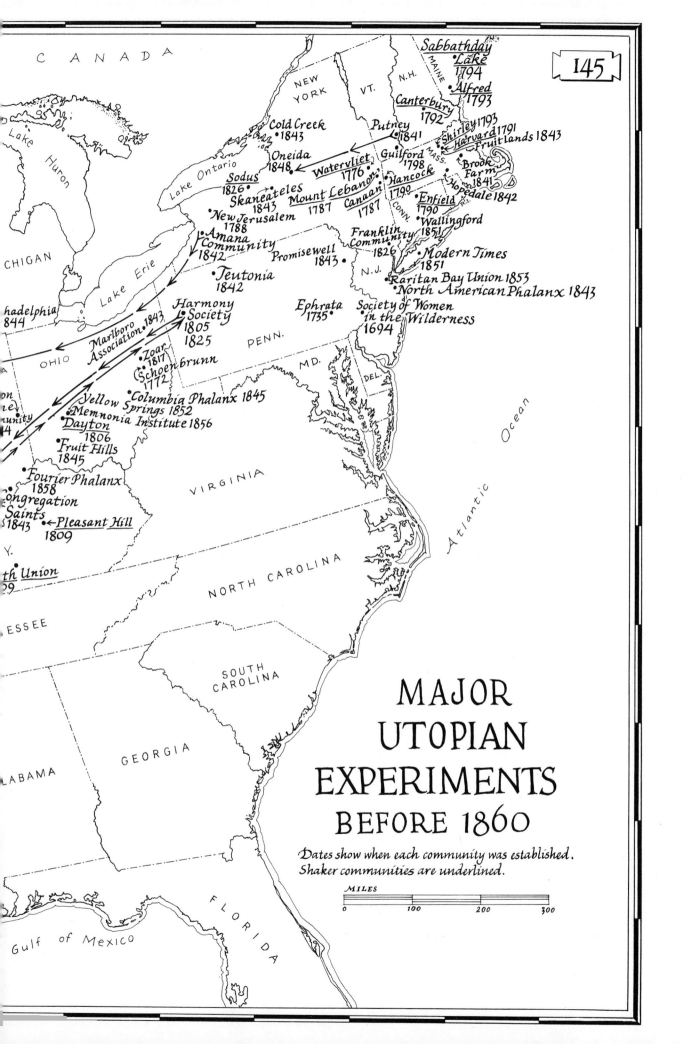

CANADA

Lake Huron

CHIGAN

Lake Ontario

NEW YORK

VT.

N.H.

MAINE

MASS.

CONN.

N.J.

PENN.

OHIO

MD.

DEL.

VIRGINIA

NORTH CAROLINA

SOUTH CAROLINA

GEORGIA

FLORIDA

ALABAMA

ESSEE

Y.

Lake Erie

Gulf of Mexico

Atlantic Ocean

Sabbathday Lake 1794

Alfred 1793

Canterbury 1792

Cold Creek 1843

Putney 1841

Shirley 1793

Harvard 1791

Fruitlands 1843

Oneida 1848

Watervliet 1776

Guilford 1798

Brook Farm 1841

Sodus 1826

Hancock 1790

Hopedale 1842

Skaneateles 1843

Mount Lebanon 1787

Canaan 1787

Enfield 1790

New Jerusalem 1788

Wallingford 1851

Amana Community 1842

Franklin Community 1826

Modern Times 1851

Promisewell 1843

Raritan Bay Union 1853

North American Phalanx 1843

Teutonia 1842

hadelphia 844

Harmony Society 1805 1825

Ephrata 1735

Society of Women in the Wilderness 1694

Marlboro Association 1843

Zoar 1817

Schoenbrunn 1772

Yellow Springs 1852

Columbia Phalanx 1845

Memnonia Institute 1856

Dayton 1806

Fruit Hills 1845

Fourier Phalanx 1858

ongregation Saints 1843

Pleasant Hill 1809

unity 4

th Union 29

MAJOR
UTOPIAN
EXPERIMENTS
BEFORE 1860

Dates show when each community was established.
Shaker communities are underlined.

MILES

0   100   200   300

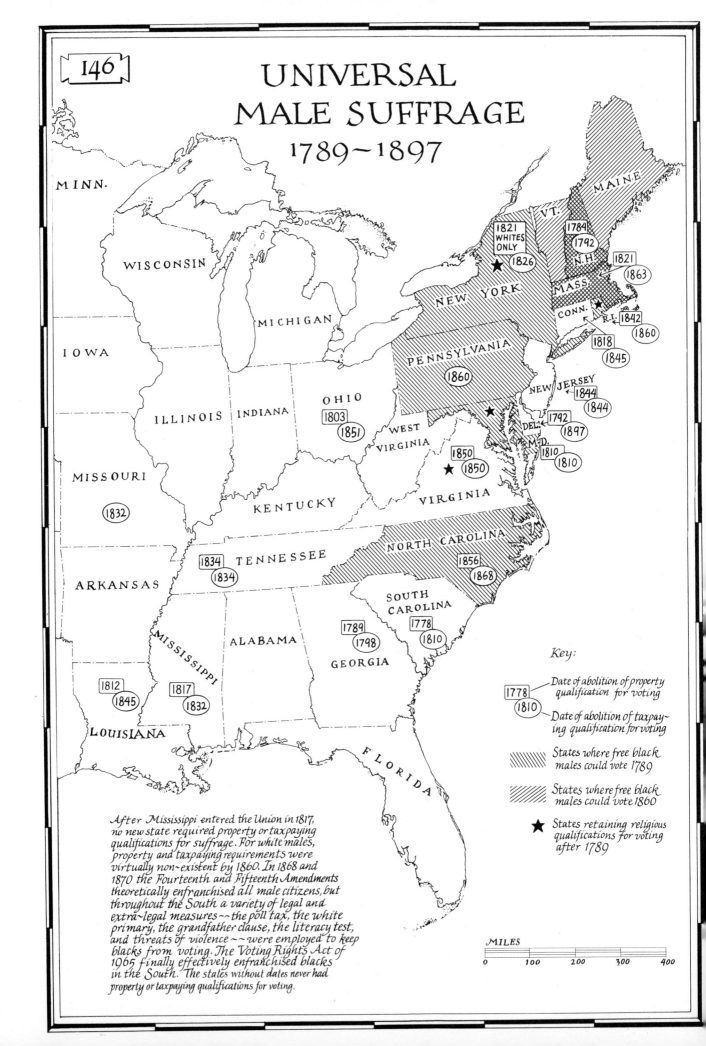

UNIVERSAL MALE SUFFRAGE
1789~1897

146

MINN.

WISCONSIN

MICHIGAN

IOWA

ILLINOIS INDIANA OHIO
1803
1851

MISSOURI
1832

KENTUCKY

WEST VIRGINIA

VIRGINIA
1850
1850

ARKANSAS TENNESSEE
1834
1834

NORTH CAROLINA
1856
1868

MISSISSIPPI ALABAMA GEORGIA
1812   1817   1789
1845   1832   1798

SOUTH CAROLINA
1778
1810

LOUISIANA

FLORIDA

MAINE
VT.
1784
1792
N.H.

1821
WHITES
ONLY
1826

NEW YORK

MASS.
CONN.
R.I.
1821
1863
1842
1860

PENNSYLVANIA
1860

1818
1845

NEW JERSEY
1844
1844

DEL.
1792
1897
MD.
1810
1810

Key:

1778   Date of abolition of property
       qualification for voting

1810   Date of abolition of taxpay-
       ing qualification for voting

///   States where free black
      males could vote 1789

///   States where free black
      males could vote 1860

★   States retaining religious
    qualifications for voting
    after 1789

After Mississippi entered the Union in 1817,
no new state required property or taxpaying
qualifications for suffrage. For white males,
property and taxpaying requirements were
virtually non~existent by 1860. In 1868 and
1870 the Fourteenth and Fifteenth Amendments
theoretically enfranchised all male citizens, but
throughout the South a variety of legal and
extra~legal measures ~~ the poll tax, the white
primary, the grandfather clause, the literacy test,
and threats of violence ~~ were employed to keep
blacks from voting. The Voting Rights Act of
1965 finally effectively enfranchised blacks
in the South. The states without dates never had
property or taxpaying qualifications for voting.

MILES
0   100   200   300   400

VII THE CIVIL WAR AND RECONSTRUCTION

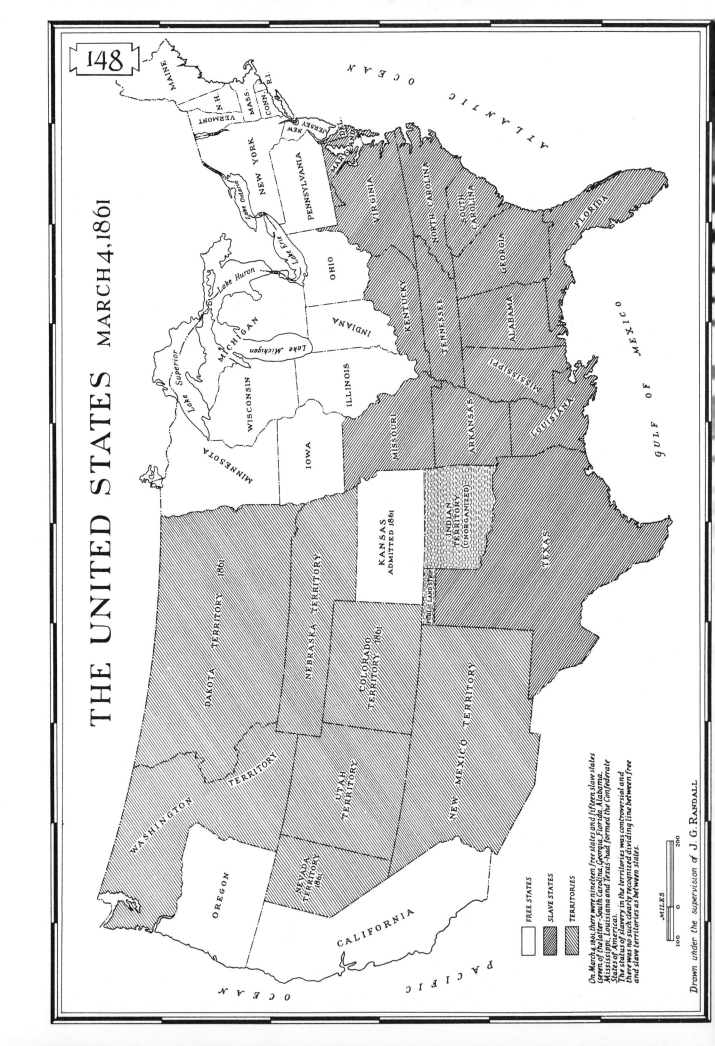

148

THE UNITED STATES MARCH 4, 1861

MAINE

N.H.
VERMONT
MASS.
CONN. R.I.

NEW YORK
NEW JERSEY

PENNSYLVANIA

Lake Ontario
Lake Erie

OHIO

INDIANA

ILLINOIS

MICHIGAN

Lake Huron

Lake Michigan

Lake Superior

WISCONSIN

MINNESOTA

IOWA

MISSOURI

MARYLAND
DEL.

VIRGINIA

NORTH CAROLINA

SOUTH CAROLINA

KENTUCKY

TENNESSEE

GEORGIA

ALABAMA

MISSISSIPPI

ARKANSAS

LOUISIANA

FLORIDA

ATLANTIC OCEAN

GULF OF MEXICO

KANSAS
ADMITTED 1861

INDIAN
TERRITORY
(UNORGANIZED)

PUBLIC LAND STRIP

TEXAS

DAKOTA TERRITORY 1861

NEBRASKA TERRITORY

COLORADO TERRITORY 1861

NEW MEXICO TERRITORY

UTAH TERRITORY

NEVADA TERRITORY 1861

WASHINGTON TERRITORY

OREGON

CALIFORNIA

PACIFIC OCEAN

On March 4, 1861, there were nineteen free states and fifteen slave states
(seven of the latter–South Carolina, Georgia, Florida, Alabama,
Mississippi, Louisiana and Texas–had formed the Confederate
States of America.
The status of slavery in the territories was controversial and
there was no such clearly recognized dividing line between free
and slave territories as between states.

FREE STATES
SLAVE STATES
TERRITORIES

MILES
100   0   200

Drawn under the supervision of J. G. RANDALL.

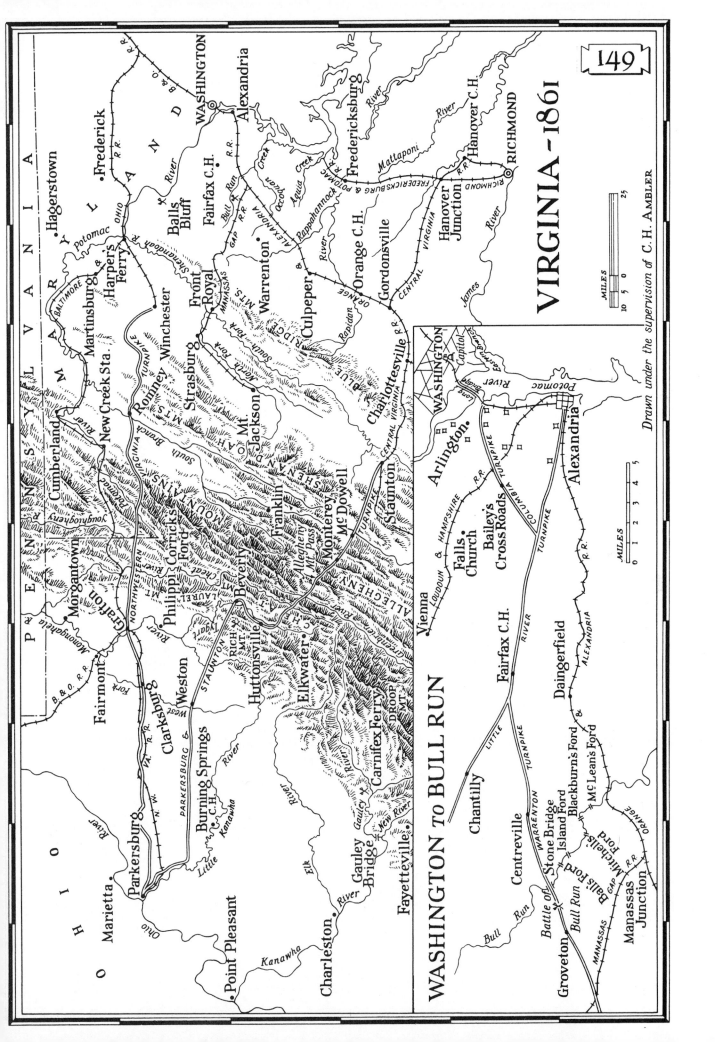

149

VIRGINIA – 1861

Drawn under the supervision of C. H. AMBLER.

MILES
10 5 0 25

WASHINGTON TO BULL RUN

MILES
0 1 2 3 4 5

PENNSYLVANIA

OHIO

MARYLAND

Hagerstown
Frederick
Cumberland
New Creek Sta.
Martinsburg
Harpers Ferry
Winchester
Romney
Strasburg
Front Royal
Warrenton
Culpeper
Orange C.H.
Gordonsville
Hanover Junction
Hanover C.H.
RICHMOND
Fredericksburg
Alexandria
WASHINGTON
Fairfax C.H.
Balls Bluff

Mt. Jackson
Franklin
Monterey
McDowell
Staunton
Charlottesville
Beverly
Huttonsville
Philippi
Corricks Ford
Elkwater
Carnifex Ferry
Gauley Bridge
Fayetteville
Weston
Clarksburg
Grafton
Fairmont
Morgantown
Parkersburg
Burning Springs
Point Pleasant
Marietta
Charleston

Blue Ridge Mts.
Shenandoah Mts.
Alleghen Mts.
Laurel Mt.
Rich Mt.
Cheat Mt.
Droop Mt.
Allegheny Mt. Pass

Potomac River
Shenandoah R.
Rappahannock River
Rapidan River
James
Mattaponi
Aquia Creek
Occoquan Creek
Bull Run
North Fork
South Fork
South Branch
Greenbrier River
Gauley River
New River
Kanawha River
Little Kanawha River
Elk River
Ohio River
Monongahela R.
Youghiogheny R.
Tygart River
Cheat River

B. & O. R.R.
BALTIMORE & OHIO
VALLEY TURNPIKE
MANASSAS GAP R.R.
ALEXANDRIA & ORANGE R.R.
ORANGE R.R.
VIRGINIA CENTRAL
CENTRAL VIRGINIA R.R.
FREDERICKSBURG & POTOMAC R.R.
NORTHWESTERN VIRGINIA R.R.
PARKERSBURG & N.W.R.R.
STAUNTON & PARKERSBURG TURNPIKE
VA. C. R.R.

Arlington
Falls Church
Baileys Cross Roads
Vienna
Fairfax C.H.
Daingerfield
Chantilly
Centreville
Stone Bridge
Island Ford
Blackburn's Ford
McLean's Ford
Balls Ford
Mitchells Ford
Manassas Junction
Groveton
Battle of Bull Run

Capitol
Long Bridge
Eastern Branch
Potomac River

LOUDOUN & HAMPSHIRE R.R.
COLUMBIA TURNPIKE
LITTLE RIVER TURNPIKE
WARRENTON TURNPIKE
MANASSAS GAP R.R.
ORANGE R.R.
ALEXANDRIA R.R.

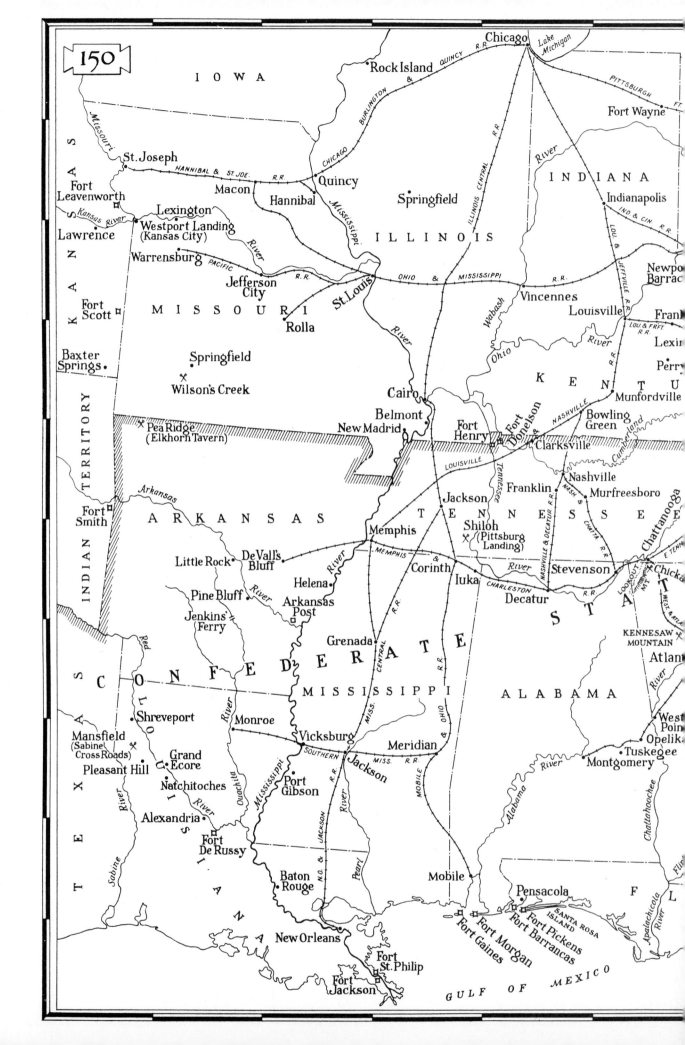

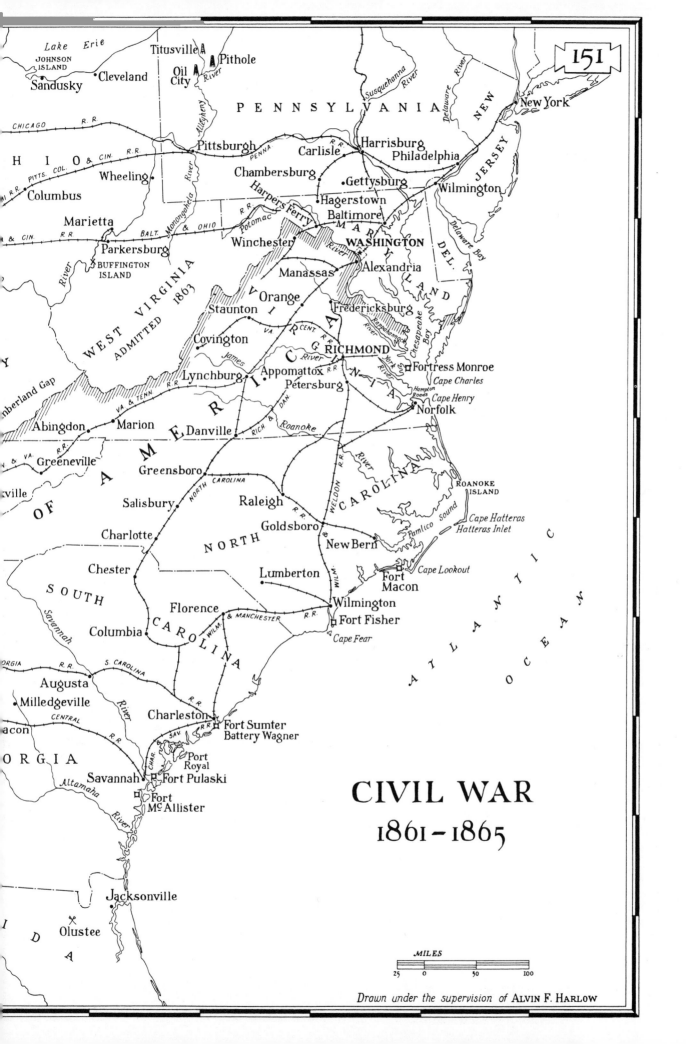

151

Lake Erie
JOHNSON ISLAND
Sandusky
Cleveland
Titusville
Oil City
Pithole
Allegheny River
PENNSYLVANIA
Susquehanna River
Delaware River
NEW
New York
CHICAGO R.R.
O H I O
PITTS. COL. R.R.
CIN. R.R.
Wheeling
Pittsburgh
PENNA. R.R.
Carlisle
Harrisburg
JERSEY
Philadelphia
Columbus
Monongahela River
Chambersburg
Gettysburg
Wilmington
Marietta
BALT. & OHIO R.R.
Harpers Ferry
Hagerstown
Baltimore
DEL.
& CIN. R.R.
Parkersburg
Winchester
Potomac River
MARYLAND
Delaware Bay
BUFFINGTON ISLAND
WASHINGTON
WEST VIRGINIA
ADMITTED 1863
Manassas
Alexandria
River
V
Orange
Staunton
I
VA. R.R.
CENT. R.R.
Fredericksburg
Rappahannock River
Chesapeake Bay
Covington
R
G
RICHMOND
James River
I
York River
Fortress Monroe
Cape Charles
mberland Gap
Lynchburg
Appomattox
N
Hampton Roads
Cape Henry
VA. & TENN. R.R.
Petersburg
I
Norfolk
A
Abingdon
Marion
Danville
RICH. & DAN. R.R.
Roanoke River
E
& VA. R.R.
Greeneville
O F
Greensboro
NORTH CAROLINA
WELDON R.R.
CAROLINA
ROANOKE ISLAND
xville
A
Salisbury
Raleigh
River
Pamlico Sound
Cape Hatteras
Hatteras Inlet
M
Charlotte
Goldsboro
New Bern
E
NORTH
Chester
Lumberton
WILM. R.R.
Cape Lookout
Fort Macon
R
SOUTH
Florence
& MANCHESTER R.R.
Wilmington
A T L A N T I C
Savannah River
CAROLINA
WILM. R.R.
Fort Fisher
Columbia
Cape Fear
ORGIA
S. CAROLINA R.R.
O C E A N
Augusta
Milledgeville
CENTRAL R.R.
River
CHAR. R.R.
Charleston
Fort Sumter
Battery Wagner
acon
SAV. R.R.
ORGIA
Port Royal
Savannah
Fort Pulaski
Altamaha River
Fort McAllister
River
Jacksonville
I
Olustee
D
A

CIVIL WAR
1861-1865

MILES
25   0   50   100

Drawn under the supervision of ALVIN F. HARLOW

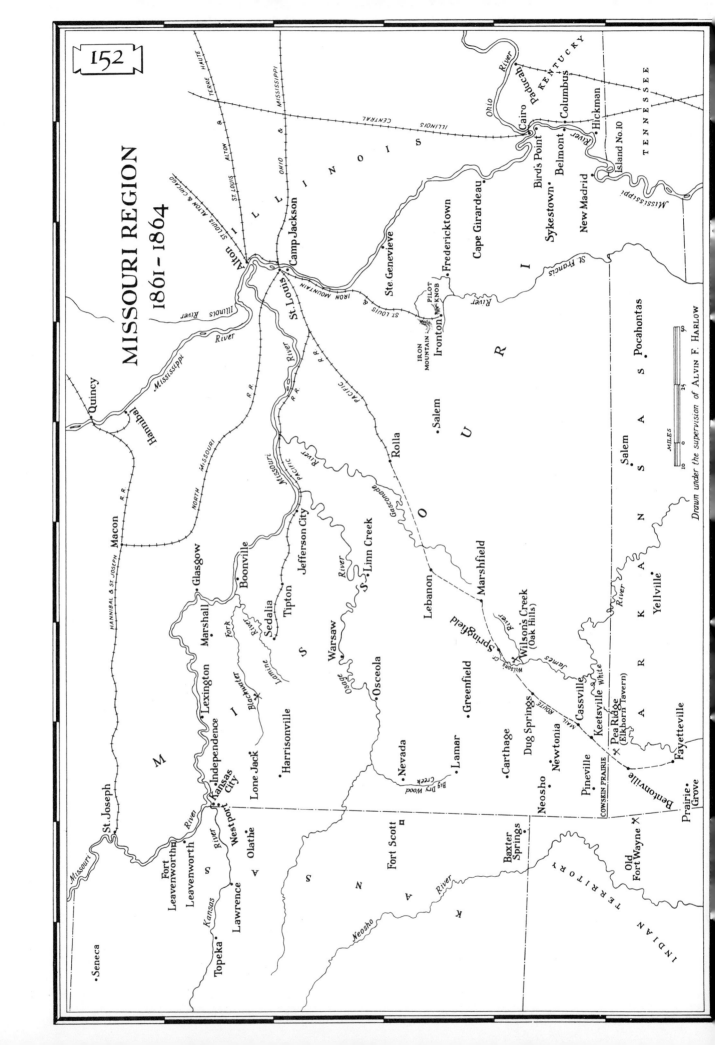

152

MISSOURI REGION
1861–1864

Drawn under the supervision of ALVIN F. HARLOW

MILES

ILLINOIS

KENTUCKY

TENNESSEE

Ohio River

Cairo
Paducah
Birds Point
Columbus
Belmont
Hickman
Sykestown
New Madrid
Island No. 10
Mississippi River

St. Louis
Camp Jackson
Alton
TERRE HAUTE
ST. LOUIS, ALTON & CHICAGO
ST. LOUIS & ALTON
ILLINOIS CENTRAL

Ste. Genevieve
Fredericktown
Cape Girardeau
ST. LOUIS & IRON MOUNTAIN R.R.
IRON MOUNTAIN
Ironton
PILOT KNOB
St. Francis River

M I S S O U R I

Quincy
Hannibal
Mississippi River
Illinois River
Missouri River
NORTH MISSOURI R. R.
HANNIBAL & ST. JOSEPH R. R.
Macon

St. Joseph
Fort Leavenworth
Leavenworth
Lawrence
Topeka
Seneca
Kansas River

K A N S A S

Westport
Olathe
Kansas City
Independence
Lone Jack
Harrisonville

Lexington
Marshall
Glasgow
Boonville
Sedalia
Tipton
Jefferson City
PACIFIC R. R.
PACIFIC R.R.
Lamine River
Blackwater Fork
Osage River
Warsaw
Osceola
Linn Creek
Gasconade River
Rolla
Salem

Fort Scott
Nevada
Big Dry Wood Creek
Lamar
Greenfield
Carthage
Neosho
Newtonia
Pineville

Baxter Springs
Neosho River

Dug Springs
Springfield
Wilsons Creek (Oak Hills)
Wilsons Cr.
James River
Marshfield
Lebanon

Cassville
Keetsville
Pea Ridge (Elkhorn Tavern)
COWSKIN PRAIRIE
MAIL ROUTE
White River
Bentonville
Prairie Grove
Old Fort Wayne
Fayetteville
Yellville

A R K A N S A S

Salem
Pocahontas

INDIAN TERRITORY

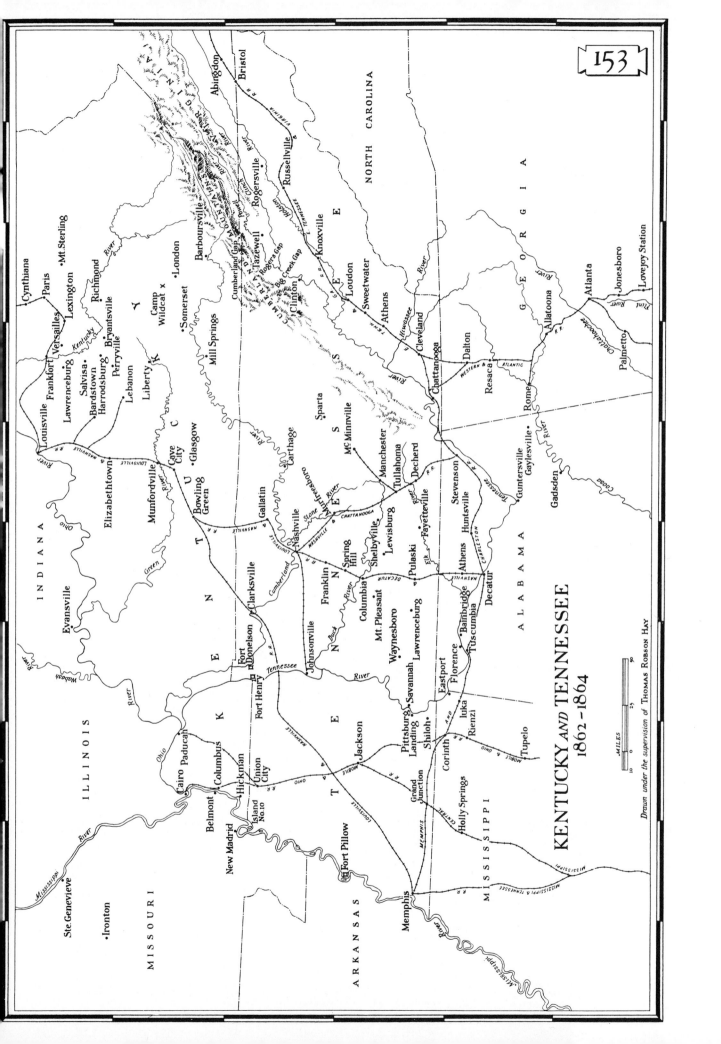

153

KENTUCKY AND TENNESSEE
1862–1864

Drawn under the supervision of THOMAS ROBSON HAY

MILES

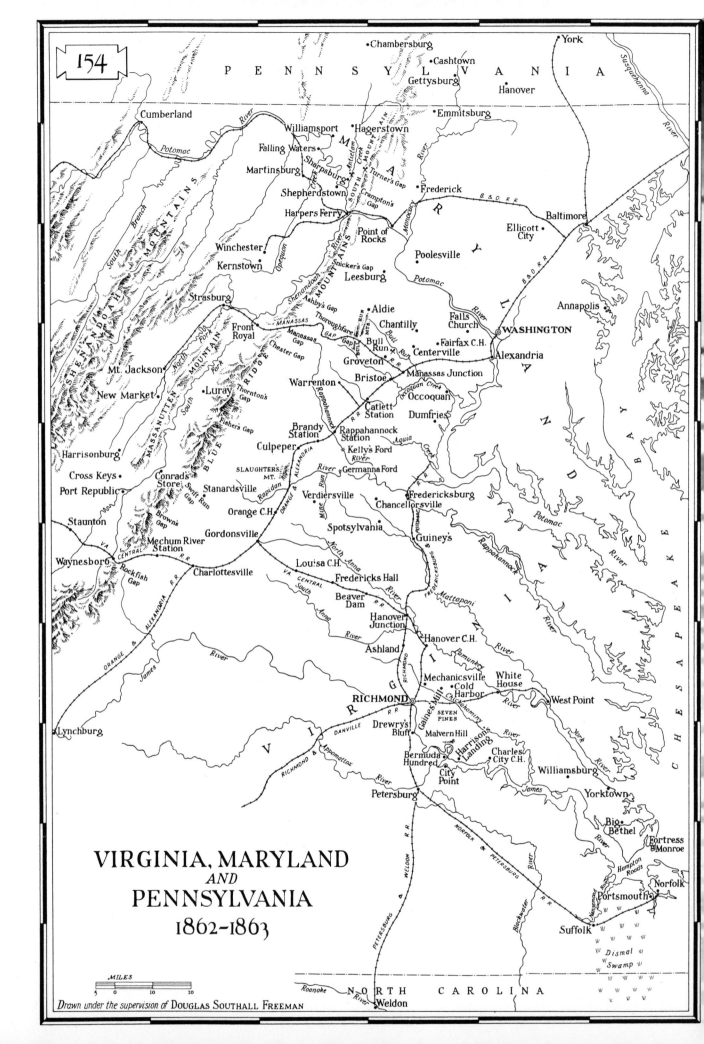

**VIRGINIA, MARYLAND
AND
PENNSYLVANIA
1862-1863**

Drawn under the supervision of DOUGLAS SOUTHALL FREEMAN

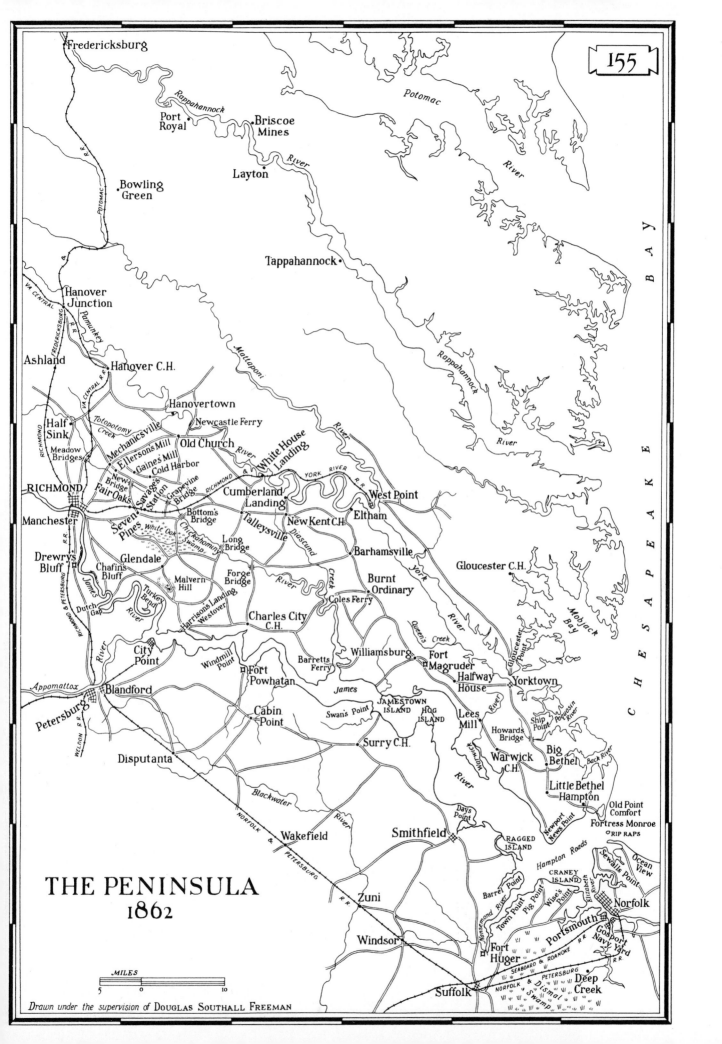

THE PENINSULA
1862

Fredericksburg

Port Royal

Briscoe Mines

Rappahannock River

Layton

Potomac River

BAY

Bowling Green

Tappahannock

Rappahannock River

Hanover Junction

Mattaponi River

Ashland

Hanover C.H.

Half Sink

Hanovertown

Newcastle Ferry

CHESAPEAKE

Meadow Bridges

Mechanicsville

Ellerson's Mill

Old Church

White House Landing

Gaines Mill

Cold Harbor

York River

RICHMOND

New Bridge

Fair Oaks

Savage's Station

Grapevine Bridge

West Point

Cumberland Landing

Eltham

Manchester

Seven Pines

Bottom's Bridge

White Oak Swamp

Chickahominy

Talleysville

New Kent C.H.

Diascund

Gloucester C.H.

Drewrys Bluff

Glendale

Long Bridge

Barhamsville

Mobjack Bay

Chafin's Bluff

Malvern Hill

Forge Bridge

Burnt Ordinary

Turkey Bend

James River

Coles Ferry

Queen's Creek

Dutch Gap

Harrisons Landing

Westover

Charles City C.H.

Gloucester Point

Williamsburg

Fort Magruder

City Point

Windmill Point

Fort Powhatan

Barretts Ferry

Halfway House

Yorktown

Appomattox

Blandford

Cabin Point

James River

Swan's Point

JAMESTOWN ISLAND

HOG ISLAND

Lees Mill

Ship Point

Poquosin River

Petersburg

Surry C.H.

Howards Bridge

Warwick C.H.

Big Bethel

Back River

Disputanta

Blackwater River

Little Bethel

Hampton

Old Point Comfort

Fortress Monroe

RIP RAPS

Wakefield

Days Point

Smithfield

RAGGED ISLAND

Newport News Point

Ocean View

Sewalls Point

Zuni

Hampton Roads

CRANEY ISLAND

Barrel Point

Wise's Point

Norfolk

Windsor

Fort Huger

Pig Point

Town Point

Nansemond River

Elizabeth River

Portsmouth

Gosport Navy Yard

SEABOARD & ROANOKE R.R.

NORFOLK & PETERSBURG R.R.

Suffolk

DISMAL SWAMP

Deep Creek

MILES

5   0   10

Drawn under the supervision of DOUGLAS SOUTHALL FREEMAN

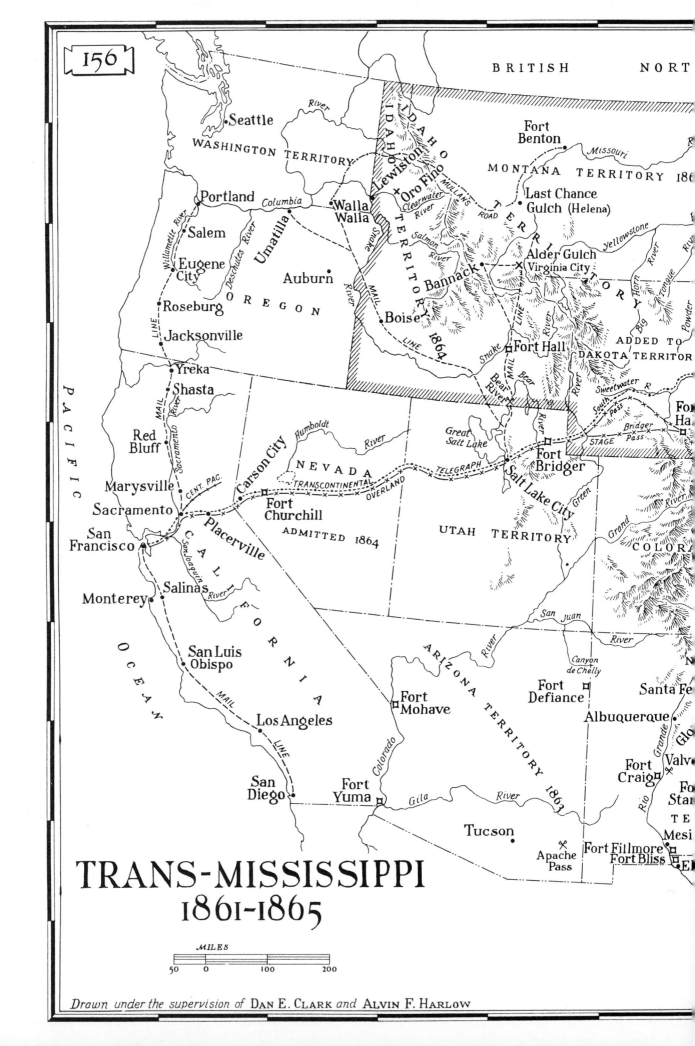

156

BRITISH   NORT

Seattle

WASHINGTON TERRITORY

Fort
Benton

Missouri

MONTANA TERRITORY 186

IDAHO

Lewiston

Oro Fino

Clearwater River

Last Chance
Gulch (Helena)

MULLANS ROAD

Yellowstone River

Portland

Columbia

Salem

Walla
Walla

Willamette River

Umatilla

Deschutes River

OREGON

Eugene
City

Auburn

Roseburg

Jacksonville

Yreka

Shasta

Red
Bluff

Marysville

Sacramento

San
Francisco

Placerville

Salinas

Monterey

San Luis
Obispo

Los Angeles

San
Diego

Fort
Yuma

MAIL LINE

Sacramento River

CENT. PAC.

Carson City

Fort
Churchill

NEVADA

Humboldt River

TRANSCONTINENTAL

ADMITTED 1864

San Joaquin River

CALIFORNIA

PACIFIC   OCEAN

MAIL LINE

MAIL LINE

IDAHO TERRITORY 1864

Salmon River

Snake River

Bannack

Boise

Fort Hall

Bear River

Great
Salt Lake

OVERLAND

TELEGRAPH

Salt Lake City

UTAH TERRITORY

Alder Gulch
Virginia City

TERRITORY

ADDED TO
DAKOTA TERRITOR

Snake River

Bear River

Fort
Bridger

Green River

Sweetwater R.

South Pass

Bridger Pass

STAGE

Fo
Ha

Fo

COLORA

San Juan River

San Juan River

Grand River

Colorado

ARIZONA TERRITORY 1863

Fort
Mohave

Gila River

Tucson

Apache
Pass

Canyon
de Chelly

Fort
Defiance

Santa Fe

Albuquerque

Rio Grande

Fort
Craig

Valv

Glo

Fo
Sta

Fort Fillmore
Fort Bliss

Mesi

T E

E

TRANS-MISSISSIPPI
1861-1865

MILES

50   0   100   200

Drawn under the supervision of DAN E. CLARK *and* ALVIN F. HARLOW

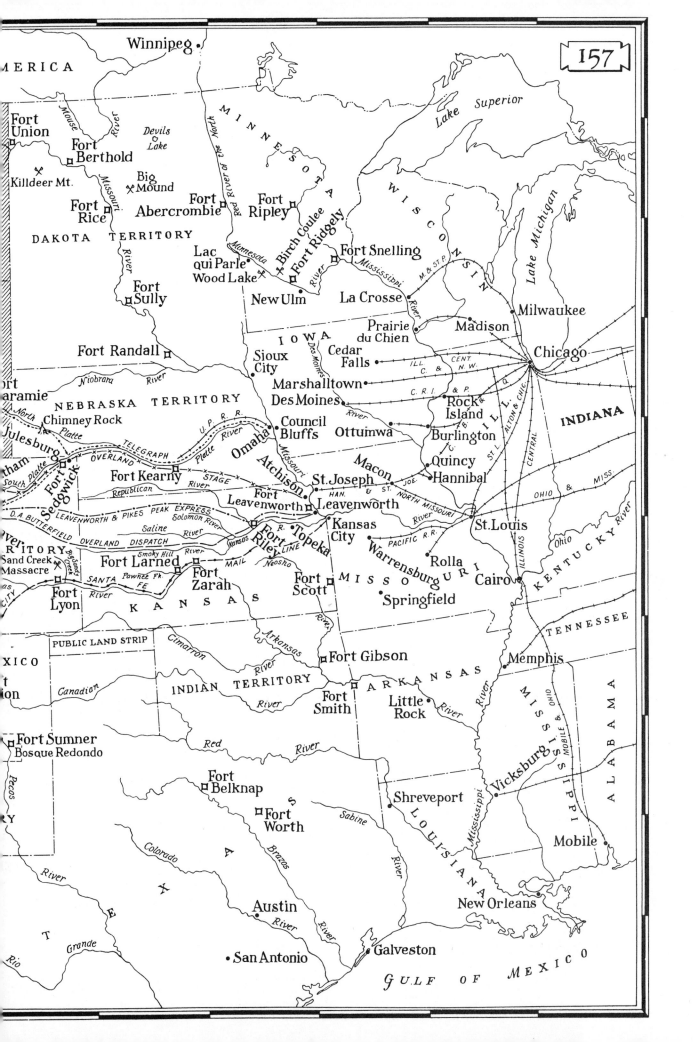

Winnipeg

MERICA

Fort
Union

Mouse River

Devils
Lake

Fort
Berthold

Killdeer Mt.

Big
Mound

Missouri River

Fort
Rice

Fort
Abercrombie

DAKOTA   TERRITORY

MINNESOTA

Red River of the North

Fort
Ripley

LAKE Superior

WISCONSIN

River

Birch Coulee
Fort Ridgely

Fort Snelling

M. & ST. P.

Fort
Sully

Lac
qui Parle
Wood Lake

Minnesota River

New Ulm

La Crosse

Mississippi River

Lake Michigan

Milwaukee

Prairie
du Chien

Madison

Fort Randall

IOWA

Sioux
City

Cedar
Falls

Chicago

ort
aramie

Niobrara   River

NEBRASKA   TERRITORY

Marshalltown

Des Moines

ILL.
C. &

CENT.
N. W.

INDIANA

Chimney Rock

North Platte

U. P. R. R.

Council
Bluffs

Ottumwa

C. R. I.   & P.

Rock &
Island

& Q.

Julesburg

TELEGRAPH

Platte River

Omaha

Des Moines River

Burlington

ST. L.
ALTON & CHIC.

tham

OVERLAND

Atchison

Missouri River

Quincy

ILL.

Fort
Sedgwick

South Platte

Fort Kearny

STAGE

St. Joseph

Macon

Hannibal

CENTRAL

Republican River

Fort
Leavenworth

HAN. & ST.
JOE.

NORTH MISSOURI

OHIO   & MISS.

LEAVENWORTH & PIKES   PEAK   EXPRESS

Leavenworth

St. Louis

KENTUCKY River

D. A. BUTTERFIELD

Saline River

Solomon River

Kansas City

River

OHIO

ver
RITORY

OVERLAND   DISPATCH

Kansas River

Fort
Riley

Topeka

LINE

PACIFIC   R. R.

ILLINOIS

Sand Creek
Massacre

Smoky Hill River

Warrensburg

Rolla

Cairo

Fort Larned

MAIL

Neosho River

Fort
Zarah

Pawnee Fk.

Fort
Scott

MISSOURI

TENNESSEE

CY

SANTA   FE

Fort
Lyon

River

KANSAS

Springfield

PUBLIC LAND STRIP

Cimarron River

Arkansas River

Fort Gibson

Memphis

XICO
t
on

Canadian River

INDIAN   TERRITORY

ARKANSAS

MISSISSIPPI

Fort
Sumner
Bosque Redondo

River

Fort
Smith

Little
Rock

River

Pecos River

Red   River

Fort
Belknap

Mississippi River

MOBILE & OHIO

ALABAMA

Fort
Worth

S

Sabine River

Shreveport

Vicksburg

Mobile

Colorado River

A

Brazos River

LOUISIANA

RY

Rio Grande

T
E
X

Austin

River

River

New Orleans

San Antonio

Galveston

GULF   OF   MEXICO

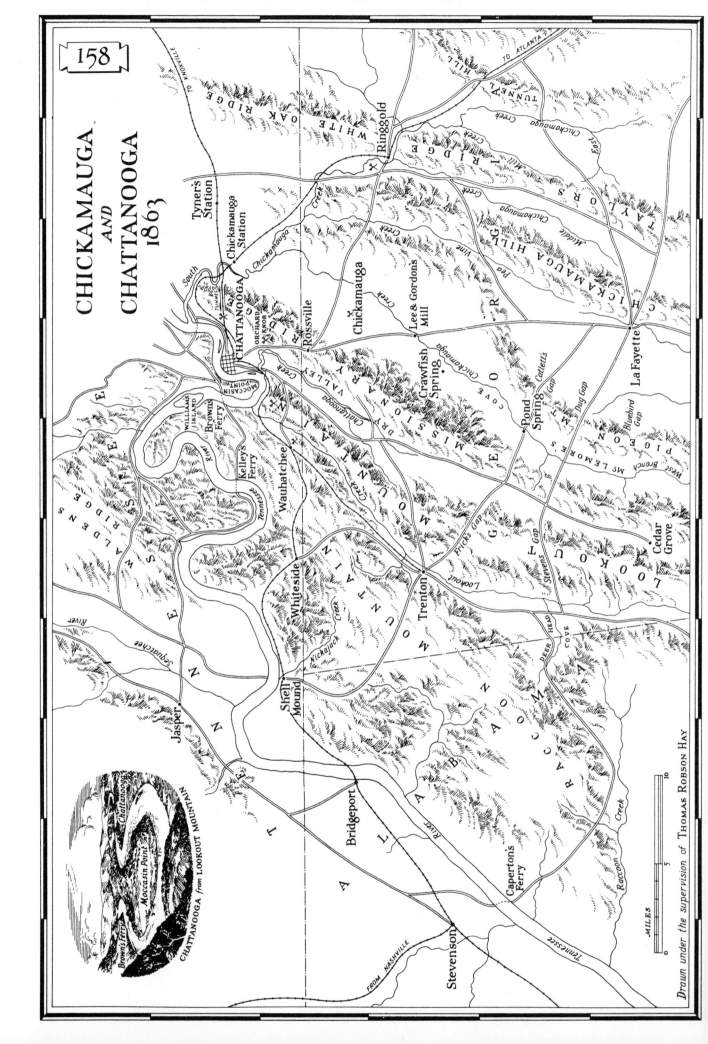

158

CHICKAMAUGA
AND
CHATTANOOGA
1863

TO KNOXVILLE

TO ATLANTA

WHITE OAK RIDGE

Ringgold

TUNNEL HILL

TAYLORS RIDGE

East Chickamauga Creek

Mill Creek

Chickamauga Creek

Tyner's Station

Chickamauga Station

Middle Chickamauga Creek

HICKAMAUGA HILL

South Chickamauga Creek

TUNNEL

CHATTANOOGA

ORCHARD KNOB

Rossville

Chickamauga

Pea Vine Creek

PIGEON Mt LEMORE'S

Bluebird Gap

Bug Gap

Catlett's Gap

La Fayette

MOCCASIN POINT

Lee & Gordons Mill

Crawfish Spring

Pond Spring

Cove Chickamauga

MISSIONARY RIDGE

DRY VALLEY

Chattanooga Creek

WILLIAMS ISLAND

Browns Ferry

Kelley's Ferry

Tennessee River

Wauhatchee

Moccasin Point

WALDENS RIDGE

Whiteside

Nickajack Creek

Lookout Creek

Fricks Gap

Stevens Gap

LOOKOUT Mt

Cedar Grove

West Branch

RACCOON MOUNTAIN

DEER HEAD COVE

Trenton

LOOKOUT MOUNTAIN

ALABAMA

Shell Mound

Jasper

Sequatchee River

TENNESSEE

Bridgeport

Caperton's Ferry

FROM NASHVILLE

Raccoon Creek

Tennessee

Stevenson

MILES
0   5   10

CHATTANOOGA from LOOKOUT MOUNTAIN

Moccasin Point

Chattanooga

Browns Ferry

Drawn under the supervision of THOMAS ROBSON HAY

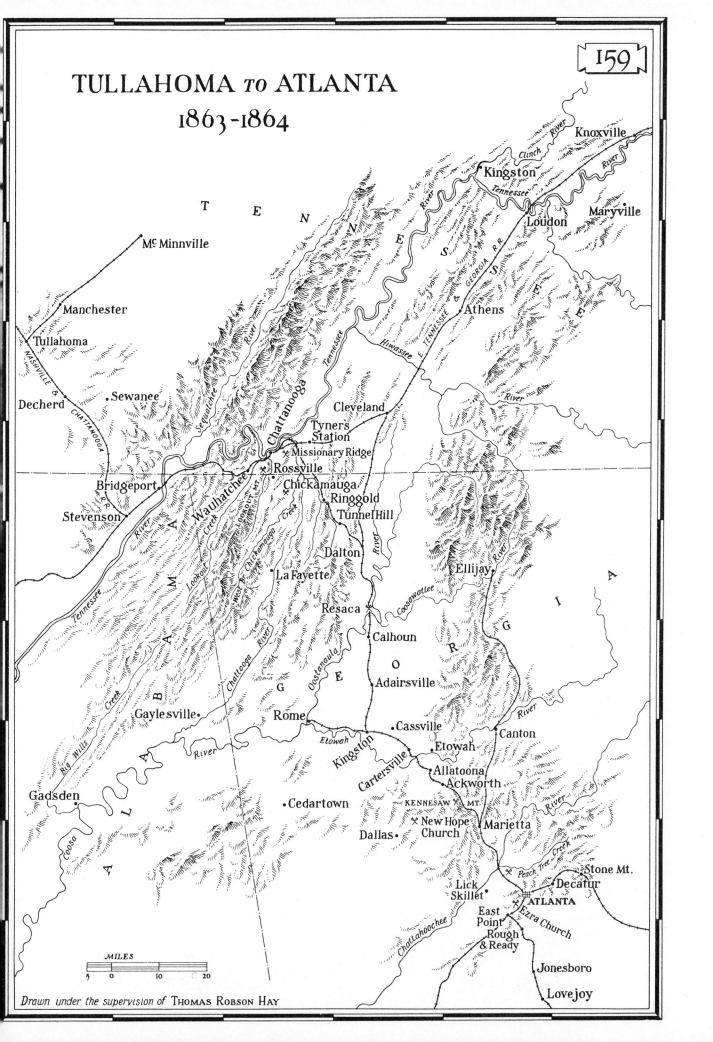

TULLAHOMA TO ATLANTA
1863-1864

T E N N E S S E E

Knoxville

Clinch River

Kingston

Tennessee River

Maryville

McMinnville

Loudon

Manchester

Athens

Hiwassee River

Tullahoma

Cleveland

Sewanee

Tyner's Station

Decherd

Missionary Ridge

Rossville

Chickamauga

Bridgeport

Ringgold

Stevenson

Tunnel Hill

Dalton

Ellijay

La Fayette

G E O R G I A

Resaca

Calhoun

Adairsville

Rome

Cassville

Canton

Gaylesville

Etowah

Etowah

Kingston

Cartersville

Allatoona

Gadsden

Ackworth

Cedartown

KENNESAW MT.

New Hope Church

Marietta

Dallas

Peach Tree Creek

Stone Mt.

Lick Skillet

Decatur

ATLANTA

East Point

Ezra Church

Chattahoochee

Rough & Ready

Jonesboro

Lovejoy

A L A B A M A

Tennessee River

Sequatchee River

Lookout Mt.

Wauhatchee Creek

West Br. Chickamauga

Chattooga River

Oostanaula River

Coosawattee

Big Wills Creek

Coosa River

NASHVILLE & CHATTANOOGA R.R.

E. TENNESSEE & GEORGIA R.R.

MILES

5   0   10   20

Drawn under the supervision of THOMAS ROBSON HAY

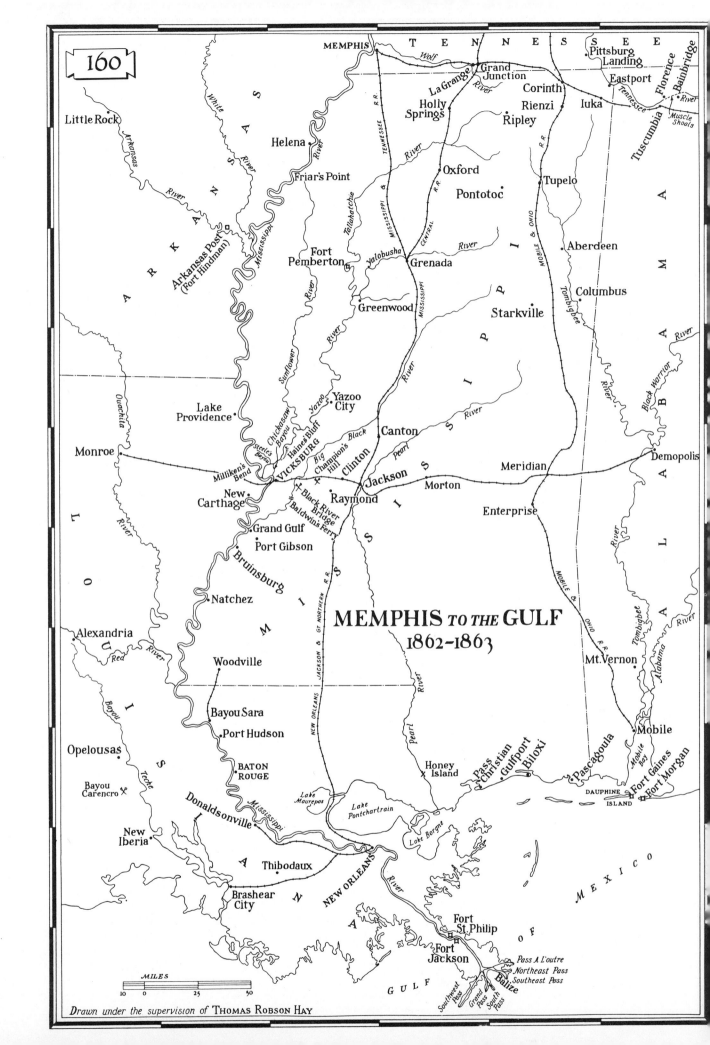

160

TENNESSEE

MEMPHIS

Little Rock

Helena

Friar's Point

ARKANSAS

Arkansas Post
(Fort Hindman)

Fort
Pemberton

Greenwood

Lake
Providence

Monroe

Milliken's
Bend

VICKSBURG

New
Carthage

Grand Gulf

Port Gibson

Bruinsburg

Natchez

Alexandria

Woodville

Bayou Sara

Port Hudson

Opelousas

Bayou
Carencro

BATON
ROUGE

New
Iberia

Donaldsonville

Thibodaux

Brashear
City

LOUISIANA

Pittsburg
Landing

Florence
Bainbridge

La Grange

Grand
Junction

Holly
Springs

Corinth

Rienzi

Eastport

Ripley

Iuka

Tuscumbia

Muscle
Shoals

Oxford

Pontotoc

Tupelo

Grenada

Aberdeen

Columbus

Starkville

MISSISSIPPI

Yazoo
City

Canton

Champion's
Hill

Clinton

Jackson

Raymond

Black River
Bridge

Baldwin's Ferry

Morton

Meridian

Enterprise

ALABAMA

Demopolis

MEMPHIS TO THE GULF
1862-1863

Mt. Vernon

Mobile

Honey
Island

Pass
Christian

Gulfport

Biloxi

Pascagoula

Mobile
Bay

Fort Gaines

Fort Morgan

DAUPHINE
ISLAND

Lake
Maurepas

Lake
Pontchartrain

Lake Borgne

NEW ORLEANS

GULF OF MEXICO

Fort
St. Philip

Fort
Jackson

Pass A L'outre

Northeast Pass

Southeast Pass

Southwest
Pass

Grand
Pass

South
Pass

Balize

MILES
10   0   25   50

Drawn under the supervision of THOMAS ROBSON HAY

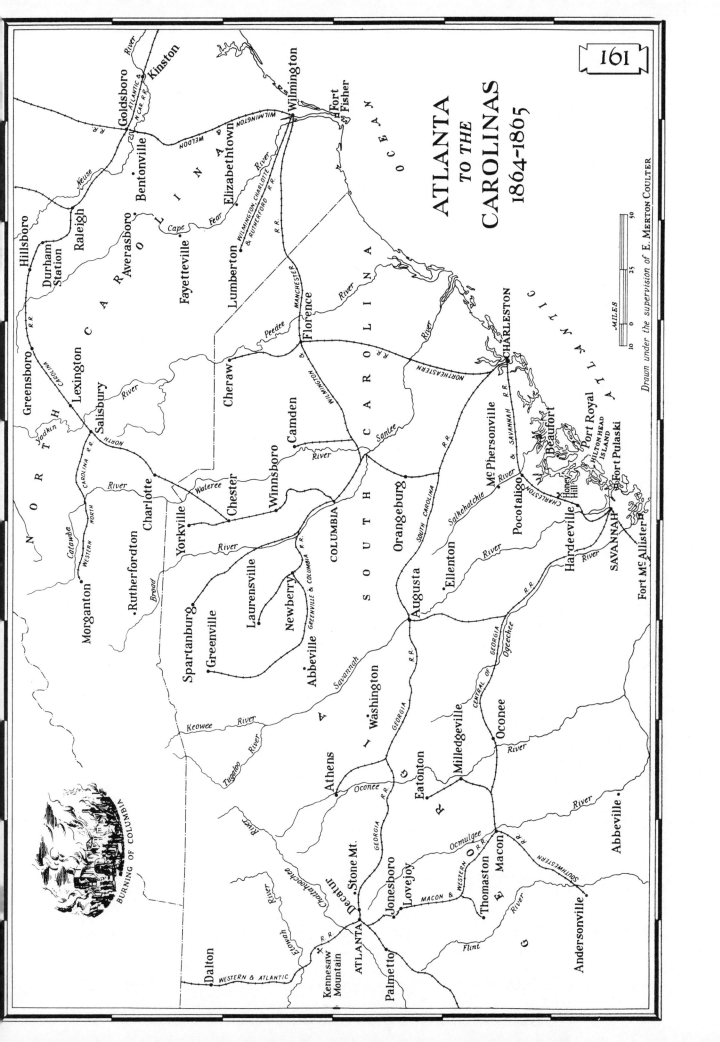

ATLANTA
TO THE
CAROLINAS
1864-1865

Drawn under the supervision of E. MERTON COULTER

MILES

NORTH CAROLINA

SOUTH CAROLINA

GEORGIA

ATLANTIC OCEAN

Kinston
Goldsboro
Hillsboro
Raleigh
Durham Station
Greensboro
Bentonville
Averasboro
Lexington
Fayetteville
Elizabethtown
Wilmington
Fort Fisher
Lumberton
Florence
Cheraw
Salisbury
Camden
Morganton
Rutherfordton
Charlotte
Yorkville
Winnsboro
Chester
COLUMBIA
Spartanburg
Greenville
Laurensville
Newberry
Abbeville
Orangeburg
CHARLESTON
McPhersonville
Beaufort
Port Royal
HILTON HEAD ISLAND
Fort Pulaski
Pocotaligo
Hardeeville
SAVANNAH
Fort McAllister
Honey Hill
Augusta
Ellenton
Washington
Milledgeville
Oconee
Athens
Eatonton
Macon
Thomaston
Abbeville
Andersonville
Dalton
Kennesaw Mountain
ATLANTA
Decatur
Stone Mt.
Jonesboro
Lovejoy
Palmetto

Meuse River
Cape Fear River
Neuse River
Peedee River
Yadkin River
Catawba River
Wateree River
Santee River
Broad River
Saluda River
Savannah River
Keowee River
Tugaloo River
Chattahoochee River
Etowah River
Ocmulgee River
Oconee River
Ogeechee River
Salkehatchie River
Flint River

WILMINGTON & WELDON R.R.
WILMINGTON CHARLOTTE & RUTHERFORD R.R.
ATLANTIC & N. CAR. R.R.
NORTH CAROLINA R.R.
WESTERN NORTH CAROLINA R.R.
MANCHESTER & WILMINGTON R.R.
NORTHEASTERN R.R.
CHARLOTTE & SOUTH CAROLINA R.R.
GREENVILLE & COLUMBIA R.R.
SOUTH CAROLINA R.R.
CHARLESTON & SAVANNAH R.R.
CENTRAL OF GEORGIA R.R.
GEORGIA R.R.
MACON & WESTERN R.R.
SOUTHWESTERN R.R.
WESTERN & ATLANTIC

BURNING OF COLUMBIA

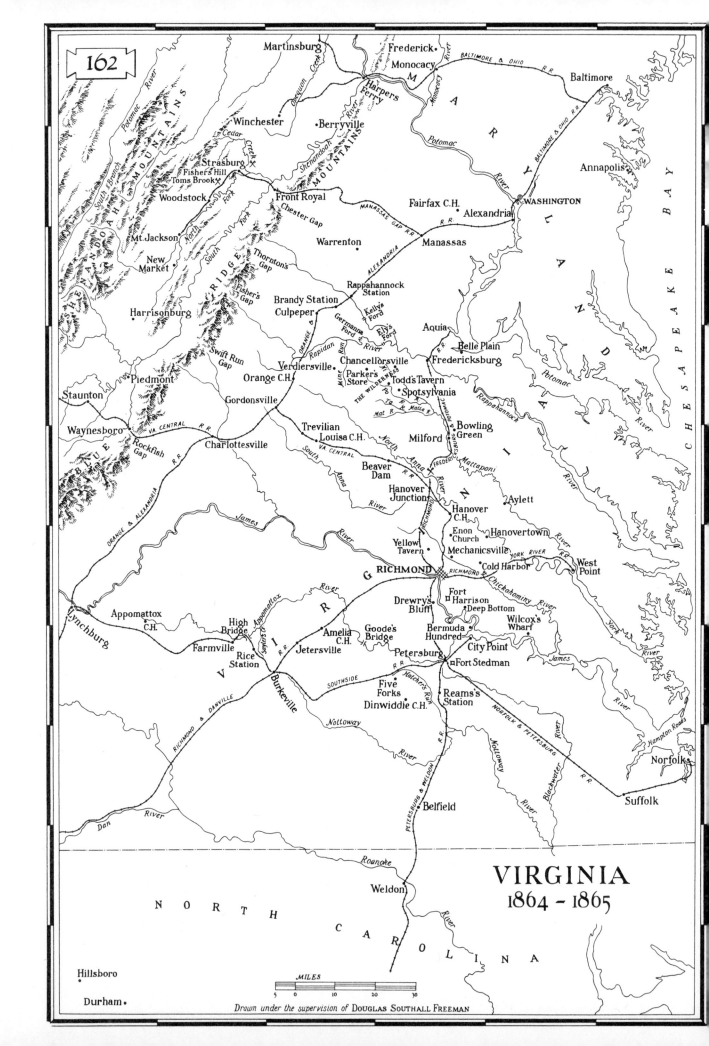

162

Martinsburg
Frederick
Monocacy
Harpers Ferry
BALTIMORE & OHIO R.R.
Baltimore
M
Potomac River
M A R Y L A N D
Annapolis
WASHINGTON
Winchester
Berryville
Fairfax C.H.
Alexandria
Strasburg
Fishers Hill
Toms Brook
Woodstock
Front Royal
Chester Gap
Warrenton
Manassas
Mt. Jackson
New Market
Thornton's Gap
Rappahannock Station
Harrisonburg
Fisher's Gap
Brandy Station
Culpeper
Kelly's Ford
Germanna Ford
Ely's Ford
Aquia
Belle Plain
Fredericksburg
Swift Run Gap
Verdiersville
Chancellorsville
Parker's Store
Todd's Tavern
Spotsylvania
Staunton
Piedmont
Orange C.H.
Gordonsville
THE WILDERNESS
Waynesboro
Rockfish Gap
Charlottesville
Trevilian
Louisa C.H.
Milford
Bowling Green
Aylett
Beaver Dam
Hanover Junction
Hanover C.H.
Enon Church
Hanovertown
Yellow Tavern
Mechanicsville
Cold Harbor
West Point
RICHMOND
Drewry's Bluff
Fort Harrison
Deep Bottom
Wilcox's Wharf
Appomattox C.H.
High Bridge
Amelia C.H.
Goode's Bridge
Bermuda Hundred
City Point
Farmville
Rice Station
Jetersville
Petersburg
Fort Stedman
Lynchburg
Burkeville
Five Forks
Dinwiddie C.H.
Reams's Station
Norfolk
Belfield
Suffolk
Weldon
Hillsboro
Durham

NORTH CAROLINA

VIRGINIA
1864 - 1865

MILES

Drawn under the supervision of DOUGLAS SOUTHALL FREEMAN

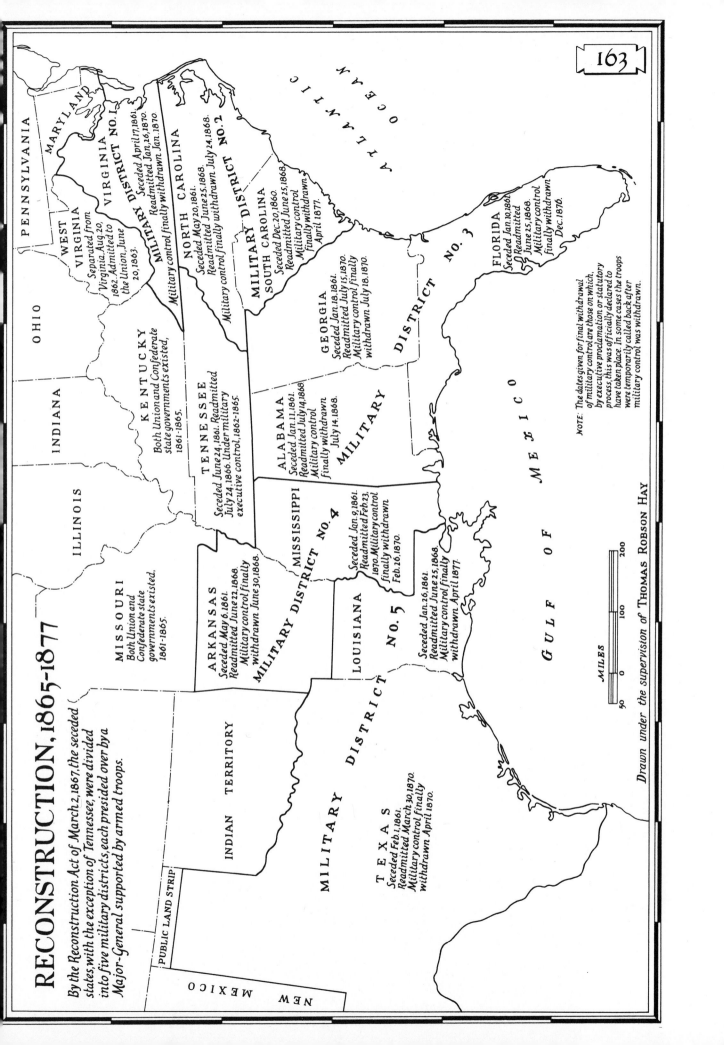

RECONSTRUCTION, 1865-1877

By the Reconstruction Act of March 2, 1867, the seceded states, with the exception of Tennessee, were divided into five military districts, each presided over by a Major-General supported by armed troops.

ATLANTIC OCEAN

PENNSYLVANIA

MARYLAND

WEST VIRGINIA
Separated from Virginia, Aug. 20, 1862. Admitted to the Union, June 20, 1863.

VIRGINIA
MILITARY DISTRICT NO. 1
Seceded April 17, 1861. Readmitted Jan. 26, 1870. Military control finally withdrawn, Jan. 1870.

OHIO

NORTH CAROLINA
Seceded May 20, 1861. Readmitted June 25, 1868. Military control finally withdrawn July 24, 1868.

MILITARY DISTRICT NO. 2

SOUTH CAROLINA
Seceded Dec. 20, 1860. Readmitted June 25, 1868. Military control finally withdrawn April 1877.

INDIANA

KENTUCKY
Both Union and Confederate state governments existed, 1861-1865.

TENNESSEE
Seceded June 24, 1861. Readmitted July 24, 1866. Under military executive control, 1862-1865.

GEORGIA
Seceded Jan. 18, 1861. Readmitted July 15, 1870. Military control finally withdrawn July 18, 1870.

MILITARY DISTRICT NO. 3

ALABAMA
Seceded Jan. 11, 1861. Readmitted July 14, 1868. Military control finally withdrawn July 14, 1868.

MILITARY

FLORIDA
Seceded Jan. 10, 1861. Readmitted June 25, 1868. Military control finally withdrawn Dec. 1876.

ILLINOIS

MISSOURI
Both Union and Confederate state governments existed, 1861-1865.

ARKANSAS
Seceded May 6, 1861. Readmitted June 22, 1868. Military control finally withdrawn June 30, 1868.

MISSISSIPPI
Seceded Jan. 9, 1861. Readmitted Feb. 23, 1870. Military control finally withdrawn Feb. 16, 1870.

MILITARY DISTRICT NO. 4

LOUISIANA
Seceded Jan. 26, 1861. Readmitted June 25, 1868. Military control finally withdrawn April 1877.

MILITARY DISTRICT NO. 5

INDIAN TERRITORY

TEXAS
Seceded Feb. 1, 1861. Readmitted March 30, 1870. Military control finally withdrawn April 1870.

PUBLIC LAND STRIP

NEW MEXICO

GULF OF MEXICO

NOTE: The dates given for final withdrawal of military control are those on which, by executive proclamation or statutory process, this was officially declared to have taken place. In some cases the troops were temporarily called back after military control was withdrawn.

MILES
50 0 100 200

Drawn under the supervision of THOMAS ROBSON HAY

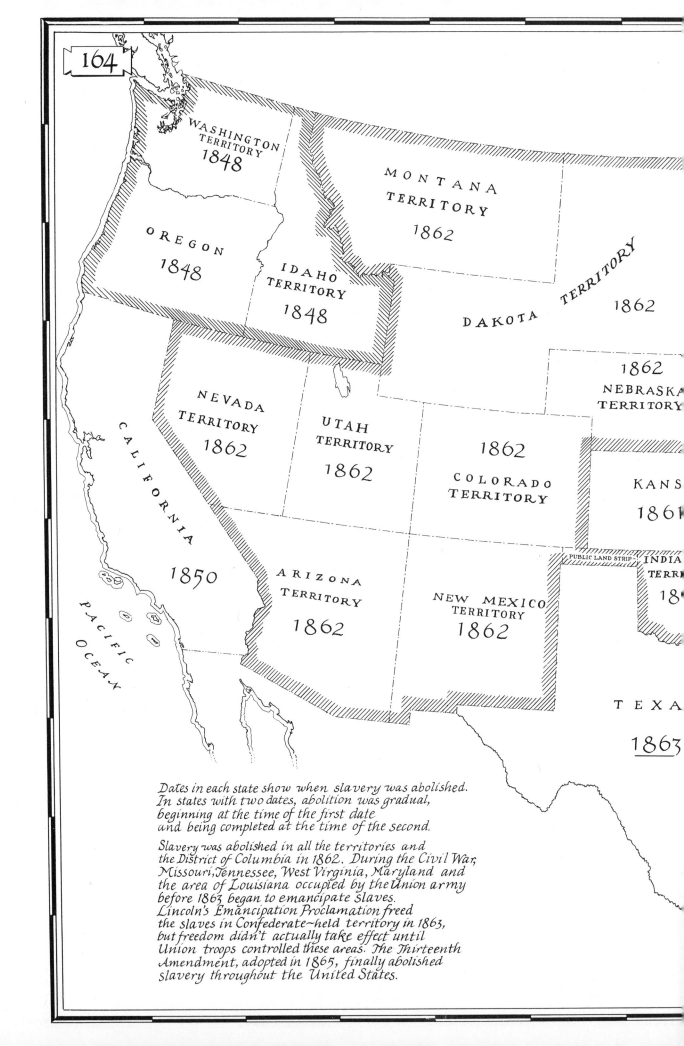

164

WASHINGTON
TERRITORY
1848

OREGON
1848

IDAHO
TERRITORY
1848

MONTANA
TERRITORY
1862

DAKOTA TERRITORY 1862

NEVADA
TERRITORY
1862

UTAH
TERRITORY
1862

1862
COLORADO
TERRITORY

1862
NEBRASKA
TERRITORY

CALIFORNIA
1850

ARIZONA
TERRITORY
1862

NEW MEXICO
TERRITORY
1862

KANS
1861

PUBLIC LAND STRIP

INDIA
TERR

PACIFIC
OCEAN

TEXA
1863

Dates in each state show when slavery was abolished.
In states with two dates, abolition was gradual,
beginning at the time of the first date
and being completed at the time of the second.

Slavery was abolished in all the territories and
the District of Columbia in 1862. During the Civil War,
Missouri, Tennessee, West Virginia, Maryland and
the area of Louisiana occupied by the Union army
before 1863 began to emancipate slaves.
Lincoln's Emancipation Proclamation freed
the slaves in Confederate-held territory in 1863,
but freedom didn't actually take effect until
Union troops controlled these areas. The Thirteenth
Amendment, adopted in 1865, finally abolished
slavery throughout the United States.

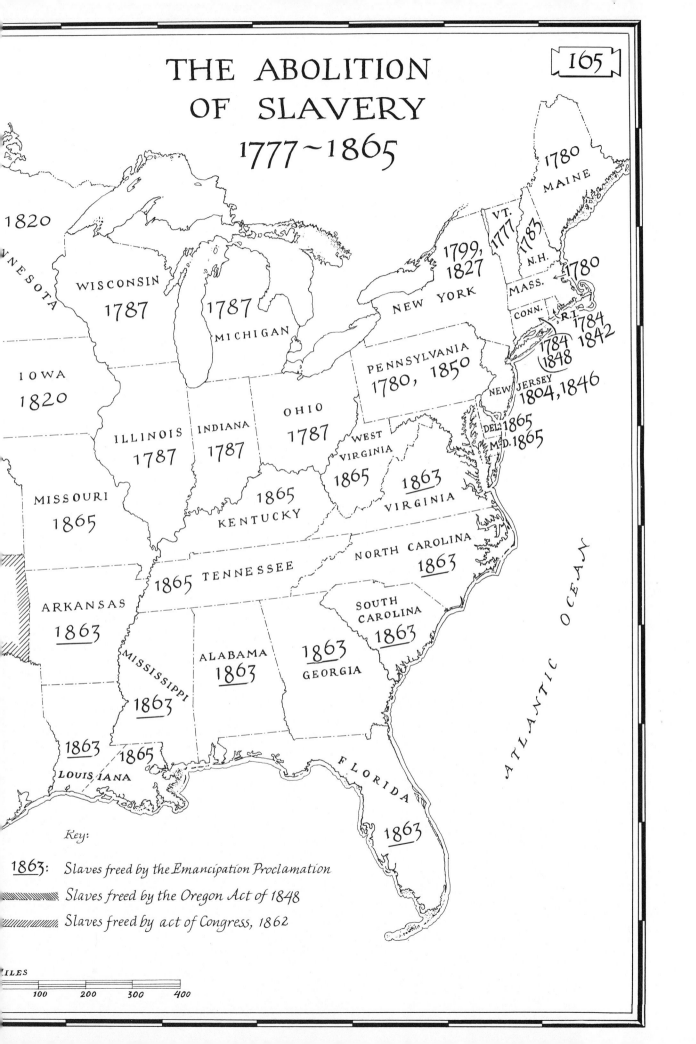

THE ABOLITION OF SLAVERY 1777~1865

Key:

<u>1863</u>: Slaves freed by the Emancipation Proclamation

Slaves freed by the Oregon Act of 1848

Slaves freed by act of Congress, 1862

MILES
100 200 300 400

1820

MINNESOTA

WISCONSIN 1787

1787 MICHIGAN

IOWA 1820

ILLINOIS 1787

INDIANA 1787

OHIO 1787

MISSOURI 1865

1865 KENTUCKY

WEST VIRGINIA 1865

<u>1863</u> VIRGINIA

ARKANSAS <u>1863</u>

1865 TENNESSEE

NORTH CAROLINA <u>1863</u>

SOUTH CAROLINA <u>1863</u>

MISSISSIPPI <u>1863</u>

ALABAMA <u>1863</u>

<u>1863</u> GEORGIA

<u>1863</u> 1865 LOUISIANA

FLORIDA <u>1863</u>

1780 MAINE

VT. 1777

1783

N.H.

1799, 1827 NEW YORK

MASS. 1780

CONN. R.I. 1784

1784 1842

1784 1848

PENNSYLVANIA 1780, 1850

NEW JERSEY 1804, 1846

DEL. 1865

MD. 1865

ATLANTIC OCEAN

VIII THE END OF THE FRONTIER

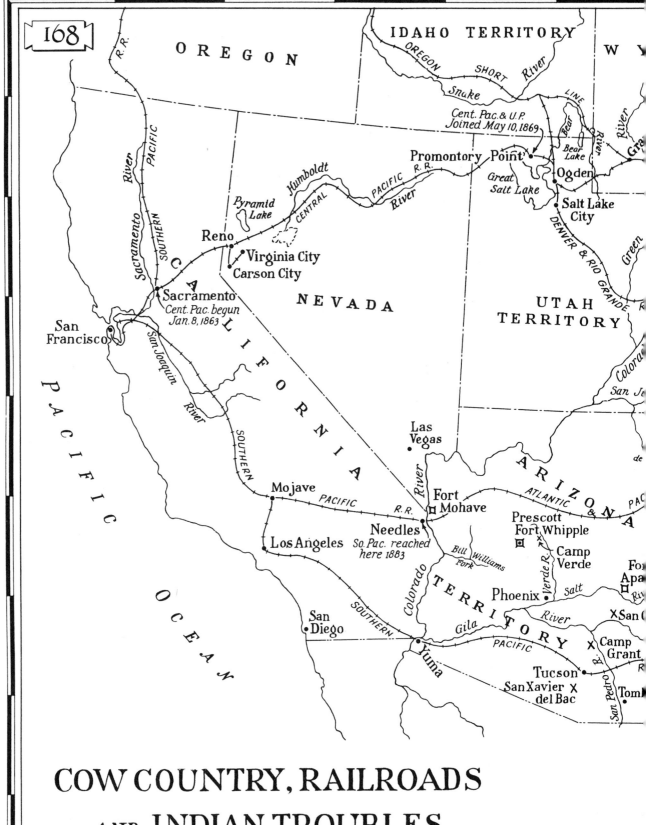

168

IDAHO TERRITORY

OREGON

W Y

Cent. Pac.& U.P.
Joined May 10, 1869

Promontory Point

Ogden

Great Salt Lake

Salt Lake City

Pyramid Lake

Humboldt River

CENTRAL

PACIFIC R.R.

Reno

Virginia City
Carson City

NEVADA

UTAH
TERRITORY

SOUTHERN PACIFIC

Sacramento
Cent. Pac. begun
Jan. 8, 1863

San Francisco

San Joaquin River

C A L I F O R N I A

Las Vegas

DENVER & RIO GRANDE

Colorado

San Jo

P A C I F I C

SOUTHERN

Mojave

PACIFIC

R.R.

Fort Mohave

ARIZONA

ATLANTIC &

PAC

Prescott
Fort Whipple

Camp Verde

Los Angeles

Needles
So. Pac. reached
here 1883

Bill Williams Fork

Verde R.

Phoenix

Salt

Fo
Apa

San C

River

San Diego

SOUTHERN

Colorado

Gila River

T E R R I T O R Y

PACIFIC

Salt

X San C

X Camp Grant

O C E A N

Yuma

Tucson
San Xavier
del Bac

San Pedro R.

Tom

COW COUNTRY, RAILROADS
AND INDIAN TROUBLES
1865-1885

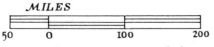

MILES

50   0   100   200

Drawn under the supervision of ALVIN F. HARLOW *and* CARL COKE RISTER

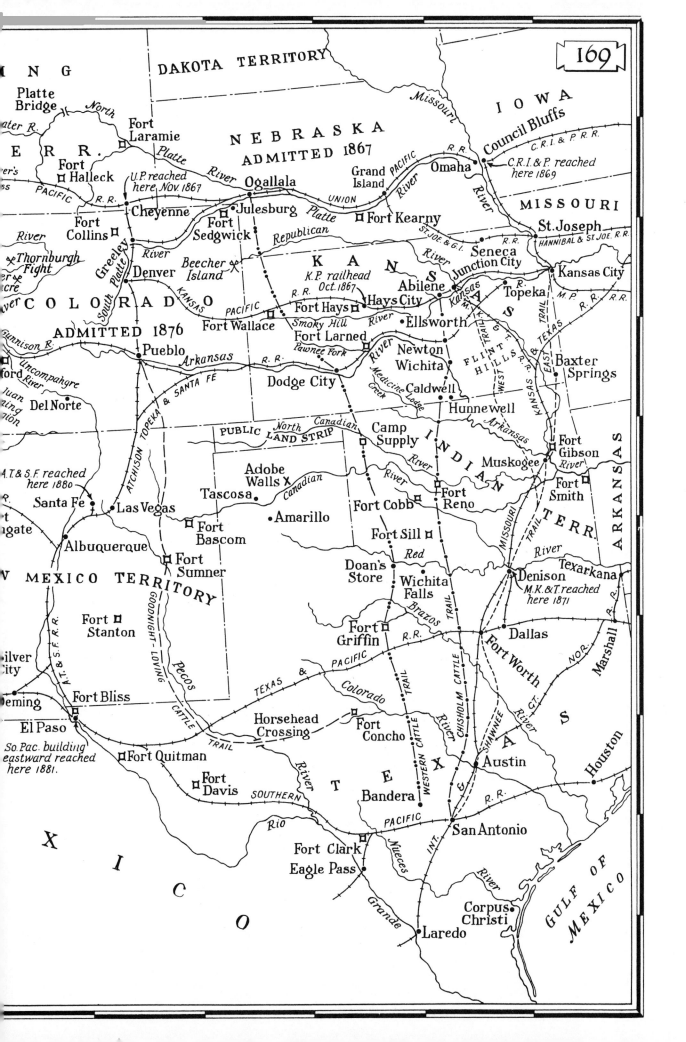

169

WYO

DAKOTA TERRITORY

Platte
Bridge
ater R.

North

ER R.
Fort
Laramie

Platte

Fort
Halleck

U.P. reached
here Nov. 1867

PACIFIC
R.R.

Cheyenne

Fort
Collins

Greeley

Thornburgh
Fight

Denver

COLORADO

ADMITTED 1876

Gunnison R.

Uncompahgre

Del Norte

Pueblo

A.T.& S.F. reached
here 1880

Santa Fe

Las Vegas

Albuquerque

N MEXICO TERRITORY

Fort
Stanton

ilver
City

A.T.& S.F. R.R.

Fort Bliss

eming

El Paso

So.Pac. building
eastward reached
here 1881.

Fort Quitman

Fort
Davis

X

I

C

O

NEBRASKA
ADMITTED 1867

Platte

River

Ogallala

Julesburg

Fort
Sedgwick

KANSAS
PACIFIC

Republican

River

Fort Wallace

Smoky Hill

Fort Hays

Hays City

River

Fort Larned

Pawnee Fork

Arkansas

R.R.

Dodge City

PUBLIC
LAND STRIP

North

Canadian

Camp
Supply

Adobe
Walls X

Tascosa

Canadian

Amarillo

ATCHISON TOPEKA & SANTA FE

GOODNIGHT-LOVING

Fort
Bascom

Fort
Sumner

Pecos

CATTLE

Horsehead
Crossing

Fort Cobb

Fort
Reno

Red

Doan's
Store

Fort Sill

Wichita
Falls

Fort
Griffin

Fort Concho

Bandera

Rio

SOUTHERN

Grande

Fort Clark

Eagle Pass

Nueces

River

TEXAS & PACIFIC

Colorado

TRAIL

WESTERN CATTLE

Brazos

R.R.

TEX

River

CHISHOLM CATTLE TRAIL

SHAWNEE CATTLE

San Antonio

INT.

River

Laredo

Grand
Island

PACIFIC

River

UNION

Fort Kearny

IOWA

Council Bluffs

Missouri

Omaha

St.Joe & G.I.

Seneca

Junction City

Abilene

Ellsworth

Newton

Wichita

Caldwell

Hunnewell

FLINT HILLS

M.K.&T. R.R.

WEST

EAST TRAIL

River

Medicine Lodge Creek

Arkansas

INDIAN

River

River

Muskogee

Fort
Smith

Texarkana

Denison

M.K.& T. reached
here 1871

Dallas

Fort Worth

Marshall

NOR.

River

Austin

Houston

Corpus
Christi

GULF OF
MEXICO

MISSOURI

St.Joseph

HANNIBAL & ST.JOE R.R.

Kansas City

Topeka

M.P. R.R.

Baxter
Springs

Fort
Gibson

River

TERR.

ARKANSAS

C.R.I.& P.R.R.

C.R.I.& P. reached
here 1869

Red River

K.P. railhead
Oct.1867

Kansas River

South Platte River

Beecher
Island

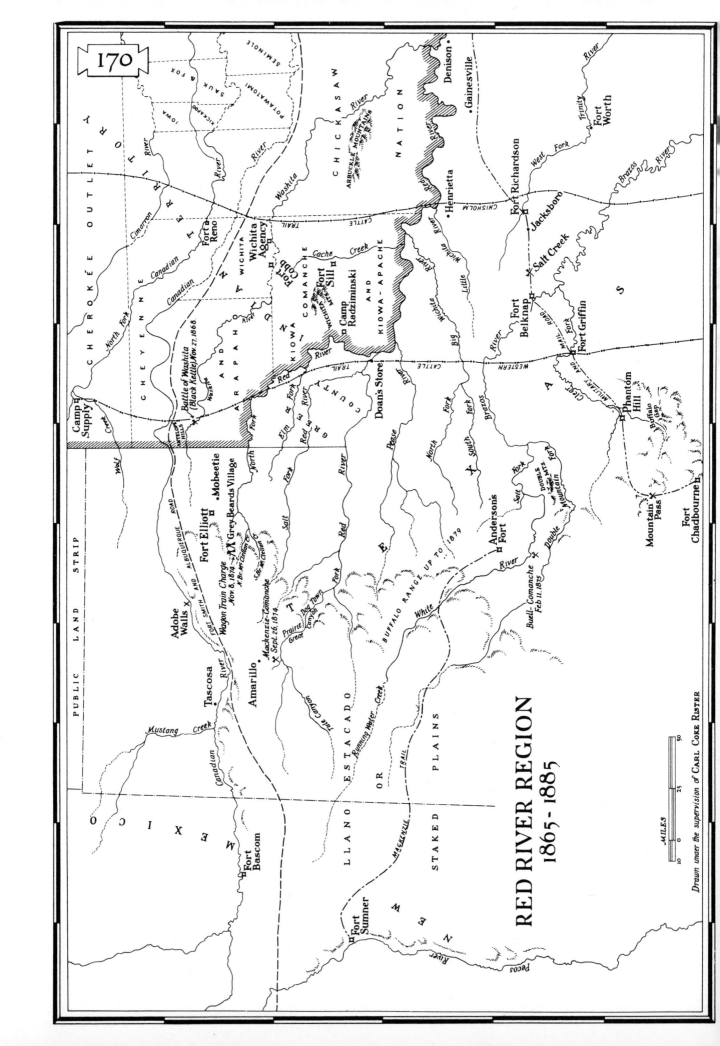

170

PUBLIC LAND STRIP

CHEROKEE OUTLET

TERRITORY

SAUK FOX
IOWA
KICKAPOO
POTAWATOMI
SEMINOLE
CHICKASAW NATION

Denison •
• Gainesville

Canadian River
Cimarron
North Fork
Canadian River

Fort Reno

CHEYENNE AND ARAPAHO

Wichita Agency
Fort Cobb
WICHITA

Cache Creek
Fort Sill
Camp Radziminski

COMANCHE KIOWA AND KIOWA-APACHE

Battle of Washita
(Black Kettle) Nov. 27, 1868

Washita River

ARBUCKLE MOUNTAINS

Red River

Henrietta •

Fort Richardson
Jacksboro

CHISHOLM TRAIL

West Fork

Trinity River
Fort Worth •

Brazos River

Salt Creek

Fort Belknap
Fort Griffin

Elk Fork
Red River

GREER COUNTY

Doan's Store

CATTLE TRAIL

WESTERN

Clear Fork

MILITARY AND MAIL ROAD

Phantom Hill

Buffalo Gap

Mountain Pass

Fort Chadbourne

Camp Supply

Wolf Creek

CAPTAIN'S HILLS

• Mobeetie
Fort Elliott

Grey Beard's Village

North Fork

Salt Fork

Red River

Pease River

North Fork Red River

Big Wichita River
Little Wichita River

South Fork Brazos River

Double Mountain Fork

DOUBLE MTS.

Anderson's Fort

BUELL COMANCHE Feb. 11, 1875

BUFFALO RANGE UP TO 1879

Adobe Walls

FORT SMITH AND ALBUQUERQUE ROAD

Wagon Train Charge
Nov. 8, 1874
N. Br. McClellan

Col. McClellan Cr.

Mackenzie-Comanche
Sept. 26, 1874

Amarillo •

Tascosa •

Canadian River

Mustang Creek

MEXICO

Fort Bascom

Fort Sumner

Dog Town
Prairie Dog Town
Great Canyon

Tule Canyon

LLANO ESTACADO OR STAKED PLAINS

Running Water Creek

White River

MACKENZIE TRAIL

N E W   M E X I C O

Pecos River

RED RIVER REGION
1865 - 1885

MILES
10   0   25   50

Drawn under the supervision of CARL COKE RISTER

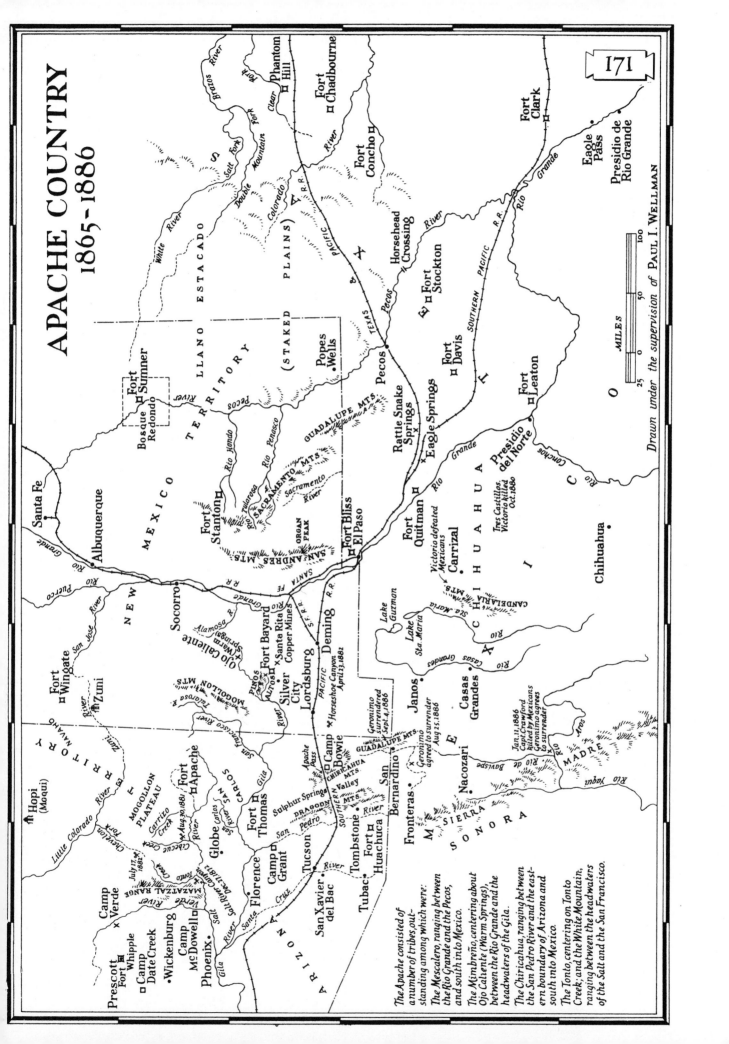

APACHE COUNTRY
1865–1886

171

Drawn under the supervision of PAUL I. WELLMAN

MILES
25 0 50 100

The Apache consisted of
a number of tribes, out-
standing among which were:
The Mescalero, ranging between
the Rio Grande and the Pecos,
and south into Mexico.

The Mimbreño, centering about
Ojo Caliente (Warm Springs),
between the Rio Grande and the
headwaters of the Gila.

The Chiricahua, ranging between
the San Pedro River and the eastern boundary of Arizona and
south into Mexico.

The Tonto, centering on Tonto
Creek; and the White Mountain,
ranging between the headwaters
of the Salt and the San Francisco.

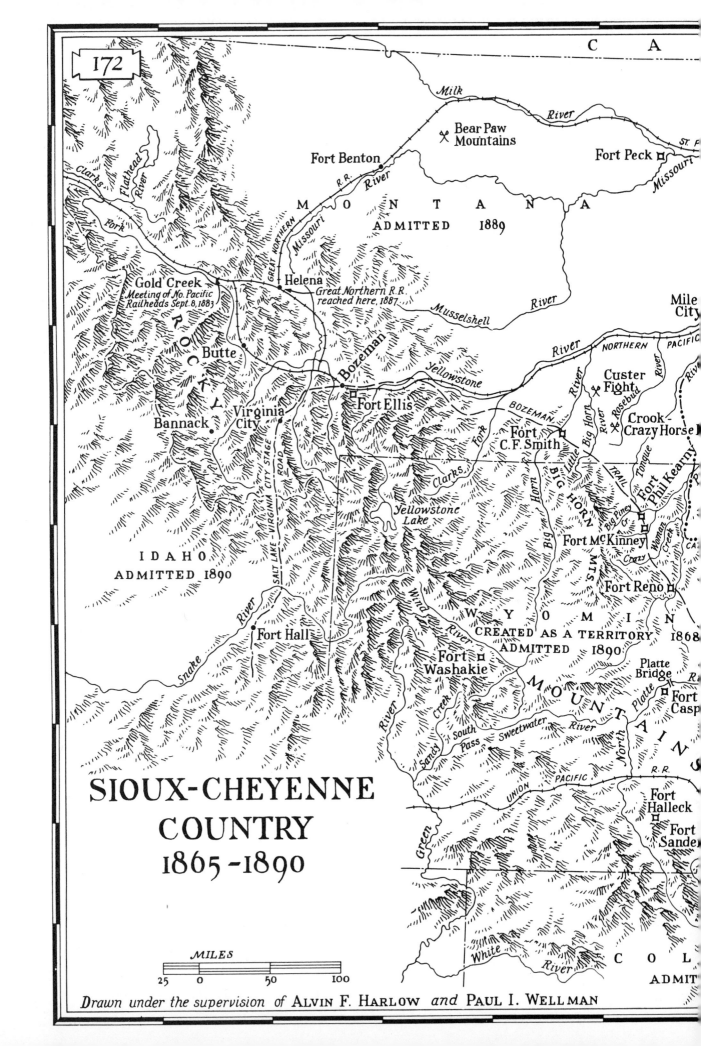

172

CA

Milk River

Bear Paw Mountains

Fort Benton

Fort Peck

ST. P

Missouri

M O N T A N A
ADMITTED 1889

GREAT NORTHERN R.R.

Missouri River

Clarks Flathead River

Fork

Gold Creek
Meeting of No. Pacific
Railheads Sept. 8, 1883

Helena

Great Northern R.R.
reached here, 1887

Musselshell River

Mile City

ROCKY

Butte

Bozeman

Yellowstone River

NORTHERN PACIFIC

Custer Fight

Rosebud

Crook-
Crazy Horse

Virginia City

Bannack

Fort Ellis

BOZEMAN

Little Big Horn River

Tongue River

SALT LAKE - VIRGINIA CITY STAGE ROAD

Clarks Fork

Fort
C.F. Smith

Big Horn

Fort
Phil Kearny

BIG HORN MTS.

Big Piney Cr.

Yellowstone Lake

Wind River

Crazy Woman Creek

Fort McKinney

I D A H O
ADMITTED 1890

Big Horn River

Fort Reno

W Y O M I N

Fort Hall

CREATED AS A TERRITORY 1868
ADMITTED 1890

Snake River

Fort
Washakie

Green River

South Pass

Sandy Creek

Sweetwater River

M O U N T A I N S

Platte Bridge

Platte River

Fort
Casp

North

UNION PACIFIC

R.R.

Fort
Halleck

Fort
Sande

SIOUX-CHEYENNE
COUNTRY
1865-1890

White River

C O L

ADMIT

Drawn under the supervision of ALVIN F. HARLOW *and* PAUL I. WELLMAN

MILES
25 0 50 100

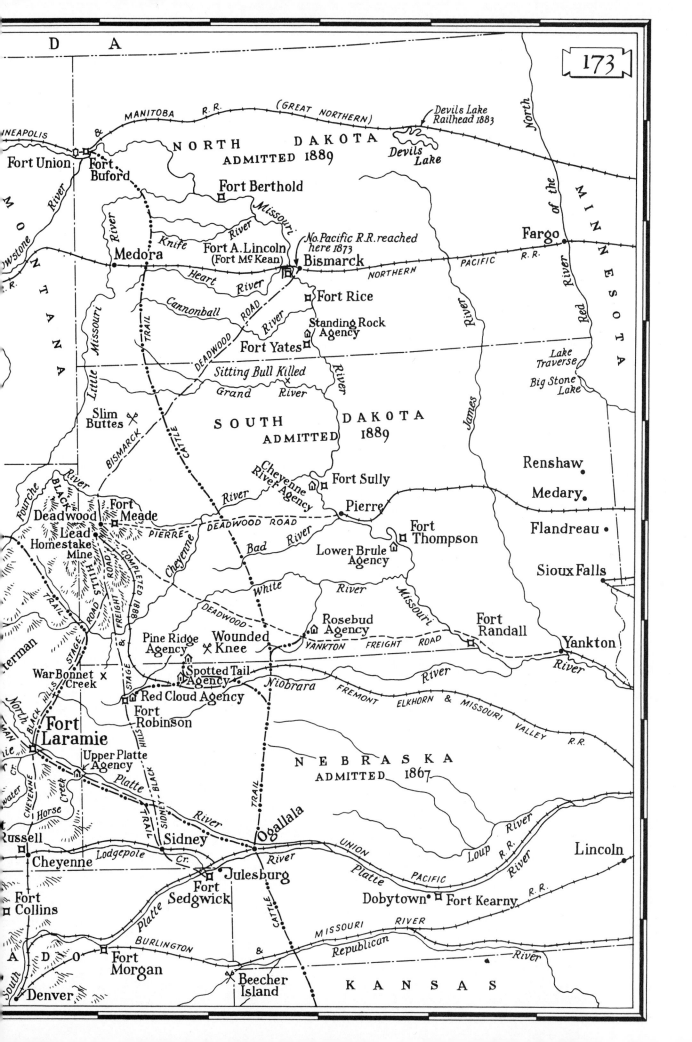

D A

MANITOBA R.R. (GREAT NORTHERN)

Devils Lake
Railhead 1883

North

MINNEAPOLIS

N O R T H   D A K O T A
ADMITTED 1889

Devils
Lake

Fort Union
Fort
Buford

River

Fort Berthold

Missouri

Fargo

River

MONTANA

Knife

River

of the

M I N N E S O T A

Yellowstone

R.R.

Little

Medora

Heart

River

Fort A. Lincoln
(Fort McKean)

No. Pacific R.R. reached
here 1873

Bismarck

PACIFIC

R.R.

NORTHERN

Red River

TRAIL

Cannonball

River

DEADWOOD

River

Fort Rice

Standing Rock
Agency

Fort Yates

River

Lake
Traverse

BISMARCK

Sitting Bull Killed

Big Stone
Lake

Grand

River

S O U T H   D A K O T A

Slim
Buttes

ADMITTED 1889

James

Missouri

CATTLE

Renshaw

Fourche

River

BLACK

Cheyenne
River Agency

Fort Sully

Medary

Fort
Meade

River

Deadwood

DEADWOOD ROAD

Pierre

Flandreau

COMPLETED 1888

PIERRE

Fort
Thompson

Lead

Homestake
Mine

HILLS

Cheyenne

Bad

River

Lower Brule
Agency

Sioux Falls

STAGE & FREIGHT ROAD

White

River

River

Missouri

Fort
Randall

TRAIL

DEADWOOD

Rosebud
Agency

STAGE

War Bonnet
Creek

Pine Ridge
Agency

Wounded
Knee

YANKTON

FREIGHT

ROAD

Yankton

Spotted Tail
Agency

Niobrara

River

River

Red Cloud Agency

BLACK

Fort
Robinson

FREMONT

ELKHORN & MISSOURI

VALLEY

R.R.

North

HILLS

Fort
Laramie

Upper Platte
Agency

N E B R A S K A

Platte

ADMITTED 1867

SIDNEY

CHEYENNE

Horse

Creek

River

BLACK

Ogallala

Loup

River

Russell

Sidney

TRAIL

River

Lincoln

Lodgepole

Cr.

Platte

UNION

PACIFIC

River

Cheyenne

Julesburg

River

R.R.

Fort
Sedgwick

CATTLE

Dobytown

Fort Kearny

Fort
Collins

BURLINGTON

&

MISSOURI

RIVER

A D O

Fort
Morgan

Beecher
Island

Republican

River

K A N S A S

South

Denver

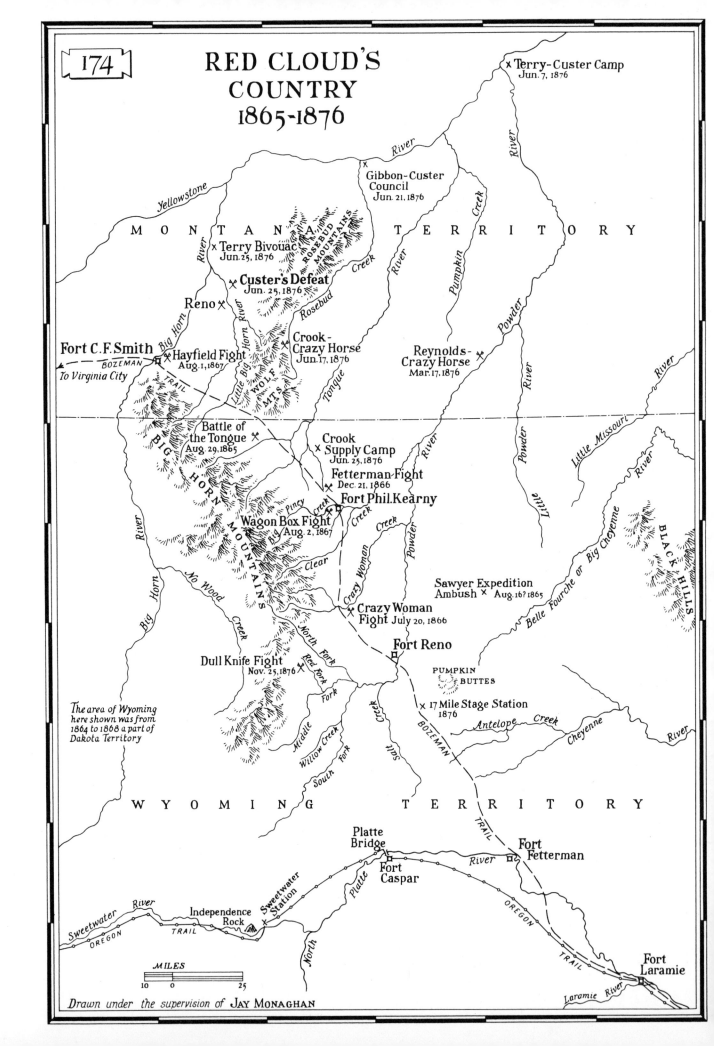

RED CLOUD'S COUNTRY 1865-1876

174

× Terry-Custer Camp
Jun. 7, 1876

M O N T A N A   T E R R I T O R Y

Yellowstone   River

River

× Gibbon-Custer
Council
Jun. 21, 1876

ROSEBUD MOUNTAINS

Creek

Pumpkin Creek

River

× Terry Bivouac
Jun. 25, 1876

✕ Custer's Defeat
Jun. 25, 1876

Rosebud

River

Powder

Reno ✕

Big Horn River

Little Big Horn River

Crook-
Crazy Horse
Jun. 17, 1876

Reynolds-
Crazy Horse ✝
Mar. 17, 1876

Fort C.F.Smith

BOZEMAN TRAIL

✕ Hayfield Fight
Aug. 1, 1867

WOLF MTS

Tongue

To Virginia City

BIG HORN MOUNTAINS

Battle of
the Tongue ✝
Aug. 29, 1865

River

Crook
✕ Supply Camp
Jun. 25, 1876

River

Fetterman Fight
✕ Dec. 21, 1866

Powder

Little

Little Missouri River

River

Piney Creek

Fort Phil. Kearny

Wagon Box Fight
Big Aug. 2, 1867

Creek

Creek

Powder

BLACK HILLS

Big Horn

No Wood

Clear

Crazy Woman

Creek

Sawyer Expedition
Ambush ✕ Aug. 16? 1865

Belle Fourche or Big Cheyenne

Crazy Woman ✝
Fight July 20, 1866

Dull Knife Fight
Nov. 25, 1876

North Fork

Red Fork

Fort Reno

PUMPKIN BUTTES

River

The area of Wyoming
here shown was from
1864 to 1868 a part of
Dakota Territory

Middle Fork

Willow Creek

South Fork

Creek

Salt

BOZEMAN TRAIL

× 17 Mile Stage Station
1876

Antelope Creek

Cheyenne River

W Y O M I N G   T E R R I T O R Y

Platte
Bridge

River

Fort
Fetterman

Fort
Caspar

OREGON TRAIL

Sweetwater River

Independence
Rock

Sweetwater
Station

Platte

North

TRAIL

Fort
Laramie

OREGON

OREGON TRAIL

Laramie River

MILES
10   0   25

Drawn under the supervision of JAY MONAGHAN

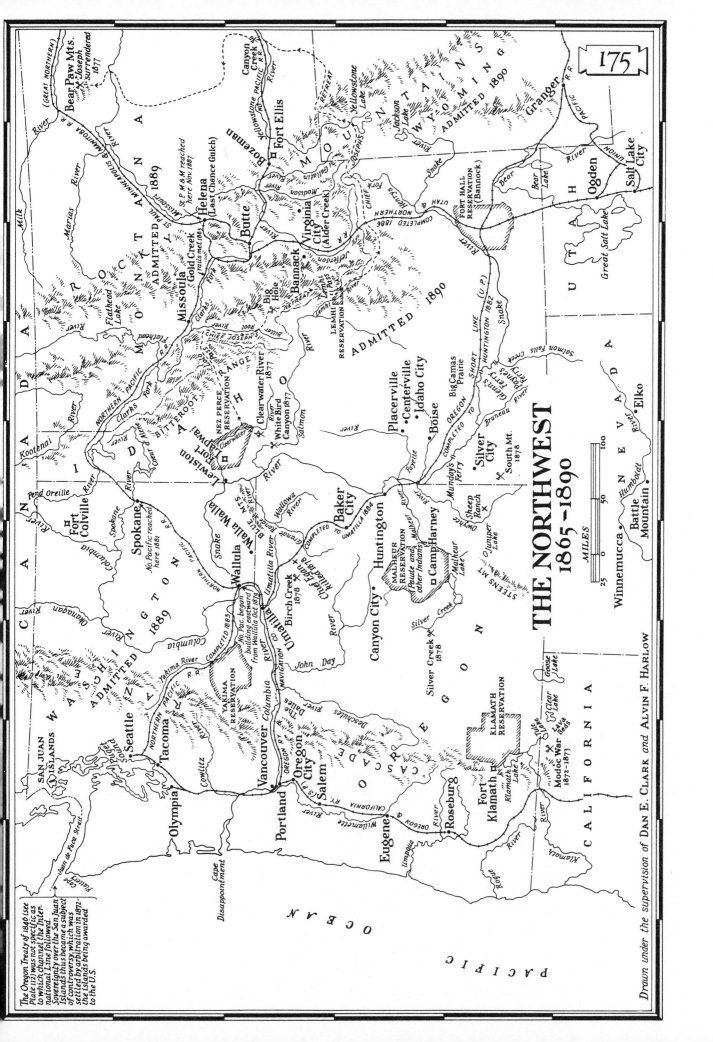

THE NORTHWEST
1865–1890

Drawn under the supervision of DAN E. CLARK and ALVIN F. HARLOW

MILES
100   50   25   0

The Oregon Treaty of 1846 (see Plate 112) was not specific as to which channel the International Line followed. Sovereignty over the San Juan Islands thus became a subject of controversy, which was settled by arbitration in 1872—the islands being awarded to the U.S.

PACIFIC OCEAN

CANADA

WASHINGTON
ADMITTED 1889

OREGON

IDAHO
ADMITTED 1890

MONTANA
ADMITTED 1889

WYOMING
ADMITTED 1890

UTAH

NEVADA

CALIFORNIA

ROCKY MOUNTAINS

Bear Paw Mts. (GREAT NORTHERN) Joseph surrendered 1877

Milk River
Marias River
Missouri River
Winnipeg & Minneapolis R.R.
Helena (Last Chance Gulch)
St.P.M.& M. reached here Nov. 1887
Gold Creek [trails met 1883]
Butte
Missoula
Flathead Lake
Clarks Fork
NORTHERN PACIFIC R.R.
BITTERROOT RANGE
CHIEF JOSEPH PASS
Big Hole RETREAT
Virginia City (Alder Creek)
Bannack
Jefferson River
Madison River
Gallatin River
Fort Ellis
Bozeman
Canyon Creek *
Yellowstone R.R.
Yellowstone Lake
Jackson Lake
Snake River
JOSEPH'S CHIEF RETREAT
NORTHERN PACIFIC R.R. COMPLETED 1886
Bear River
Bear Lake
FORT HALL RESERVATION (Bannock)
UTAH & NORTHERN R.R.
Granger R.R.
UNION PACIFIC
Ogden
Salt Lake City
Great Salt Lake

Pend Oreille
Kootenai River
Columbia River
Fort Colville
Spokane
No. Pacific reached here 1881
Spokane River
Okanogan River
Coeur d'Alene River
Clarks Fork
Lemhi Pass
LEMHI RESERVATION
CHIEF JOSEPH RETREAT
Clearwater River 1877
NEZ PERCE RESERVATION
White Bird Canyon 1877
Lewiston
Fort Lapwai
Clearwater River
Salmon River
Salmon River
Placerville
Centerville
Idaho City
Boise
Payette River
OREGON SHORT LINE COMPLETED TO HUNTINGTON 1882 (U.P.)
Silver City
South Mt.
Glenn's Ferry
Payne's Ferry
Salmon Falls Creek
Bruneau River
Snake River
Winnemucca
Battle Mountain
Humboldt River
Elko

Seattle
Tacoma
Olympia
Puget Sound
San Juan Islands
Cape Flattery
Strait of Juan de Fuca
Cape Disappointment
NORTHERN PACIFIC R.R.
Yakima River
YAKIMA RESERVATION
OREGON RY. & NAVIGATION CO.
Wallula
Walla Walla
BLUE MTS.
Umatilla River
UMATILLA CO.
Birch Creek
Chief Egan killed 1878
Grande Ronde River
Wallowa River
Wallowa Mts.
Snake River
Baker City
Huntington
COMPLETED TO UMATILLA 1884
No. Pac. began building eastward from Wallula Oct. 1879
No. Pac. COMPLETED 1883
Vancouver
Portland
Oregon City
Salem
Eugene
Columbia River
Cowlitz River
Willamette River
The Dalles
Deschutes River
John Day River
MALHEUR RESERVATION (Paiute and other Indians) 1878
Camp Harney
Malheur Lake
Malheur River
Owyhee River
Sheep Ranch
Juniper Lake
Steens Mt.
Canyon City
Silver Creek 1878
Silver Creek
CASCADE RANGE
OREGON RY.
Roseburg
Fort Klamath
KLAMATH RESERVATION
Klamath Lake
Tule Lake
Lava Beds
Modoc War 1872-1873
Clear Lake
Goose Lake
Umpqua River
Rogue River
Klamath River
CALIFORNIA R.Y.

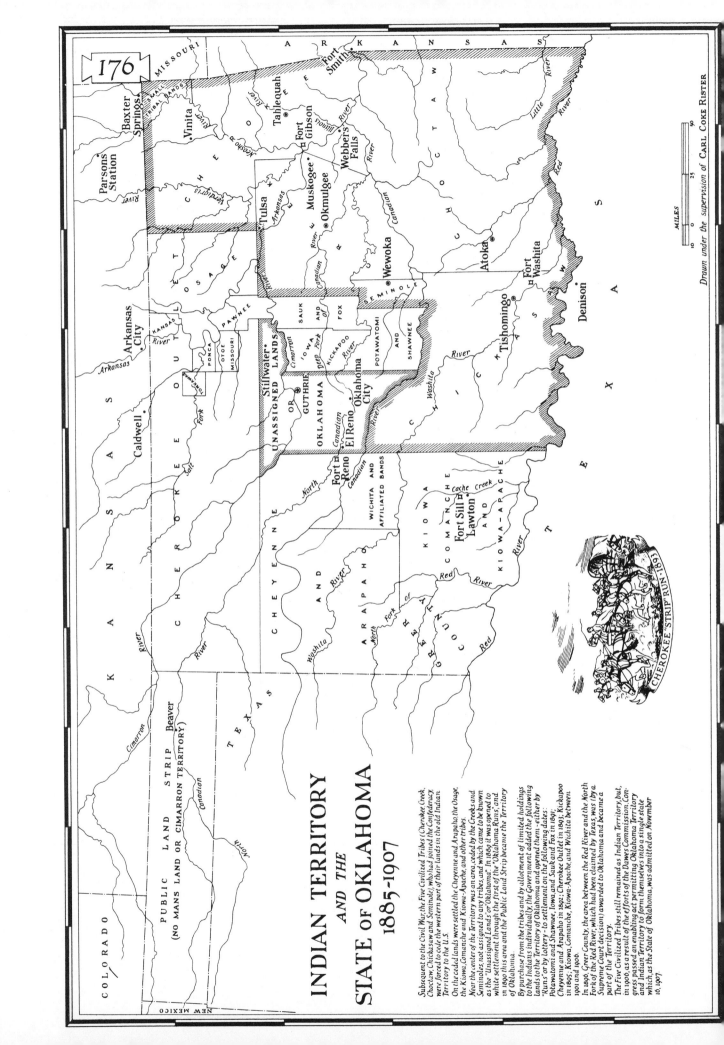

176

C O L O R A D O

MISSOURI

A R K A N S A S

K A N S A S

Baxter Springs

Parsons Station

Vinita

Tahlequah

Fort Smith

SMALL TRIBAL BANDS

C H E R O K E E

Fort Gibson

Webbers Falls

Tulsa

Muskogee

Okmulgee

C H O C T A W

Arkansas City

O S A G E

C H E R O K E E   O U T L E T

KANSAS

PAWNEE

PONCA

OTOE MISSOURI

TONKAWA

Stillwater

UNASSIGNED LANDS

SAUK AND of FOX

IOWA

KICKAPOO

POTAWATOMI AND SHAWNEE

SEMINOLE

Wewoka

Atoka

Fort Washita

Denison

Caldwell

GUTHRIE

OR

OKLAHOMA

Oklahoma City

El Reno

Fort Reno

Tishomingo

C H I C K A S A W

T E X A S

C H E Y E N N E

A N D

A R A P A H O

WICHITA AND AFFILIATED BANDS

K I O W A

C O M A N C H E

A N D

K I O W A - A P A C H E

G R E A T   C O U N T R Y

Fort Sill

Lawton

Cache Creek

Red River

PUBLIC LAND STRIP Beaver

(NO MANS LAND OR CIMARRON TERRITORY)

NEW MEXICO

CHEROKEE "STRIP" RUN 1893

MILES

Drawn under the supervision of CARL COKE RISTER

INDIAN TERRITORY
AND THE
STATE of OKLAHOMA
1885-1907

Subsequent to the Civil War, the Five Civilized Tribes (Cherokee, Creek, Choctaw, Chickasaw and Seminole) who had joined the Confederacy, were forced to cede the western part of their lands in the old Indian Territory to the U.S.

On the ceded lands were settled the Cheyenne and Arapaho, the Osage, the Kiowa, Comanche and Kiowa-Apache, and other tribes.

Near the center of the Territory was an area, ceded by the Creeks and Seminoles, not assigned to any tribes, and which came to be known as the "Unassigned Lands" or "Oklahoma." In 1889 it was opened to white settlement through the first of the "Oklahoma Runs," and in 1890 this area and the Public Land Strip became the Territory of Oklahoma.

By purchase from the tribes and by allotment of limited holdings to the Indians individually, the Government added the following lands to the Territory of Oklahoma and opened them – either by "Runs or by lottery – to settlement on the following dates:
Potawatomi and Shawnee, Iowa, and Sauk and Fox in 1891;
Cheyenne and Arapaho in 1892; Cherokee Outlet in 1893; Kickapoo in 1895; Kiowa, Comanche, Kiowa-Apache and Wichita between 1901 and 1906.

In 1896, Greer County, the area between the Red River and the North Fork of the Red River, which had been claimed by Texas, was (by a Supreme Court decision) awarded to Oklahoma and became a part of the Territory.

The Five Civilized Tribes still remained as Indian Territory, but, in 1900 as result of the efforts of the Dawes Commission, Congress passed an enabling act, permitting Oklahoma Territory and Indian Territory to form themselves into a single state which, as the State of Oklahoma, was admitted on November 10, 1907.

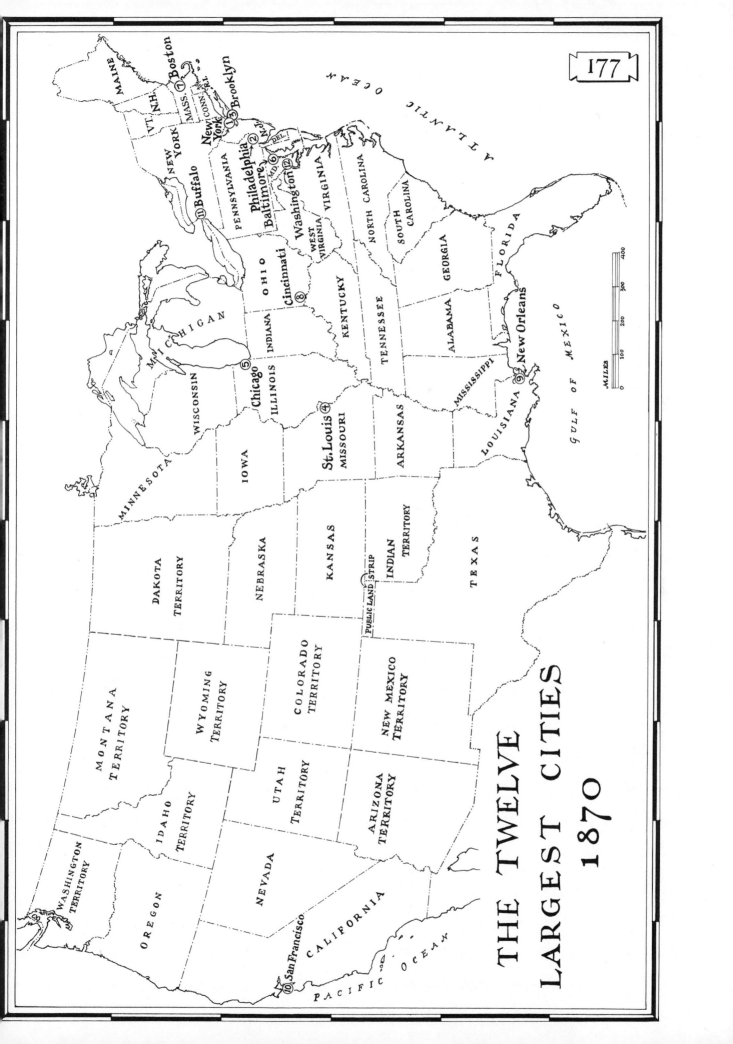

THE TWELVE
LARGEST CITIES
1870

ATLANTIC OCEAN

MAINE

VT. N.H.
MASS.
CONN. R.I.
N.J.
DEL.

Boston ⑦
Brooklyn ③
New York ①
②
Philadelphia ⑥
Baltimore ⑫
Washington

NEW YORK

Buffalo ⑪

PENNSYLVANIA

WEST VIRGINIA
VIRGINIA

NORTH CAROLINA

SOUTH CAROLINA

OHIO

Cincinnati ⑧

INDIANA

ILLINOIS

Chicago ⑤

MICHIGAN

WISCONSIN

MINNESOTA

IOWA

St.Louis ④

MISSOURI

KENTUCKY

TENNESSEE

ARKANSAS

MISSISSIPPI

ALABAMA

GEORGIA

FLORIDA

LOUISIANA

New Orleans ⑨

GULF OF MEXICO

MILES
0 100 200 300 400

DAKOTA TERRITORY

NEBRASKA

KANSAS

PUBLIC LAND STRIP

INDIAN TERRITORY

TEXAS

MONTANA TERRITORY

WYOMING TERRITORY

COLORADO TERRITORY

NEW MEXICO TERRITORY

IDAHO TERRITORY

UTAH TERRITORY

ARIZONA TERRITORY

WASHINGTON TERRITORY

OREGON

NEVADA

CALIFORNIA

San Francisco ⑩

PACIFIC OCEAN

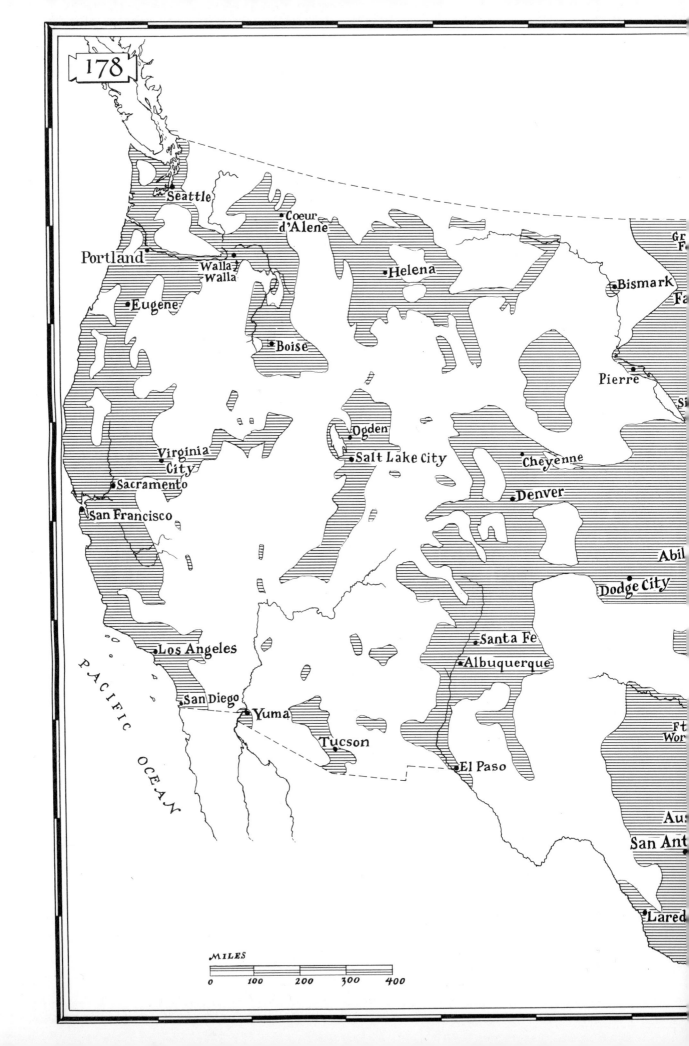

178

Seattle

Coeur
d'Alene

Portland

Walla
Walla

Eugene

Helena

Gr
F

Bismark

Fa

Boise

Pierre

Si

Ogden

Virginia
City

Salt Lake City

Cheyenne

Sacramento

Denver

San Francisco

Abil

Dodge City

Los Angeles

Santa Fe

Albuquerque

San Diego

Yuma

Tucson

Ft
Wor

P
A
C
I
F
I
C

El Paso

O
C
E
A
N

Au

San Ant

Lared

MILES

0   100   200   300   400

SETTLED
AREAS
1890

*This map does not show
areas settled by Indians.*

Duluth

Sault Ste. Marie

St. Paul

Green
Bay

Buffalo

Albany

Portland

Boston

New
Haven

Providence

Milwaukee

Detroit

Dubuque

Chicago

Toledo Cleveland

Harrisburg
Pittsburgh

Brooklyn
New York

Philadelphia
Wilmington

Des Moines

Columbus

Baltimore

uncil Bluffs
naha

Indianapolis

Washington

Kansas
City

Cincinnati

Richmond

Norfolk

eka

St. Louis

Louisville

Evansville

Lexington

Raleigh

Nashville

Knoxville

Chattanooga

Ft.
Smith

Memphis

Little Rock

Atlanta

Charleston

Montgomery

Savannah

Natchez

Jacksonville
St. Augustine

Mobile

New
Orleans

Pensacola

Galveston

ATLANTIC OCEAN

Gulf of Mexico

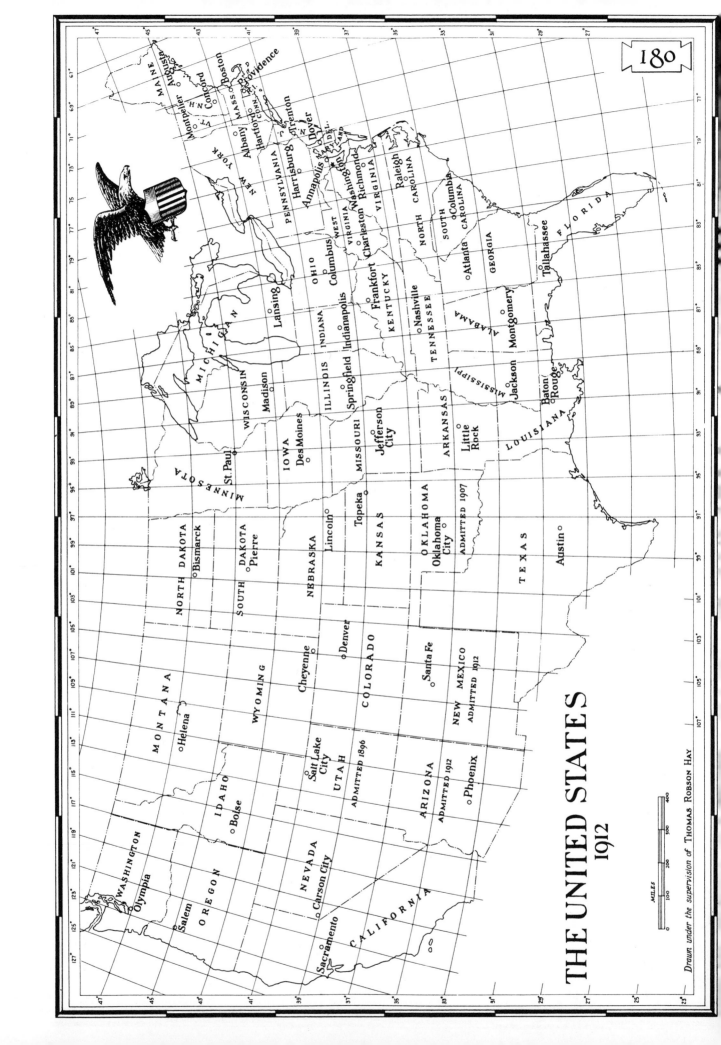

THE UNITED STATES
1912

Drawn under the supervision of THOMAS ROBSON HAY

180

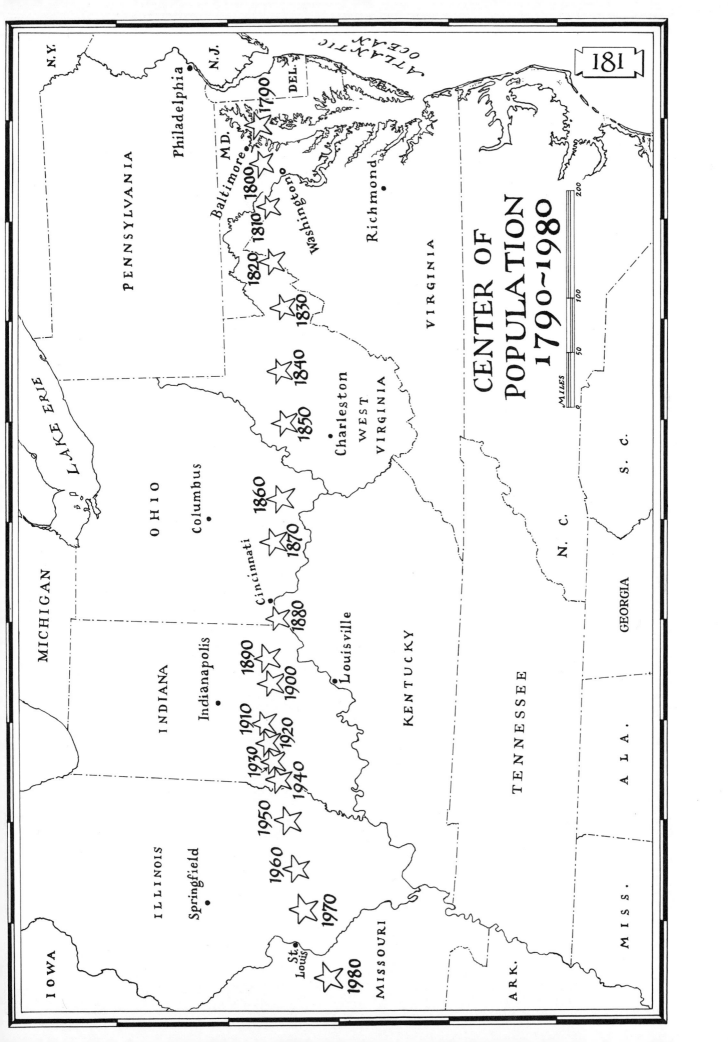

CENTER OF
POPULATION
1790~1980

181

IX THE UNITED STATES AS A WORLD POWER,
1898–1984

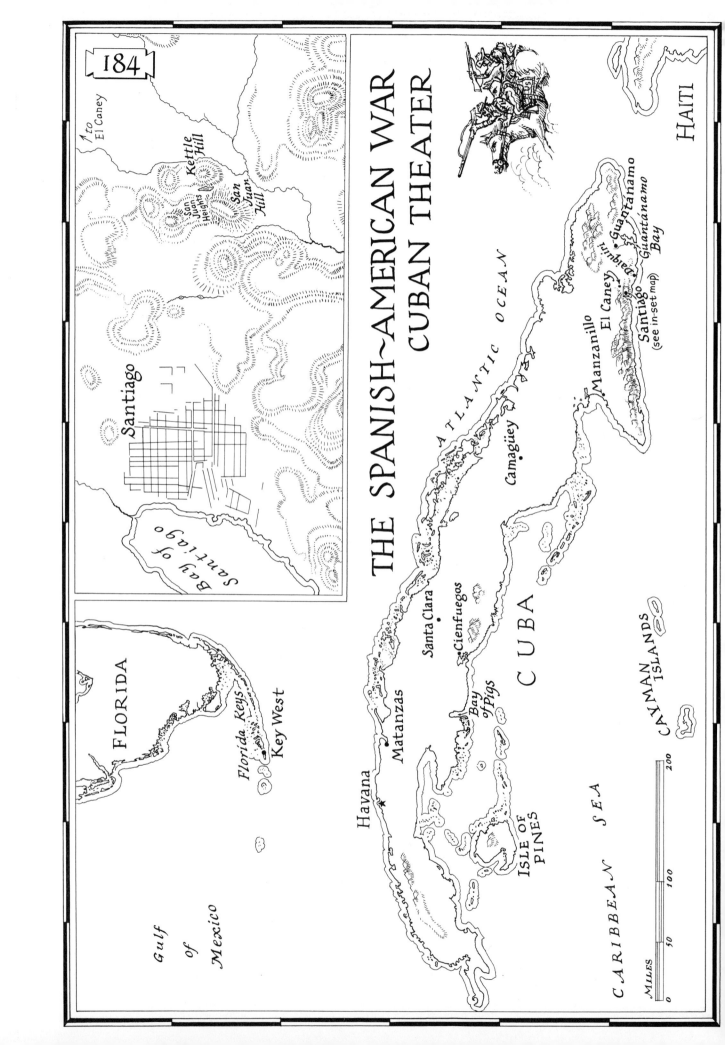

THE SPANISH-AMERICAN WAR CUBAN THEATER

184

Kettle Hill

to El Caney

San Juan Hill

San Juan Heights

Santiago

Bay of Santiago

FLORIDA

Gulf of Mexico

Florida Keys

Key West

Havana

Matanzas

Santa Clara

Cienfuegos

Bay of Pigs

ISLE OF PINES

CUBA

CARIBBEAN SEA

CAYMAN ISLANDS

ATLANTIC OCEAN

Camagüey

Manzanillo

El Caney

Santiago (see in-set map)

Siboney

Guantánamo

Guantánamo Bay

HAITI

MILES

0   50   100   200

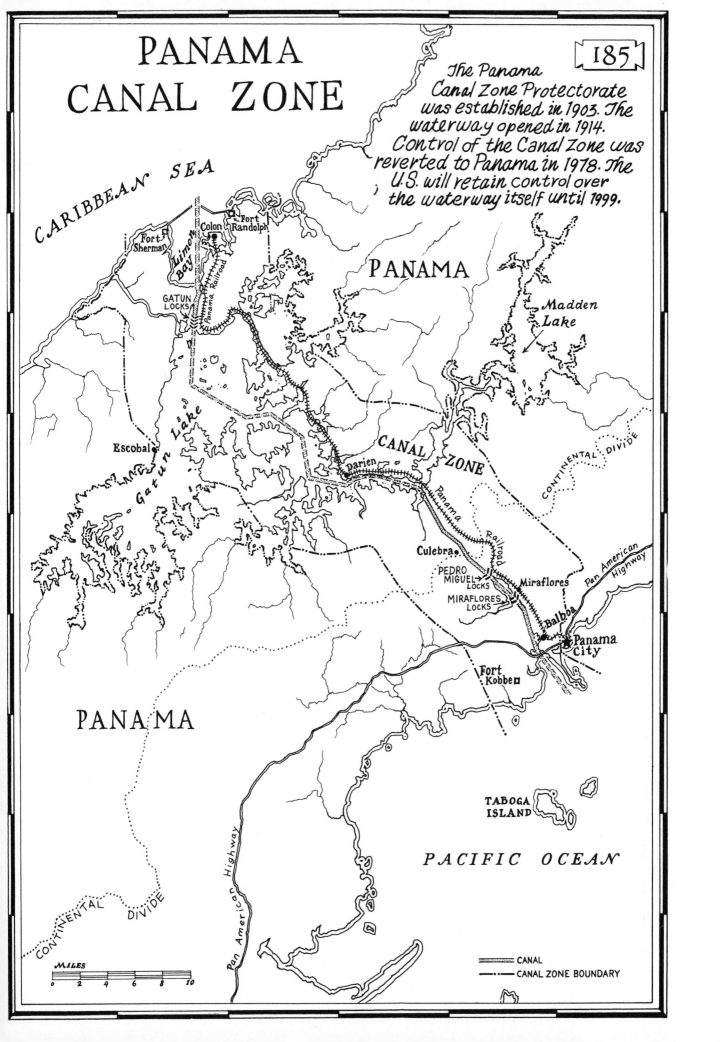

PANAMA CANAL ZONE

The Panama Canal Zone Protectorate was established in 1903. The waterway opened in 1914. Control of the Canal Zone was reverted to Panama in 1978. The U.S. will retain control over the waterway itself until 1999.

CARIBBEAN SEA

PANAMA

Fort Sherman

Colon

Fort Randolph

Limon Bay

GATUN LOCKS

Panama Railroad

Madden Lake

Escobal

Gatun Lake

CANAL ZONE

CONTINENTAL DIVIDE

Darien

Panama Railroad

Culebra

PEDRO MIGUEL LOCKS

Miraflores

MIRAFLORES LOCKS

Pan American Highway

Balboa

Panama City

Fort Kobbe

PANAMA

Pan American Highway

TABOGA ISLAND

PACIFIC OCEAN

CONTINENTAL DIVIDE

MILES

0 2 4 6 8 10

CANAL

CANAL ZONE BOUNDARY

Columbus
Hachita

NEW MEXICO

Fort Bliss
El Paso

UNITED   STAT

Carrizal

Madera

Chihuahua

C H I H U A H U A

Rio Grande

New Orleans

Parral

1916~1917 U.S. punitive expedition
in Northern Mexico.

M E X I C O

Gulf of Mexico

PACIFIC

OCEAN

Mexico City

1914 U.S. occupation
of Veracruz

Vera Cruz

BRITISH
HONDUR

HONDURAS

GUATEMALA
1954 U.S.-supported
revolution
overthrows government

EL
SALVADOR

L.A.
NICAR.

1954~1976 & 1982~1984
U.S. Military support

EL SALVADOR
1980~1984
U.S. strengthens economic
and political support

Managua
NICARAGUA

1912~1925 U.S. occupation;
finances
under U.S. control
1926~1933 U.S. occupation
1981~1984 U.S. military
support

MILES
0   100   200   400

UNITED STATES INTERVENTIONS *IN THE* CARIBBEAN *AND* MIDDLE AMERICA 1898~1984

ATLANTIC

OCEAN

Tampa

Miami

Key West

Havana

C U B A

Bay of Pigs

Isle of Pines
1903~1925 Formally
claimed by U.S.

Caimanera Guantánamo

CUBA
1898~1902 U.S. occupation
1902~1934 U.S. maintains right to
   intervene under
   Platt Amendment
1906~1909 U.S. occupation
1917 U.S. occupation

1961 Unsuccessful anti~Castro
   invasion, supported by the U.S.
1962 U.S. blockade

JAMAICA

Port-au-
Prince
HAITI
1915~1934
U.S. occupation

DOMINICAN
REPUBLIC

Samaná
Bay

1916~1924 U.S.
   occupation
1965~1966
U.S. occupation

PUERTO
RICO
1898
Annexed

U.S. VIRGIN
ISLANDS
1917
Purchased

HONDURAS
1981~1984
U.S. supported
antigovernment
forces

CARIBBEAN   SEA

1983 U.S.
led invasion
of GRENADA

PANAMA
1903 U.S. supported revolution
   against Colombia

1903 Control of Canal Zone
   granted to U.S.

1978 Treaty reverts control of the
Canal Zone to Panama. U.S. retains
control over the canal itself until 1999.

TA
ICA

CANAL
ZONE

Colon

P A N A M A

C O L O M B I A

VENEZUELA

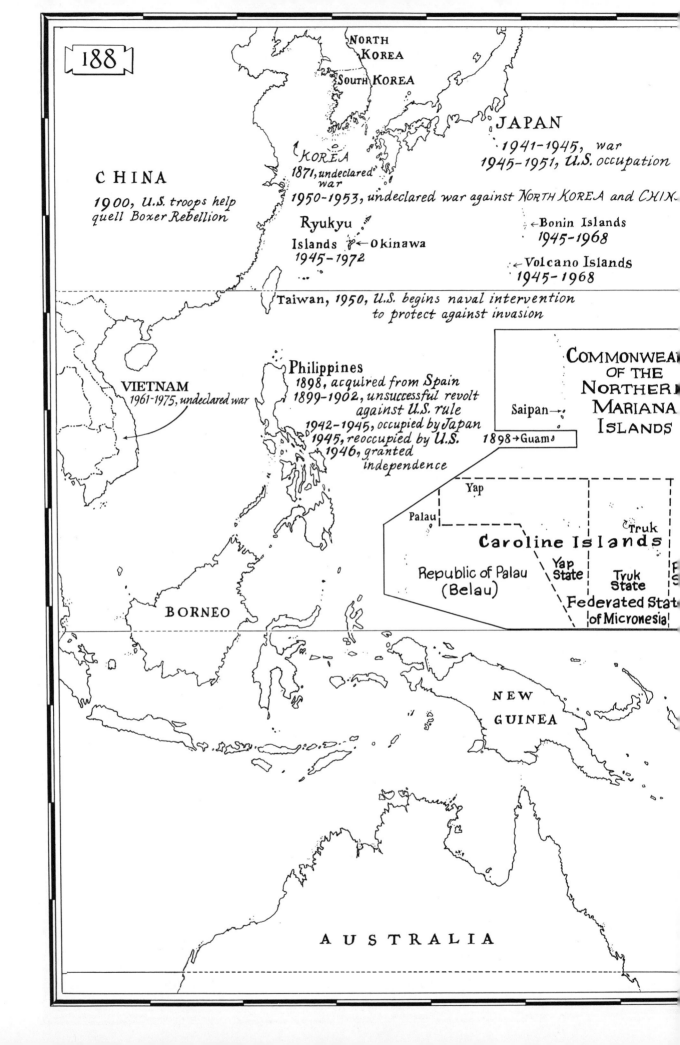

188

NORTH KOREA

SOUTH KOREA

JAPAN
1941–1945, war
1945–1951, U.S. occupation

KOREA
1871, undeclared war
1950–1953, undeclared war against NORTH KOREA and CHIN...

CHINA
1900, U.S. troops help quell Boxer Rebellion

Ryukyu Islands ←Okinawa
1945–1972

←Bonin Islands
1945–1968

←Volcano Islands
1945–1968

Taiwan, 1950, U.S. begins naval intervention to protect against invasion

COMMONWEA...
OF THE
NORTHER...
MARIANA...
ISLANDS

Saipan→

VIETNAM
1961–1975, undeclared war

Philippines
1898, acquired from Spain
1899–1902, unsuccessful revolt against U.S. rule
1942–1945, occupied by Japan
1945, reoccupied by U.S.
1946, granted independence

1898→Guam

Yap

Palau

Caroline Islands

Truk

Republic of Palau
(Belau)

Yap State

Truk State

Federated State
of Micronesia

BORNEO

NEW
GUINEA

AUSTRALIA

THE UNITED STATES
IN THE PACIFIC
1867 ~ 1980

Dates indicate the date of U.S. annexation or occupation

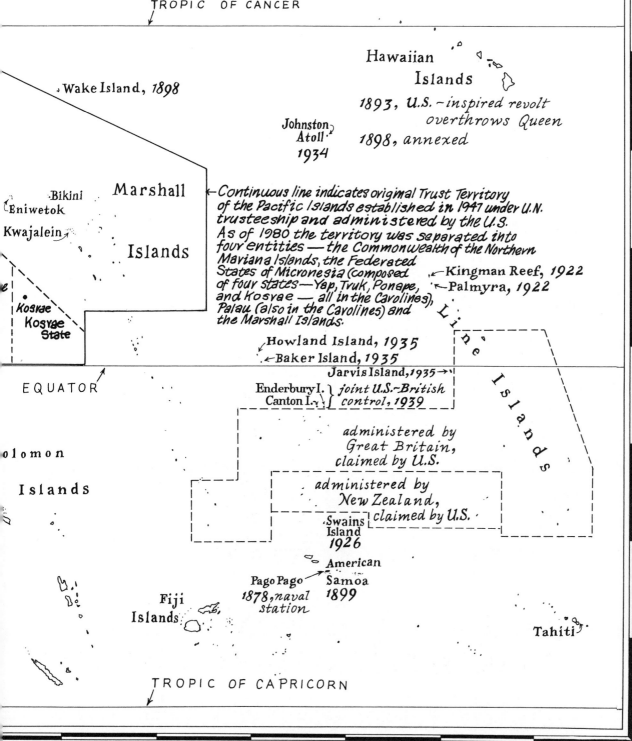

· Midway
Island, *1867*

TROPIC OF CANCER

Hawaiian

Islands

1893, U.S. ~ inspired revolt
overthrows Queen

1898, annexed

· Wake Island, *1898*

Johnston
Atoll
1934

· Bikini
Eniwetok

Kwajalein

Marshall

Islands

←*Continuous line indicates original Trust Territory*
of the Pacific Islands established in 1947 under U.N.
trusteeship and administered by the U.S.
As of 1980 the territory was separated into
four entities — the Commonwealth of the Northern
Mariana Islands, the Federated
States of Micronesia (composed ←*Kingman Reef, 1922*
of four states — Yap, Truk, Ponape, ←*Palmyra, 1922*
and Kosrae — all in the Carolines),
Palau (also in the Carolines) and
the Marshall Islands.

Kosrae
Kosrae
State

· Howland Island, *1935*
←·Baker Island, *1935*

Jarvis Island, *1935* →
Enderbury I. ⎱ *joint U.S.-British*
Canton I. ⎰ *control, 1939*

Line Islands

EQUATOR

administered by
Great Britain,
claimed by U.S.

olomon

Islands

administered by
New Zealand,
claimed by U.S.

·Swains
Island
1926

· American
Samoa
1899

PagoPago
1878, naval
station

Fiji
Islands

Tahiti

TROPIC OF CAPRICORN

NORTH
SEA

ENGLAND

•Calais

Pass
Ypres•   M
Armentières•
        Lille
        •N
        Ch
        •Ar
        Cam
        Le

Somme River

Amiens•
Cantigny•

ENGLISH   CHANNEL

Le Havre

Compiègne•

Be
V

Seine River

Paris

Versailles•

FRANCE

WORLD WAR I
THE WESTERN FRONT, 1917 ~1918

NETHERLANDS

Antwerp

Brussels
☆

Liège

Coblenz

BELGIUM

Sambre R.

Meuse River

Rhine River

Moselle River

LUX-
EMBOURG

GERMANY

uentin

Sedan

 ons

River

 sons

Rheims

esches

Marne

River

Argonne
Forest

Armistice Line

Verdun

Metz

LORRAINE

âteau-
ierry

Bar-
le-Duc

Saint-
Mihiel

Pont-à-Mousson

Strasbourg

Seicheprey

Meuse River

Moselle River

ALSACE

Rhine River

Chaumont

SWITZERLAND

MILES

0   50   100

192

WORLD WAR II
MEDITERRANEAN THEATER

Dates indicate when and
where American invasion
troops landed

FLYING FORTRESS

PORTUGAL

SPAIN

MAJOR

Strait of Gibraltar

Gibraltar

M E

SPANISH
MOROCCO

Algi
Nov. 8

Rabat
Fedala
Nov. 8, 1942

Oran
Nov. 8, 1942

Port
Lyautey
Nov. 8,
1942

Casablanca

Fez

Safi
Nov. 8, 1942

FRENCH MOROCCO

ALGERIA

FRANCE

Po River

Ferrara

Bologna

Marseille

St. Raphael
St. Maxime
St. Tropez
Cavalaire
Cap Negre
Toulon
ALL AUGUST 15, 1944

Pisa
Arno R.
Florence
Gothic
Line
Ancona

ELBA

ITALY

CORSICA
SEPT. 13-30, 1943

ADRIATIC

Pescara
Gustav
Line
Rome
Termoli

SEA

Anzio
Nettuno
JAN. 22, 1944
Monte
Cassino
Foggia

MINORCA

SARDINIA

Naples
Bari

TYRRHENIAN

Salerno

SEA

Amalfi
SEPT. 9, 1943
Paestum
SEPT. 9, 1943
Taranto

MEDITERRANEAN

SEA

Palermo
Messina

Marsala
Reggio di Calabria

Bougie
Bizerte
Strait of Messina

Bone
SICILY
Catania

Cape Bon
Licata
JULY 10, 1943
Gela
JULY 10,
1943
Syracuse

Tunis
Scoglitti
JULY 10, 1943

Enfidaville

MALTA

Sbeitla
Kasserine
Pass
MEDITERRANEAN

Gafsa
SEA

Mareth

TUNISIA

LIBYA

Miles
0   50   100   200

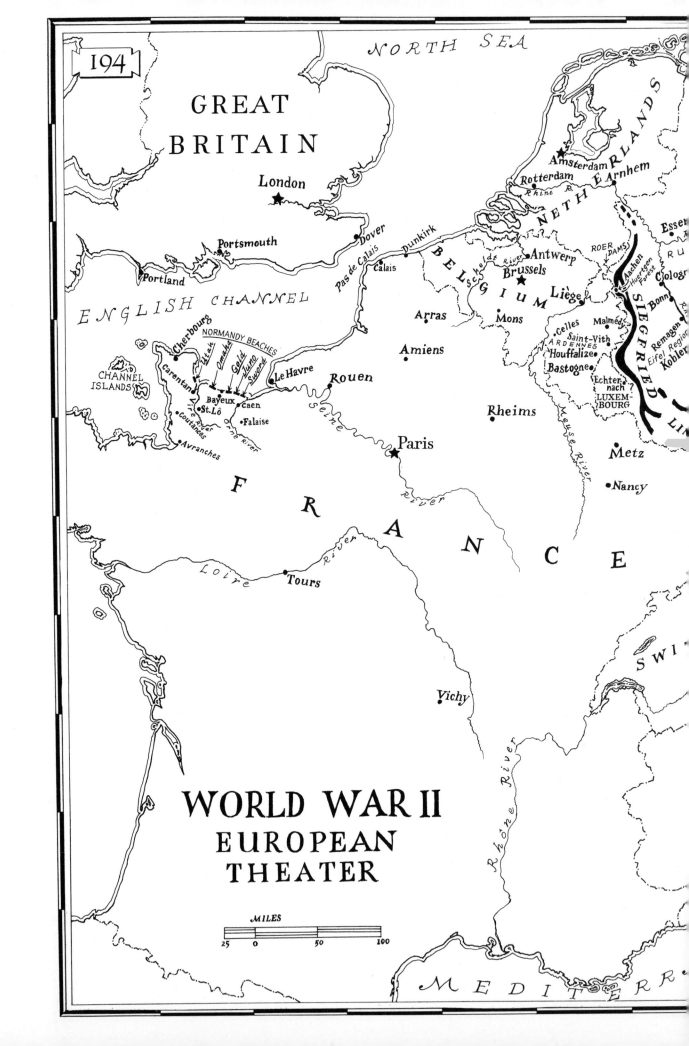

NORTH SEA

GREAT BRITAIN

London

Portsmouth

Dover

Portland

Dunkirk

Calais

Pas de Calais

ENGLISH CHANNEL

Amsterdam

Rotterdam

NETHERLANDS

Arnhem

Rhine R.

ROER DAMS

Antwerp

Scheldt River

Brussels

BELGIUM

Liège

Essen

RU

Aachen

Hüertgen Forest

Cologne

Bonn

Remagen

Eifel Region

Koblen

SIEGFRIED LI

Arras

Mons

Amiens

Celles

Malmédy

Saint-Vith

ARDENNES

Houffalize

Bastogne

Echter-nach

LUXEM-BOURG

Cherbourg

NORMANDY BEACHES

Utah

Omaha

Gold

Juno

Sword

Le Havre

Rouen

CHANNEL ISLANDS

Carentan

Bayeux

St.Lô

Vire River

Coutances

Caen

Orne River

Falaise

Avranches

Rheims

Seine River

Metz

Nancy

F R A N C E

Loire River

Tours

Vichy

SWI

Rhône River

WORLD WAR II
EUROPEAN
THEATER

MILES

25   0   50   100

M E D I T E R R

195

Hamburg

Bremen

Elbe River

Bergen-Belsen

POLAND

Berlin
Potsdam

Magdeburg

G E R M A N Y

Paderborn

Mulde River

Torgau

Leipzig

Dresden

Buchenwald

nkfurt

Prague

CZECHOSLOVAKIA

UNITED STATES
ZONE OF OCCUPATION

Linz
Mauthausen

Dachau

Vienna

Munich

HUNGARY

A U S T R I A

BRENNER PASS

LAND

ITALY

YUGOSLAVIA

ADRIATIC SEA

EAN
SEA

ALEUTIAN ISLANDS

ATTU
KISKA
UNALASKA
Dutch Harbor

WORLD WAR II
PACIFIC
THEATER

U.S. DIVE BOMBER

PACIFIC

OCEAN

MIDWAY

HAWAIIAN ISLANDS
Haleiwa
OAHU
PEARL HARBOR

WAKE ISLAND

ENIWETOK
MARSHALL ISLANDS
KWAJALEIN

K
LANDS

MAKIN
GILBERT ISLANDS
TARAWA

EEN ISLANDS
BOUGAINVILLE
SOLOMON ISLANDS
Tassafaronga
press
gusta
ay
NEW GEORGIA
E ESPERANCE
GUADALCANAL

SANTA CRUZ ISLANDS

SAMOA

ORAL
SEA

Miles
0   500   1000

198

KOREA
1950-1953

CHINA

Yalu River

•Chongjin

•Chosan

Changjin Reservoir

DEMOCRATIC PEOPLE'S REPUBLIC OF KOREA
(NORTH KOREA)

Chongchon R.

Taedong River

•Hungnam

SEA

OF

JAPAN

Pyongyang★
(Heijo)

Nan River

Wonsan

Pyonggang•

Chorwon• Kumhwa•

38°   38°

Kaesong•
•Panmunjom   •Chunchon

Seoul★

YELLOW

Inchon•

SEA

•Osan   •Wonju   *Han River*

REPUBLIC OF
KOREA
(SOUTH KOREA)   *Line: Aug.5, 1950*

Taejon•   *Naktong River*

•Pusan

Koje Island•

MILES

0   50   100

CHINA

DEMOCRATIC REPUBLIC
OF
VIETNAM
(NORTH VIETNAM)

Dien Bien Phu

★ Hanoi
• Haiphong

GULF OF
TONKIN

Mekong River

Mekong R.

• Vientiane

L A O S

✈ Udon Thani (Udorn)

Demilitarized Zone

17°

—Quang Tri
• Khe Sanh
• Hue
Da Nang

THAILAND

Chu Lai•
My Lai•   VAN TUONG
• Quang Ngai   PENINSULA

Ubon Ratchathani ✈

• Dak To

✈ Nakhon Ratchasima
(Korat)

• Kontum

IA DRANG VALLEY

• Pleiku
• Qui Nhon

CENTRAL

✕ Nakhon Phanom
★ Bangkok

C A M B O D I A

HIGHLANDS

REPUBLIC
OF
VIETNAM
(SOUTH VIETNAM)

• Nha Trang

CAM RANH
BAY

Mekong River

GULF
OF
SIAM

Phnom
Penh ★

• An Loc

Tan Son Hut
Air
Base   • Bien Hoa
       ★ Saigon

• Sihanoukville

SOUTH CHINA
SEA

• Long Xuyen

MEKONG
DELTA

VIETNAM
1961-1975

• Phuoc Long

Miles
0   50   100

✈ Air Force bases in Thailand

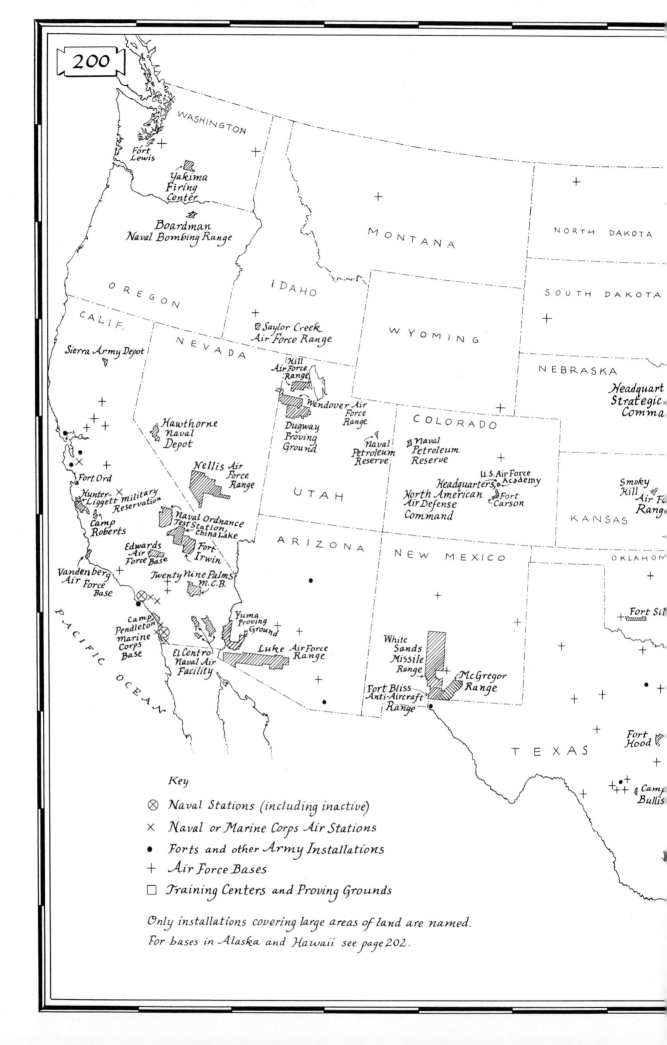

200

WASHINGTON

Fort Lewis

Yakima Firing Center

Boardman Naval Bombing Range

OREGON

IDAHO

MONTANA

NORTH DAKOTA

SOUTH DAKOTA

WYOMING

CALIF.

NEVADA

Saylor Creek Air Force Range

NEBRASKA

Sierra Army Depot

Hill Air Force Range

Wendover Air Force Range

Dugway Proving Ground

Naval Petroleum Reserve

COLORADO

Naval Petroleum Reserve

Headquarters Strategic Comma

Hawthorne Naval Depot

UTAH

U.S. Air Force Academy

Headquarters North American Air Defense Command

Fort Carson

KANSAS

Smoky Hill Air Fo Rang

Nellis Air Force Range

Fort Ord

Naval Ordnance Test Station, China Lake

Hunter-Liggett military Reservation

Camp Roberts

ARIZONA

NEW MEXICO

OKLAHOM

Edwards Air Force Base

Fort Irwin

Vandenberg Air Force Base

Twenty Nine Palms m.C.B.

Yuma Proving Ground

PACIFIC OCEAN

Camp Pendleton Marine Corps Base

Luke Air Force Range

El Centro Naval Air Facility

Fort Sil

White Sands Missile Range

McGregor Range

Fort Bliss Anti-Aircraft Range

TEXAS

Fort Hood

Camp Bullis

Key

⊗ Naval Stations (including inactive)

× Naval or Marine Corps Air Stations

• Forts and other Army Installations

+ Air Force Bases

□ Training Centers and Proving Grounds

Only installations covering large areas of land are named.
For bases in Alaska and Hawaii see page 202.

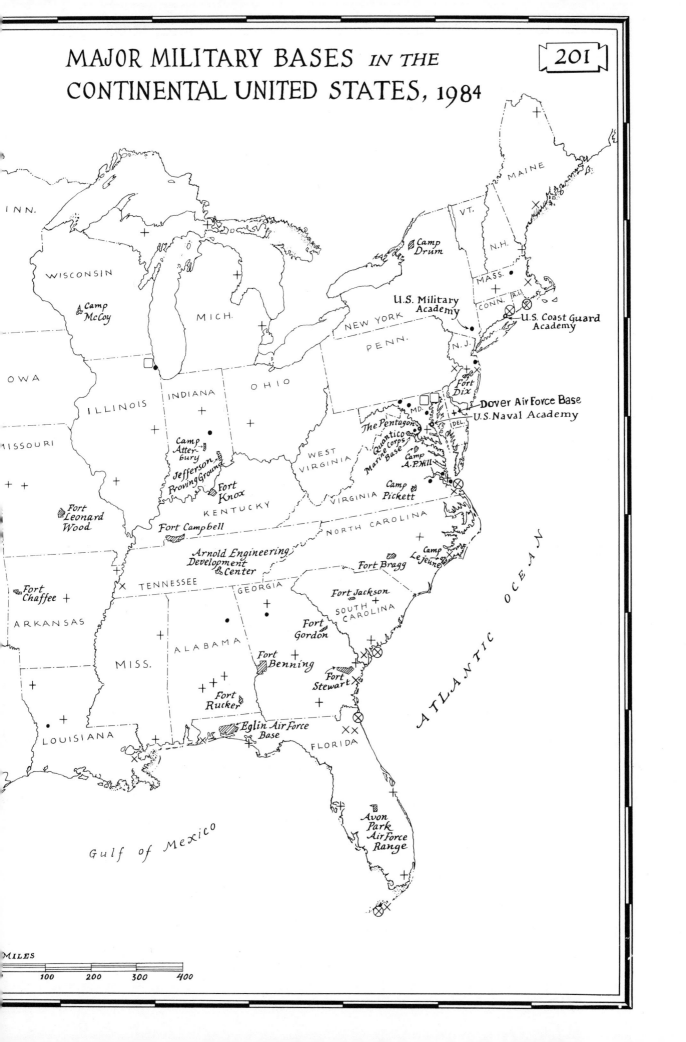

MAJOR MILITARY BASES *IN THE* CONTINENTAL UNITED STATES, 1984

MINN.

WISCONSIN

Camp McCoy

MICH.

IOWA

ILLINOIS

INDIANA

OHIO

MISSOURI

Camp Atterbury

Jefferson Proving Ground

Fort Knox

KENTUCKY

Fort Leonard Wood

Fort Campbell

Fort Chaffee

ARKANSAS

TENNESSEE

Arnold Engineering Development Center

MISS.

ALABAMA

Fort Benning

Fort Rucker

LOUISIANA

Eglin Air Force Base

FLORIDA

Gulf of Mexico

MAINE

VT.

N.H.

MASS.

Camp Drum

NEW YORK

U.S. Military Academy

CONN.

R.I.

U.S. Coast Guard Academy

PENN.

N.J.

Fort Dix

MD.

DEL.

Dover Air Force Base

U.S. Naval Academy

The Pentagon

Quantico Marine Corps Base

WEST VIRGINIA

Camp A.P. Hill

Camp Pickett

VIRGINIA

NORTH CAROLINA

Fort Bragg

Camp Lejeune

GEORGIA

Fort Jackson

SOUTH CAROLINA

Fort Gordon

Fort Stewart

Avon Park Air Force Range

ATLANTIC OCEAN

MILES

100   200   300   400

MAJOR AMERICAN MILITARY INSTALLATIONS ABROAD, 1984

Shemya, AF

Alaska

Fairbanks,
Eielson, A
AF

Elmendorf,
AF
Anchorage,
A

Big Delta,
A

Midway Island, N

Oahu
Hawaii, N, A, AF

Johnston
Island, AF

Thule, AF

GREENLAND

CANADA

DEW (DISTANT EARLY WARNING) LINE
Sondrestrom,
AF

ICELAND

Keflavik, N, AF

Bermuda, N

Azores,

CUBA

Guantanamo
Bay, N

Fort Buchanan, A
Puerto Rico
Roosevelt Roads, N

Canal Zone,
N, A, AF

Key

N: NAVY

A: ARMY

AF: AIR FORCE

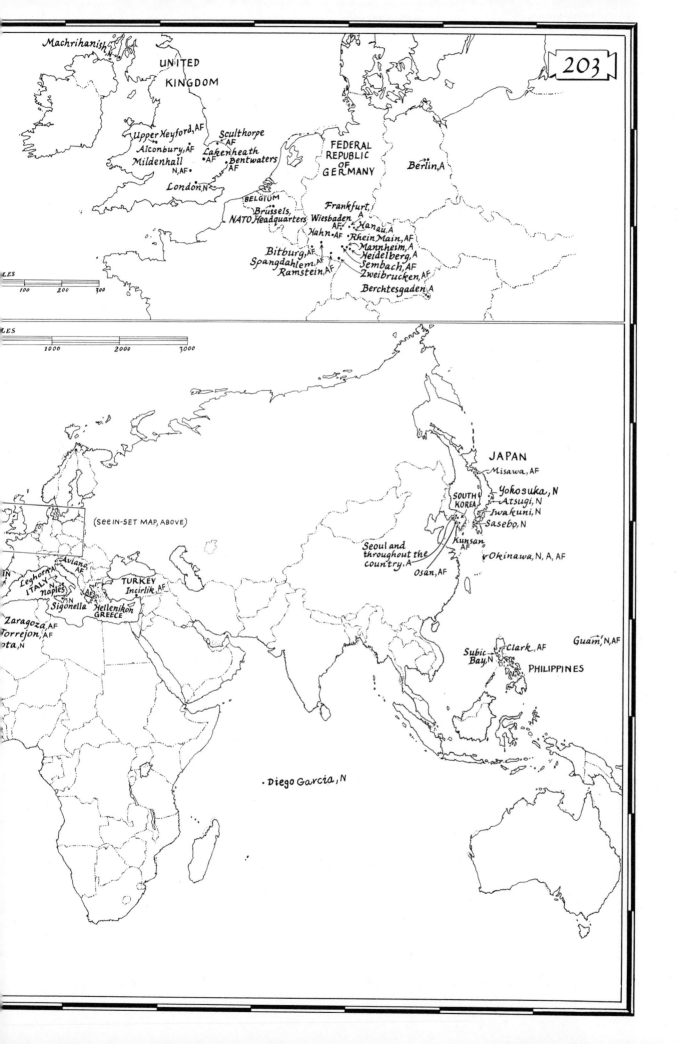

Machrihanish, N

UNITED
KINGDOM

Upper Heyford, AF   Sculthorpe
Alconbury, AF   AF
Mildenhall   Lakenheath
   N, AF   AF   Bentwaters
                              AF

London, N

FEDERAL
REPUBLIC
OF
GERMANY

Berlin, A

BELGIUM

Brussels,
NATO Headquarters   Wiesbaden
                              AF
                    Hahn, AF

Frankfurt,
A
Hanau, A
Rhein Main, AF
Mannheim, A
Heidelberg, A
Sembach, AF
Zweibrucken, AF

Bitburg, AF
Spangdahlem, AF
Ramstein, AF

Berchtesgaden, A

LES
100   200   300

LES
1000   2000   3000

JAPAN
Misawa, AF

Yokosuka, N
Atsugi, N
Iwakuni, N
Sasebo, N

SOUTH
KOREA

Kunsan
AF

Okinawa, N, A, AF

(SEE IN-SET MAP, ABOVE)

Aviano,
AF
Leghorn, A
ITALY   N
Naples   N
Sigonella   Hellenikon
         GREECE
         TURKEY
         Incirlik, AF

Seoul and
throughout the
country, A

Osan, AF

Zaragoza, AF
Torrejon, AF
ota, N

Guam, N, AF

Subic   Clark, AF
Bay, N

PHILIPPINES

Diego Garcia, N

X SOCIAL AND ECONOMIC DEVELOPMENTS

MAJOR
INDIAN RESERVATIONS
IN THE
CONTINENTAL U.S.
1984

MILES

0   100   200   300   400

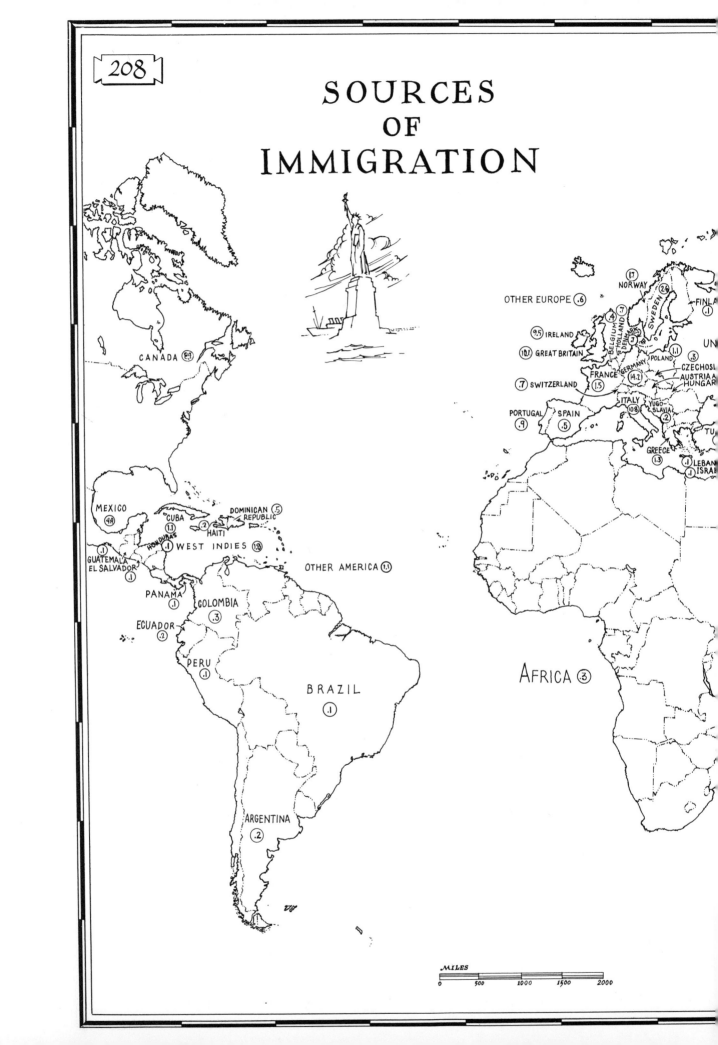

208

SOURCES
OF
IMMIGRATION

CANADA 29.1

OTHER EUROPE .6

NORWAY 1.7

SWEDEN 2.6

FINLA .1

IRELAND 9.5

BELGIUM .4
HOLLAND .7
DENMARK 1.7

POLAND 1.1

GREAT BRITAIN 10.1

CZECHOSL .3
AUSTRIA A
HUNGAR

FRANCE 1.5

GERMANY 14.2

UN

SWITZERLAND .7

PORTUGAL .9

SPAIN .5

ITALY 10.8

YUGO-SLAVIA .2

TU

GREECE 1.3

LEBAN .1
ISRA .1

MEXICO 4.4

DOMINICAN REPUBLIC .5

CUBA 1.1

HAITI .2

HONDURAS .1
GUATEMALA .1
EL SALVADOR .1

WEST INDIES 1.9

OTHER AMERICA 1.1

AFRICA .3

PANAMA .1

COLOMBIA .3

ECUADOR .2

PERU .1

BRAZIL .1

ARGENTINA .2

MILES
0   500   1000   1500   2000

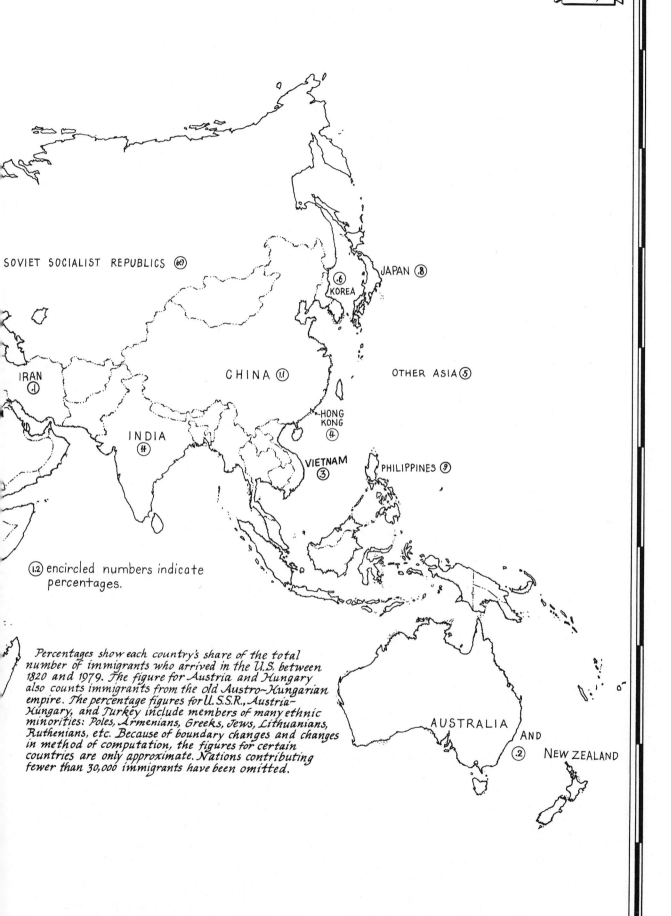

SOVIET SOCIALIST REPUBLICS ⑥

KOREA ⑥

JAPAN ⑧

IRAN ①

CHINA ⑪

OTHER ASIA ⑤

INDIA ④

HONG KONG ④

VIETNAM ③

PHILIPPINES ⑨

⑫ encircled numbers indicate
percentages.

AUSTRALIA AND

② NEW ZEALAND

Percentages show each country's share of the total
number of immigrants who arrived in the U.S. between
1820 and 1979. The figure for Austria and Hungary
also counts immigrants from the old Austro~Hungarian
empire. The percentage figures for U.S.S.R., Austria-
Hungary, and Turkey include members of many ethnic
minorities: Poles, Armenians, Greeks, Jews, Lithuanians,
Ruthenians, etc. Because of boundary changes and changes
in method of computation, the figures for certain
countries are only approximate. Nations contributing
fewer than 30,000 immigrants have been omitted.

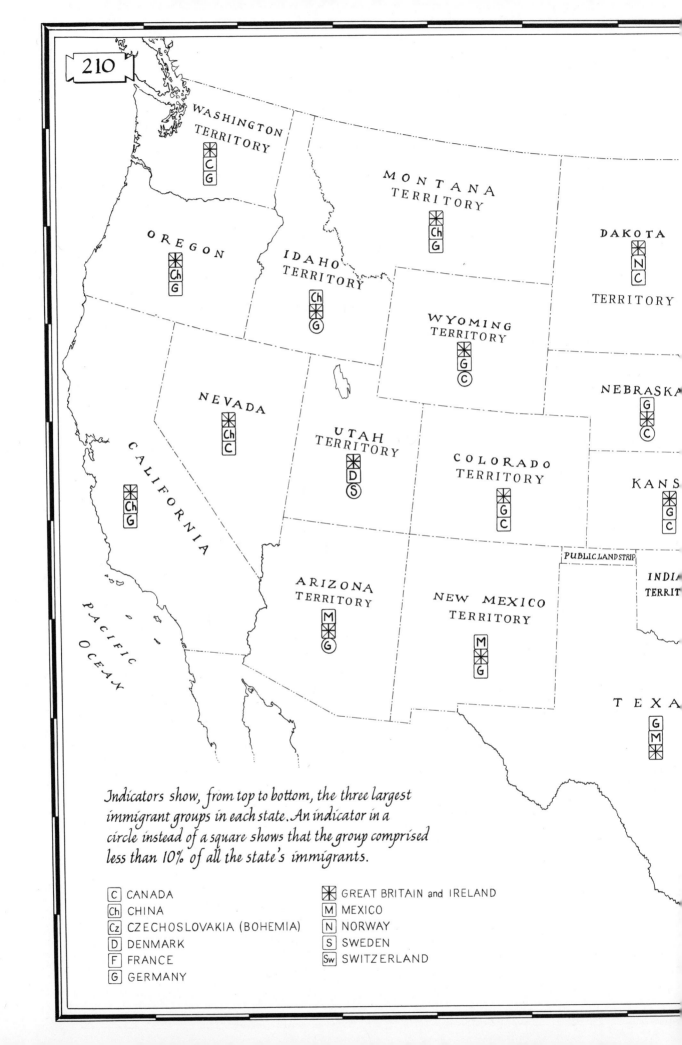

210

WASHINGTON TERRITORY

OREGON

MONTANA TERRITORY

IDAHO TERRITORY

DAKOTA TERRITORY

WYOMING TERRITORY

NEBRASKA

NEVADA

UTAH TERRITORY

COLORADO TERRITORY

KANSAS

CALIFORNIA

PACIFIC OCEAN

ARIZONA TERRITORY

NEW MEXICO TERRITORY

PUBLIC LAND STRIP

INDIAN TERRIT

TEXAS

Indicators show, from top to bottom, the three largest immigrant groups in each state. An indicator in a circle instead of a square shows that the group comprised less than 10% of all the state's immigrants.

C CANADA
Ch CHINA
Cz CZECHOSLOVAKIA (BOHEMIA)
D DENMARK
F FRANCE
G GERMANY

✴ GREAT BRITAIN and IRELAND
M MEXICO
N NORWAY
S SWEDEN
Sw SWITZERLAND

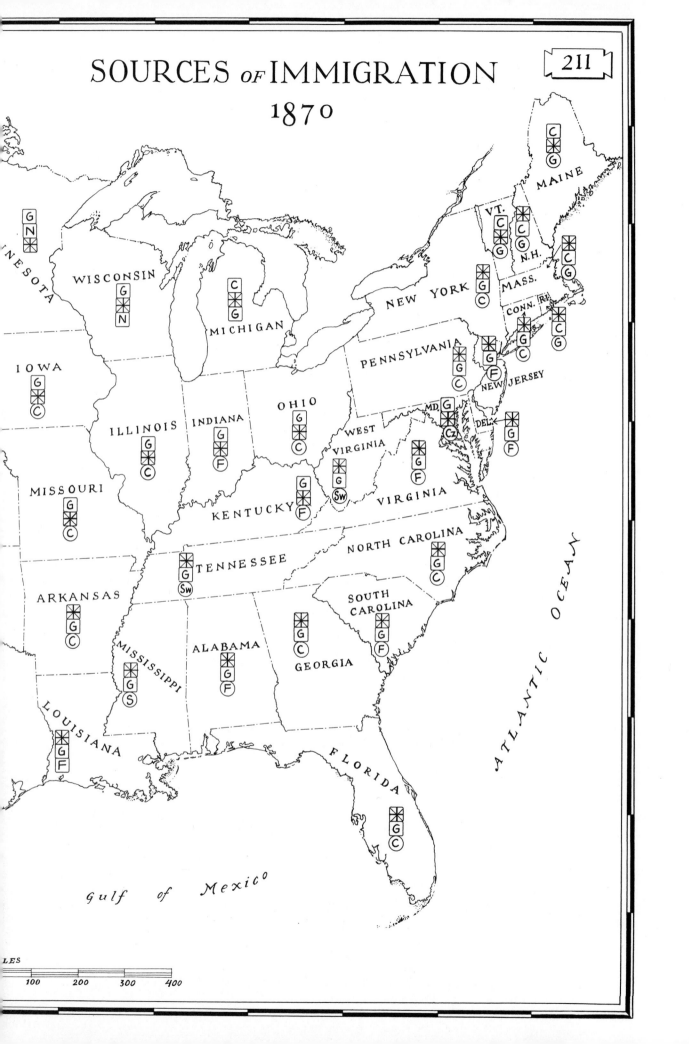

SOURCES OF IMMIGRATION
1870

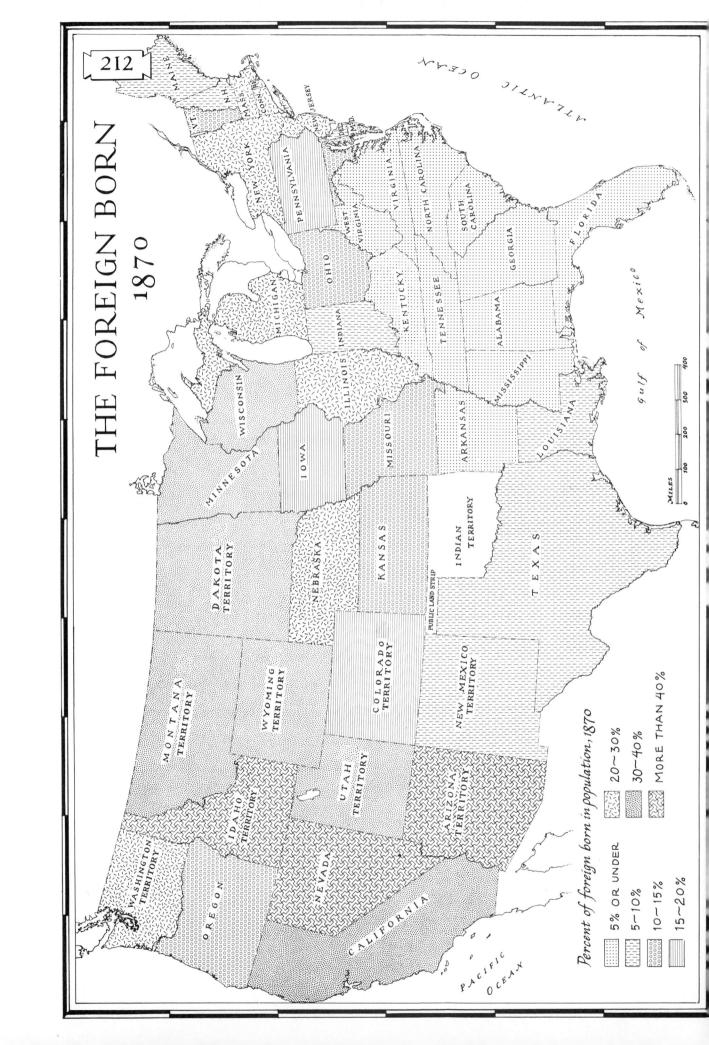

THE FOREIGN BORN
1870

212

Percent of foreign born in population, 1870

5% or under
5–10%
10–15%
15–20%
20–30%
30–40%
More than 40%

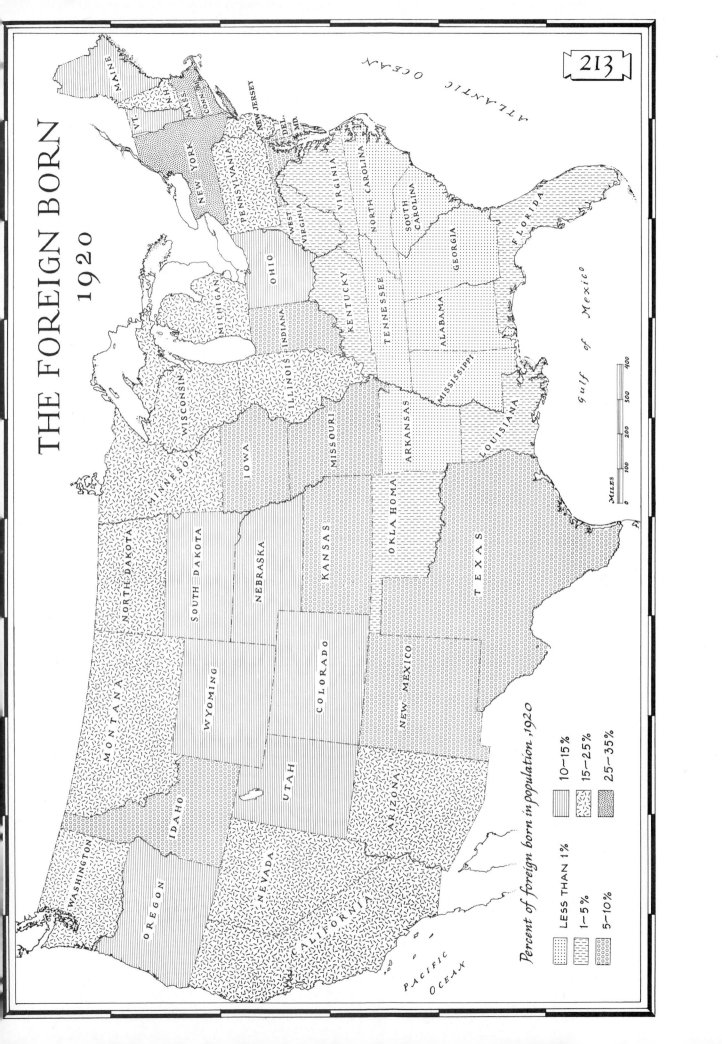

THE FOREIGN BORN
1920

213

Percent of foreign born in population, 1920

LESS THAN 1%
1–5%
5–10%
10–15%
15–25%
25–35%

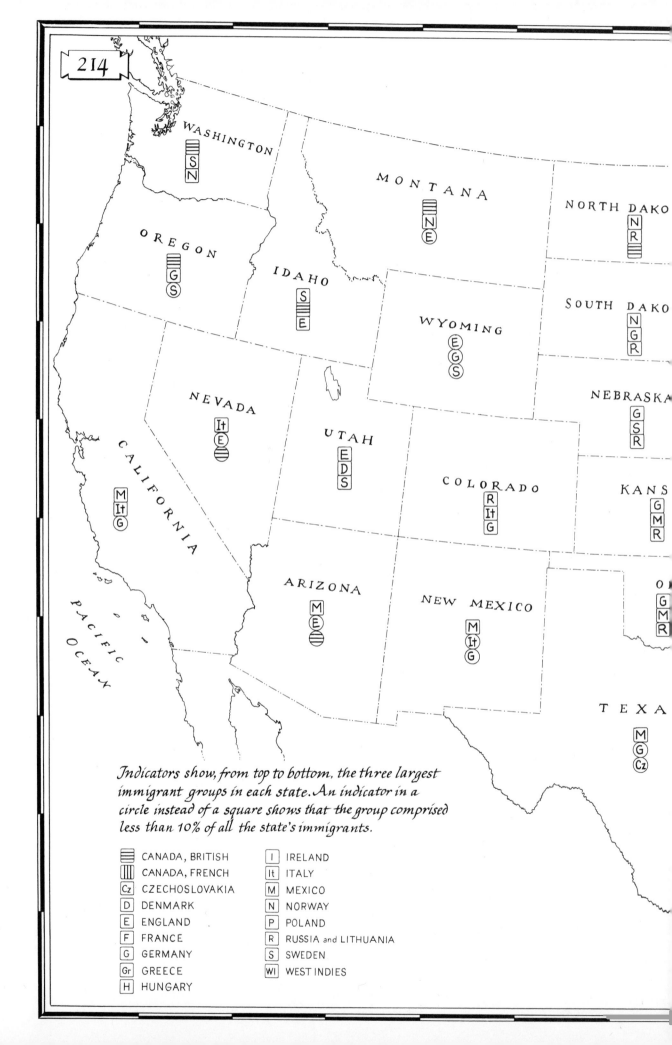

WASHINGTON
S
N

MONTANA
N
E

NORTH DAKO
N
R

OREGON
G
S

IDAHO
S
E

WYOMING
E
G
S

SOUTH DAKO
N
G
R

NEVADA
It
E

UTAH
E
D
S

COLORADO
R
It
G

NEBRASKA
G
S
R

CALIFORNIA
M
It
G

ARIZONA
M
E

NEW MEXICO
M
It
G

KANS
G
M
R

O
G
M
R

PACIFIC OCEAN

TEXA
M
G
Cz

Indicators show, from top to bottom, the three largest immigrant groups in each state. An indicator in a circle instead of a square shows that the group comprised less than 10% of all the state's immigrants.

☰	CANADA, BRITISH	I	IRELAND
⦀	CANADA, FRENCH	It	ITALY
Cz	CZECHOSLOVAKIA	M	MEXICO
D	DENMARK	N	NORWAY
E	ENGLAND	P	POLAND
F	FRANCE	R	RUSSIA and LITHUANIA
G	GERMANY	S	SWEDEN
Gr	GREECE	WI	WEST INDIES
H	HUNGARY		

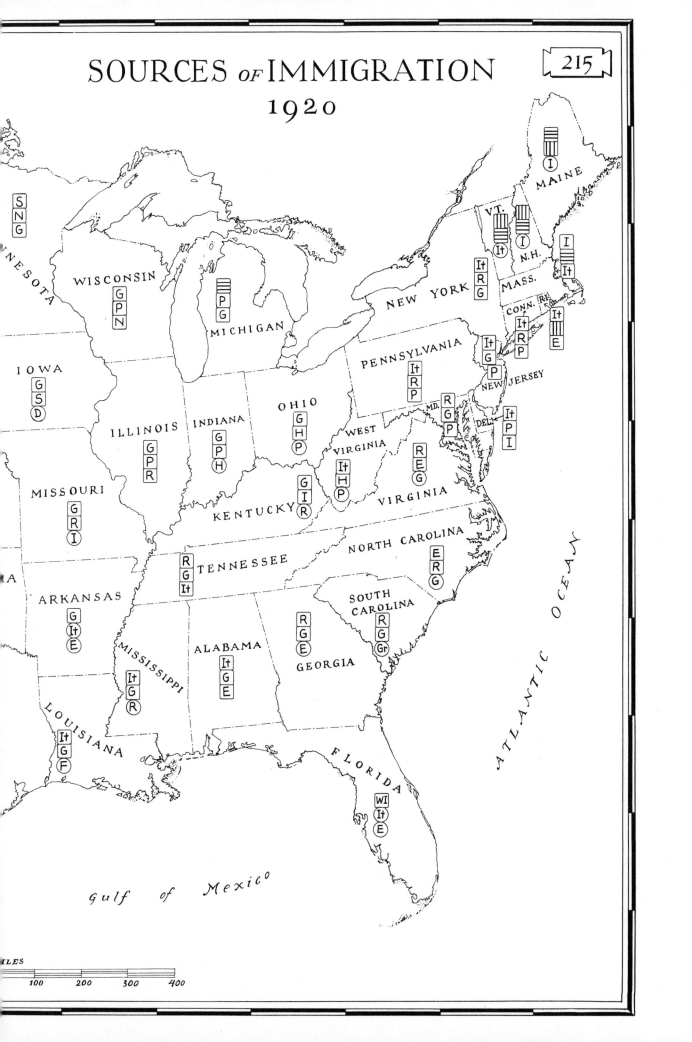

SOURCES of IMMIGRATION
1920

215

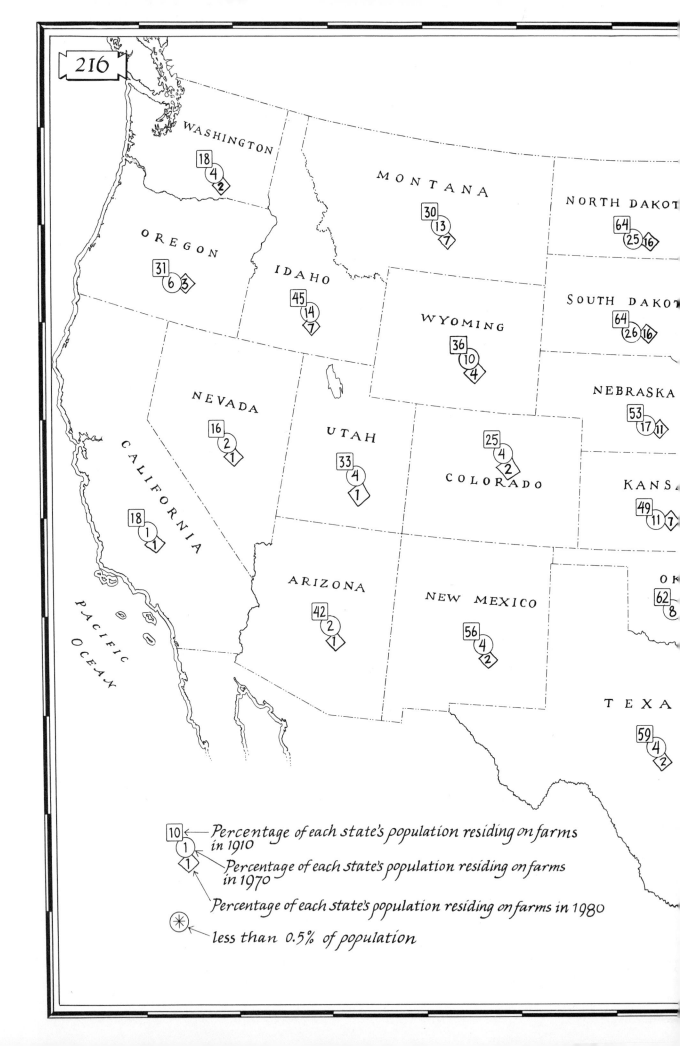

216

WASHINGTON
18
4
2

OREGON
31
6
3

MONTANA
30
13
7

NORTH DAKOT
64
25
16

IDAHO
45
14
7

WYOMING
36
10
4

SOUTH DAKOT
64
26
16

NEBRASKA
53
17
11

NEVADA
16
2
1

UTAH
33
4
1

COLORADO
25
4
2

KANSA
49
11
7

CALIFORNIA
18
1
1

ARIZONA
42
2
1

NEW MEXICO
56
4
2

OK
62
8

TEXA
59
4
2

PACIFIC
OCEAN

10 ← *Percentage of each state's population residing on farms in 1910*

1 ← *Percentage of each state's population residing on farms in 1970*

1 ← *Percentage of each state's population residing on farms in 1980*

✳ ← *less than 0.5% of population*

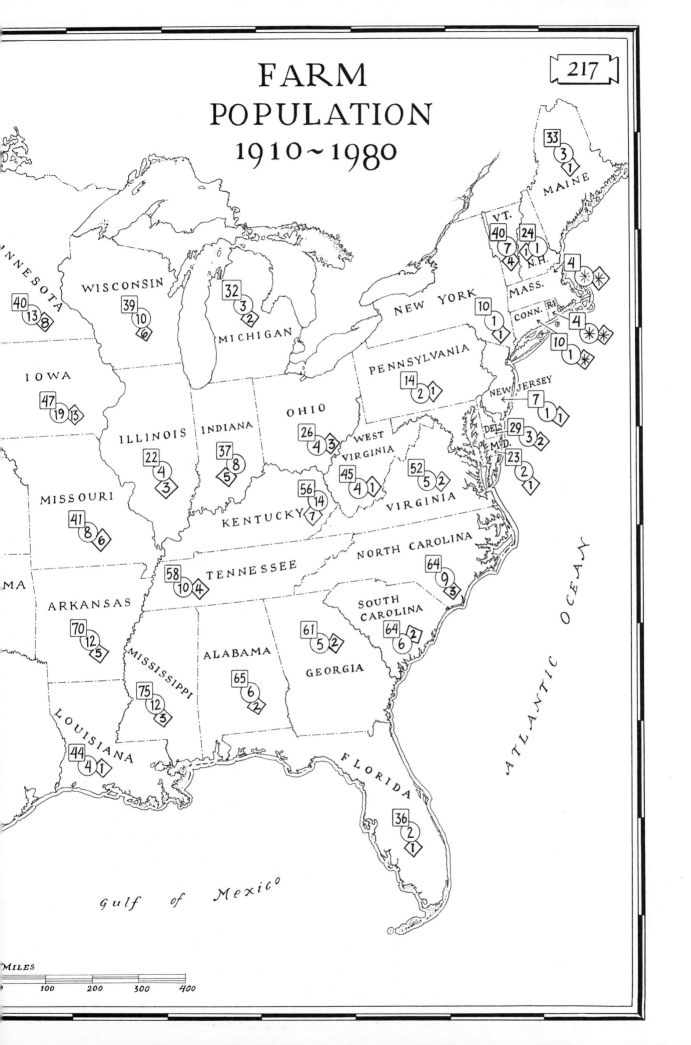

FARM
POPULATION
1910~1980

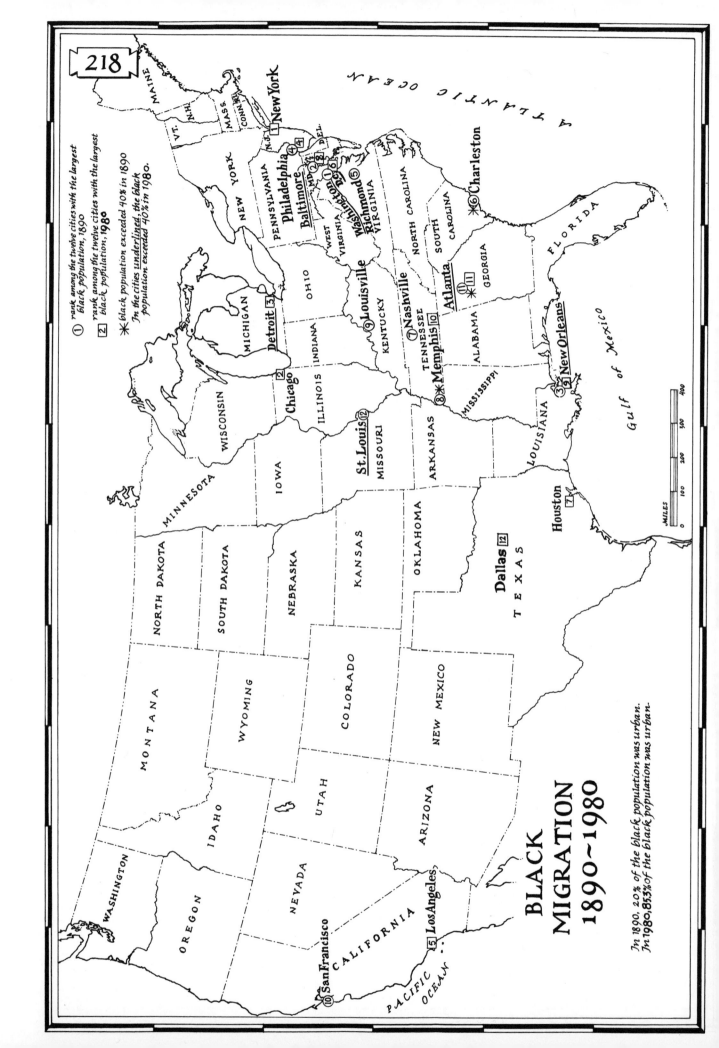

218

① rank among the twelve cities with the largest black population, 1890

② rank among the twelve cities with the largest black population, 1980

✳ black population exceeded 40% in 1890
In the cities underlined, the black population exceeded 40% in 1980.

ATLANTIC OCEAN

MAINE
VT. N.H. MASS. CONN. R.I.
NEW YORK
N.J.
PENNSYLVANIA
DEL.
MD.
WEST VIRGINIA
VIRGINIA
NORTH CAROLINA
SOUTH CAROLINA
GEORGIA
FLORIDA

① New York
④ ② Philadelphia
Baltimore
② ① ⑧ ⑥ Washington D.C.
⑤ Richmond
⑥ Charleston ✳
⑪ ⑪ Atlanta ✳

OHIO
MICHIGAN
INDIANA
ILLINOIS
KENTUCKY
TENNESSEE
ALABAMA
MISSISSIPPI
LOUISIANA

③ Detroit
② Chicago
⑨ Louisville
⑦ ⑦ Nashville
⑩ Memphis
⑧ ✳
③ ② New Orleans
Houston ⑦
Dallas ⑫

WISCONSIN
MINNESOTA
IOWA
MISSOURI
NORTH DAKOTA
SOUTH DAKOTA
NEBRASKA
KANSAS
OKLAHOMA
ARKANSAS
TEXAS

St.Louis ⑫

Gulf of Mexico

MONTANA
WYOMING
COLORADO
NEW MEXICO
IDAHO
UTAH
ARIZONA
NEVADA
OREGON
WASHINGTON
CALIFORNIA

⑩ San Francisco
⑤ Los Angeles

PACIFIC OCEAN

MILES
0 100 200 300 400

BLACK
MIGRATION
1890~1980

In 1890, 20% of the black population was urban.
In 1980, 85.3% of the black population was urban.

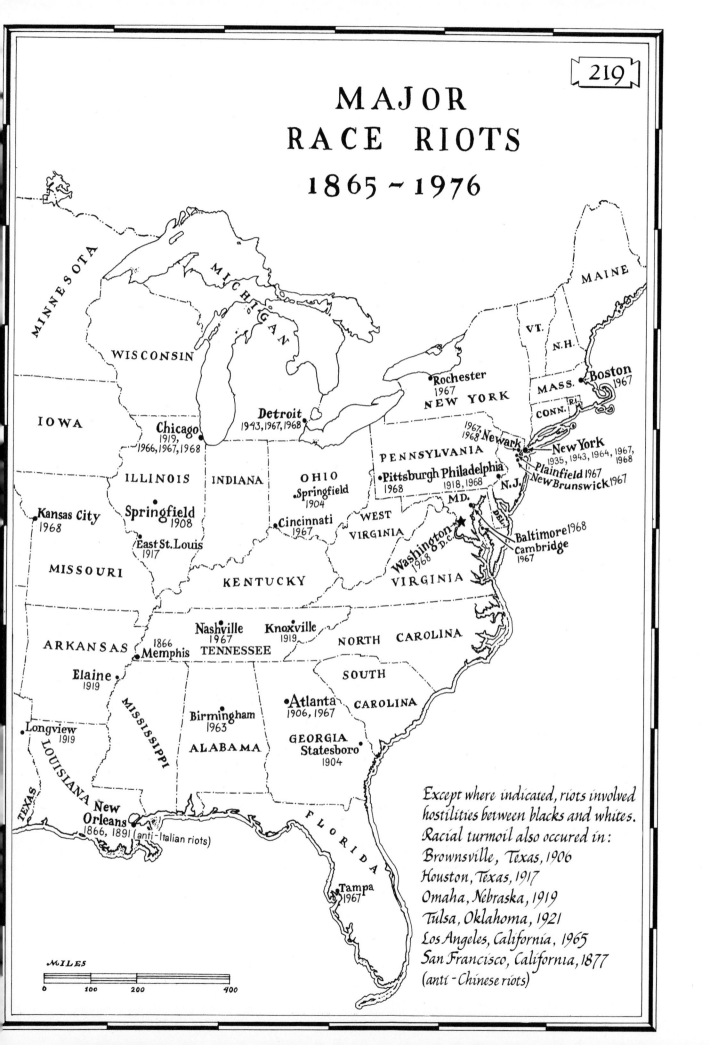

MAJOR
RACE RIOTS
1865 ~ 1976

219

Rochester 1967

Boston 1967

Detroit 1943, 1967, 1968

Chicago 1919, 1966, 1967, 1968

1967, 1968 Newark

New York 1935, 1943, 1964, 1967, 1968

Pittsburgh 1968   Philadelphia 1918, 1968

Plainfield 1967
New Brunswick 1967

Springfield 1904

Kansas City 1968

Springfield 1908

Cincinnati 1967

East St. Louis 1917

Washington D.C. 1968

Baltimore 1968
Cambridge 1967

Nashville 1967   Knoxville 1919

1866 Memphis

Elaine 1919

Atlanta 1906, 1967

Birmingham 1963

Longview 1919

GEORGIA Statesboro 1904

New Orleans 1866, 1891 (anti-Italian riots)

Tampa 1967

Except where indicated, riots involved
hostilities between blacks and whites.
Racial turmoil also occured in:
Brownsville, Texas, 1906
Houston, Texas, 1917
Omaha, Nebraska, 1919
Tulsa, Oklahoma, 1921
Los Angeles, California, 1965
San Francisco, California, 1877
(anti-Chinese riots)

MILES

0   100   200   400

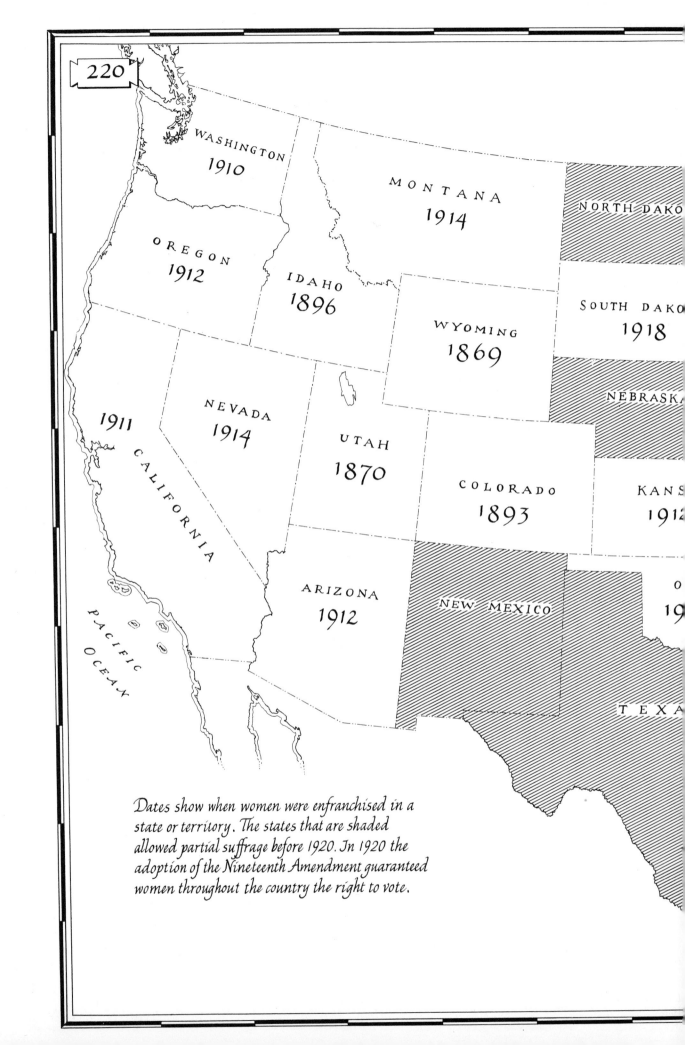

WASHINGTON
1910

MONTANA
1914

NORTH DAKO

OREGON
1912

IDAHO
1896

WYOMING
1869

SOUTH DAKO
1918

NEBRASK

1911

NEVADA
1914

UTAH
1870

COLORADO
1893

KANS
191

CALIFORNIA

PACIFIC
OCEAN

ARIZONA
1912

NEW MEXICO

O
19

TEXA

Dates show when women were enfranchised in a
state or territory. The states that are shaded
allowed partial suffrage before 1920. In 1920 the
adoption of the Nineteenth Amendment guaranteed
women throughout the country the right to vote.

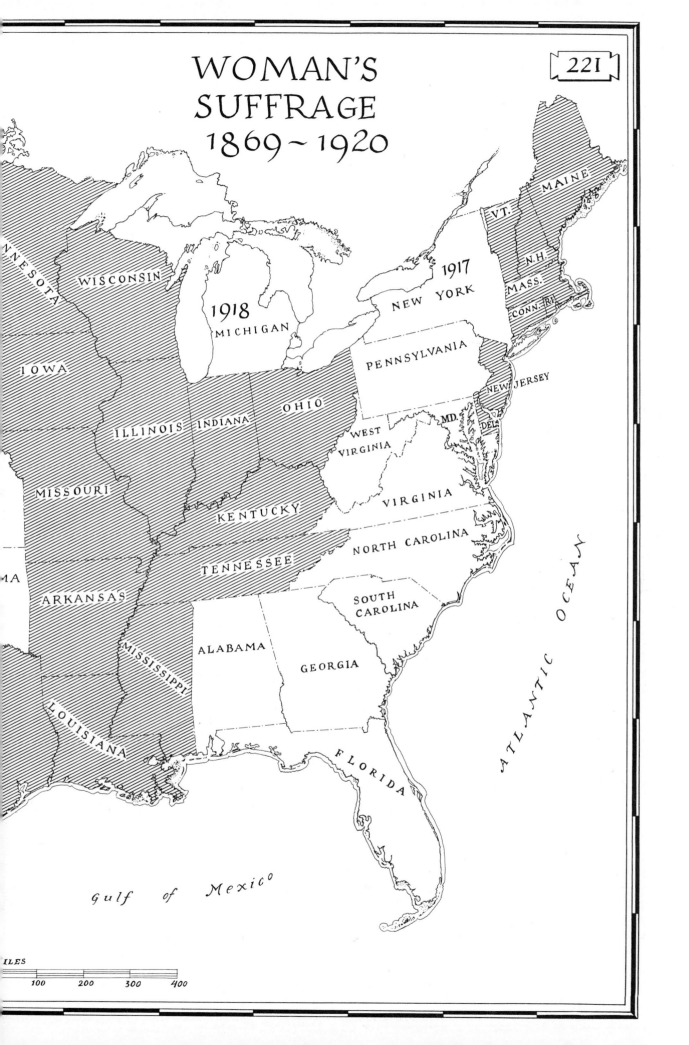

WOMAN'S SUFFRAGE
1869~1920

1917

1918

MAINE

VT.

N.H.

MASS.

CONN. R.I.

NEW YORK

MICHIGAN

WISCONSIN

MINNESOTA

IOWA

PENNSYLVANIA

NEW JERSEY

ILLINOIS INDIANA OHIO

MD.

DEL.

WEST VIRGINIA

MISSOURI

KENTUCKY

VIRGINIA

NORTH CAROLINA

TENNESSEE

ARKANSAS

SOUTH CAROLINA

ALABAMA

GEORGIA

MISSISSIPPI

LOUISIANA

FLORIDA

ATLANTIC OCEAN

Gulf of Mexico

MILES

100   200   300   400

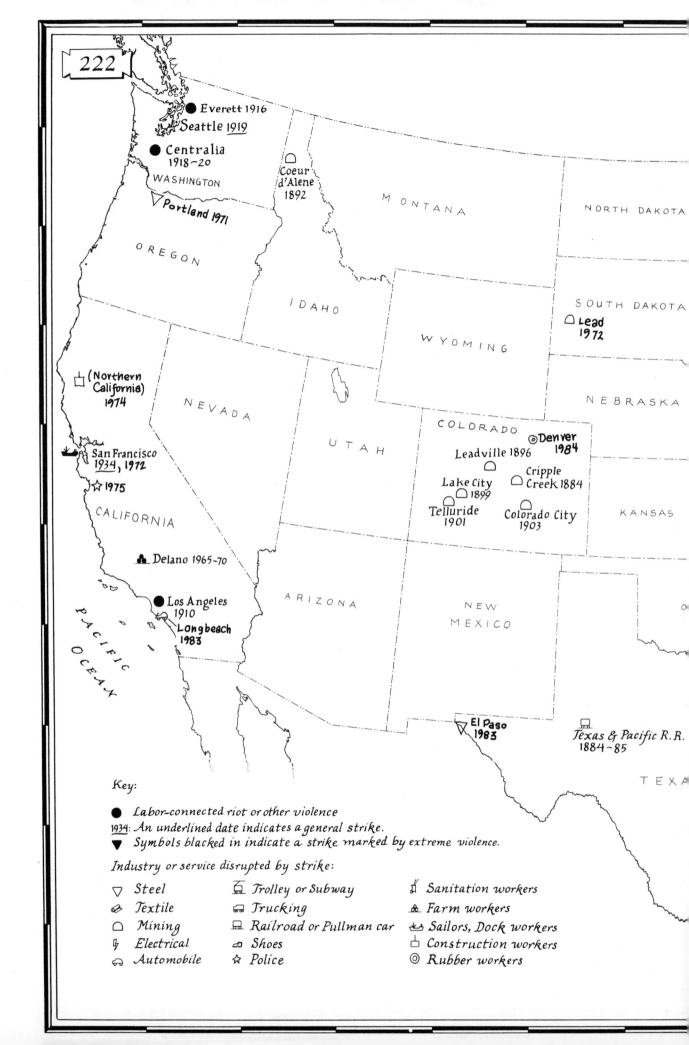

222

Everett 1916
Seattle 1919
Centralia 1918~20
WASHINGTON
Coeur d'Alene 1892
MONTANA
NORTH DAKOTA
Portland 1971
OREGON
IDAHO
WYOMING
SOUTH DAKOTA
Lead 1972
(Northern California) 1974
NEVADA
UTAH
COLORADO
Denver 1984
Leadville 1896
NEBRASKA
San Francisco 1934, 1972
Lake City 1899
Cripple Creek 1884
1975
Telluride 1901
Colorado City 1903
KANSAS
CALIFORNIA
Delano 1965~70
Los Angeles 1910
Longbeach 1983
ARIZONA
NEW MEXICO
PACIFIC OCEAN
El Paso 1983
Texas & Pacific R.R. 1884~85
TEXA

Key:

● Labor-connected riot or other violence
1934: An underlined date indicates a general strike.
▼ Symbols blacked in indicate a strike marked by extreme violence.

Industry or service disrupted by strike:

▽ Steel
🚊 Trolley or Subway
🗡 Sanitation workers
🖋 Textile
🚐 Trucking
♣ Farm workers
◠ Mining
🚃 Railroad or Pullman car
⚓ Sailors, Dock workers
⚡ Electrical
👞 Shoes
⊔ Construction workers
🚗 Automobile
☆ Police
◎ Rubber workers

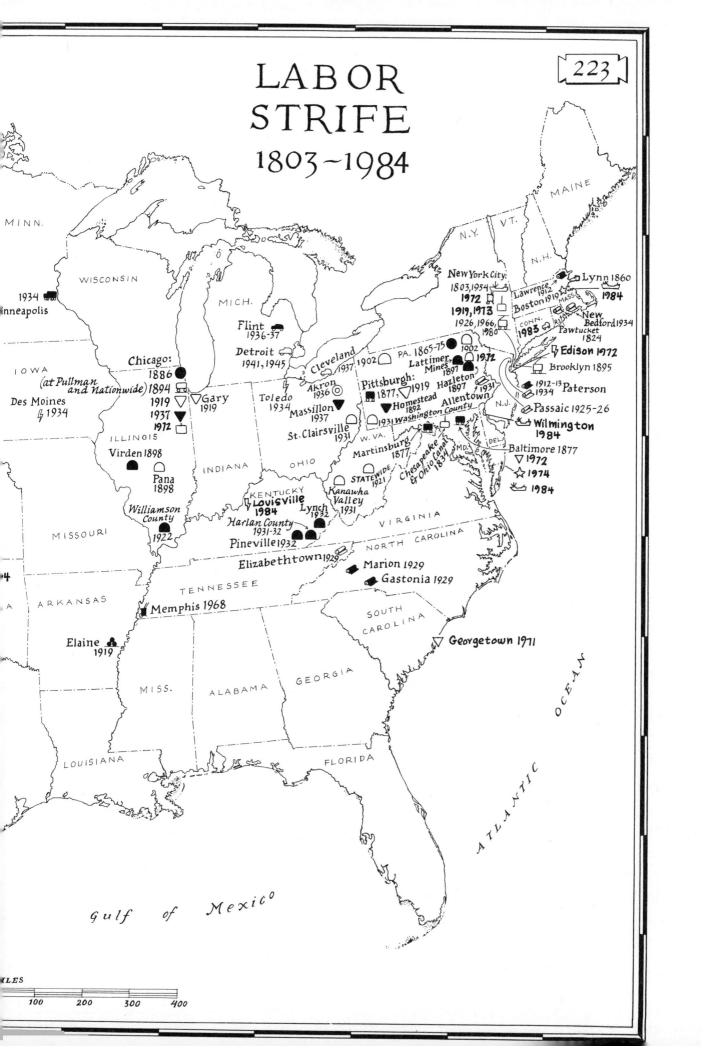

LABOR STRIFE
1803-1984

MINN.

WISCONSIN

MICH.

MAINE

N.Y.

VT.

N.H.

1934 Minneapolis

Flint 1936-37

New York City: 1803, 1954
1972
1919, 1973
1926, 1966, 1980

Lynn 1860
1984

Lawrence 1912
Boston 1919
MASS.
CONN. 1983

New Bedford 1934
Pawtucket 1824

IOWA

Detroit 1941, 1945

Cleveland 1937 1902

PA. 1865-75 1902
Lattimer Mines 1897

1972

Edison 1972

Chicago:
1886
(at Pullman and Nationwide) 1894
1919
1937
1972

Des Moines 1934

Gary 1919

Toledo 1934

Akron 1936

Pittsburgh: 1877, 1919
Massillon 1937
Homestead 1892
Washington County 1931

Hazleton 1897 1931
Allentown

Brooklyn 1895

1912-13 1934 Paterson

Passaic 1925-26

N.J.

DEL.

Wilmington 1984

ILLINOIS

St. Clairsville 1931

W. VA.

Virden 1898
Pana 1898

INDIANA

OHIO

Martinsburg 1877

MD.

Baltimore 1877
1972
1974
1984

Williamson County 1922

MISSOURI

KENTUCKY
Louisville 1984

Lynch 1932

STATEWIDE 1921

Kanawha Valley 1931

Chesapeake & Ohio Canal 1834

Harlan County 1931-32
Pineville 1932

VIRGINIA

NORTH CAROLINA

Elizabethtown 1929

Marion 1929
Gastonia 1929

TENNESSEE

ARKANSAS

SOUTH CAROLINA

Memphis 1968

Elaine 1919

MISS.

ALABAMA

GEORGIA

Georgetown 1971

LOUISIANA

FLORIDA

ATLANTIC OCEAN

Gulf of Mexico

MILES
100   200   300   400

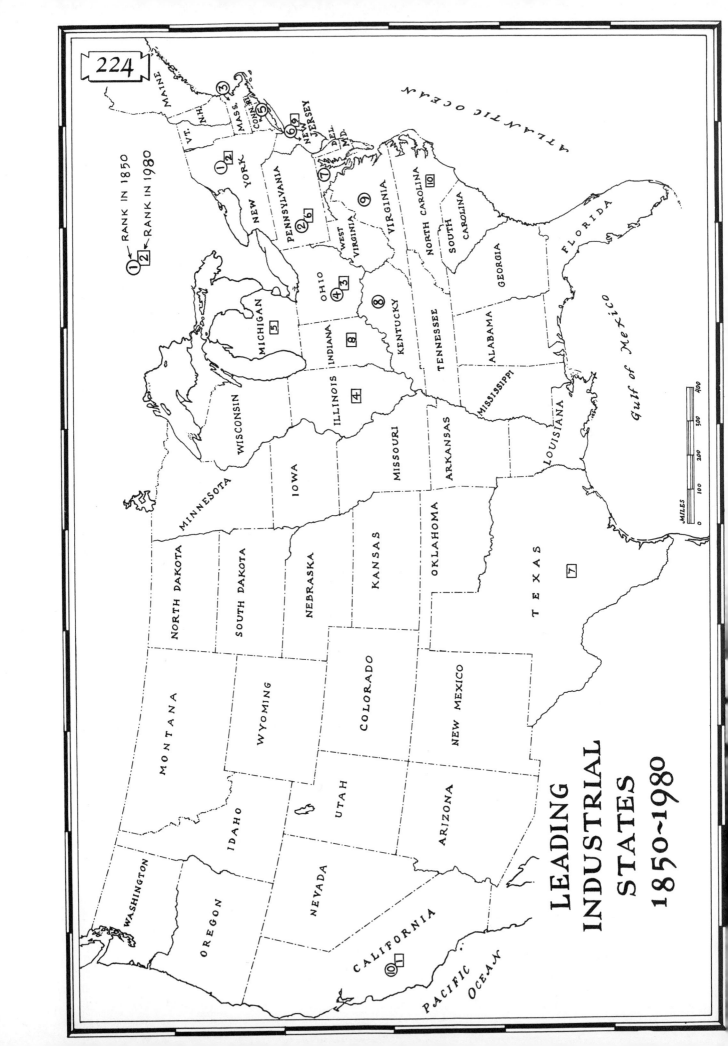

224

RANK IN 1850
RANK IN 1980

LEADING
INDUSTRIAL
STATES
1850~1980

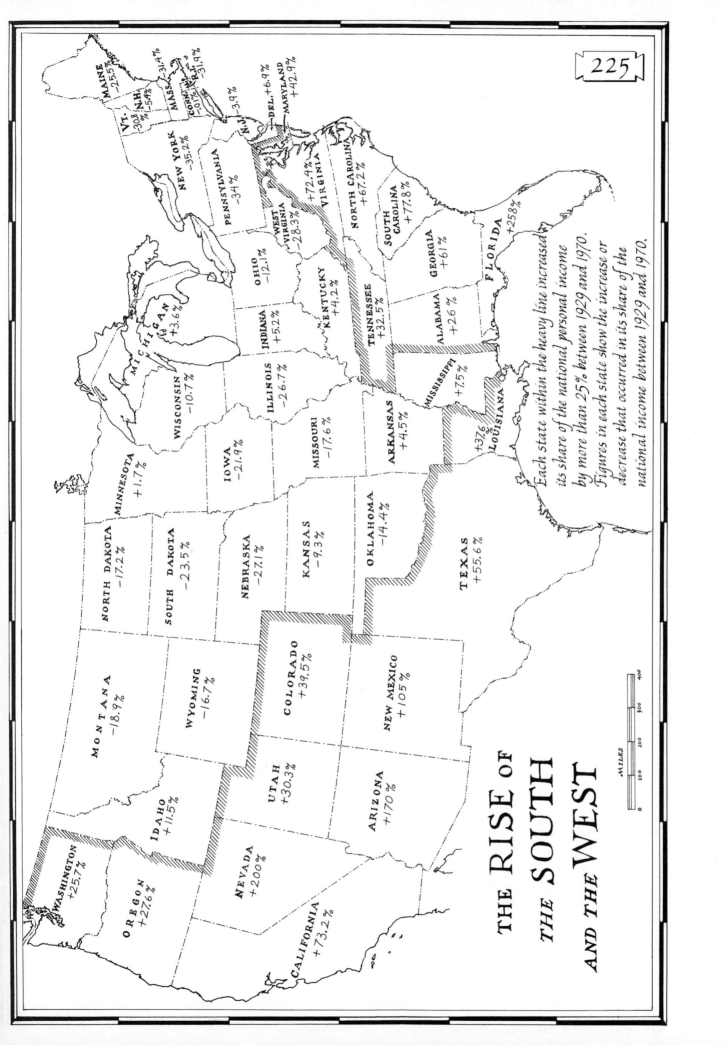

THE RISE OF THE SOUTH AND THE WEST

Each state within the heavy line increased its share of the national personal income by more than 25% between 1929 and 1970. Figures in each state show the increase or decrease that occurred in its share of the national income between 1929 and 1970.

MILES
0 100 200 300 400

MAINE −25.5%
N.H. −54%
VT. −30.8%
MASS. −31.4%
CONN. −31.9%
R.I. −0%
NEW YORK −35.2%
PENNSYLVANIA −34%
N.J. −3.9%
DEL. +6.9%
MARYLAND +42.9%
WEST VIRGINIA −28.3%
VIRGINIA +72.4%
NORTH CAROLINA +67.2%
SOUTH CAROLINA +77.8%
GEORGIA +61%
FLORIDA +258%
OHIO −12.1%
KENTUCKY +4.2%
TENNESSEE +32.5%
ALABAMA +26%
MISSISSIPPI +7.5%
LOUISIANA +37.6%
INDIANA +5.2%
ILLINOIS −26.7%
MICHIGAN +3.6%
WISCONSIN −10.7%
MINNESOTA +1.7%
IOWA −2.9%
MISSOURI −17.6%
ARKANSAS +4.5%
NORTH DAKOTA −17.2%
SOUTH DAKOTA −23.5%
NEBRASKA −27.1%
KANSAS −9.3%
OKLAHOMA −14.4%
TEXAS +55.6%
MONTANA −18.9%
WYOMING −16.7%
COLORADO +39.5%
NEW MEXICO +105%
IDAHO +11.5%
UTAH +30.3%
ARIZONA +170%
WASHINGTON +25.7%
OREGON +27.6%
NEVADA +200%
CALIFORNIA +73.2%

OREGON

CALIFORNIA
1900-1984

Redwood
National
Park

TULE LAKE
RESERVOIR

Lassen
Volcanic
National
Park

MAJOR IRRIGATED AREAS

OIL FIELDS

NEVADA

•Reno

LAKE TAHOE

Sacramento

San Francisco

Berkeley
Oakland

•San Jose

HETCH
HETCHY
RESER
VOIR

Yosemite
National
Park

Coalinga

Fresno

Kings
Canyon
Nat'l.
Park

Sequoia
Nat'l.
Park

Las Vegas•

HOOVER DAM

DEATH
VALLEY

SEARLES
LAKE (DRY SALT)

LAKE
MOJAVE

Bakersfield

•Mojave
•Boron

DAVIS
DAM

MOJAVE DESERT

Needles

PACIFIC

Santa
Barbara

Hollywood

SAN ANDREAS FAULT

Mount Wilson
Pasadena

Los Angeles

Santa Monica
Watts
Wilmington
Long Beach
Hunting
ton Beach

Whittier
Anaheim

San Clemente
△Mount Palomar

Riverside

COLORADO RIVER AQUEDUCT

LAKE
HAVASU

PARKER DAM

San Diego

IMPERIAL
VALLEY

IMPERIAL DAM

MEXICO

OCEAN

MILES
25   0   50   100

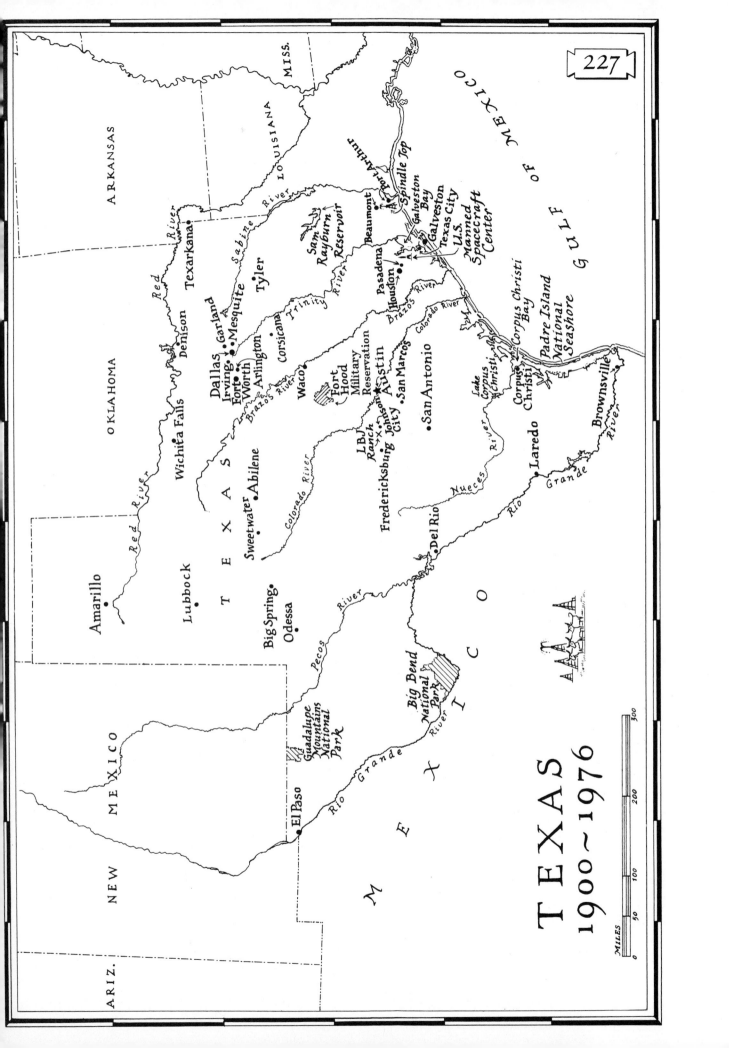

ARIZ.

NEW MEXICO

ARKANSAS

OKLAHOMA

LOUISIANA

MISS.

Red River

Red River

Red River

Sabine River

Trinity

Texarkana

Denison

Wichita Falls

Amarillo

Lubbock

Big Spring

Odessa

Sweetwater

Abilene

T E X A S

Dallas

Irving

Fort Worth

Garland

Mesquite

Arlington

Corsicana

Tyler

Waco

Brazos River

Colorado River

Pecos River

Fort Hood Military Reservation

Austin

Fredericksburg

LBJ Ranch

Johnson City

San Marcos

San Antonio

Beaumont

Port Arthur

Spindle Top

Galveston Bay

Galveston

Texas City

U.S. Manned Spacecraft Center

Pasadena

Houston

Brazos River

Colorado River

Sam Rayburn Reservoir

Del Rio

Nueces River

Rio Grande

Laredo

Corpus Christi

Corpus Christi Bay

Lake Corpus Christi

Padre Island National Seashore

Brownsville

Rio Grande River

Big Bend National Park

Guadalupe Mountains National Park

El Paso

Rio Grande

M   E   X   I   C   O

G U L F   OF   M E X I C O

T E X A S
1900~1976

MILES

0   50   100   200   300

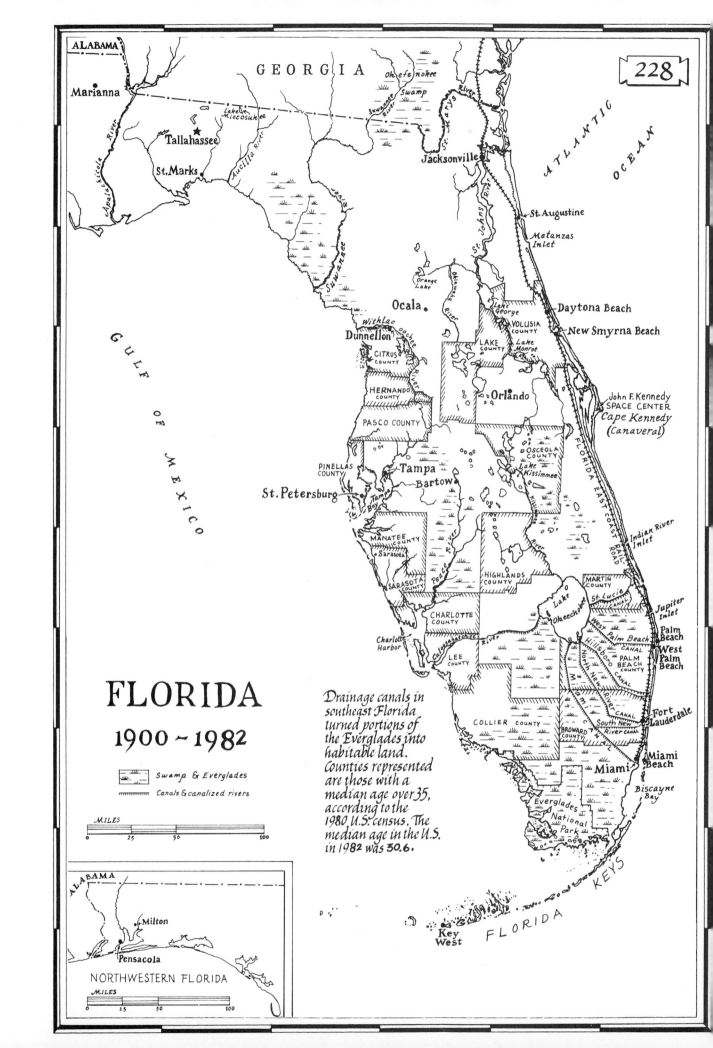

ALABAMA

GEORGIA

Marianna

Lake Miccosukee

Apalachicola River

Tallahassee

St.Marks

Aucilla River

Suwannee River

Okefenokee Swamp

St. Marys River

ATLANTIC

Jacksonville

St. Augustine

Matanzas Inlet

OCEAN

Orange Lake

St. Johns River

Ocala

Dunnellon

Withlacoochee River

CITRUS COUNTY

HERNANDO COUNTY

PASCO COUNTY

PINELLAS COUNTY

Oklawaha River

Lake George

Lake Monroe

VOLUSIA COUNTY

LAKE COUNTY

Daytona Beach

New Smyrna Beach

Orlando

John F. Kennedy SPACE CENTER

Cape Kennedy (Canaveral)

OSCEOLA COUNTY

Lake Kissimmee

GULF OF MEXICO

Tampa

Bartow

St. Petersburg

Tampa Bay

MANATEE COUNTY

Sarasota

SARASOTA COUNTY

Peace River

Kissimmee River

FLORIDA EAST COAST RAILROAD

Indian River Inlet

HIGHLANDS COUNTY

MARTIN COUNTY

St. Lucie Canal

Jupiter Inlet

CHARLOTTE COUNTY

Charlotte Harbor

Caloosahatchee River

LEE COUNTY

Lake Okeechobee

West Palm Beach Canal

Hillsboro Canal

North New River Canal

PALM BEACH COUNTY

Palm Beach

West Palm Beach

FLORIDA

1900 ~ 1982

COLLIER COUNTY

Miami Canal

South New River Canal

BROWARD COUNTY

Fort Lauderdale

Miami

Miami Beach

Biscayne Bay

Swamp & Everglades

Canals & canalized rivers

Drainage canals in southeast Florida turned portions of the Everglades into habitable land. Counties represented are those with a median age over 35, according to the 1980 U.S. census. The median age in the U.S. in 1982 was 30.6.

Everglades National Park

MILES

0   25   50   100

FLORIDA KEYS

Key West

ALABAMA

Milton

Pensacola

NORTHWESTERN FLORIDA

MILES

0   25   50   100

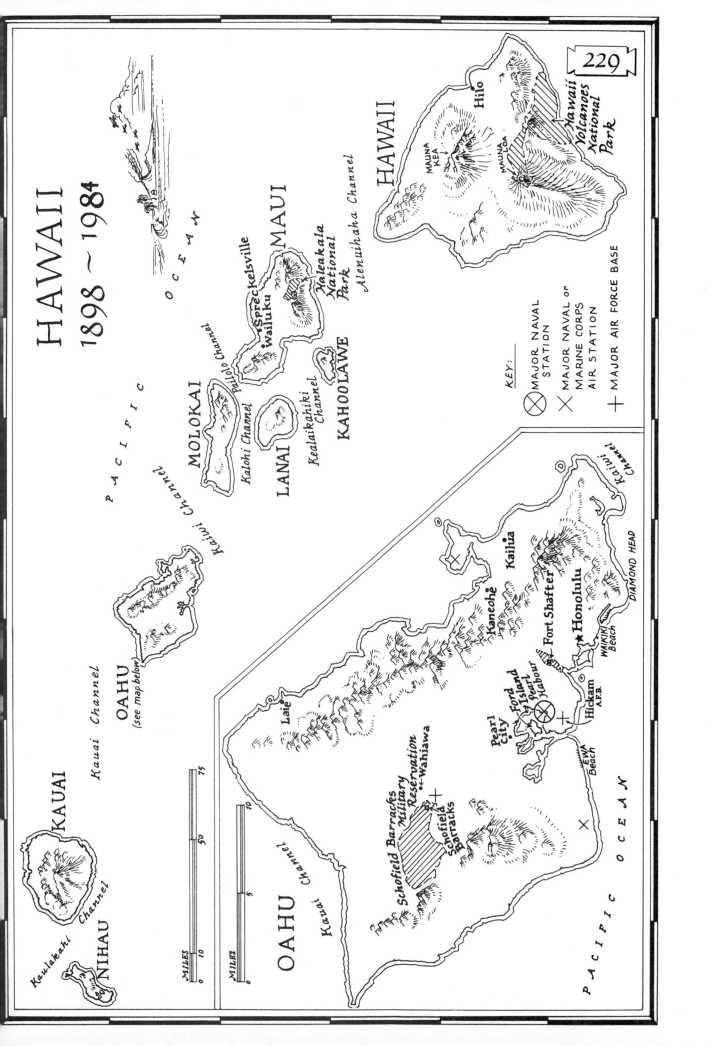

HAWAII
1898 ~ 1984

KAUAI

NIHAU

Kaulakahi Channel

Kauai Channel

OAHU
(see map below)

Kaiwi Channel

PACIFIC

OCEAN

MOLOKAI

Pailolo Channel

Kalohi Channel

MAUI

Spreckelsville
Wailuku

Haleakala
National
Park

LANAI

Kealaikahiki Channel

KAHOOLAWE

Alenuihaha Channel

HAWAII

Hilo

MAUNA
KEA

MAUNA
LOA

Hawaii
Volcanoes
National
Park

KEY:

⊗ MAJOR NAVAL
STATION

✕ MAJOR NAVAL or
MARINE CORPS
AIR STATION

+ MAJOR AIR FORCE BASE

MILES
0   50   75   10

MILES
0   5   10

OAHU

Kauai Channel

Kaiwi Channel

Laie

Kaneohe

Kailua

Fort Shafter

Honolulu

WAIKIKI
Beach

DIAMOND HEAD

Pearl
City

Ford
Island

Pearl
Harbour

Hickam
A.F.B.

EWA
Beach

Wahiawa

Schofield Barracks
Military
Reservation

Schofield
Barracks

PACIFIC OCEAN

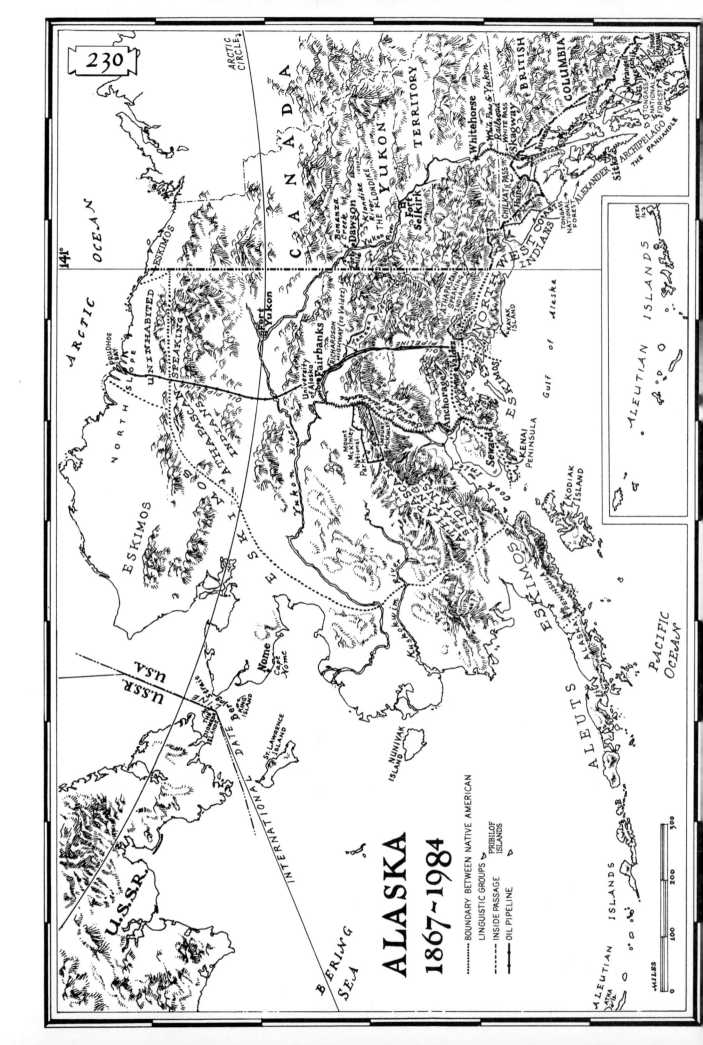

ALASKA
1867~1984

- - - - BOUNDARY BETWEEN NATIVE AMERICAN
LINGUISTIC GROUPS
· · · · INSIDE PASSAGE
—→ OIL PIPELINE

PRIBILOF
ISLANDS

MILES
0   100   200   300

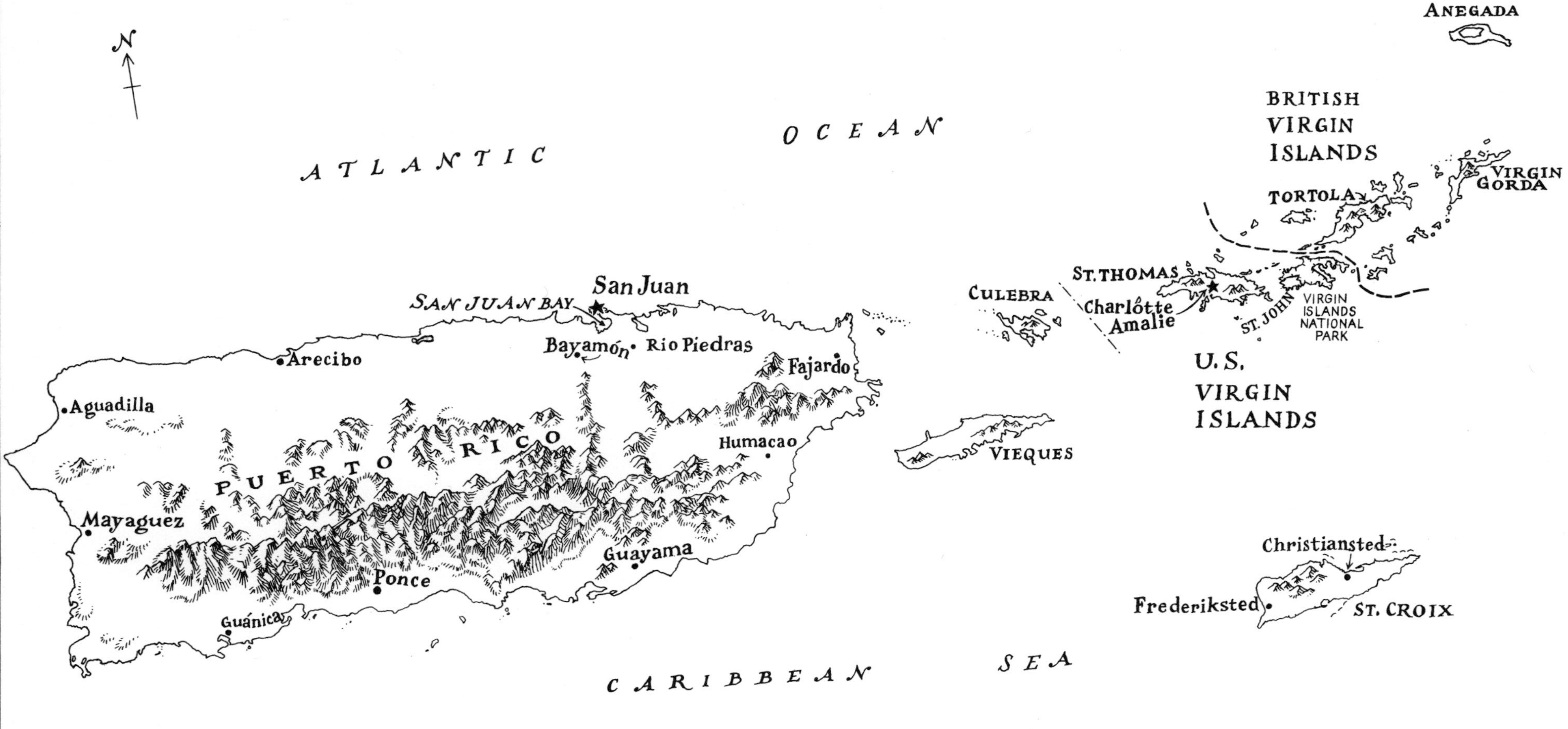

ANEGADA

VIRGIN GORDA

BRITISH VIRGIN ISLANDS

TORTOLA

VIRGIN ISLANDS NATIONAL PARK

NHP

ST. JOHN

ST. THOMAS

Charlotte Amalie

U.S. VIRGIN ISLANDS

Christiansted

St. Croix

Frederiksted

CULEBRA

VIEQUES

S E A

OCEAN

Fajardo

Humacao

San Juan

Rio Piedras

Bayamón

SAN JUAN BAY

Guayama

Ponce

P U E R T O R I C O

C A R I B B E A N

Arecibo

Guánica

Aguadilla

Mayagüez

A T L A N T I C

N

MILES

0   10   20   30   40

PUERTO RICO AND THE UNITED STATES VIRGIN ISLANDS

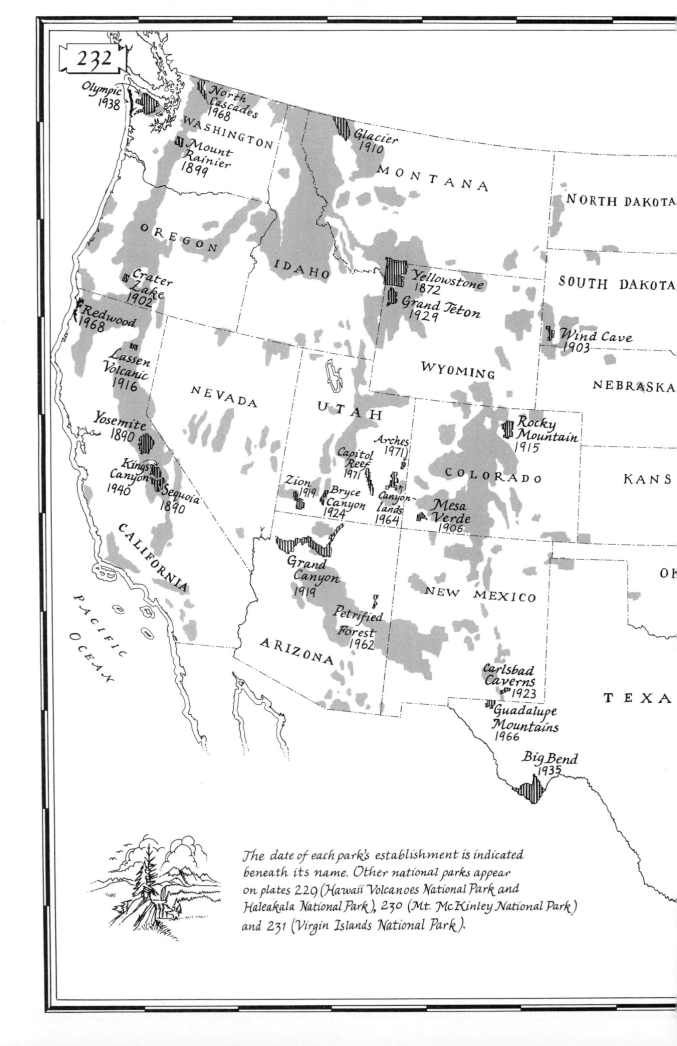

Olympic
1938

North
Cascades
1968

WASHINGTON

Glacier
1910

MONTANA

Mount
Rainier
1899

NORTH DAKOTA

OREGON

IDAHO

SOUTH DAKOTA

Crater
Lake
1902

Yellowstone
1872

Redwood
1968

Grand Teton
1929

WYOMING

Wind Cave
1903

Lassen
Volcanic
1916

NEBRASKA

NEVADA

UTAH

Rocky
Mountain
1915

Yosemite
1890

KANS

Arches
1971

Capitol
Reef
1971

COLORADO

Kings
Canyon
1940

Sequoia
1890

Zion
1919

Bryce
Canyon
1924

Canyon
lands
1964

Mesa
Verde
1906

CALIFORNIA

Grand
Canyon
1919

NEW MEXICO

OK

Petrified
Forest
1962

PACIFIC
OCEAN

ARIZONA

Carlsbad
Caverns
1923

TEXA

Guadalupe
Mountains
1966

Big Bend
1935

The date of each park's establishment is indicated
beneath its name. Other national parks appear
on plates 229 (Hawaii Volcanoes National Park and
Haleakala National Park), 230 (Mt. McKinley National Park)
and 231 (Virgin Islands National Park).

NATIONAL
PARKS AND FORESTS
1872~1984

Voyageurs 1971

Isle Royale 1931

MAINE

Acadia 1919

VT.

N.H.

MASS.

CONN.

MINNESOTA

WISCONSIN

MICHIGAN

NEW YORK

IOWA

PENNSYLVANIA

NEW JERSEY

OHIO

MD.

DEL.

ILLINOIS · INDIANA

WEST VIRGINIA

Shenandoah 1926

MISSOURI

KENTUCKY

Mammoth Cave 1926

VIRGINIA

NORTH CAROLINA

TENNESSEE

Great Smoky Mountains 1926

ARKANSAS

SOUTH CAROLINA

tt 906

Hot Springs 1921

MISSISSIPPI

ALABAMA

GEORGIA

AA

LOUISIANA

FLORIDA

ATLANTIC OCEAN

Everglades 1934

Gulf   of   Mexico

ILES

100   200   300   400

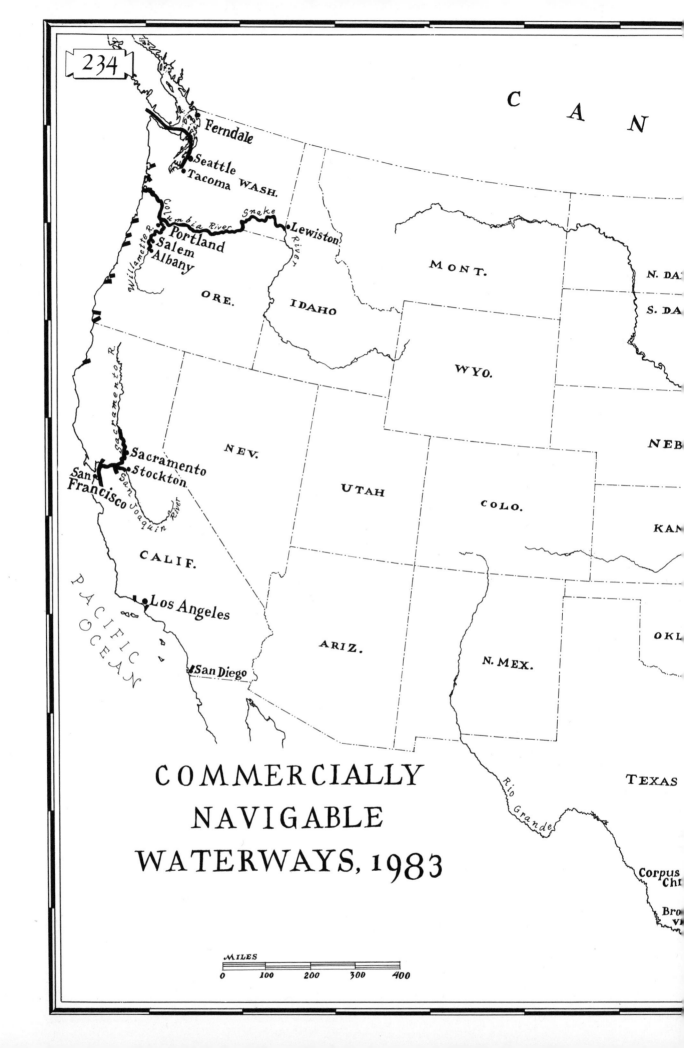

234

Ferndale
• Seattle
• Tacoma WASH.

Columbia River *Snake* • Lewiston

Willamette R. • Portland
• Salem
• Albany

ORE. IDAHO MONT. N. DA

S. DA

WYO.

Sacramento R.

NEV. NEB

• Sacramento
• Stockton

San
Francisco *San Joaquin River*

UTAH COLO.

KAN

CALIF.

• Los Angeles

ARIZ. N. MEX. OKL

• San Diego

PACIFIC
OCEAN

C A N

TEXAS

Rio Grande

Corpus
Chr

Bro
Vi

COMMERCIALLY
NAVIGABLE
WATERWAYS, 1983

MILES

0   100   200   300   400

ADA

LAKE SUPERIOR

Duluth

MINN.

Minneapolis

WIS.

Green Bay
Appleton

Milwaukee

Sault Ste. Marie

LAKE MICHIGAN

MICH.

Saginaw

Chicago

Detroit

LAKE HURON

LAKE ONTARIO

Toronto

Buffalo   Syracuse

Oswego

Albany

LAKE ERIE

Toledo   Cleveland

N.Y.

MAINE

Penobscot R.

St. Lawrence River

Kennebec R.

Bangor

Belfast

VT.

N.H.

Bath   Augusta

Connecticut R.

MASS.   Portsmouth

Boston

Hudson R.

CONN.   R.I.   Providence
New London

New York

IOWA

ux City

ILL.   IND.

OHIO

PA.

Pittsburgh

Philadelphia

Baltimore

N.J.

DEL.

Illinois River

Mississippi River

Cincinnati

Ohio River

Allegheny River

W. VA.

Washington
D.C.

Potomac R.

MD.

Missouri River

nsas City

St. Louis

MO.

Louisville

Kentucky R.

KY.

Bowling Green

Kanawha River

Charleston

Rappahannock

Richmond

James River

York River
Norfolk
Elizabeth City

OCEAN

Cumberland R.

Nashville

TENN.

Knoxville

Tennessee R.

VA.

Roanoke River

N.C.

Fayetteville

Cape Fear R.

Wilmington

ulsa

ko
ee

Arkansas River

ARK.

Memphis

Little Rock

Ouachita River

MISS.

Camden

Pearl River

Birmingham

Selma

Black Warrior R.

Tombigbee River

Alabama R.

Chattahoochee River

Columbus

ALA.

Apalachicola R.

GA.

Augusta

Savannah R.

S.C.

Charleston

Savannah

Jacksonville

FLA.

St. Johns River

Beaumont
uston

oria

LA.

Baton
Rouge

Atchafalaya R.

New Orleans

Mobile

St.
Marks

Gulf of Mexico

Tampa

Caloosahatchee
River

Miami

ATLANTIC

Navigable waterway

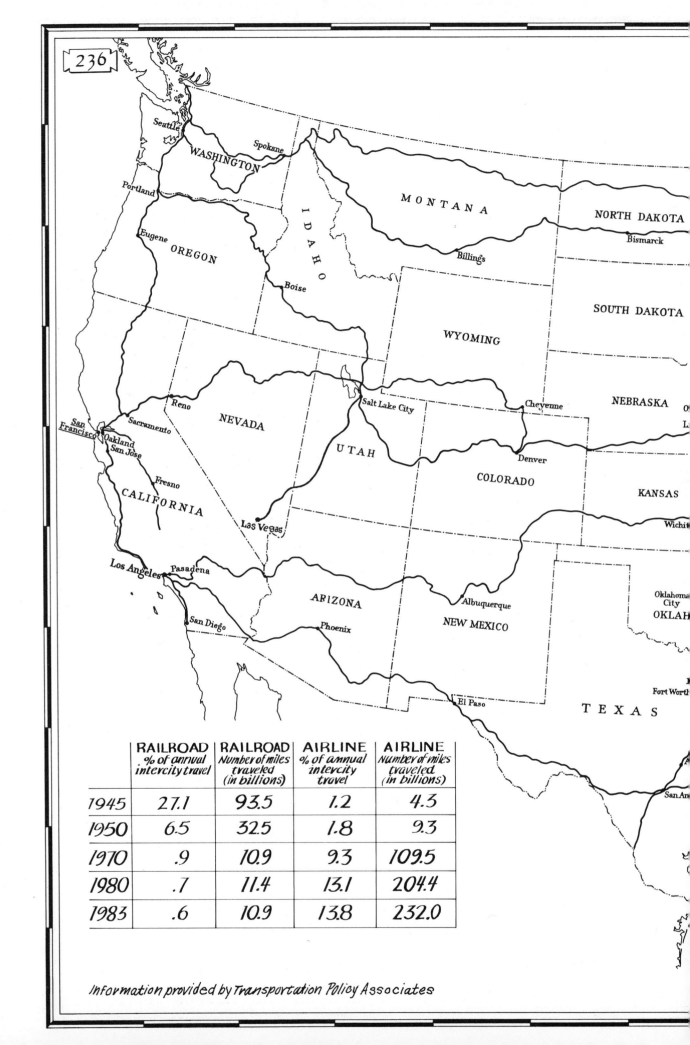

	RAILROAD % of annual intercity travel	RAILROAD Number of miles traveled (in billions)	AIRLINE % of annual intercity travel	AIRLINE Number of miles traveled (in billions)
1945	27.1	93.5	1.2	4.3
1950	6.5	32.5	1.8	9.3
1970	.9	10.9	9.3	109.5
1980	.7	11.4	13.1	204.4
1983	.6	10.9	13.8	232.0

Information provided by Transportation Policy Associates

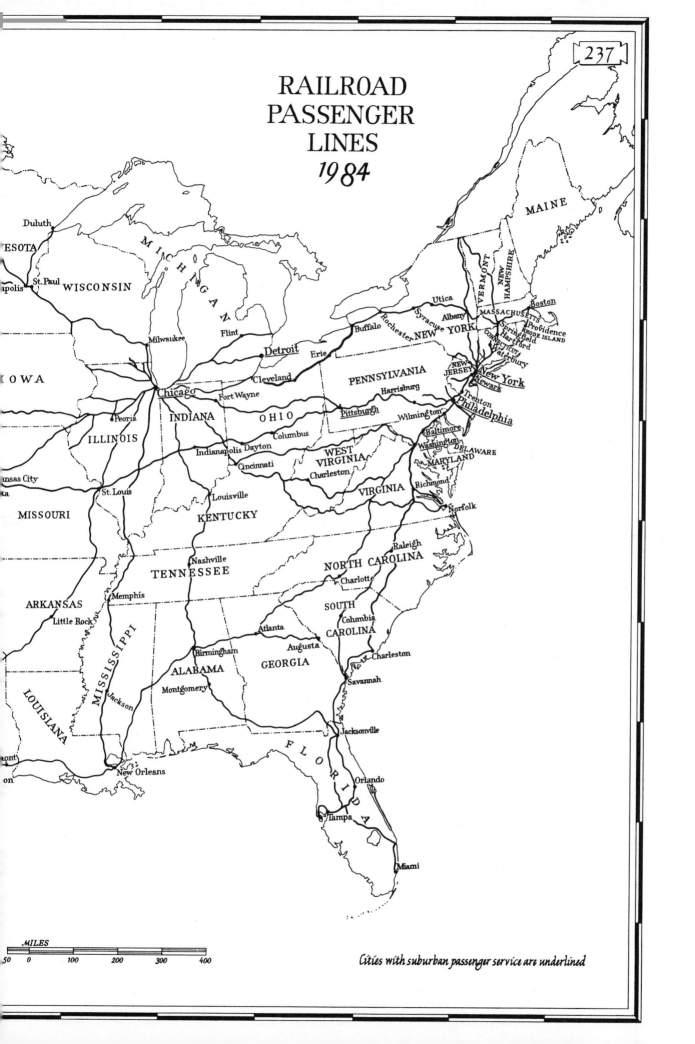

RAILROAD PASSENGER LINES
1984

MILES

50   0   100   200   300   400

Cities with suburban passenger service are underlined

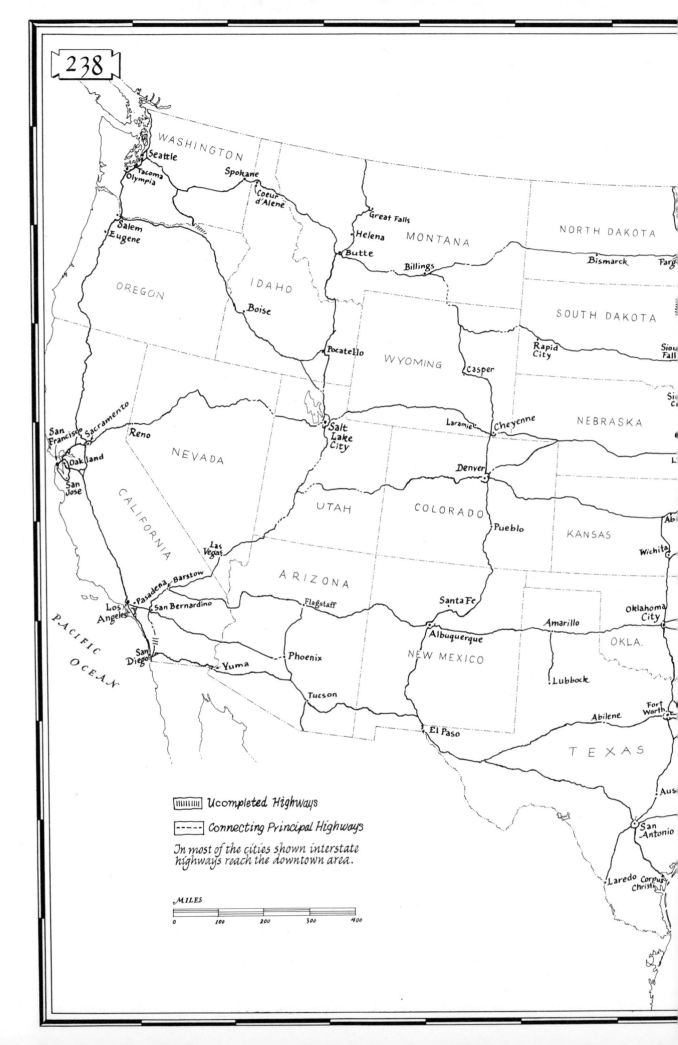

238

WASHINGTON

Seattle
Tacoma
Olympia

Spokane

Coeur
d'Alene

Great Falls

Helena

Butte

MONTANA

NORTH DAKOTA

Bismarck   Farg

Salem
Eugene

OREGON

IDAHO

Boise

Billings

SOUTH DAKOTA

Pocatello

WYOMING

Casper

Rapid
City

Siou
Fall

San
Francisco
Sacramento

Reno

NEVADA

Oakland

San
Jose

CALIFORNIA

Las
Vegas

Salt
Lake
City

Laramie   Cheyenne

Denver

UTAH

COLORADO

Pueblo

NEBRASKA

L

Si
C

KANSAS

Wichita

Ab

Pasadena Barstow

Los
Angeles

San Bernardino

ARIZONA

Flagstaff

Santa Fe

Amarillo

Oklahoma
City

OKLA.

San
Diego

Yuma

Phoenix

Tucson

Albuquerque

NEW MEXICO

Lubbock

El Paso

Abilene

Fort
Worth

PACIFIC
OCEAN

TEXAS

Aus

San
Antonio

Laredo Corpus
Christi

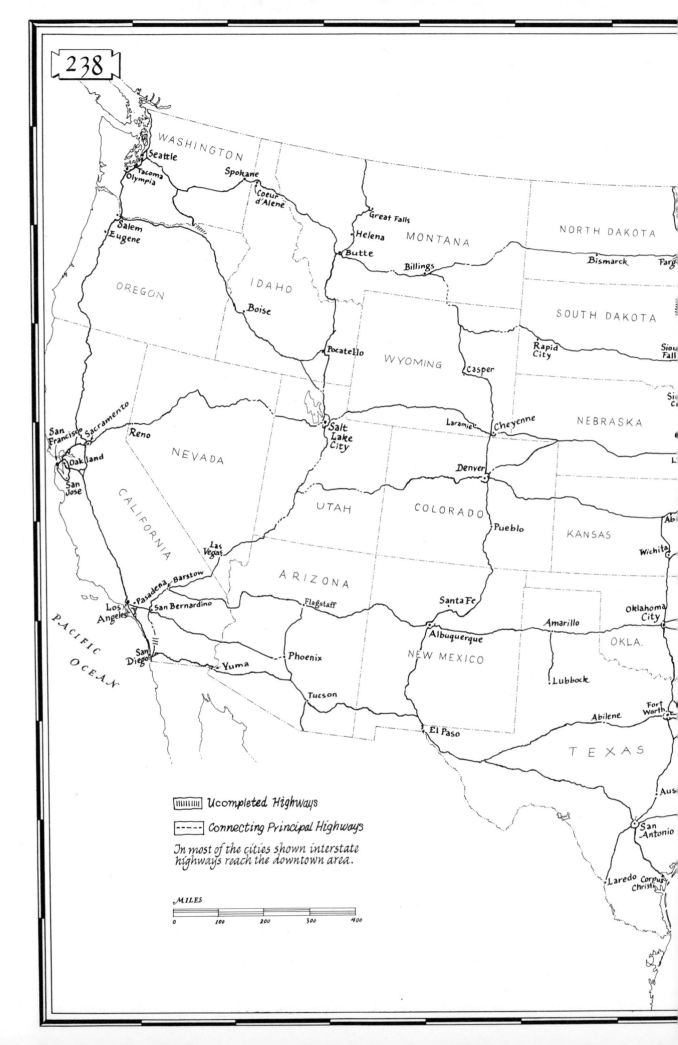

Ucompleted Highways

Connecting Principal Highways

In most of the cities shown interstate
highways reach the downtown area.

MILES

0   100   200   300   400

INTERSTATE HIGHWAY SYSTEM 1984

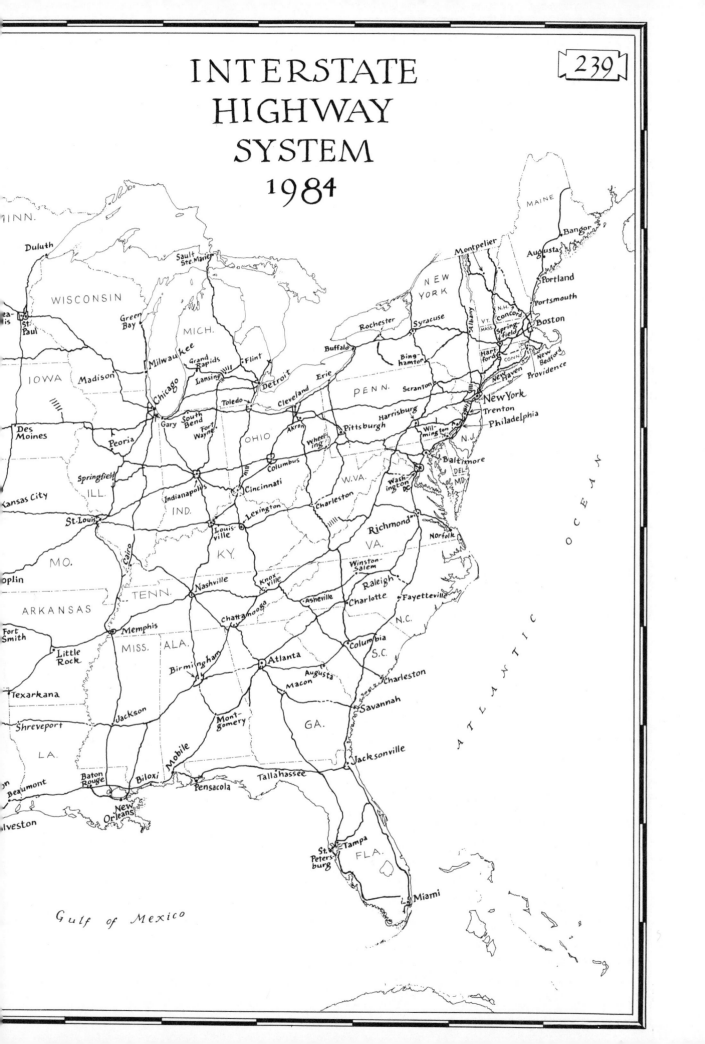

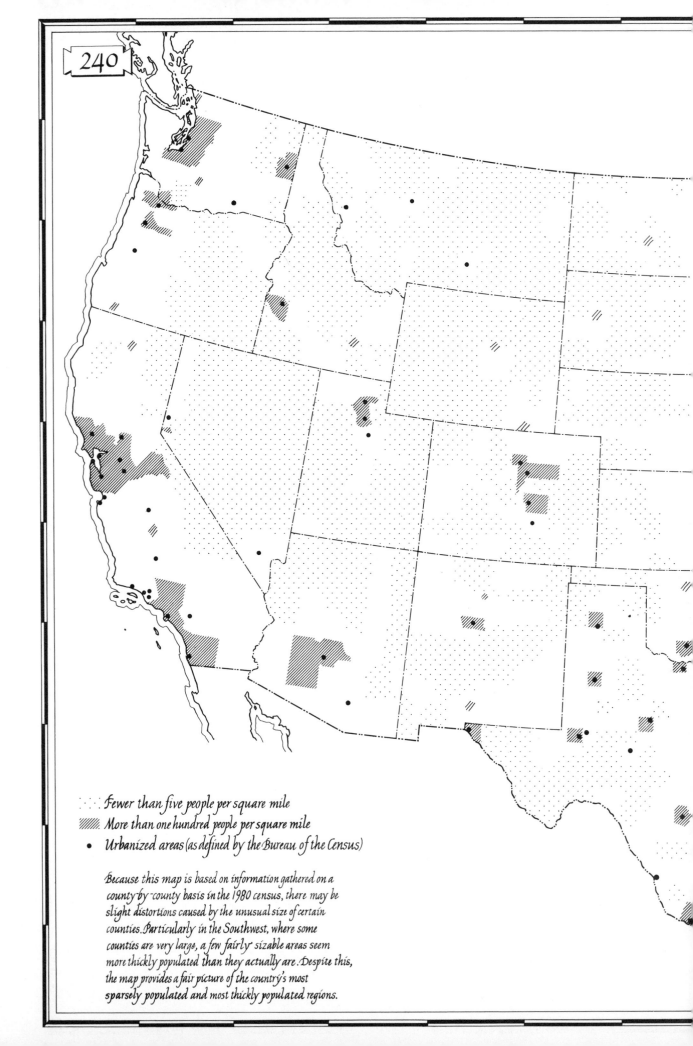

240

..... Fewer than five people per square mile

///// More than one hundred people per square mile

• Urbanized areas (as defined by the Bureau of the Census)

Because this map is based on information gathered on a
county-by-county basis in the 1980 census, there may be
slight distortions caused by the unusual size of certain
counties. Particularly in the Southwest, where some
counties are very large, a few fairly sizable areas seem
more thickly populated than they actually are. Despite this,
the map provides a fair picture of the country's most
sparsely populated and most thickly populated regions.

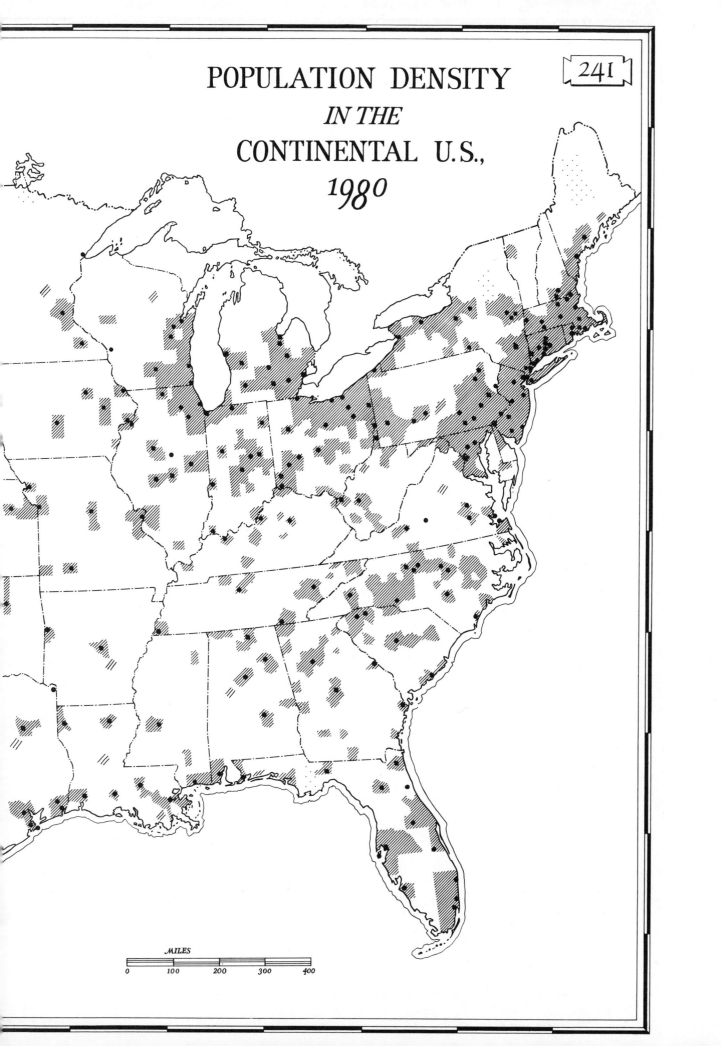

POPULATION DENSITY
IN THE
CONTINENTAL U.S.,
1980

241

MILES

0   100   200   300   400

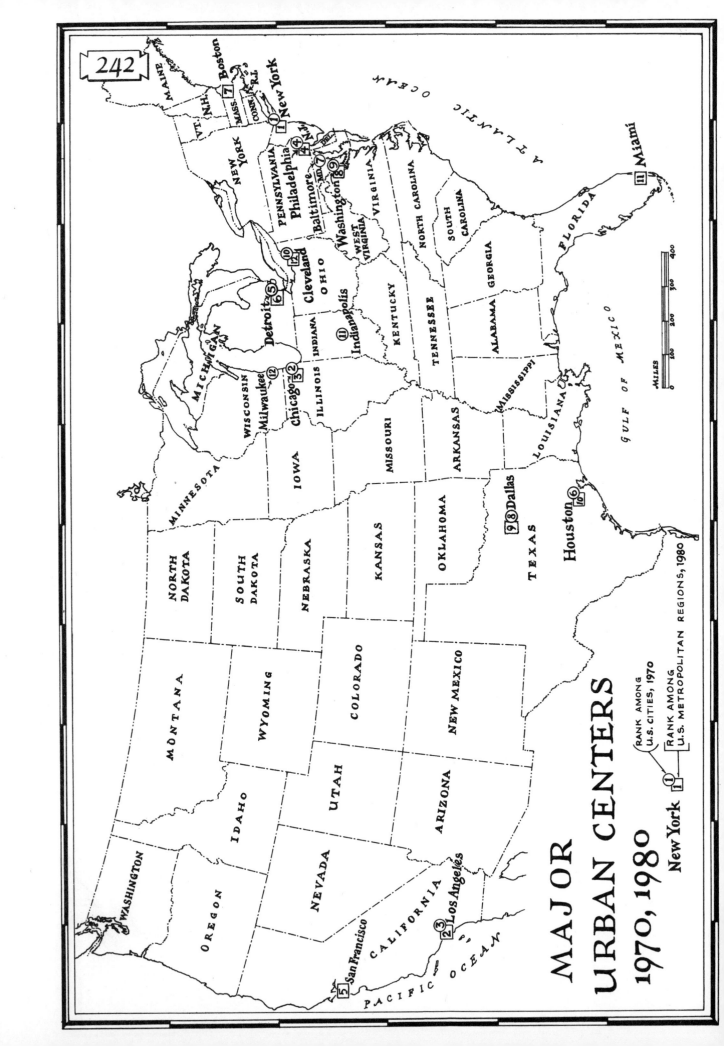

MAJOR URBAN CENTERS 1970, 1980

XI CURRENT ISSUES,
1978–1984

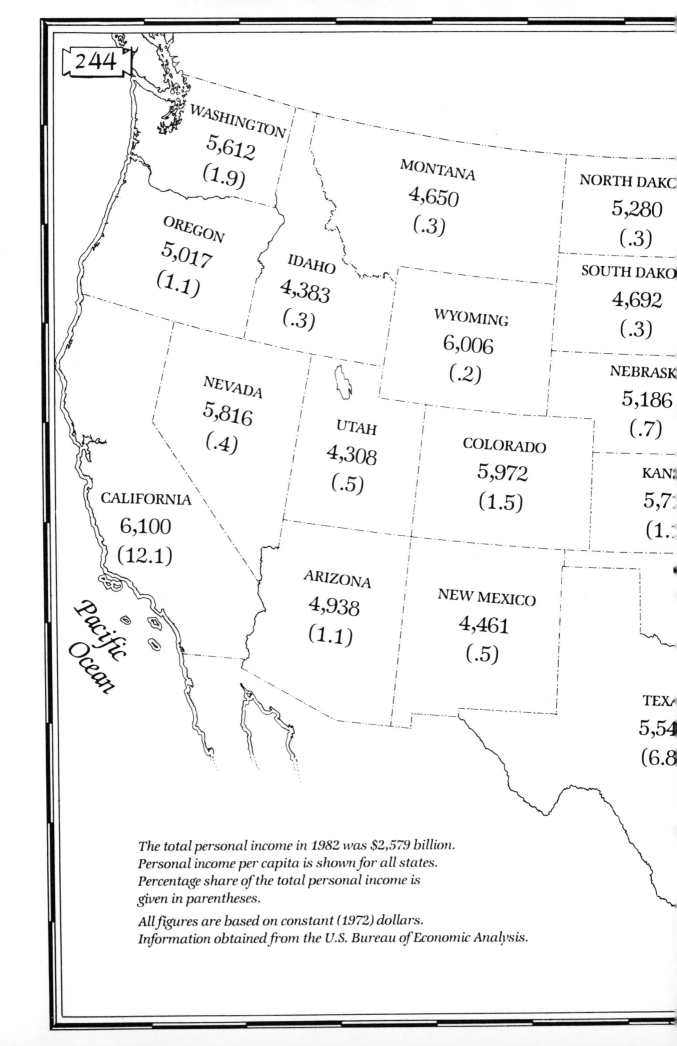

WASHINGTON
5,612
(1.9)

OREGON
5,017
(1.1)

IDAHO
4,383
(.3)

MONTANA
4,650
(.3)

NORTH DAKO
5,280
(.3)

SOUTH DAKO
4,692
(.3)

WYOMING
6,006
(.2)

NEBRASK
5,186
(.7)

NEVADA
5,816
(.4)

UTAH
4,308
(.5)

COLORADO
5,972
(1.5)

KAN
5,7
(1.

CALIFORNIA
6,100
(12.1)

ARIZONA
4,938
(1.1)

NEW MEXICO
4,461
(.5)

Pacific Ocean

TEX
5,54
(6.8

The total personal income in 1982 was $2,579 billion.
Personal income per capita is shown for all states.
Percentage share of the total personal income is
given in parentheses.

All figures are based on constant (1972) dollars.
Information obtained from the U.S. Bureau of Economic Analysis.

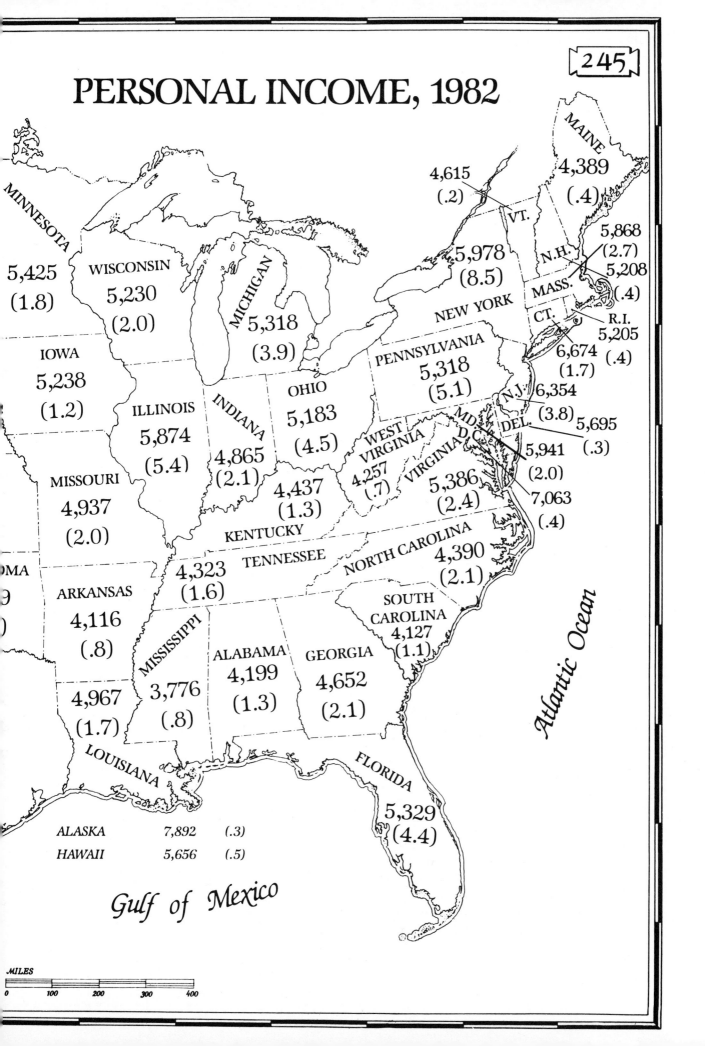

PERSONAL INCOME, 1982

MAINE
4,389
(.4)

4,615
(.2)

VT.

5,868
(2.7)

N.H.

5,208
(.4)

5,978
(8.5)

MASS.

NEW YORK

CT.

R.I.
5,205
(.4)

PENNSYLVANIA
5,318
(5.1)

6,674
(1.7)

N.J. 6,354
(3.8)

MINNESOTA
5,425
(1.8)

WISCONSIN
5,230
(2.0)

MICHIGAN
5,318
(3.9)

MD.
D.C.

DEL.

5,695
(.3)

5,941
(2.0)

7,063
(.4)

IOWA
5,238
(1.2)

OHIO
5,183
(4.5)

ILLINOIS
5,874
(5.4)

INDIANA
4,865
(2.1)

WEST
VIRGINIA
4,257
(.7)

VIRGINIA
5,386
(2.4)

MISSOURI
4,937
(2.0)

4,437
(1.3)

KENTUCKY

NORTH CAROLINA
4,390
(2.1)

OMA
9
)

ARKANSAS
4,116
(.8)

TENNESSEE
4,323
(1.6)

SOUTH
CAROLINA
4,127
(1.1)

MISSISSIPPI
3,776
(.8)

ALABAMA
4,199
(1.3)

GEORGIA
4,652
(2.1)

Atlantic Ocean

4,967
(1.7)

LOUISIANA

FLORIDA
5,329
(4.4)

ALASKA   7,892   (.3)
HAWAII   5,656   (.5)

Gulf of Mexico

MILES
0   100   200   300   400

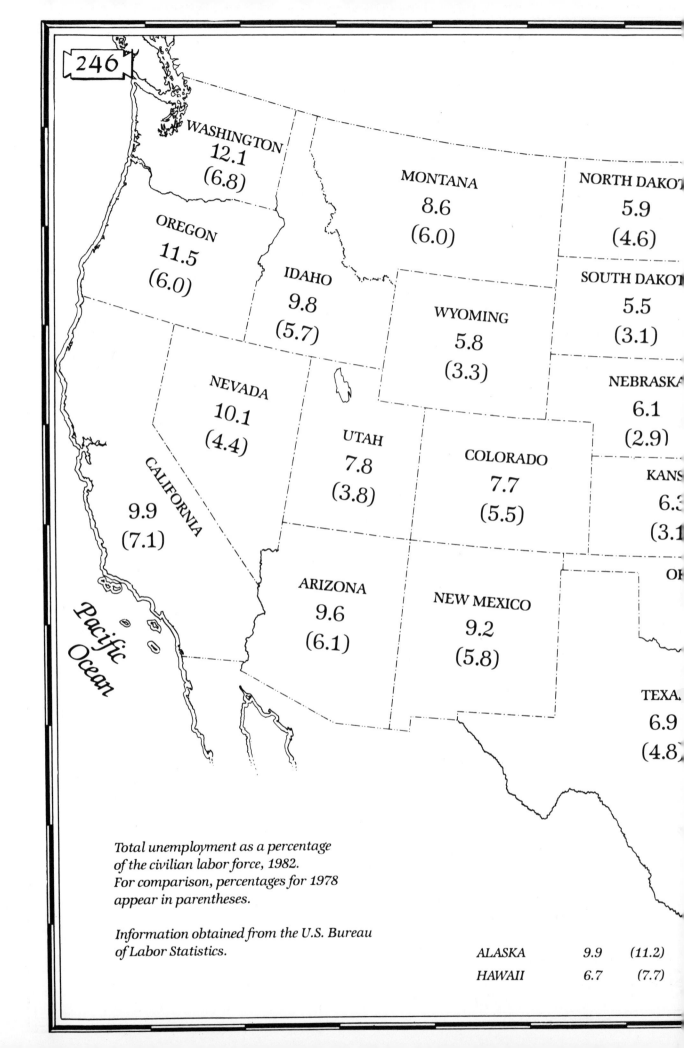

246

WASHINGTON
12.1
(6.8)

OREGON
11.5
(6.0)

IDAHO
9.8
(5.7)

MONTANA
8.6
(6.0)

NORTH DAKOT
5.9
(4.6)

SOUTH DAKOT
5.5
(3.1)

WYOMING
5.8
(3.3)

NEBRASKA
6.1
(2.9)

NEVADA
10.1
(4.4)

UTAH
7.8
(3.8)

COLORADO
7.7
(5.5)

KANS
6.3
(3.1

CALIFORNIA
9.9
(7.1)

ARIZONA
9.6
(6.1)

NEW MEXICO
9.2
(5.8)

OK

TEXA
6.9
(4.8)

Pacific
Ocean

*Total unemployment as a percentage
of the civilian labor force, 1982.
For comparison, percentages for 1978
appear in parentheses.*

*Information obtained from the U.S. Bureau
of Labor Statistics.*

ALASKA	9.9	(11.2)
HAWAII	6.7	(7.7)

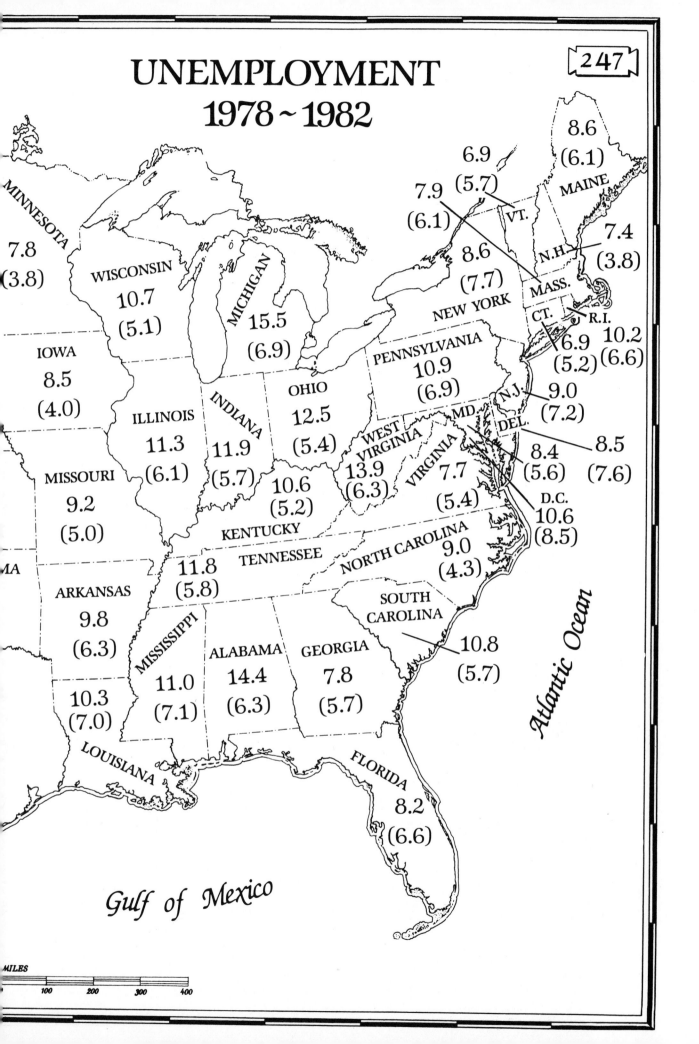

UNEMPLOYMENT
1978 ~ 1982

247

MINNESOTA
7.8
(3.8)

WISCONSIN
10.7
(5.1)

MICHIGAN
15.5
(6.9)

IOWA
8.5
(4.0)

ILLINOIS
11.3
(6.1)

INDIANA
11.9
(5.7)

OHIO
12.5
(5.4)

MISSOURI
9.2
(5.0)

KENTUCKY
10.6
(5.2)

TENNESSEE
11.8
(5.8)

ARKANSAS
9.8
(6.3)

MISSISSIPPI
11.0
(7.1)

ALABAMA
14.4
(6.3)

GEORGIA
7.8
(5.7)

10.3
(7.0)

LOUISIANA

PENNSYLVANIA
10.9
(6.9)

NEW YORK
8.6
(7.7)

6.9
(5.7)

7.9
(6.1)

VT.

MAINE
8.6
(6.1)

N.H.

7.4
(3.8)

MASS.

CT.
6.9
(5.2)

R.I.
10.2
(6.6)

N.J.
9.0
(7.2)

MD
8.4
(5.6)

DEL.
8.5
(7.6)

D.C.
10.6
(8.5)

WEST
VIRGINIA
13.9
(6.3)

VIRGINIA
7.7
(5.4)

NORTH CAROLINA
9.0
(4.3)

SOUTH
CAROLINA
10.8
(5.7)

FLORIDA
8.2
(6.6)

Atlantic Ocean

Gulf of Mexico

MA

MILES
100   200   300   400

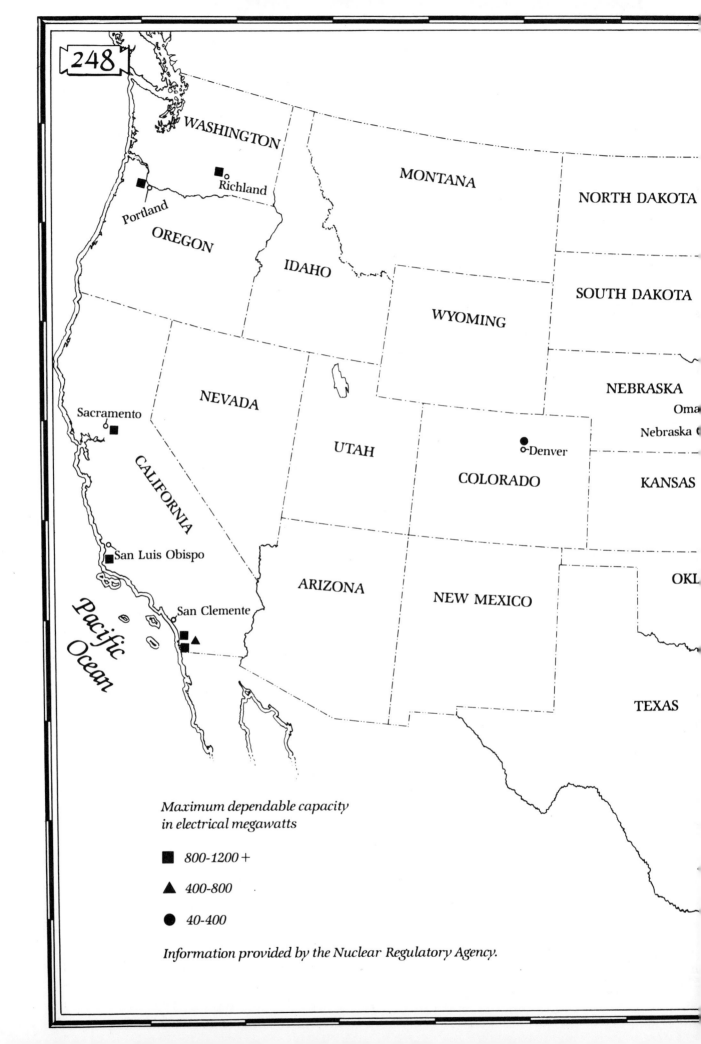

248

WASHINGTON

Richland

Portland

OREGON

IDAHO

MONTANA

NORTH DAKOTA

SOUTH DAKOTA

WYOMING

NEVADA

Sacramento

UTAH

COLORADO

NEBRASKA

Oma

Nebraska C

Denver

KANSAS

CALIFORNIA

San Luis Obispo

Pacific Ocean

San Clemente

ARIZONA

NEW MEXICO

OKL

TEXAS

*Maximum dependable capacity
in electrical megawatts*

■ *800-1200 +*

▲ *400-800*

● *40-400*

Information provided by the Nuclear Regulatory Agency.

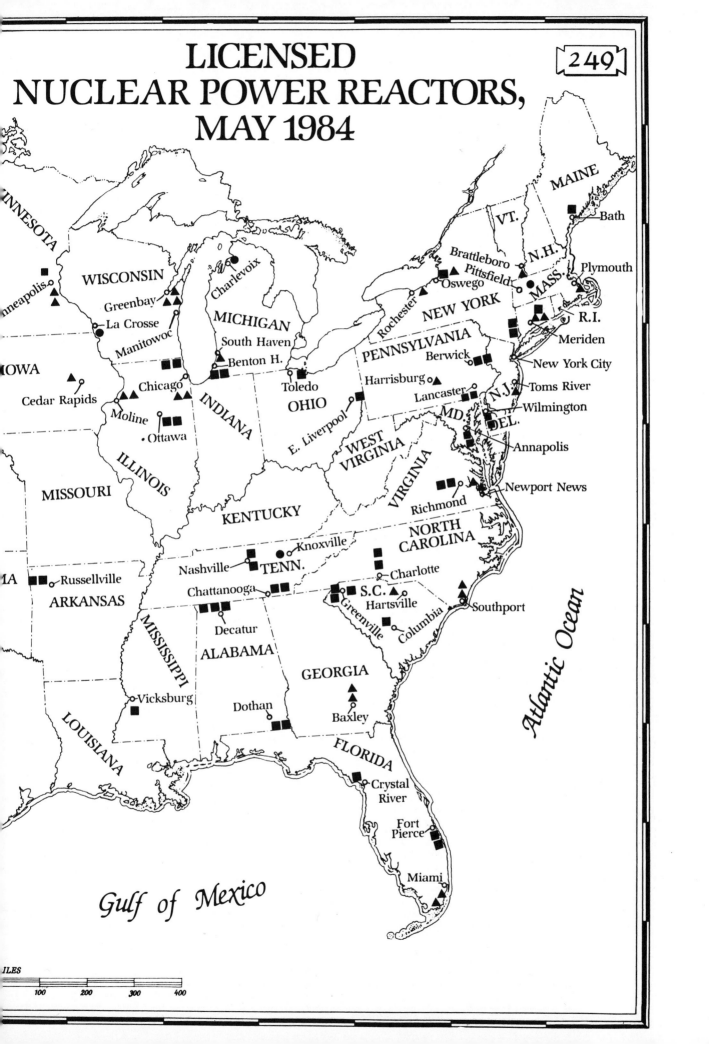

LICENSED NUCLEAR POWER REACTORS, MAY 1984

MAINE

MINNESOTA

WISCONSIN

Charlevoix

VT.

N.H.

Bath

Brattleboro
Pittsfield
Oswego

MASS.

Plymouth

nneapolis

Greenbay

MICHIGAN

La Crosse

South Haven

Manitowoc

Benton H.

Rochester

NEW YORK

R.I.

Meriden

IOWA

Cedar Rapids

Chicago

Toledo

OHIO

PENNSYLVANIA

Harrisburg

Berwick

New York City

Moline

INDIANA

Lancaster

N.J.

Toms River

Ottawa

E. Liverpool

Wilmington

MD.

DEL.

ILLINOIS

WEST
VIRGINIA

Annapolis

MISSOURI

KENTUCKY

VIRGINIA

Newport News

Richmond

NORTH
CAROLINA

Knoxville

Nashville

TENN.

Charlotte

Russellville

Chattanooga

S.C.

Southport

ARKANSAS

Greenville

Hartsville

Columbia

Decatur

ALABAMA

GEORGIA

Vicksburg

Dothan

Baxley

MISSISSIPPI

LOUISIANA

FLORIDA

Crystal
River

Gulf of Mexico

Fort
Pierce

Miami

Atlantic Ocean

ILES

100   200   300   400

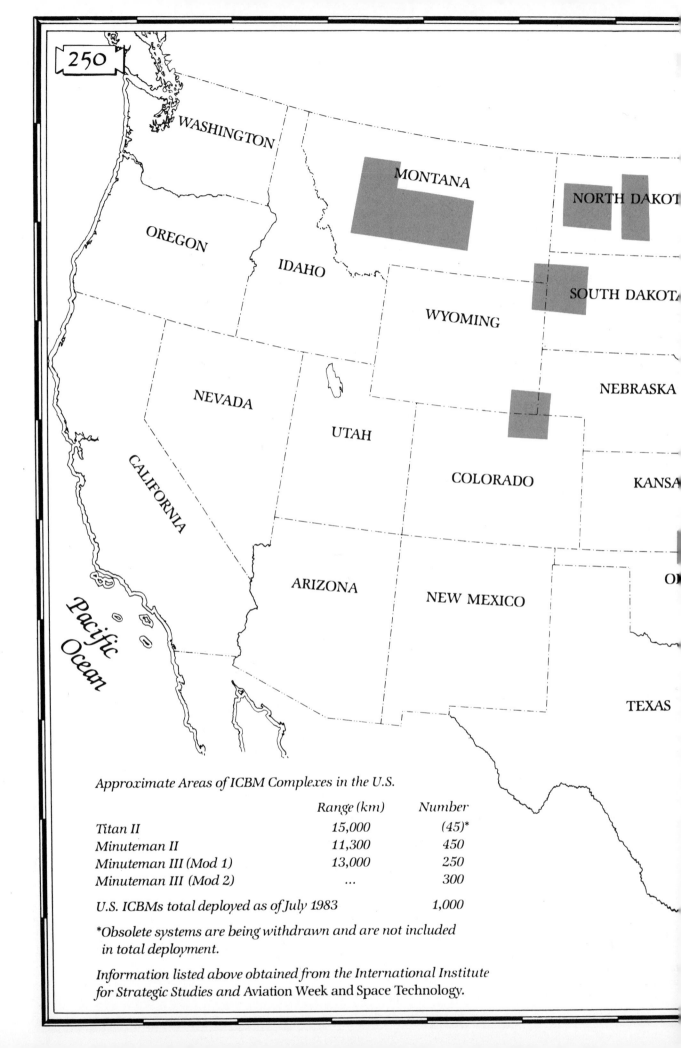

WASHINGTON

MONTANA

NORTH DAKOT

OREGON

IDAHO

SOUTH DAKOTA

WYOMING

NEBRASKA

NEVADA

UTAH

CALIFORNIA

COLORADO

KANSA

Pacific Ocean

ARIZONA

NEW MEXICO

O

TEXAS

Approximate Areas of ICBM Complexes in the U.S.

	Range (km)	Number
Titan II	15,000	(45)*
Minuteman II	11,300	450
Minuteman III (Mod 1)	13,000	250
Minuteman III (Mod 2)	...	300
U.S. ICBMs total deployed as of July 1983		1,000

Obsolete systems are being withdrawn and are not included in total deployment.

Information listed above obtained from the International Institute for Strategic Studies and Aviation Week and Space Technology.

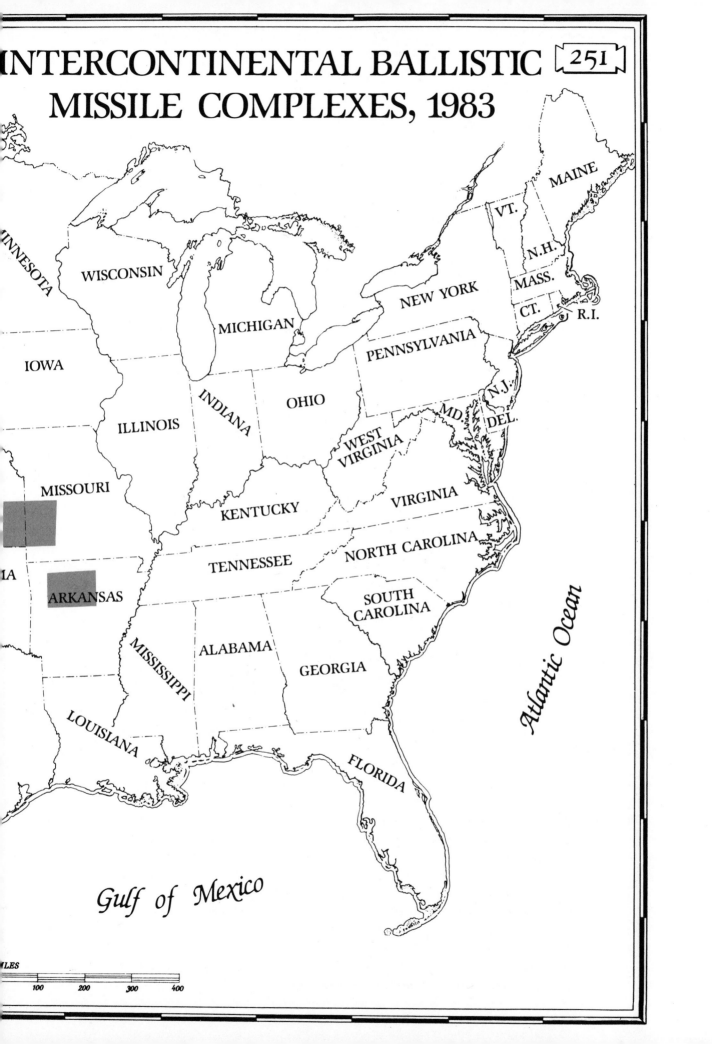

INTERCONTINENTAL BALLISTIC MISSILE COMPLEXES, 1983

MAINE

MINNESOTA

WISCONSIN

VT.

N.H.

MASS.

NEW YORK

CT.

R.I.

MICHIGAN

PENNSYLVANIA

IOWA

INDIANA

OHIO

N.J.

ILLINOIS

MD.

DEL.

WEST
VIRGINIA

MISSOURI

VIRGINIA

KENTUCKY

TENNESSEE

NORTH CAROLINA

IA

ARKANSAS

SOUTH
CAROLINA

MISSISSIPPI

ALABAMA

GEORGIA

Atlantic Ocean

LOUISIANA

FLORIDA

Gulf of Mexico

MILES

100   200   300   400

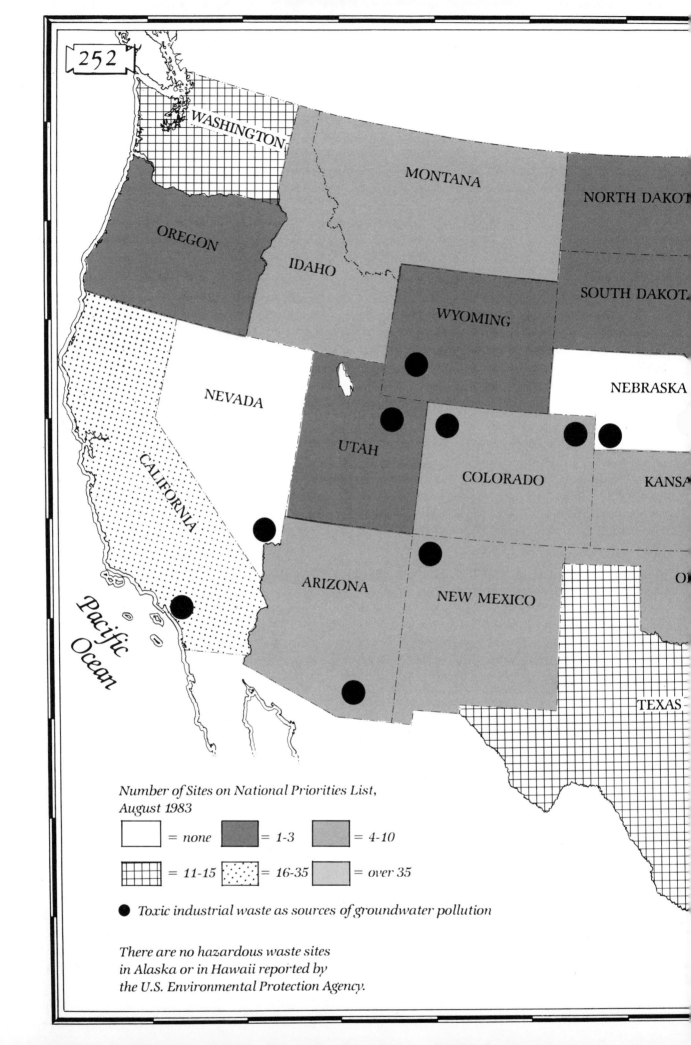

252

WASHINGTON

MONTANA

NORTH DAKOT

OREGON

IDAHO

SOUTH DAKOT

WYOMING

NEVADA

NEBRASKA

UTAH

COLORADO

KANSA

CALIFORNIA

ARIZONA

NEW MEXICO

OK

Pacific
Ocean

TEXAS

*Number of Sites on National Priorities List,
August 1983*

☐ = *none* ▨ = *1-3* ▨ = *4-10*

▦ = *11-15* ▨ = *16-35* ▨ = *over 35*

● *Toxic industrial waste as sources of groundwater pollution*

*There are no hazardous waste sites
in Alaska or in Hawaii reported by
the U.S. Environmental Protection Agency.*

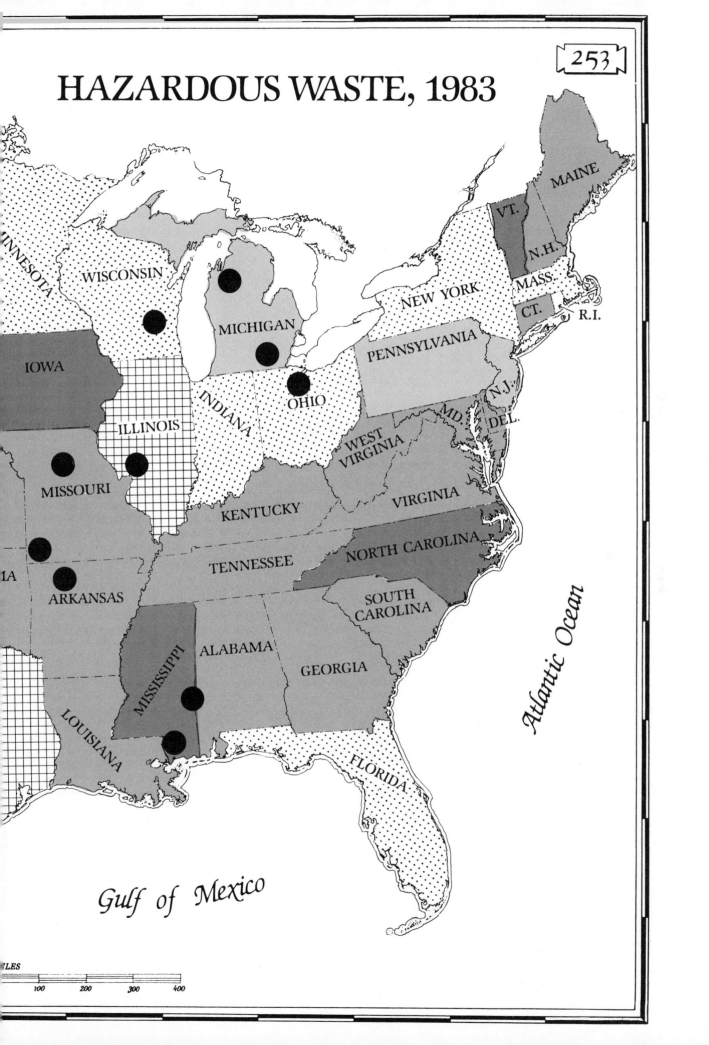

HAZARDOUS WASTE, 1983

253

MAINE

VT.

N.H.

MASS.

CT.

R.I.

MINNESOTA

WISCONSIN

MICHIGAN

NEW YORK

PENNSYLVANIA

N.J.

IOWA

INDIANA

OHIO

MD.

DEL.

ILLINOIS

WEST VIRGINIA

MISSOURI

KENTUCKY

VIRGINIA

NORTH CAROLINA

TENNESSEE

IA

ARKANSAS

SOUTH CAROLINA

MISSISSIPPI

ALABAMA

GEORGIA

LOUISIANA

Atlantic Ocean

FLORIDA

Gulf of Mexico

ILES

100   200   300   400

INDEX

This Index is designed to serve two main purposes. First, it enables the user of the *Atlas* to turn, quickly and definitely, to the map or maps on which a given location is shown.

Second, it serves as a cross reference, enabling the user of the work to follow, from map to map, the development of areas in succeeding periods of our history. Thus, the advance of the frontier may be visualized; or the evolution of a Territory, in its changing extents, may be followed through to the final creation of the State; or the migrations and removals of the various Indian tribes may be traced.

In the indexing of historical locations some inconsistencies are inevitable. An Indian village of the time of DeSoto can scarcely be listed as being in a present-day state. On the other hand, Harpers Ferry was important historically long before the existence of the state of West Virginia; Vincennes was a French frontier post sixty years before the Territory of Indiana was formed; yet, for the purposes of an index, it would be confusing to identify these places other than in their present states. Again, as between towns which have had a continuing existence and those which have disappeared or which are not direct descendants of existing towns of the same name, a distinction in the form of listing is desirable—although the basis for decision is often very slight indeed.

Also, there is the matter of spellings, accents and possessives. No uniformity existed, nor is it the province of an atlas of American history to establish uniformity, but rather, in each case, to follow the form most used over the greatest period of time, and, where distinct variations occur, to list those variations with a reference to the form used.

Thus, without departing too greatly from consistency, the editors, in compiling the following Index, have endeavored to so list each location that it may be readily found in the Index—from which the user will turn to the proper map, where the status of the place, during the period of the map, will be amply evident.

INDEX

INDEX

Boston Ten Townships, 109
Boswyck, N. Y., 35
Botetourt County, Va., 72
Botetourt C. H., Va., 72
Bottom's Bridge, Va., 155
Bougainville Island, 197
Bougie, Algeria, 193
Boulder, Colo., 142
Boulder Creek, 142
Bound Brook, N. J., 43, 83
Boundaries: With Canada, 94, 110,
  111, 112–113, 118–119, 132, 133,
  134–135, 175; with Mexico, 112–
  113, 118–119, 122, 134–135, 136–
  137, 140; with Spanish Florida,
  94, 106–107; with Spanish Louis-
  iana, 94
Bourbon County, Ga., 106
Bouresches, France, 191
Bourgmont Expedition (1714–
  1724), 23
Bowie, Camp (Ariz.), 171
Bowlegs Town, Fla., 107, 121
Bowling Green, Ky., 124, 150, 153,
  235
Bowling Green, Va., 155, 162
Bowyer, Fort, 106, 116
Boydton Plank Road. See Hatcher's
  Run
Bozeman, Mont., 172, 175
Bozeman Trail, 172–173, 174
Braddock's Defeat, 63, 69
Braddock's Grave, 69
Braddock's Road, 63, 69
Bradford, Colo., 142
Bradford, Mass., 46
Bradford, N. H., 127
Brady, Fort, 111
Bragg, Fort, N. C., 201
Braintree, Mass., 37, 46, 58, 127
Branchville, S. C., 126
Brandon, Miss., 126
Brandy Station, Va., 154, 162
Brandywine, Del., 131
Brandywine Creek, 41, 83
Branford, Conn., 38, 46, 90
Brashear City, La., 160
Brasseaux, Ruisseau de, 65
Brattleboro, Vt., 51, 127, 249
Brazil, 208
Brazito, N. Mex., 137
Brazoria, Tex., 123, 137

Brazos River, 12, 20, 23, 99, 113,
  119, 122, 123, 137, 141, 157, 169,
  170, 171, 227
Breakneck Mountain, 85
Breckenridge, Colo., 142
Breed's Hill, 78
Brenner Pass, Italy-Austria, 195
Breton, Cape, 60
Breuckelen, N. Y., 35
Brewerton, Fort, 73
Briar Creek, 86
Briar Creek, Battle of, 86
Bridgeport, Ala., 158, 159
Bridgeport, Conn., 127, 131
Bridgeport, N. J., 43
Bridger, Fort, 134, 138, 140, 156
Bridger's Camp, Wyo., 120
Bridger's Pass, Wyo., 156, 169
Bridgeton, N. J., 43, 45
Bridgewater, Mass., 46, 58
Bridgman's Fort, 50
Brighton Reservation, Fla., 207
Briscoe Mines, Va., 155
Bristoe, Va., 154
Bristol, Conn., 131
Bristol, Maine, 36
Bristol, Pa., 45, 125
Bristol, R. I., 39
Bristol, Tenn.-Va., 153
British Canadian immigration, 214–
  215
British Columbia, Can., 230
British Honduras, 186
British imimgration, 208, 210–211,
  214–215
British Virgin Islands, 231
Broad River (Ga.), 107
Broad River (at Port Royal, S. C.),
  15
Broad River (a tributary of the
  Santee River), 44, 52, 54, 66, 71,
  86, 87, 161
Broad River, First, 54
Brockton, Mass., 131
Bronx River, 82
Brook Farm, Mass., 145
Brooke, Fort, 121
Brookfield, Mass., 46, 50, 51, 58
Brookhaven, N. Y., 38
Brookline, Mass., 77 78
Brooklyn, N. Y., 35, 82, 101, 127,
  129, 177, 179, 223

Brooklyn Heights, N. Y., 82
Brookville, Ind., 110
Broward County, Fla., 228
Brown, Fort, 137
Brown, John, Raid (1859), 102
Brown Claims, Kans., 143
Brown's Bank, 95
Brown's Ferry, Tenn., 158
Brown's Gap, Va., 154
Browns Hole, 118, 134
Brownstown, Mich., 114
Brownsville, Tex., 227, 234
Bruinsburg, Miss., 160
Brule River, 20
Bruneau River, 175
Brunswick, Maine, 50, 76
Brunswick, N. J., 83, 91
Brunswick, N. C., 24, 44, 80
Brussels, Belg., 191, 194, 203
Bryans Station, Ky., 55
Bryantsville, Ky., 153
Bryce Canyon National Park, Utah,
  232
Buade, Fort de, 21, 25
Buade, Lake, 20
Bucareli, Tex., 99
Buchanan, Fort (P. R.), 202
Buchanan, Va., 125
Buchanan County, Mo., 143
Buchenwald, Ger., 195
Buck Tooth, N. Y., 73
Buckaloons, Pa., 52, 73
Buckfield, Maine, 127
Bucks County, Pa., 102
Buckskin, Colo., 142
Buell-Comanche Battle (Feb. 11,
  1875), 170
Buena Vista, Battle of, 137
Buffalo, N. Y., 114, 125, 127, 129,
  130, 177, 179, 235, 237, 239
Buffalo and Rochester Railroad,
  127
Buffalo Bayou, 123
Buffalo Creek, 87
Buffalo Gap, Tex., 170
Buffalo Gap, Va., 53
Buffalo Range, 170
Buffington Island, 151
Buford, Fort, 173
Bull Run, 149, 154
Bull Run, Battle of, 149
Bull Run, Second Battle of, 154

260

INDEX

INDEX

INDEX

INDEX

INDEX

South Pass (Mississippi Delta), 26, 116, 160
South Pass (Wyo.), 118, 120, 134, 138, 140, 156, 173
South Platte River, 23, 113, 119, 135, 141, 142, 157, 169, 173
South River (Delaware River), 41
South River (N.C.), 80
South Toe River, 87
South Union, Ky., 145
South Vietnam, 199
Southampton, N. Y., 35, 38, 46, 90
Southampton County, Va., 102
Southeast Pass (Mississippi Delta), 116, 160
Southern Mississippi Railroad, 150
Southern Pacific Railroad, 168, 171, 175
Southern Ute Reservation, Ariz.-Colo., 206
Southold, N. Y., 35, 38, 46, 90
Southport, N. C., 249
Southport, Wis., 133
Southside Railroad, 162
Southwest Pass (Mississippi Delta), 26, 116, 160
Southwest Point, Tenn., 96
Southwest Territory (Territory South of the River Ohio), 94
Southwestern Railroad, 161
Soviet Union, 208–209, 230
Sowams, R. I., 39
Spain, 192, 203, 208
Spangdahlem, Ger., 203
Spanish-American War (1898), 184
Spanish Explorations, 12–13
Spanish Fort, Ga., 22
Spanish Morocco, 192
Spanish Peaks, 122
Spanish Trail. See Old Spanish Trail
Sparta, Tenn., 153
Spartanburg, S. C., 161
Spencer, Ind., 110
Spindle Top Oil Field, Tex., 227
Spirit Lake, 133
Spokane, Wash., 175, 236, 238
Spokane House, Wash., 112
Spokane Reservation, Wash., 206
Spokane River, 134, 175
Spotswood, N. J., 43, 83
Spotswood Expedition, 44, 53

Spotsylvania, Va., 86, 154, 162
Spotted Tail Agency, Nebr., 173
Spreckelsville, Hawaii, 229
Spring Hill, Tenn., 153
Spring Wells, Mich., 114
Springfield, Ill., 126, 150, 180, 181, 219, 239
Springfield, Mass., 38, 46, 51, 58, 102, 127, 131, 237, 239
Springfield, Mo., 141, 150, 152, 157,
Springfield, N. J., 83
Springfield, N. Y., 51, 73
Springfield, Ohio, 124, 126, 219
Squakeag, Mass., 58
Stadacona (Site of City of Quebec), 6, 19
Staked Plains, 119 122, 137, 170, 171
Stalnakers, Va., 52, 54, 71, 72
Stamford, Conn., 38, 46, 90
Stanardsville, Va., 154
Standing Rock Agency, N. Dak., 173
Standing Rock Reservation, S. Dak., 206
Stanislaus River, 139
Stanton, Fort, 122, 141, 156, 169, 171
Stanton, Kans., 143
Stanwix, Fort, 51, 59, 71, 73, 84, 108, 109
Stanwix, Fort, Treaty of (1768), 70, 73
Stanwix, Fort, Treaty of (1784), 108
Starkville, Miss., 160
Starved Rock, 20, 27
Staten Island, 35, 43, 82, 83, 91
Staunton, Va., 51, 52, 53, 66, 71, 72, 86, 101, 149, 151, 154, 162
Staunton River, 52, 54, 71, 72, 86
Stedman, Fort, 162
Steele's Bayou, 160
Steens Mountain, 175
Stephenson, Fort, 114
Sterling, Mass., 127
Sterling Iron Works, N. Y., 47
Steuben, Fort, 103
Steubenville, Ohio, 130
Stevens Gap, Ga., 158
Stevenson, Ala., 150, 153, 158, 159
Stewart, Fort (Ga.), 201
Stewarts Crossing, 69
Stillwater, Minn., 133

Stillwater, N. Y., 84
Stillwater, Okla., 176
Stockbridge Reservation, Wis., 207
Stockton, Calif., 139
Stockton, Fort, 171
Stoddert, Fort, 106
Stone Arabia, N. Y., 84
Stone Bridge, Va., 149
Stone Mountain, Ga., 159, 161
Stone River, 153
Stoney Creek, Battle of, 114
Stonington, Conn., 46, 117, 127
Stonington Railroad, 127
Stono Rebellion (1739), 102
Stono River, 81
Stony Brook, 77, 78
Stony Point, N. Y., 73, 85, 91
Strait of Gibraltar, 193
Strait of Messina, 193
Strandviken, 41
Stranger Creek, 143
Strasbourg, Alsace, 191
Strasburg, Va., 53, 149, 154, 162
Strategic Air Command, Headquarters (Omaha, Nebr.), 200
Stratford, Conn., 38, 46, 90
Strawberry Bank, N. H., 36
Strother, Fort, 107
Stuart River, 134
Stuart's Town, S. C., 44
Subic Bay, Philippines, 203
Sublette's Cutoff, 138
Sudbury, Mass., 37, 46, 58
Sudbury River, 77
Suffern, N. Y., 91
Suffolk, N. Y., 90
Suffolk, Va., 51, 86, 154, 155, 162
Suffrage, Universal Male (1789–1897), 146; Woman's (1869–1920), 220–221
Sullivan, Fort, 73
Sullivan C. H., Tenn., 96
Sullivan's Island, 81
Sully, Fort, 157, 173
Sulphur Springs Valley (Ariz.), 171
Sulu Sea, 196
Sumatra, 196
Summit Lake Reservation, Nev., 206
Sumner, Fort, 157, 169, 170, 171
Sumter, Fort, 151
Sunbury, Fort, 86